What Next for Britain in the Middle East?

Security, Trade and Foreign Policy after Brexit

Edited by
Christopher Phillips and Michael Stephens

I.B.TAURIS
LONDON • NEW YORK • OXFORD • NEW DELHI • SYDNEY

I.B. TAURIS
Bloomsbury Publishing Plc
50 Bedford Square, London, WC1B 3DP, UK
1385 Broadway, New York, NY 10018, USA
29 Earlsfort Terrace, Dublin 2, Ireland

First published in Great Britain 2022

Cover design by Adriana Brioso
Cover image: Map of the Near and Middle East from The Times Atlas. (© Print
Collector/Getty Images)

A catalogue record for this book is available from the British Library.

A catalog record for this book is available from the Library of Congress.

ISBN: HB: 978-0-7556-1715-9
PB: 978-0-7556-1716-6
ePDF: 978-0-7556-1717-3
eBook: 978-0-7556-1718-0

Typeset by Integra Software Sevices Pvt. Ltd.
Printed and bound in Great Britain

What Next for Britain in the Middle East?

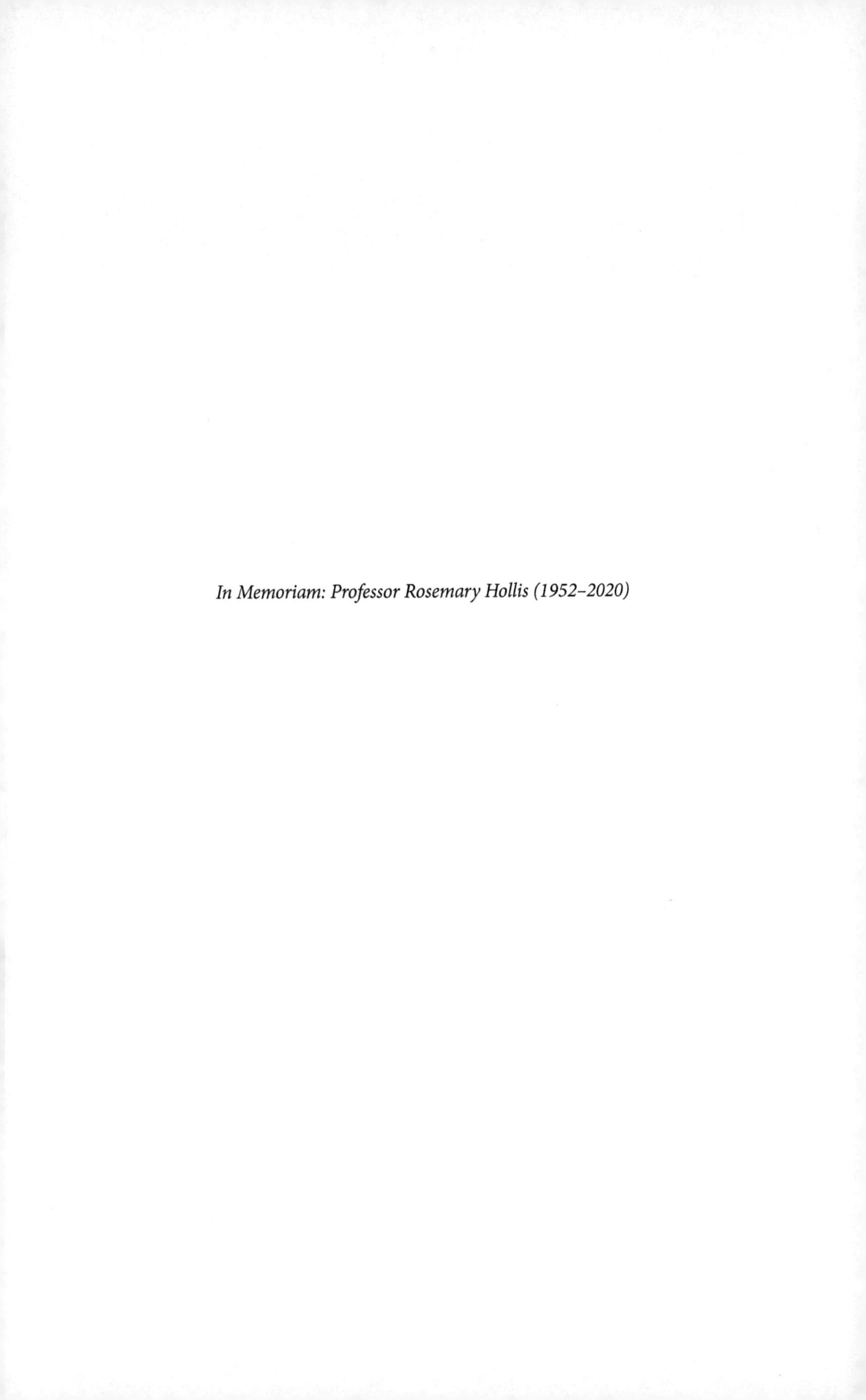

In Memoriam: Professor Rosemary Hollis (1952–2020)

Contents

List of Contributors viii
Map of the Middle East xi
Acknowledgements xii

1 Introduction *Christopher Phillips and Michael Stephens* 1

Part 1 Still searching for a role – The UK in the Middle East from East of Suez to Brexit

2 Britain and the Middle East since the end of Empire *Rosemary Hollis* 13
3 Britain's foreign policy landscape in the post-Brexit era *Michael Clarke* 27
4 Still special? The UK and United States in the Middle East *Michael Stephens* 41

Part 2 Principles and pragmatism – The debates over the UK's Middle East priorities

5 Values *James Lynch* 55
6 Prosperity *David Butter* 69
7 Security *Louise Kettle* 81

Part 3 Britain and the non-Arab powers

8 Turkey *Bill Park* 97
9 Israel *Ian Black* 109
10 Iran *Sanam Vakil* 123

Part 4 Britain and the Middle Eastern Arab states

11 Syria and the Levant *Christopher Phillips* 139
12 Iraq *Jack Watling* 151
13 The Gulf *Tobias Borck and Michael Stephens* 165
14 Egypt *Emman El-Badawy* 181
15 Conclusion *Christopher Phillips and Michael Stephens* 199

Notes 206
Select Bibliography 243
Index 245

Contributors

Dr Ian Black

Ian Black is a Visiting Senior Fellow at the Middle East Centre of LSE and a former Middle East Editor, European Editor, Diplomatic Editor and Jerusalem Correspondent of *The Guardian* newspaper. He has also written for the *Washington Post*, *The Economist* and *The New York Times*. His latest book is *Enemies and Neighbours: Arabs and Jews in Palestine and Israel, 1917–2017*. He appears regularly on British, international and regional TV and radio channels commenting on current affairs.

Dr Tobias Borck

Tobias Borck is an Associate Fellow at the Royal United Services Institute in London, and an independent analyst and consultant specializing in Middle East politics and security. His main research interests include the foreign policies of the Arab Gulf states; the post-2011 political and security developments in North Africa (especially in Libya); and European – specifically German and British – foreign policy towards the Middle East. He holds degrees in Arabic and Middle East Studies (BA) and Applied Security Strategy (MA); he received his PhD from Exeter University, which focused on stability and regional order in the Middle East from the perspective of Saudi Arabia, the UAE and Qatar.

David Butter

David Butter is an analyst of politics, economics and business in the Middle East & North Africa (MENA) region. He has worked as regional director for the Middle East at the Economist Intelligence Unit, and for *MEED* magazine, where he was editor between 2000 and 2002. He holds an MA in comparative politics from Sussex University and a BA in Arabic and Persian from Oxford University.

Professor Michael Clarke

Michael Clarke is a former Director General of the Royal United Services Institute and now a RUSI Distinguished Fellow. He is a Visiting Professor at King's College London, and Associate Director of the Strategy and Security Institute, University of Exeter.

Dr Emman El-Badawy

Emman El-Badawy is Head of Research at the Tony Blair Institute and a British Academy Postdoctoral Fellow at King's College London's Grand Strategy Department in War Studies. Emman specializes on the Middle East and the Arab-Muslim world and holds a doctorate in Arab and Islamic studies from the University of Exeter. She leads the work at the Tony Blair Institute on security and extremism, as well as a programme on the Middle East. Her current research with KCL's Professor John Bew is funded by the British Academy and explores the roots of Islamism and its global manifestations today. She is a BBC Expert Voice on the Middle East, terrorism and extremism, and has served as consultant and adviser on a number of projects, commissions and boards focused on conflict, insurgency and state-building in the last few years.

Professor Rosemary Hollis
Rosemary Hollis was a British Political Scientist and Professor of Middle East Policy Studies at City University London until her retirement in 2018. Hollis was known for her decades of expertise and scholarship on the relations between the European Union, the UK and the United States with the Middle East. She was formerly the Research Director at Chatham House.

Dr Louise Kettle
Louise Kettle is an Assistant Professor of International Relations at the University of Nottingham. Her research focuses on the relationship between Britain and the Middle East, particularly related to military operations since the 1956 Suez crisis. Her latest book *Learning from the History of British Interventions in the Middle East* examines how lessons can be learned from past operations to inform current and future policy in the region.

James Lynch
James Lynch is a Founding Director of FairSquare, a human rights-focused research and advocacy organization. He began his career working on the Middle East for the Foreign and Commonwealth Office, studying Arabic in Damascus, working in the British Embassy in Doha and leading the FCO's Gulf team in the early months of the coalition government in 2010. He moved to Amnesty International in 2011 and spent seven years there, including as Middle East Deputy Director and Head of Arms Control and Human Rights. He has written on human rights in the Middle East for *The Guardian*, *CNN* and *Middle East Eye*.

Bill Park
Bill Park is Visiting Research Fellow at King's College, London. He sits on the British Institute at Ankara's (BIAA) research council, was an editorial board member for the journal *Mediterranean Politics*, sits on the international advisory panel for the journal *Turkish Studies* and is an adviser to the Centre for Turkish Studies (CEFTUS). He was Visiting Scholar at TOBB-ET University in Ankara (January–April 2016), and is an adviser to the Centre for Turkish Studies, Shaanxi Normal University, Xian, China.

Dr Christopher Phillips
Christopher Phillips is Reader in International Relations at Queen Mary, University of London, where he is also Deputy Dean. He was formerly a Fellow at Chatham House and is author of several books, including *The Battle for Syria: International Rivalry in the New Middle East* (London: Yale University Press, 2016 [3rd ed. 2020]).

Michael Stephens
Michael Stephens is a Senior Research Fellow at the Foreign Policy Research Institute (FPRI), an Associate Fellow at Bright Blue and Associate Fellow at RUSI where he

previously worked as the Research Fellow for Middle East Studies. Michael was seconded to the Foreign and Commonwealth in 2017 serving as the Senior Research Analyst for Lebanon and Syria.

Dr Sanam Vakil

Sanam Vakil is the Deputy Director of the Middle East North Africa Programme at Chatham House, where she leads the Future Dynamics in the Gulf project and the Iran Forum. Sanam's research focuses on regional security, Gulf geopolitics and on future trends in Iran's domestic and foreign policy. She is also the James Anderson Professorial Lecturer in the Middle East Studies department at the Johns Hopkins School of Advanced International Studies (SAIS Europe) in Bologna, Italy.

Dr Jack Watling

Jack Watling is Research Fellow for Land Warfare at RUSI. Jack has recently conducted studies of deterrence against Russia, force modernization, partner force capacity building, the future of corps operations, the future of fires and Iranian strategic culture. Jack's PhD examined the evolution of Britain's policy responses to civil war in the early twentieth century. Prior to joining RUSI Jack worked in Iraq, Mali, Rwanda, Brunei and further afield.

Map of the Middle East

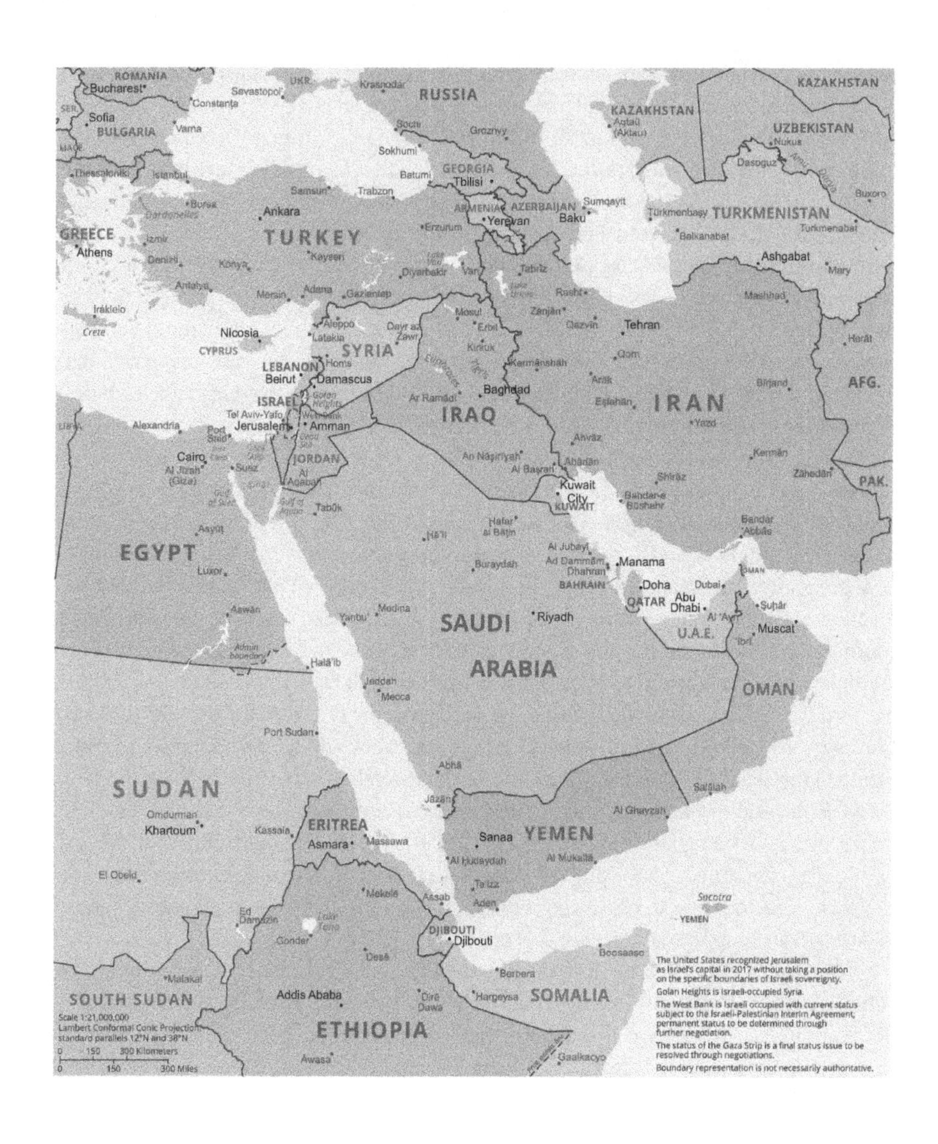

Acknowledgements

This volume originated with a conversation between the two editors during a long bus journey in Lebanon. The UK had recently voted to leave the European Union and both authors wondered what that would mean for Britain's future involvement with the Middle East? Would it make little difference, mark a significant departure or something in between? As London plans its post-EU 'Global Britain' strategy, where should the Middle East feature, or are other regions now a greater priority? Although we had our own thoughts on these questions, we also knew the limits of our expertise and so sought out a range of specialists from the scholarly and policy community to offer their perspectives. The initial result was a forum hosted by the Royal United Services Institute (RUSI), which eventually developed into this book. The authors would like to extend a huge thanks to RUSI for facilitating those opening phases and for being engaged and gracious hosts. We would also like to thank IB Tauris and Sophie Rudland for their faith in the project and support in bringing it to life. We would also like to express our enormous gratitude to all the authors for their timely and deeply insightful contributions, especially given the state of flux and uncertainty in both British, Middle Eastern and global politics, which have necessitated several updates to the manuscript.

Christopher would like to add further thanks to the School of Politics and International Relations at Queen Mary, University of London, which funded some of his research and continues to be a stimulating and supporting place to work; to his colleague Karl Pike for assisting with research; and to Mike Stephens for being an excellent collaborator and for his hard work and ingenuity in getting the book over the line. Finally, he'd like to thank Lindsay and Margot, as well as his wider family and friends for all their support. Michael would like to especially thank Alistair Burt, Sir Mark Lyall-Grant, Sir Christopher Meyer, Sir Malcolm Rifkind and Sir John Scarlett for their invaluable time and wise counsel; Tobias Borck for being a sounding board for ideas, and a great co-author; Chris Phillips, whose ideas and energy have pushed this project through to its completion; and lastly Victoria Friedlander for her help and support, and his family for being a constant source of strength and support all through this process.

This book is dedicated to Professor Rosemary Hollis who passed away soon after submitting her chapter for this volume, which we have sought to leave untouched in her honour. Her inspiration and support have been central to both authors in seeking to continue the legacy of British Scholarship on the Middle East region. Indeed, it was her book *Britain and the Middle East: Policy in the 9/11 Decade* that was the primary work that the authors discussed when deciding to produce this volume. Rosemary was not just a great authority on the Middle East region, but the moral conscience for many who wished to see more accountability, fairness and justice in British Middle East policy. The authors hope that this volume will stand as a tribute to her legacy.

Christopher Phillips and Michael Stephens, London, March 2021

1

Introduction

Christopher Phillips and Michael Stephens

For good or ill, Brexit has transformed the UK's place in the world. Whether it will become the buccaneering 'Global Britain' promised by the Leave campaign, or the gloomy 'sick man of Europe' cautioned by Remainers, London's outlook and priorities abroad are changing as a result of its departure from the European Union (EU). As the public adjust to new realities and policymakers seek to redefine Britain's international role, it is an opportune moment to re-examine the UK's relations with a region in which it has complex recent and historical ties: The Middle East.

Though Britain's footprint in the Middle East rescinded in the decades after the end of its colonial occupation, recent decades have seen a noticeable increase in British activity. The military has been deployed against enemy governments and terrorist organizations; diplomats have worked with allies to seek conflict resolution; trade and investment have been actively courted; British culture and values, such as governance and human rights, have been encouraged, albeit selectively. However, can these policies be considered successful? The picture is mixed at best. While Western coalitions that included Britain seem to have contained terror threats like ISIS and Al-Qaeda, they also helped create the instability that helped them thrive in Iraq, Libya and elsewhere. For all the UK's efforts, the Israeli–Palestinian conflict is no closer to resolution, nor are the wars in Syria and Yemen that British diplomats sought to settle. British trade and investment with certain Gulf states have grown steadily, but the region as a whole offers a limited contribution to the British economy. Though Britain retains some soft power via cultural institutions like the BBC and British Council, London's attempts to promote 'British values' have largely fallen on deaf ears, with the region's already weak human rights and governance record getting worse in most states.

As an introspective Britain reflects on its changing global position and recent policy failures, it must also reckon with the changes underway in the Middle East and wider world. An era of US dominance is giving way to one of renewed great power competition – made more complex by an international economy which, despite the impact of the coronavirus pandemic, remains globalized and interconnected. The Middle East is one arena for this competition, but it is also home to a range of medium powers like Iran, Saudi Arabia and Turkey that are increasingly interventionist. Since the 2011 Arab Uprisings the numbers of unstable Middle Eastern states have increased, providing new arenas for their rivalries to play out. Moreover, the region continues to be plagued by the poor governance and limited development that prompted the 2011 uprisings in the first place, with even the prosperous Gulf states looking more vulnerable after a sustained drop in oil prices.

Revisiting Britain's approach to the Middle East is therefore both timely and necessary, but it is a topic that has been surprisingly neglected in published works. Academics have tended to focus on British foreign policy in general or on a particular Middle Eastern issue or arena.[1] The same is true of Britain's foreign policy think tanks and research centres, which largely produce detailed reports on particular issues, but rarely attempt broad analyses of the UK's overall strategy towards the Middle East.[2] One exception was Rosemary Hollis' 2010 volume, *Britain and the Middle East: Policy in the 9/11 Decade*, a strong survey of the Blair and Brown governments' engagement with the region, though now somewhat dated. Another was the House of Lords Select Committee on International Relations report of May 2017, 'The Middle East: Time for New Realism,' which stated:

> British policy as it stands has not always adjusted to new conditions: dilemmas abound and we find there are inconsistencies, half-hearted attempts and sometimes neglect. The UK's engagement should be sustained and developed, but based on substantially revised assumptions from those that have guided British policy, some of them for the last century.[3]

In many ways the chapters that follow echo these sentiments and expand in more detail on the report's general findings that the UK needs to re-evaluate its role in the Middle East.

The volume brings together a collection of leading scholars and policy experts on British foreign policy and Middle Eastern politics. Each offers a unique contribution discussing how the UK might respond to its changed position and the transformations underway in the Middle East and wider world, whether focusing on a particular theme, such as security, or on a particular regional actor, like Iran. Though the contributors each offer their own perspective, they are united in seeking to answer the same question: what next for the UK in the Middle East after Brexit? To answer this, we have posed a series of sub-questions to feed into this debate: which regions and issues should the UK prioritize? Is there any room for or even advantage in pursuing certain principles or 'British values', or should security and economic benefit always take precedence? Who are Britain's optimal partners from inside and outside the Middle East, and will this remain the case in the coming decades? In an era of relative decline, can British influence be revitalized and is this even desirable? How should the UK best engage with the Middle East in the coming decades with the resources at its disposal? This book considers what Britain's priorities and capabilities in the Middle East are and offers suggestions for what they should be.

In many ways this book muses on an even bigger question to emerge from Brexit: what is Britain's place in the world? By focusing on one of the regions the UK has historically been most engaged in, this forward-looking volume assesses the drivers of foreign policy successes and failures, outlining a range of possible routes to maximize future British influence.

Changing world, changing Middle East, changing Britain

While the chapters that follow offer a range of assessments on Britain's various future challenges and opportunities in the Middle East, several themes recur. The first is the changing global, regional and local context in which Britain must now operate. Globally, the liberal order is under severe strain. The post-Cold War 'unipolar moment' of US dominance has given way to a new era of great power rivalry, characterized by US–Chinese competition, a more militarily interventionist Russia, a retreating Washington (even after the election of the multilateralist Joe Biden) and increased activism by medium regional powers like Turkey and Iran. The UK's historic role of oscillating between its European and American allies will likely continue, though in a context where the Western alliance as a whole is likely to be weaker than it has been in decades compared to other global players. Britain's departure from the EU complicates this as London may have to pursue foreign policy based on achieving short-term goals such as trade deals rather than long-term strategy. The Middle East, one of several likely arenas for great power competition in the coming decade, could be one region where the UK struggles to find its own path in the face of rival US, EU and Chinese interests.

This global shift interacts with significant regional changes in the last decade. When the UK was intervening in the Middle East during the 1990s and 2000s, the region was broadly ordered into two blocs. Most states were allies of the United States and the West, but a collection of relatively weak states, variously led by Iran, Syria and non-state actors like Hezbollah, rejected US hegemony. Since 2011 that pro-Western bloc has split with a Turkish-Qatari-Muslim Brotherhood faction challenging one led by Saudi Arabia and the UAE that includes Egypt and has ever-warming ties with Israel. These blocs are quite fluid and states within them frequently follow their own agendas often without consulting either regional or global allies. Moreover, while both the Turkey-Qatar and the Saudi-UAE-led bloc remain Western allies, none is as firmly wedded to Washington (or London) as in the past and both Russia and China have considerably enhanced their ties to each. Moscow and Beijing have also deepened their involvement in the third bloc, led by Iran but with close ties to Syria, Lebanon and Iraq. In the 2020s then, the West will be less important to Middle Eastern states than it once was, and the UK is less important within the West.

In addition to this, the UK's interest in the Middle East is diminished. Public appetite to be involved in the Middle East was low even before the 2003 Iraq War and has plummeted since. MPs decision not to endorse a proposed strike on Syria in 2013 indicated how much such scars continue to be felt. The main exception to this public reluctance is on areas of security, with the public largely in support of anti-ISIS operations, especially bombing campaigns that posed less risk to UK troops.[4] There is sporadic public concern on certain Middle East issues, such as human rights violations, the Israel–Palestine conflict, women's rights, arms sales and isolated events like the murder of journalist Jamal Khashoggi, but these rarely translate to sustained pressure on ministers to act. That said, Britain's leaders are also less interested in the Middle East than they once were. The declining salience of oil with a shift to more renewable energy has lessened interest in the region in general. With Brexit and post-EU trade deals taking up most foreign policy bandwidth, the region has fallen further down the priority list except for when sudden crises return it to the front page, often prompting short-term reactive responses. The decision-makers have changed too. While the UK has long had a highly centralized policymaking structure, recent changes have amplified this. The newly merged Foreign, Commonwealth and Development Office has steadily lost influence under successive prime ministers (with the possible exception of David Cameron), with the Cabinet Office and No. 10 increasingly the centre of foreign policymaking. With most policies made by a small handful of individuals, this gives even less bandwidth for the Middle East. Despite a recent boost to defence spending, few expect the Middle East to be the MoD's primary focus. The UK's capacity and interest in the region therefore look increasingly limited.

The obvious conclusion from this changing context is for the UK to be more realistic and less ambitious in its engagement with the Middle East. This need not mean disinterest, but rather a recognition of its limited capacity and to be more selective in its engagement. While in the past the UK has sought to be influential in multiple Middle East arenas, it will spread itself too thinly to be effective if it repeats this path. A better approach, so believe the editors and many of the contributors to this volume, is to focus on a limited number of achievable goals in specific areas of Britain's interest and then channel resources into those areas. In short, to favour depth over breadth: to do less, but to do it well.

Difficult choices: Principles and pragmatism

But what are Britain's interests in the Middle East upon which this new narrower capacity should focus? A second theme of this volume is an exploration of the three areas that the UK has historically prioritized in the region: security, trade and values. Of these, security has been the most recently valued, partly due to proximity. As Michael Clarke notes in his chapter, unlike the United States, the MENA region is on Europe's doorstep and the potential for instability to spill over directly means it cannot be ignored. And although both US and UK foreign policies increasingly place emphasis on the Subcontinent and East Asia as part of the so-called Indo-Pacific tilt, this should not mean that the Middle East suddenly becomes unimportant.

Despite leaving the EU, Britain remains one of the wealthiest and biggest defence spenders in Europe, meaning it is likely to play a role in any urgent short-term security concerns that emerge. Beyond such occasional reactive commitments, however, the UK must be selective on which security areas it will focus on. As Louise Kettle notes, after Britain's own security, its next priority has been to support crucial allies, and this requires uncomfortable choices as the region sees more conflict. Would Britain send military assistance to the Gulf states, for example, if a war with Iran broke out? Likewise, would it join a US-led coalition against Tehran, even if it opposed conflict, but was worried about losing favour with Washington? Such outcomes are distinct possibilities in the coming decade and the UK would do well to plan for such an eventuality, establishing how it might viably support its allies in a means that it can afford, or how it can avoid such interventions without rupturing key alliances. This will require a delicate balancing act of trade-offs and calculations.

While the Middle East has historically not been a vital economic region for the UK, the recent increase in Gulf trade alongside the centrality of trade deals after Brexit has amplified London's financial concerns. As David Butter discusses in his chapter, Britain faces a choice over whether to build on the existing but limited trade successes it has – mostly arms and services and with the Gulf states – or to seek new markets and focus on new sectors. Gulf trade is heavily linked to a buoyant oil and gas sector, and with both suffering from the impact of Covid-19 and a global shift away from fossil fuels, there may be slimmer pickings than in the past. Beyond the Gulf, there are comparatively limited options for British businesses, although Turkey and Egypt, with which it already has decent economic links, are the most obvious places to step up. As Sanam Vakil notes, Iran could be a further attractive market for Britain, but the current political climate makes any serious increase unlikely. Exploring possible areas for increased economic activity in Iran or preparing for any future change in political circumstances that would allow greater market penetration might be one area for UK planners to explore; however, given the limited resources available it is unlikely. Again, the question of bandwidth and resources is vital. Any increase in British trade requires more resources, energy and focus from London especially given the growing competition from other global powers, and the UK must weigh up if the Middle East is the best target for such efforts.

The final driver of UK Middle East policy is values which, as James Lynch notes in his chapter, have historically been the 'third wheel' – prioritized only when it doesn't seriously hinder security or trade. In the post-Brexit landscape, it is highly possible that values will diminish even further in importance as the hunt for trade partners and sustaining military alliances necessitates turning a blind eye towards human rights abuses and poor governance. That said, values seem likely to retain rhetorical importance. Foreign Secretary Dominic Raab made a point of emphasizing how post-Brexit Britain will prioritize sanctions against human rights abusers. Similarly, any future Labour government would likely vocalize the importance of values in foreign policy, as it did in the past. Yet whatever the rhetoric, Britain's currently diminished global and regional importance, and its prioritization of trade and security, will limit the chances for such protestations to cut through to regional governments. That does not mean the statements should not be made, but a recognition that any value-driven policy requires more than rhetoric and symbolic action. With its imperial past the UK has never had the automatic moral authority that many of its leaders often assume, but its behaviour in the Middle East, especially the Iraq War, as well as the internal strife over Brexit, has damaged Britain's reputation further. Rebuilding will require concerted effort. This need not mean jettisoning allies with unpalatable governing records, but being consistent in criticism of those policies, while seeking other routes to rebuild Britain's reputation. Seeking to lead by example rather than by instruction might be a start. As both Christopher Phillips and Emma El-Badawy note, Britain's pre-existing soft power institutions, such as the BBC, British Council and the UK university sector, could also be valuable assets, as could closer horizontal diplomatic and military relations, a point made by Jack Watling. However, these institutions remain under threat of cuts in the UK for domestic reasons, with politicians often unaware or unbothered by the potential foreign policy implications, and when combined with a cut in the UK's foreign aid spending from 0.7 per cent of GDP to 0.5 per cent the picture is not a happy one. Cuts to key public institutions – which will be inevitable given the enormous government spending undertaken during the course of the pandemic – will make the UK less attractive, hindering attempts to rebrand and rebuild the UK's global and regional reputation.

Targeted engagement

Alongside exploring the changing context in which Britain operates, and the changes and continuities in its main interests, a third theme of this volume concerns where the UK should direct its attention. Where should it focus its narrower bandwidth? There is already an unofficial hierarchy of interest in the Middle East with more resources dedicated to some states over others. The authors in this volume suggest that some of this is justified, while others are a relic from an earlier era and require a rethink. The Gulf is and should remain the number one area of UK interest, given its overlap of both security and economic priorities. As Tobias Borck and Michael Stephens note, this necessitates some uncomfortable compromises on values as these governments are becoming more rather than less autocratic. The internal fissures within the Gulf Cooperation Council (GCC) over the Qatar Blockade and other disputes have made managing relations in this region more complex, requiring a focus on a series of individual bilateral relationships rather than with a single bloc. Even so, the Gulf is a region where the UK enjoys some genuine and unique deep relationships. While it comes with the cost of appearing cosy with autocratic governments, there is merit in seeking to strengthen and deepen these ties further, while continuing to at least speak out against any human rights or governance abuses.

After the Gulf, the next most important states to the UK are Iran, Turkey and Israel. As Vakil notes, Iran's importance to London is closely tied to security concerns in the region as a whole and the Gulf specifically. Its involvement as a guarantor of the JCPOA is one of Britain's few prominent diplomatic roles in the region, but the possibility of conflict relating to Iran is increasing. The UK is more likely to be a follower than a leader on events, but it still needs to develop suitable contingency plans. Turkey's importance is primarily economic though, as Bill Park notes, the UK is one of the few Western states enjoying favourable ties with an increasingly isolated Ankara. While again this requires some trade-offs on values as the Turkish government becomes increasingly despotic, London is well placed to build on this relationship for economic and possible security gains. Similar trade-offs will be necessary to expand its ties with an Israeli government that seems ever-more uncompromising on its occupation of the West Bank. As Ian Black notes, trade, tech and intelligence collaboration with Israel is at an all-time high and should continue. The challenge for London will be how to build on this relationship without abandoning the Palestinians. While the UK should recognize that its ability to influence the peace process, while never much, is now even less, that shouldn't mean capitulation. A firm line on settlements and a human rights-based critique of Israel may be one means to enhance ties without unpalatable compromises.

The authors note some regions where Britain might hedge its bets: to dedicate resources if circumstances are right, but to avoid if not. Watling identifies Iraq as one. While a degree of security cooperation is likely to continue given the potential for instability and the possible return of ISIS or similar organisations, economic conditions make Iraq's potentially valuable market unattractive without reform. Similarly, El-Badawy notes the challenges for the UK in Egypt. The potential implosion of Egypt poses a serious security threat to Europe and the UK and necessitates a degree of engagement irrespective. However, with the military regime suspicious of Britain and generally closed and opaque, London may find considerable investment will not generate either the reforms or the access it hopes for, prompting a more cautious approach. In contrast, Phillips argues Britain should heavily reduce its involvement in Syria. While security concerns will necessitate some monitoring of the situation and occasional involvement, the UK's political influence over the conflict is minimal. With more powerful players involved and dwarfing Britain's influence, taking a back seat and refocusing elsewhere would be a better use of resources. Phillips also argues that London might reconsider how involved in Lebanon it wishes to be given the heavy competition from other powers.

In contrast, smaller states with less immediate security or economic concerns might be worth enhancing Britain's footprint in. Jordan and Oman in particular are two historic allies that London has deep horizontal ties with. Indeed, Muscat and Amman might be interesting testbeds of the 'do less but better' approach recommended in this volume. It is unlikely such investments in resources will reap any immediate material benefit, and so might not find favour with politicians looking for short-term gains. Such an approach would be a mistake however, as building close ties to these states could help boost the UK's reputation and give London genuine friends in the region that would prove valuable long into the future.

In approaching the Middle East in the 2020s, it is important to strike the right tone that acknowledges the changed circumstances. For the generation of leaders coming to power in the Middle East and their youthful population, the British Empire is ancient history and most have grown up in an era when the UK was not a powerful player. At the same time, Britain has been portrayed negatively in many school history classes. The somewhat superior approach of some British leaders and bureaucrats towards the Middle East, an echo of the colonial mindset, needs to be totally expunged from policymaking as it adds no value and frequently hinders British interests. London needs to view Middle Eastern states and their peoples as friends, allies and equal partners, not as clients. Some may wish to learn from British expertise, but many do not, and resent being lectured. Equally the UK could learn from the Middle East if it is open to it. The opportunities for Britain in the coming decade will be less than in the past due to factors beyond the UK's control. However, how London approaches the region, where it targets its limited resources and with what priorities, will determine how well Britain achieves its goals.

Book structure

To explore these views, this volume is divided into four sections each dealing with a distinct set of contained concepts, themes or geographically distinct areas. The authors feel this best breaks down Britain's diverse interests and policies, across a vast expanse of the world in which there are many distinct cultures and identities.

The first section entitled 'Still searching for a role – the UK in the Middle East from East of Suez to Brexit' sets the scene for subsequent chapters by assessing Britain's historical relationships in the Middle East and outlines the current geostrategic environment that Britain faces as it leaves the EU. In the opening chapter the late Professor Rosemary Hollis traces Britain's relationships in the Middle East since the 1971 withdrawal from East of Suez up until the present day. Professor Michael Clarke follows this with a focus on the main contours of global politics at the beginning of the 2020s and addresses some of the major policy questions that Britain must come to terms with as power shifts from West to East. To end the section Michael Stephens analyses the state of the Special Relationship between the UK and its closest ally, the United States, looking at areas of continuity and change for London as it balances its diplomatic relations with a superpower that appears reluctant to be as involved in the Middle East as before.

The second section entitled 'Principles and pragmatism – the debates over the UK's Middle East priorities' looks at the three key thematic questions that govern British policy in the region: values, economics and security. James Lynch opens the section by looking at the moral questions Britain must tackle in its regional policy, arguing that this will be a difficult balance for the UK in the years ahead. David Butter looks at Britain's economic interests in the region, suggesting that there are indeed opportunities ahead for the UK if it looks smartly at where and how to invest. Louise Kettle closes the section by assessing the myriad of security threats that still emanate from the Middle East region, ranging from international terrorist organizations to the threat of a nuclear Iran, all of which Britain must contend with alongside its allies in the decade to come.

The third section entitled 'Britain and the non-Arab powers' focuses on the three major powers in the Middle East whose identities and histories are both external, but critically linked to the Arab Middle East: Turkey, Israel and Iran. In Chapter 8, Bill Park assesses the current relationship between Britain and Turkey, which has become of more interest to Britain after Brexit, yet is also problematic as Erdogan's Turkey clashes with crucial British allies like the United States and France. In Chapter 9, Ian Black looks at Britain's relationship with Israel, assessing its involvement in the stalled Middle East Peace Process and looking at how London has forged closer links particularly in the economic sphere. To finish the section Sanam Vakil provides an overview of Britain's checkered relationship with Iran, which is replete with historical setbacks and challenges, but is still one of the most critical today given the ongoing global concern over Iran's nuclear programme.

The fourth section looks at the heart of the Arab World, analysing Britain's continued interests in a region that was heavily shaped by its imperialist designs, the ramifications of which are still present today. In Chapter 11 Christopher Phillips assesses the state of British policy in Syria and the Levant region, looking at ways Britain could improve its position by better balancing its interests in Jordan while drawing down in Syria, and by extension Lebanon. Jack Watling looks at the challenges for Britain in Iraq in Chapter 12, which are many. Continued state fragility, corruption and the ever-present dynamic between the United States and Iran present a whole host of issues for Britain to tackle, with Watling asserting that some of these challenges may be too great for London, requiring a rethink. In Chapter 13 Tobias Borck and Michael Stephens assess the relationship between Britain and its historically close partners in the Gulf. Noting that although years of interlinkages provide a strong footing for good relations in the future, the Gulf states have changed in mindset and outlook from years past, and Britain will need to better adjust to these states' more assertive stances than it has done previously. In Chapter 14 Emman El-Badawy looks at British–Egyptian relations: as the most populous country in the Middle East, Egypt's importance cannot be underestimated. El-Badawy suggests that Britain must strike a better balance between engaging with Egypt's young population and its continued support for Egypt's authoritarian government. In the final chapter, Phillips and Stephens present their conclusions, arguing that Britain's Middle East Policy post-Brexit should be narrowed and more tightly focused in areas that Britain can have the most impact, as opposed to trying to be involved in all regional questions as part of a regional policy that cannot ever be successfully implemented.

Part One

Still searching for a role – The UK in the Middle East from East of Suez to Brexit

2

Britain and the Middle East since the end of Empire

Rosemary Hollis

The record shows that whatever role Britain might aspire to play in the Middle East, its options have been determined by the machinations of regional players, both state and non-state actors, and the ambitions of its leading ally the United States and, increasingly, those of Russia and China. As a result, the British have tended to prioritize pragmatism over idealism.

Between 1945 and 1971 Britain's erstwhile imperial predominance in the Middle East was transformed into a set of bilateral relationships with individual states. Over the same period, Britain itself transited from an imperial power to what one British politician termed 'a major power of the second rank'.[1] British ambitions in and for the Middle East were adjusted accordingly.

From the 1970s, the principal objective repeatedly invoked by Her Majesty's Government (HMG) was for regional stability, in the interests of British commerce and the free flow of oil to British and other Western economies. HMG also shared with the United States a commitment to curbing the influence of the Soviet Union in the region, and when the latter eventually collapsed and the United States emerged as unrivalled regional hegemon in the 1990s, the British developed a niche role under the US umbrella.

Its alliance with the United States nonetheless impelled the British into a series of military interventions alongside the Americans, notably in 1991 to reverse the Iraqi invasion of Kuwait and subsequently, following the attacks on New York and Washington of 11 September 2001 (9/11), in the context of Washington's declared 'war on terror'. The interventions since 9/11 have largely failed to achieve either regional or regime stability. Instead, conflict and agitation for change have become more widespread, and dealing with the repercussions of Islamist-inspired terrorism both at home and abroad has become a central British policy imperative.

End of the Imperial Era

Britain's 'imperial moment' in the Middle East[2] was short-lived, especially when compared to the duration of the Ottoman Empire. Yet, because the British managed to drive out the Ottomans during the First World War and establish control across much of the region, until the aftermath of the Second World War, HMG did have what might be termed a regional approach to the Middle East.

Even though victorious in the Second World War, in the aftermath the UK was burdened with debts and unable to maintain its extensive imperial commitments in the face of mounting pressures for independence. When they left India in 1947, the British lost what they had regarded as 'the jewel in the imperial crown' and, along with it, the Indian navy hitherto used by Britain to police the Indian Ocean and Persian Gulf.

The decision to relinquish the Mandate for Palestine in 1947 was driven by lack of resources to hold on in the face of both Arab and Jewish opposition to Britain's continued presence. As the British withdrew, Israeli independence was declared and in the first Arab–Israeli war that followed, the fledgling Jewish state was established and the Palestinians suffered their catastrophe or *Nakba*. For years thereafter Arabs across the region saw fit to hold Britain primarily responsible for that outcome, at least until the United States attained regional hegemony.

Anti-imperialism and the appeal of Arab nationalism drove the British authorities out of Egypt in 1952, paving the way for the rise of Gamal Abdel Nasser as a direct challenge to the British. They nearly lost their predominance in Iran in 1953, when the elected government of Mohammed Mosaddeq supplanted the Shah and nationalized the Iranian energy industry, thereby dispossessing what had become a British monopoly. HMG responded by colluding with the Americans to topple Mosaddeq and reinstate the Shah. In the process the British retrieved a stake in Iranian oil, though only in conjunction with American companies. In Iran, the legacy of this episode was an abiding distrust of the British as well as the Americans.

British action against Nasser proved more damaging to British self-esteem. When the government of Anthony Eden colluded with Israel and France to try to seize control of the Suez Canal by force in 1956, the result was humiliating for HMG. Excluded from and outraged by this plot, the United States intervened forcing Britain, and thence France and Israel, to withdraw their forces. Thereafter the British resolved never again to risk crossing swords so directly with Washington. Their days of doing as they pleased in the Middle East were over, and by 1958 they had lost their influence in Iraq and were obliged to reduce their profile in Jordan.

In 1961 the British conceded to Kuwait's demands for independence and in 1967 they gave up the campaign to stay in Yemen and evacuated the British colony in Aden. Only in the Arab Gulf states of Bahrain, Qatar, what became the United Arab Emirates (UAE) and Oman did they linger on, but they sensed their days were numbered there too.[3]

Adjusting to decline

According to the report of a government committee on Britain's representational services overseas (*the Plowden Report*) of 1964:

> Britain retains many wide responsibilities and a high degree of world-wide influence. We believe that the British people wish to sustain that influence and

> share Sir Winston Churchill's view that Britain could not be content to be relegated to a tame and minor role in the world.[4]

Plowden nonetheless concluded that Britain could no longer meet its extended commitments and needed to consolidate its overseas representation and charge its diplomats with prioritizing trade promotion.

After a Labour government came to power in 1964, Parliament debated the implications of the loss of empire. Not only was overt imperialism no longer a viable or ideologically justifiable way of organizing the global order, but super-power rivalry had become the driving force in international relations. In the Middle East this meant competition for clients between the United States and the Soviet Union such that, by 1967, they were ranged on opposite sides in the Arab–Israeli conflict.

Reflecting on Britain's identity and prospects, Labour Foreign Secretary Michael Stuart called for adjustment to a new position as a 'major power of the second rank', because 'Britain's former dominating position is gone. But … Britain retains a position of considerable influence all over the world'.[5]

In terms of defence spending, in 1964 it was the initial intention of the new Labour government to make cuts that would shore up the depleted national coffers and many party members advocated a withdrawal from British bases East of Suez. However, Prime Minister Harold Wilson and Defence Secretary Denis Healey chose a different path. Faced with a fall in gold reserves, a widening trade gap and stagnation in industrial production, they were intent upon warding off a devaluation in sterling. They identified the United States as best placed to help rescue the situation.

This was effectively the beginning of the era in which the British would adjust to acting with others in the Western alliance and prioritize the 'special relationship' with the United States in particular. That said, the United States proved a demanding ally. On a visit to Washington in 1965 Wilson and Healey deduced that President Lyndon Johnson looked to Britain to defend Western interests East of Suez, including in the Gulf, partly because British forces were already in place to do so and partly because the United States was preoccupied with the war in Vietnam.

As a result, no significant cuts were made in British defence spending and the government tried to continue to meet all its existing overseas commitments with depleted resources. By the end of the 1960s however, the government had to conclude that a withdrawal 'East of Suez' was unavoidable. A new Conservative government tried to row back on this assessment, only to reach the same conclusion and in 1971 Britain withdrew its forces, including from the Gulf, while Bahrain, Qatar and the UAE gained formal independence. The British did, however, retain forces in Oman to help the Omani government defeat a rebellion, backed by socialist Yemeni factions in the south of the Sultanate.[6]

Britain's response to the Arab–Israeli war of 1967 was more that of a bystander than a participant, though Britain's ambassador to the United Nations, Lord Caradon, played a leading role in drafting UN Security Council Resolution 242 that called for Israel to relinquish captured territory in return for peace with its Arab neighbours. In this respect HMG acted in accordance with Britain's avowed new identity as 'a major power of the second rank'; that is, a permanent member of the UN Security

Council with an influential role in determining international norms and the rule of law; a leading member of NATO and, from 1973, a member of the European Economic Community (EEC).

The oil boom years

Starting with Libya, in the early 1970s, the major Arab oil-producing states, as well as Iran, nationalized their energy industries. In contrast to 1953, there was no British attempt to resist this development, and control over the process of determining the market price of oil shifted from the major international energy companies, including BP and Shell, to the producer governments and thence the Organization of Petroleum Exporting Countries (OPEC). In fact, the energy companies adapted to the new circumstances, not least because they were global operations and new technologies enabled them to drill for oil in previously inaccessible sites, including the North Sea.

For the producer states nationalization spelled new wealth. The international banking sector, including British-based banks, responded quickly to coax the producer governments in the Gulf to deposit their surplus petro-dollars with Western finance houses. British-based infrastructure developers and consumer-goods producers followed up with a push to gain new contracts in the oil-rich Gulf states. Thus began what became known as the 'oil boom' years, with major British companies and finance houses among the main beneficiaries. The British government and consumers were less fortunate, however.

The boom turned to crisis in 1973, when Arab oil-producers imposed an oil embargo on the United States and other state-supporters of Israel during the 1973 Arab–Israeli war. Global oil prices tripled between 1973 and 1975. The impact on the British economy and response of the Conservative government led by Edward Heath, including restrictions on energy usage that reduced industrial production to a 'three-day week', contributed to Heath's fall from power in 1974.

The subsequent Labour government lost its narrow majority in Parliament by 1977 and an election in 1979 delivered a victory for the Conservative Party led by Margaret Thatcher. That year also saw another oil shock – triggered by the revolution in Iran and fall of the Shah. The same year the Soviets invaded Afghanistan. These developments prompted the US administration to take direct responsibility for protecting US interests and designing security arrangements in the Gulf, to which the British duly accommodated.

The Thatcher years

During her first term in office Prime Minister Margaret Thatcher consolidated her hold on power through her successful prosecution of the Falklands War. The first Thatcher government also initiated an expansion of the budget for defence and a contraction in that for diplomacy. By her own admission, Thatcher was not impressed by 'the grandees' at the Foreign and Commonwealth Office (FCO) and did not automatically defer to them on foreign policy issues.

By 1985 expenditure on the FCO had been reduced by 9.4 per cent over a seven-year period by running down staff levels by 17 per cent and by applying cost-effectiveness measures to all diplomatic functions.[7] As a result, commercial work became the best-resourced task of the FCO's overseas staff and pursuit of bilateral trade agreements became the main focus for the British in the Middle East.

In the 1983 election, the Conservative Party adopted a slogan 'to put the Great back in Great Britain!' Meanwhile, Thatcher formed a close relationship with US President Ronald Reagan and together they championed liberal market capitalism, including deregulation of the banking sector and privatization of state enterprises, which in Thatcher's case included selling off government shares in British Aerospace (later to become BAE Systems), British Gas, British Airways and BP. State revenues were boosted by the sale of state-run enterprises and tax returns on North Sea oil production. In the 1980s Britain became a net exporter of energy, reliant on Middle East producers only for a specific type of crude.

New opportunities for business in the Gulf states meanwhile attracted many companies to set up branches there, and the number of British expats living in the Gulf increased exponentially compared with imperial times, creating a new form of British 'interest' in the region.[8] Safeguarding British and Western interests in the Gulf was a stated objective of HMG's 'out-of-NATO-area' strategy. As explained by Foreign Minister Francis Pym in March 1980:

> We shall continue to contribute to the security and stability of the Indian Ocean and Gulf areas through the provision of military training assistance and advice, and defence equipment. From time to time we deploy units from all three Services for visits to friendly countries and undertake exercises with their forces.[9]

Thatcher personally was instrumental in securing for Britain its largest single defence sales contract on record. The two-part deal, Al Yamamah I of 1985 and Al Yamamah II of 1988, was signed between HMG and the government of Saudi Arabia and involved the supply of seventy-two Tornado fighters and fifty Hawk jet trainers, helicopters, naval vessels, the construction of two airbases, associated equipment, spare parts, training and support services.[10] It was a counter-trade deal, paid for in oil supplies to BP and Shell, to be sold at market prices by them, the proceeds of which were then transferred to the Ministry of Defence and thence to BAE Systems, which in turn paid various British sub-contractors. The deal also included an 'offset' component, whereby HMG would encourage British companies, helped by BAE Systems, to invest in the production of their products in the Saudi Kingdom.

The significance of this and subsequent UK arms sales to the Saudis was threefold. First, it provided a major source of funding for the British defence sector. Second, it enabled BAE Systems with revenue to cover the transition from production of Tornados to that of its successor, the Eurofighter or Typhoon, and thereby ensured the survival and sustainability of Britain's independent defence industrial base.[11] Third, this government-to-government deal bound Britain more closely to Saudi Arabia and formed the bedrock of their bilateral relationship, which included intelligence sharing, and a mutual interest in the stability and longevity of the Saudi rulers.

Though not on the same scale, there were to be other defence sales contracts signed between HMG and the governments of the other Arab Gulf states in the 1980s and more yet in subsequent decades. On a lesser scale Britain sold arms to Iran and Iraq, even though these countries were at war between 1980 and 1988 and Britain's official position was one of neutrality. In keeping with US policy, Britain supplied arms to Iraq in order to prevent Iraq losing to the Islamic Republic. However, the British parliament was not made aware of this policy and when the sales were revealed the government was obliged to instigate an enquiry.[12]

Turning to the Arab–Israeli sector, the UK government cited the unresolved conflict as a source of instability in the wider region. Interviewed in 1981, then Foreign Office Minister Douglas Hurd said:

> Our friends in the Gulf have always made clear that the Palestine issue is enormously important to them, and that it is difficult for them to be counted on as friends of the West so long as it appears that the West is simply supporting Israel. That's one reason why we Europeans, in the Venice Declaration last year, tried to take an even-handed line and tried to advance matters.[13]

While the FCO was generally perceived (not least by the Israelis) as tilting towards the Arab perspective rather than that of the Israelis, Thatcher distinguished herself with a more nuanced position.[14] She disliked PLO Chairman Yasser Arafat and shunned the PLO as a terrorist organization, but recognized the right to self-determination of Palestinians in the West Bank and Gaza, though she did not advocate a Palestinian state. She had a frosty relationship with Israeli Prime Minister Yitzhak Shamir, yet established a rapport with Foreign Minister Shimon Peres and encouraged him to forge an agreement with King Hussein of Jordan, who became her personal friend and frequent confidante. Thatcher's attempt to facilitate a secret deal (the 'London Agreement') between Peres and Hussein in 1987 foundered when Peres informed Shamir of the plan.[15]

Thatcher maintained that continuance of the Israeli–Palestinian conflict gave the Soviets a lever to instigate instability in the region, and she was critical of the Reagan administration's inattention to the issue and disdain for King Hussein. Her vision was the reinstatement of Jordanian rule over most of the West Bank. Overall, Thatcher overestimated her own, and by extension Britain's, power to manipulate or dragoon the principal actors. Hers was the last unilateral attempt by the British to orchestrate a resolution to the Israeli–Palestinian conflict.

It was near the very end of Thatcher's time in office that Iraq invaded Kuwait, in August 1990, and she personally helped galvanize US President George Bush to take a decisive stand on this challenge to international law and to stability in the Gulf. However, Thatcher was forced from office by members of her own party, and it was left to her successor John Major to oversee Britain's contribution to the US-led coalition that ousted the Iraqis from Kuwait in 1991.

In retrospect, the Thatcher era might be considered a template for a post-Brexit Britain: providing a distinctive and self-confident voice in international affairs, championing free trade and 'the rule of law', yet contributing Britain's weight to a broader Western agenda through NATO, the World Bank and IMF, and at the UN Security Council. That said, during the Thatcher years there was a niche role for the British under the US umbrella in terms of defence sales and military alliances with the Gulf states which Thatcher understood and capitalized on, aided by her strong rapport with the US president. However, Reagan did not pay attention to her theories about resolving the Israeli–Palestinian conflict.

To replicate the distinctive role that Britain attained during the Thatcher era would require an alignment of interests and goals with those of the United States which seems less likely under a US president averse to new military entanglements overseas and lacking a clear strategy for US engagement in the region to which the British could commit support.

Perhaps the best illustration of how Britain was able to distinguish itself as positively instrumental in the Middle East, while accepting US leadership, was in the Gulf War of 1990–1. HMG marshalled the largest single overseas deployment of British forces since the Second World War to join the US-led coalition that eventually liberated Kuwait in 1991. According to the commander of the British forces, General Sir Peter de la Billiere, the logic of fielding such a large force was to ensure British participation in US planning for Operation Desert Storm.[16] In this respect the British were successful, though their voice turned out to be far less influential in subsequent military operations.

Under the oversight of US Secretary of Defense, General Colin Powell, a veteran of Vietnam, the US strategy to reverse the Iraqi occupation of Kuwait favoured the deployment of vastly superior forces to deliver a quick and decisive victory. This was accomplished with very few coalition casualties, though the frontline Iraqi forces in and around Kuwait were hammered in a massive aerial bombardment ahead of the allied ground offensive.

The crack troops of Iraq's Republican Guard Corps, by contrast, were kept back from the frontline and largely survived unscathed. They were not engaged or pursued, because President Bush called a halt to the Coalition offensive once the Iraqis took flight from Kuwait. Military and political analysts were subsequently to question the wisdom of calling off the offensive before delivering a more crushing blow to Iraq's armed forces. Had US and British forces proceeded further into Iraq there would have been anger among their Arab allies, who refused to enter Iraqi territory at all. Bush was also criticized for calling for an uprising against the leadership of Iraqi President Saddam Hussein, which he did once the fighting stopped. By this he apparently envisaged a coup d'état, rather than the mass uprisings that actually occurred, involving both the predominantly Shia Arab population of Southern Iraq and the Kurds in north, both of which communities had been repressed under Saddam's rule.

Under the terms of the ceasefire at the end of the war, the Iraqi armed forces were permitted to keep their helicopter forces and used these to suppress the revolt in the south of Iraq. By contrast, US, British and French forces did come to the rescue of Kurds fleeing the regime's counter-offensive in the north and eventually set up a no-fly zone wherein the Kurds would subsequently establish an autonomous enclave. There was also to be a no-fly zone established along the Iraqi side of the border with Kuwait, policed by US, British and French aircraft based in the Gulf. However, this did not protect the population of Southern Iraq from renewed repression by the regime of Saddam Hussein.

Legacies of the 1990–1 Gulf War

There were many lessons to be derived from this war. In purely military terms it was considered a success, including by the British, except that is, for the fact that the regime and armed forces of Saddam Hussein were allowed to survive. The benefits of the deployment of overwhelming military strength ahead of the fighting were ignored when it came to the subsequent decision to invade Iraq in 2003. Equally overlooked in that context were the lessons drawn by Iraqi opponents of Saddam Hussein, in Southern Iraq, who found themselves abandoned by the Coalition when they revolted. That tempered their enthusiasm for the return of US and UK forces in 2003.

Also ignored was the effect of the 1991 war on Osama bin-Laden, leader of what became Al-Qaeda. He and his followers saw the whole Coalition operation as a manifestation of Western imperialism. Al-Qaeda became self-appointed champions of Arabs opposed to the imposition of Western control over the region. In particular, the methods chosen by the US and its Western allies to contain Saddam Hussein's Iraq after 1991 fuelled the ire of Al-Qaeda.

Blanket sanctions were maintained in the name of forcing Baghdad to renounce its programme for the development of Weapons of Mass Destruction (WMD). UN weapons inspectors were sent into Iraq to execute this imperative but failed to secure full Iraqi cooperation. US, British and, for a while, French forces periodically bombed Iraqi targets, all of them represented as military assets, in a vain attempt to reinforce the message. Meanwhile, the Iraqi general population, aside from the Kurds, languished, and Arabs around the region became more sympathetic to their plight. Subsequent attempts by the United States to instigate a coup against Saddam failed.

For the duration of the 1990s, the British remained heavily involved in the American strategy for Iraq and sought to coordinate with the United States when it came to devising new security arrangements for the Arabian Peninsula states. Yet the British were essentially minor players under the US umbrella. The Americans established bases in all the smaller Arab Gulf states, where they pre-positioned US-made equipment paid for by Gulf governments. In a sense, the United States picked up where the British had left off in 1971, but on a grander scale. Also like the British before them, they concentrated their forward positions in the peripheral states rather than in Saudi Arabia. This was because Saudi citizens were considered hostile to an overt US presence there, especially after a US-manned base near Riyadh and then a housing complex for US personnel in Dahran came under terrorist attack, variously attributed to Saudi dissidents or Iran.

The British had no part in the Madrid peace conference sponsored by the United States and, nominally, Russia in 1991. Clearly, Washington saw no value in involving the UK – and initially the European Union (EU) was kept on the sidelines. The conference brought together Israel, Arab neighbouring states and others, including some Palestinians attached to the Jordanian delegation. The conference launched what became the US-sponsored Middle East Peace Process (MEPP), in fulfilment of a promise made by the Bush administration to address the Arab–Israeli conflict once Kuwait had been liberated. The delegations proceeded from Madrid to formal talks in Washington. However, when it was revealed that the Israelis and the PLO had agreed a peace formula at secret talks in Norway, the so-called Oslo process was adopted by the US administration of Bill Clinton and the first Oslo Accord was signed on the White House lawn in 1993.

To protect that process from anticipated opposition from Iran, the Clinton administration initiated what was called 'Dual Containment' of both Iraq and Iran. The latter came under US unilateral sanctions which were intended to pressure Iran to change its policies, including its support for Hezbollah in Lebanon – a Shia militia that had come into being in opposition to the Israelis after they invaded Lebanon in 1982. Britain was among the European countries which had consistently called for the Israelis to withdraw from Lebanon, under the terms of UN Resolution 425, which they did only partially. Despite US objections, in the 1990s the British also sided with other members of the EU in pursuing a policy of engagement with Iran. HMG encouraged British companies to ignore the US sanctions and managed to deter Washington from imposing a secondary boycott on those companies.

Looking back, perhaps the best way to characterize how British decision-makers saw Britain's place in the world in the 1990s is provided by the Conservative Foreign Secretary Douglas Hurd. He claimed Britain was 'punching above its weight'.[17] In the Middle East the reality of US hegemony was acknowledged, but HMG retained a distinctive position on Iran and Lebanon. It was most closely aligned with the United States on Iraq and continued to operate alongside US arms manufacturers when it came to pursuing contracts in the Arab Gulf states.

On the MEPP, HMG deferred to the US lead, while increasingly aligning its stance with the rest of the EU. For a while, the UK was a bridge-builder *within* the EU, between those members most critical of Israel, which in the 1990s included Greece, Spain and France, and those most sympathetic, that is Germany and the Netherlands. After Tony Blair came to office in 1997, however, it became one of his ambitions to position Britain as a bridge between Europe and the United States. Yet he ended up so closely aligned to Washington that he lost the ear and respect of some of Britain's European allies.

The advent of New Labour

In the general election of 1997, the Labour Party, rebranded under the leadership of Blair as 'New Labour', swept to power with a resounding majority. Together Blair and his Chancellor Gordon Brown set a new tone for the relationship between their party and the British business community, managing to maintain business confidence at the same time as attending to aspects of the domestic agenda that the Tories had been accused of neglecting.

Brown led on economic issues, while Blair led on policy presentation and increasingly, over time, on foreign policy. Blair was also instrumental in concluding the Good Friday Agreement that brought peace to Northern Ireland. Brown took a personal interest in international development and the formulation and pursuit of the UN's Millennium Development Goals. Under new labour a new Department for International Development was established with, over time, a budget larger than that of the FCO.

The comparative youth of the prime minister and many of the newly elected members of parliament was celebrated as representing a new beginning. Blair called Britain 'a young country' and made no apology for his poor knowledge of history. He and his closest associates in government positively welcomed the phenomenon of 'globalization'. They borrowed the jargon of business management to describe their mission in government and Blair revolutionized the decision-making process to dispense with traditional procedures, including minute-taking, when discussing issues with his circle.[18] No. 10 Downing Street (the Prime Minister's office) became the centre of a decision-making process which frequently bypassed the Cabinet, Cabinet Committees and Government Departments.

In his first years at No. 10, Blair and his advisers adopted the idea that they would make Britain 'a force for good' in the world, and this objective appeared in his government's first Strategic Defence Review. This meant that British actions abroad, particularly interventions to curb the powers of dictatorial regimes, would enhance the reputation of Britain as a champion of good causes. Britain's intervention in Sierra Leone was the first such venture under Blair, to be followed up, on a much more significant scale, with the intervention in Kosovo. In that instance Blair virtually bounced the administration of US President Bill Clinton into committing ground forces, as well as shouldering the main burden of aerial bombardment.

In 1998 British forces joined the Americans in Operation Desert Fox, whereby they bombed a series of Iraqi military positions and installations, in the name of forcing the Iraqi government to comply with UN weapons inspections. The actual effect was to prompt Saddam Hussein to expel the inspectors. Over the next couple of years HMG became even more energetic than the Americans in enforcing the sanctions regime on Iraq, claiming that this was necessary to contain Iraq and would in time lead either to Iraqi cooperation or prompt a coup d'état against Saddam.

However, the US administration had lost faith in the sanctions policy and was more actively pursuing ways to topple the regime. In addition, most Arab governments had ceased to regard Iraq as a dangerous threat and were more worried about the toll sanctions were taking on the Iraqi people. They withheld cooperation with the scheme favoured by HMG and enshrined in UN Resolution 1284 of 1999, to switch from denying Iraq the importation of any goods except those explicitly permitted by the UN to permitting it to import all goods except those explicitly denied.

There was to be a dramatic shift in Blair's orientation on international affairs following 9/11. After that, Blair dropped his talk of making Britain 'a force for good' and instead began talking about the imperative to combat 'evil'. He flew to Washington and pledged to 'stand shoulder to shoulder' with the US administration of President George W Bush in what became 'the war on terror'.

British forces, at the time engaged in a joint exercise with the armed forces of Oman, were directed to support the US invasion of Afghanistan, in pursuit of Al-Qaeda, which took place in the immediate aftermath of 9/11. British forces would later lend their weight to the NATO forces deployed in Afghanistan – some of whom would subsequently suffer gruelling encounters with the Taliban in Helmand province. Meanwhile, Blair was among the first to be alerted to Bush's intentions to follow up the Afghanistan operation with the invasion of Iraq.

As was revealed subsequently, by Spring 2002 Blair had pledged to Bush that the British would be with him come what may, though he kept the Cabinet and the British people in the dark about this undertaking. Over the following summer and into the autumn, strenuous efforts were made by the British to secure a UN resolution that would give legal cover to Bush's plans for Iraq. Eventually, the UN Security Council adopted Resolution 1441 and obliged Iraq to receive a new team of weapons inspectors.

When those inspectors failed to find evidence of the WMD programme that Blair was convinced existed, Washington was determined to go ahead with an invasion anyway. So eager was Blair to be part of the invasion that he persuaded his Attorney General to deem such action legal, under previous UN Resolutions, in contradiction to his earlier position. The invasion, with British forces included, began on 20 March 2003. The fateful consequences are well-known and the Chilcott Inquiry published in 2016 provides a detailed account of the decision-making process by which the British became embroiled in the whole endeavour.

To compound his damaged record on Iraq, Blair also presided over a rapprochement with Libya's Muammar Qadhafi in the aftermath of the Iraq invasion. British officers from MI6 worked with their CIA counterparts to convince Qadhafi to relinquish his WMD programme. This paved the way for the lifting of sanctions imposed on Libya after the Lockerbie bombing in 1988. British companies were then able to sign contracts to redevelop the Libyan energy sector and supply arms to the Colonel's regime. As would be revealed later, M16 also helped 'render' to Libya two individuals wanted by the Qadhafi regime for dissident activities. The men were subjected to torture and later brought a case in the UK courts against the MI6 officer involved, as well as then Foreign Secretary Jack Straw.[19]

What this case demonstrated was that the Blair government lied about its role in the extrajudicial rendition to third countries of suspected terrorists after 9/11. This discovery was but one aspect of the whole saga of HMG's activities in the early 2000s that damaged Britain's reputation for adherence to the rule of law and government accountability.

A somewhat less contentious aspect of Blair's legacy was his role in the MEPP, though his impact proved limited. He apparently saw himself as qualified to make a positive contribution because of his experience with Northern Ireland but found that both the Israeli and the Palestinian leaderships looked to the Americans as their preferred mediator. Blair therefore sought to exercise his influence on the process by supporting the efforts of the Clinton administration. As it transpired, those efforts failed to seal a deal before Clinton left office.

Blair persisted in his self-appointed role when George W. Bush replaced Clinton in 2000. By then Ariel Sharon had become Israeli prime minister and instituted a crackdown on Palestinian resistance in the occupied territories, which led to the near elimination of the Palestinian Authority. Only support from the EU kept it afloat. Nonetheless, Blair sought to persuade Bush to restart the MEPP and worked with the EU to produce the so-called Road Map that Bush eventually agreed to adopt, with caveats, after the start of the Iraq invasion. Blair later offered to help Secretary of State Condoleezza Rice with another initiative, the Annapolis Conference, though his efforts were never credited as decisive.

Perhaps the most remarkable outcome of all Blair's efforts was his nomination, by Bush, for appointment as envoy for the Quartet (the US, Russia, the EU and the UN) after Blair left office in 2007. He served in that role, with no substantial achievement, until 2015. Much more significant, however, was Blair's role in the war on terror. As reported in the Chilcot enquiry, Blair chose not to heed the warnings of Britain's intelligence community that the invasion of Iraq would increase the threat to Britain of terrorist groups like Al-Qaeda. On 7 July 2005 (7/7) a series of suicide bombings on the London transport system, carried out by British citizens claiming affiliation to Al-Qaeda, obliged HMG to review its whole approach to counterterrorism. One result was the rollout of a series of initiatives to counter the so-called radicalization of British Muslims, attributed variously to radical preachers and internet chat rooms.[20]

Another consequence was to step up intelligence sharing with Britain's allies, including Saudi Arabia.[21] So anxious was Blair that this latter arrangement be protected, that in 2007 he called off a Serious Fraud Office enquiry into weapons sales to Saudi Arabia, for fear the Kingdom would halt intelligence cooperation.

Britain's responses to the 'Arab Spring'

In 2010 the Labour Party, under the leadership of Gordon Brown since 2007, lost the general election and a coalition government of the Conservatives, led by David Cameron, and the Liberal Democrats, was formed. In December 2010 public demonstrations in Tunisia marked the beginning of the Arab uprisings which toppled Tunisian President Zein al-Abidine Ben Ali and obliged President Mubarak of Egypt to step down. In an election in 2012, Muslim Brotherhood leader Mohamed Morsi won the Egyptian presidency. He lasted until his ousting by the army in 2013.

While welcoming the developments in Tunisia, the Cameron government was more circumspect about the fall of Mubarak in Egypt. HMG was in any case powerless to influence events in Egypt and followed the US lead in eventually recognizing the Morsi presidency, though without enthusiasm. There, and in Jordan and Morocco, the British sought to promote political and economic reform but were more reticent when it came to the Arab Gulf states. In a statement to the House of Commons in October 2012, Foreign Secretary William Hague said:

> There is no one model for democratic development in the Middle East. We must work with the grain of each society while standing up for universal human rights, recognising that the pace of change will vary in each country, and offering our assistance where we can and where it is requested.[22]

This statement encapsulated HMG's stance on the Arab uprisings, that is, to profess general support for democratic change, but to evaluate the implications and appropriate response on a case-by-case basis. With respect to the uprising in Yemen the British chose to defer to a joint initiative of the Gulf Cooperation Council (GCC) states. In Bahrain they condemned the use of live fire against demonstrators but said they preferred to exercise their influence with the government behind the scenes. They were much more fulsome in their condemnation of President Assad's brutal repression of demonstrators in Syria, and when they witnessed Qadhafi's preparations to crack down hard on rebels in Benghazi, Cameron swiftly joined French President Sarkozy in calling for armed intervention.[23]

The US administration of Barak Obama was persuaded to join other NATO members in the Libyan intervention, though Obama characterized his commitment as 'leading from behind'. HMG reasoned that because this military action was sanctioned by a UN Security Council resolution, approved by the Arab League, and would not involve NATO troops on the ground, it would not constitute a repetition of the mistakes made with Iraq. However, NATO airpower enabled rebel militia to topple Qadhafi and they subsequently began fighting among themselves. The net result was to turn Libya into a 'failed state' and a new base of operations for the Islamic State group (IS). By 2015, Libya had also become the main staging post for African migrants attempting to reach Europe by sea.

The Cameron government was at one with the Americans and French in condemning the Assad regime in Syria, as that country descended into civil war. Fatefully, the Western allies also predicted that Assad's 'days were numbered'. In fact, his regime was rescued first by Hezbollah, then Iran and, by 2015, by the Russians. The latter claimed to have been deceived by the Western powers over the intervention in Libya and held to the view that the Assad regime was the legitimate government of Syria and that there was no credible substitute. Among the rebels, extremist groups began to make the running and an offshoot of Al-Qaeda (the Nusra Front) and IS captured vast swathes of Syrian territory.

Having lost a vote in Parliament in August 2013, intended to clear the way for Britain to join the Americans in bombing the Assad regime for its alleged use of chemical weapons, Cameron and thence Obama missed an opportunity to uphold what Obama had called his 'red lines' on the use of WMD. The United States and, eventually the British, decided to commit forces to counter IS in Syria. This they did with the tacit approval of not only the Russians and Iranians but also Assad, thereby, effectively, contributing to the latter's survival.

In all other respects, the coalition government and then a Conservative one – after Cameron won an outright majority in 2015 – could not be credited with any distinctive policy shifts or achievements in the Middle East, apart perhaps for their part in the military defeat of IS in Syria and Iraq. Britain was also not directly affected by the flow of refugees out of Syria that rocked the political fortunes of the governments of Germany and Italy from 2015. In May 2016 the British people voted to leave the EU and between then and Britain's formal departure on 31 January 2020 preoccupation with 'Brexit' meant that there were no major British policy initiatives on or in the Middle East.

To conclude, the UK has signed a free trade agreement with Turkey, and hopes to sign further deals with Israel, Saudi Arabia and the UAE post-Brexit. Such deals could therefore become the new defining feature of British policy in the Middle East. If they do, Britain's profile in the region will be understood as definitely prioritizing pragmatism over principle. If there is a single thread running through Britain's dealings with the Middle East over the decades, it is that HMG has tried consistently to find a way to manage its relations with the numerous dictatorial regimes and power brokers in the region, while adhering to the norms it likes to espouse, without much success.

3

Britain's foreign policy landscape in the post-Brexit era

Michael Clarke

The post-Brexit era will take some time to arrive. Regardless of the end of the 2020 'transition phase', with Britain outside the European Union, the strategic outcomes of the Brexit decision will take a decade or more to become clear. It will take that time for Britain to prove to the world, and to itself, that there is a viable future for it as a unique type of major, contemporary European power – strategically integrated, economically decoupled but vibrantly independent. Alternatively, it will take that time to limit the damage and compensate for its failings if such a role proves beyond its reach. Or, it may simply take that time for Britain to decline to a new 'sick man of Europe' status and withdraw from front-line world politics if the Brexit decision turns out to be a strategic disaster. All three scenarios are possible and the coming decade will test them all – probably simultaneously as the country works to overcome the economic damage, and adjust to the transformative effects of the Covid-19 crisis that hit it with such force after April 2020.

But geopolitics in the rest of the world will be moving on apace at the same time, and though the fate of post-Brexit Britain is intimately involved with its immediate international context, it is also important to acknowledge the external power and momentum that is turning the geopolitical wheels of world politics ever faster in the 2020s. In short, the coming decade was always likely to be a more challenging time for the European powers, including the European Union, and not least for Britain. The effect of the Brexit process is to increase all the stakes – and the risks – that the country was in any case facing in its future foreign policies. Since the onset of the economic crisis in 2008, Britain has faced an increasingly challenging strategic path than in the years since 1991 when the Cold War ended. But Brexit has thrown into this path a series of snakes and ladders – pitfalls and opportunities – that will leave little room for strategic error.

This chapter is not concerned with Britain and the Middle East, as such, but rather with the general strategic context the country faces, which thereby becomes the backdrop for subsequent considerations of Britain's policy in the Middle East. Britain has to deal with a changing global landscape, and within that picture, to try to make a success of the Brexit process. The Middle East is not the essence of that conundrum for British policymakers. The Brexit gamble will not be won or lost there. But the way in which Brexit plays out against Britain's global strategic landscape will have a major impact on what the country is subsequentially able to achieve in the Middle East and how it may frame its policy around the region.

The major powers in Britain's landscape

In the decade just ended, many geopolitical trends came to some evident fruition. The major powers were again competing directly with each other, and significant second-rank players in the world, like Britain and most other European states, now struggle to exercise their strategic choices in the diminishing space between the new great power competitions.

The single most important geopolitical mega-trend in Britain's foreign policy landscape, as that for all its partners, will be the way the relationship between the United States and China plays out. In 2017 President Xi Jinping made it abundantly clear at the 19th Party Congress that China was thereafter ready to assume its (rightful) 'global role' and that it would project power accordingly.[1] In fact, Washington and Beijing both sent out contradictory signals about their intentions towards each other. The key geopolitical question is whether the direction of their bilateral relationship will tend towards a new accommodation – resetting a relationship that has become antagonistic on many fronts including trade, technology, espionage and military operations in the Pacific – or else emerge as a determined effort on Washington's part to limit the rise of China on the world stage. Certainly, President Donald Trump's intention was always to reset the relationship in terms of a new strategic deal more favourable to the United States.[2] President Joe Biden, driven by the same Congressional pressures, is no less committed to this aim, though the strategy to achieve it is evidently different.

If accommodation is not possible, a new US–China Cold War could be starting that would not favour the United States in the way of the old US–Soviet Cold War.[3] At worst, a 'Thucydides trap' may be awaiting them both – whereby a rising and a declining global power are predetermined towards military conflict.[4] The Covid-19 crisis sharpened all the political antagonisms between Washington and Beijing, and increased the demands that the United States should further 'decouple' its economy from China in all aspects of their mutual economic dependence. Though some decoupling is clearly underway, there are limits to which such a process can be pushed, pending some rough, new economic accommodation between the United States and China. Another way of interpreting such a hybrid relationship between the two superpowers is as a 'new medievalism' – taking place in a more fluid and less organized world that mirrors many of the conditions of medieval Europe, but which is nonetheless intensely competitive.[5] The relevance of this view to Europe is that as it declines in relative terms, 'Eurasia', it is thought, will cohere as a region and become a renewed arena of great power competition. The United States, already rethinking its commitments in Pacific Asia, may or may not take up the challenge of competing with China in Eurasia, and in a minor key also with Russia.[6] Either way, European middle-rank powers will struggle to maintain their own freedom of action within any new US–China nexus.

From a defence and security perspective, this is some distance from Britain, but it matters in a broader strategic sense. One of the greatest game-changers in modern world politics is the attempt by Beijing to create a meaningful 'Belt and Road Initiative' (BRI) to link China across the Eurasian heartland with Europe, Africa and Southeast Asia. Launched in 2013 with close on $1 trillion in a first round of foreign loans and investment, and around $6 trillion likely to be invested in the next two decades, the BRI potentially involves sixty-eight countries, 65 per cent of global population and 40 per cent of global GDP, with key economic hubs in Kazakhstan as a gateway to Europe; Pakistan to the Indian Ocean; and Djibouti into Eastern and Central Africa.[7] It sweeps up many existing schemes and initiatives and re-packages them with renewed drive and cash. The BRI hit some significant hurdles after 2018 but it is already a geopolitical force in Asia and some parts of Africa, and is likely to become so in the Middle East.[8] The BRI represents nothing less than a 'Eurasian pivot' for China, aiming to create multiple infrastructure and connectivity projects to facilitate trade and commercial cooperation. In practical terms, it covers oil and gas projects to help secure China's energy needs; connectivity, in creating rail, road and seaport links going West and South West; trade and business stimulation, through the creation of 'special economic zones'; and joint ventures in manufacturing and production in high growth sectors.[9] The BRI grandly expresses China's historic view of the world. Its domestic economy needs to expand, and it has an Asiatic destiny that is quite distinct from its future in the Pacific. In Beijing's view, there is a bigger and longer game to play, including in the Middle East, than mere economic competition with the United States.[10]

More predictably, China is determined to be a dominant geopolitical force in Pacific Asia. This can be seen in the rapid development of the Chinese military and the way Beijing chooses to use its military power to assert sovereignty in the East and South China seas. Coral atolls in disputed waters have been reclaimed and made into powerful military bases despite UN rulings that found against it. Over the last decade it has weaponized new technologies more quickly than expected and already has enough military capacity to deny easy (or safe) access for the military forces of other states – including the United States – to operate in what China defines as the 'first island chain' running from Japan to Malaysia, and in due course – it is believed – in a 'second island chain' running from Japan to Indonesia. It is an undisguised sphere of influence approach that threatens to impinge on the sovereignty of other Pacific countries.

China's rise to world power is not unconstrained, however, given its ongoing problems as a one-party state, its sovereign paranoia over historic territorial claims and an economy that is only semi-reformed. But China's current geopolitical weight is essentially based on its status as the second biggest economy in the world, the biggest internal market and the biggest single source of investment capital as Chinese sovereign wealth funds and private entrepreneurs look to invest their cash abroad. For European countries, the China of the 2020s is rich and powerful, but still trying to catapult itself from an under-developed twentieth-century country to a new type of twenty-first-century post-modern economy. Chinese leaders think of regional security in largely traditional, territorial terms but they also want to enjoy the benefits of the global economy – and China's new place in it – very much on their own terms. China's foreign and security policy is no cleverer or more long-sighted than anyone else's.

Its incipient power has been exercised crudely in many parts of the world and it has provoked some powerful resistance. But everyone understands that, unless the state somehow collapses, China's economic size and political power will only grow stronger in the coming decades and that Beijing can afford to make mistakes along the way.

The particular security challenges of this for Britain take different forms. The deepening British security partnership with Japan, for example, its traditional links with Brunei or Malaysia, or its new friendship with Vietnam, is all affected by Chinese sovereign claims in the East and South China seas. Britain takes a view on these claims based on international law and UN rulings, which normally draw thinly veiled threats of economic retaliation from Beijing. And China competes for influence around the world in what may be regarded as fair political competition, but which also sets a series of 'debt for equity' traps in some regions of natural interest to Britain – in Malaysia, Sri Lanka, Pakistan, the Horn of Africa or West Africa, where China lends profusely to governments that the IMF and World Bank regard as simply unable to sustain commercial borrowing.

China also poses some novel challenges to British security, even as Britain adjusts to the opportunities of Chinese public and private investment in its own domestic economy. For years, China's industrial and political espionage efforts throughout the world have been legendary in their scale and intentions. China has used significant segments of its civilian elite to create a different kind of state intelligence effort. Its commercial espionage and the blatant theft of intellectual property (hotly denied by Beijing) are credited with helping China achieve such rapid technological progress and are regarded as unpleasant facts of life by leaders and industrialists throughout the Western world. It is impossible to tell whether these fears are exaggerated, though they are certainly believed by senior officials in many different countries. But China's reputation for espionage and widespread attempts at the technical penetration of industrial control systems in Western countries created strong Western suspicions. In 2018 the 'Huawei controversy' erupted as Western countries were about to embark on creating 5G telecommunications systems. Fears over the use of Huawei's competitive and advanced components in Western 5G networks were partly driven by China's draconian 2017 National Intelligence Law, that made it a legal requirement under Article 7 for Chinese 'individuals', 'citizens' and 'organisations' to 'support, cooperate and collaborate in national intelligence work'.[11] As a result, the United States, Australia, New Zealand and eventually Britain (all within the Five-Eyes intelligence community) banned the use of Huawei components in their 5G systems, while the European Union continued to be very cautious in the use of their products.

For Britain, the Huawei case represents a particular example of the vulnerability that all European countries face one way or another. China is invested in three new British nuclear power plants, its companies take shares in transport infrastructure, and its own giant suppliers operate right across the British retail sector.[12] It indicates a different dimension in British foreign policy and security – one that links the functioning of Britain's critical national infrastructure and investment in British industry and society with the volatile geopolitical impact of a rising power on the other side of the world. The Covid-19 crisis created a desire across most Western countries to re-examine their reliance on cheap Chinese imports in their own various supply chains – not just in public health sectors but across the board. But it remains to be seen how far they are genuinely committed to significant levels of economic decoupling.

Not least, China's rise seems likely to affect the ways the 'rules-based international order', in which Britain invests so much commitment, evolves over the coming years. There is a vigorous argument over whether China's rise will re-write the prevailing rules, as dominant powers eventually do, in its own interests. One school of thought believes that Western powers can pursue an effective 'lock-in' strategy that stresses the universal applicability and mutual advantages of the prevailing rules-based order.[13] Others have observed that China operates 'both within and outside the existing international system while at the same time, in effect, sponsoring a new China-centric international system which will exist alongside the present system and probably slowly begin to usurp it'.[14] The truth is that a political and ethical vacuum has opened up within the international system that China naturally moves to fill. The vacuum has arisen because the Western world has been less than punctilious in observing its own rules, the economic crisis of 2008 deprived Western capitals of so much moral authority, and under President Trump the United States made dramatic efforts to reshape and reduce the framework of international institutions and customary commitments.[15]

The role of Russia in Britain's foreign and security policy landscape is more direct and immediate than that of China. Russia figures unambiguously as an explicitly revanchist great power. President Vladimir Putin made it clear in 2014 as Crimea was annexed by force of arms that the dissolution of the old Soviet Union was 'a catastrophe'.[16] Russia would try to recover its power and influence over the territories it formerly controlled and oppose the Western powers that he believed were determined to keep Russia subordinate.

Russia is a big, important and special power in global politics, but it is weakening in a strategic sense.[17] With plentiful natural resources, a population of 144 million, continental space across Europe, Asia and the Arctic, a powerful culture and great social cohesion, Russia's economy is nevertheless considerably smaller than that of Britain.[18] It is cash-rich, when oil and gas prices are high, but investment-poor in general, since global companies don't trust its commercial environment or its rule of law. Russian military capabilities can be overstated. Though it increased the proportion of its GDP spent on defence by more than half in the decade after 2008 (hitting a peak of 5.8 per cent in 2016), its GDP was falling, or static, during these years as energy prices tumbled. Military reform was given high priority by the Kremlin, though the results were patchy. Nevertheless, Western observers note clear improvements in some sectors of Russia's nuclear, air and maritime forces. Trends among the troubled ground forces are, however, equally indicative. Here, there is a determination to move away from fielding the old Red Army, of moderate quality but high numbers, to develop a new force designed primarily for offensive, very high intensity and short conflicts in and around Russia's 'near abroad'.[19] Compared to its neighbours and counterparts, Russia places disproportionate weight on its military prowess as a source of influence in world politics.

The world of the 2020s, however, seems not to be moving in Russia's favour. China progressively displaces its former influence in Central Asia. Western powers did not welcome it into a new society of post-communist nations after the Cold War and its soft-power influence in the rest of the world is low. For all its natural assertiveness, Russia is relatively isolated in world politics. In Michael Burleigh's words, it is a 'decayed, resentful nation' though its challenge to Western powers should be handled no less carefully for all that.[20] And it is all the more revanchist since, one suspects, Russian leaders know that time is not on their side and they are driven by motives that are both defensive and offensive.

They are defensive because Putin and his leadership group see the hand of Western powers in all the 'colour revolutions' of the post-Soviet states that would take them out of Russia's natural orbit. They see the same hand in any significant civil dissent in Russia. They see that NATO goes on enlarging itself – nine times since 1949 – to encompass more of the states over which Moscow used to have either complete control or heavy influence.[21] Despite what NATO leaders say, Moscow argues, the Atlantic Alliance is structurally programmed to keep on growing; it simply cannot help itself. The idea that Georgia, still less Ukraine – or, God help them, Belarus – might join NATO sometime in the future is viewed as a strategic nightmare by Russian leaders. And they remember a decade of weakness and near-chaos after 1991, which might have dismembered Russia itself and in which Western powers seemed content to ride a wave of 'wild-west capitalism' in Russia without ever trying to integrate it properly into the international system.[22] A defensive mindset progressively became something close to a national paranoia as Russians tried to explain to themselves why they were subject to so many international sanctions, why their government was vilified across the world and why Russia is perceived as being on the wrong side of history.

This defensive national paranoia is also tactically offensive for equally compelling reasons. Presented with difficult policy choices the Putin leadership group characteristically opt for risky opportunism. They act in surprising and decisive ways that keep their adversaries off-balance, and they have the political will to use military force whatever the humanitarian cost. Putin's leadership was established in 1999 through his willingness, as new Russian prime minister, to destroy the Russian city of Grozny in order to crush the separatist Chechen rebellion. Russian leaders were prepared to go into a brief war with Georgia in 2008, with Ukraine in 2013, creating 'frozen conflicts' that could be manipulated as opportunity arose, in Abkhazia and South Ossetia, within Ukraine's Donbass region, and alongside pre-existing tensions in Transnistria. Russia provoked international incidents in the Kerch Strait – an international waterway but claimed as Russian territory following the annexation of Crimea – seizing Ukrainian shipping and blocking the strait in an ill-disguised attempt to strangle Ukraine's ports on the Sea of Azov. Russia intervened decisively in the Syrian civil war in 2015 to prop up the regime of Bashar al-Assad when it was close to collapse, and through a ruthless use of airpower supporting Syrian government forces and Iranian militias, it effectively displaced Western diplomacy in the war and renewed Russian military presence in the region for the first time since the 1980s. The same leadership invested heavily in Russian mercenary forces, such as the large 'Wagner Group' officially identified in 2019 operating in Eastern Libya – technically a private security company but using Russian military transports and, reportedly, being awarded individual medals in the Kremlin.[23] There is also, by most accounts, a symbiotic relationship between the biggest Russian criminal gangs operating internationally and the Kremlin leadership.[24]

Russian policy in its immediate neighbourhood is strategically consistent with its evident attitudes to the wider European region. It extends to dark threats and hostile military gestures towards the former Soviet republics of the Baltic states. In 2016 Russia introduced nuclear-capable *Iskandar-M* missiles into the Kaliningrad enclave bordering Lithuania and Poland in reaction to NATO's increased readiness levels. After 2017, large Russian military exercises were held along the borders of all three Baltic states and Poland – the forces clearly rehearsing offensive operations as well as defensive 'anti-access' strategies. Meanwhile, Moscow sought to weaken the collective strength of the Central and West European allies both in their NATO and EU forums, by wooing allies such as Hungary, Bulgaria, even Austria and Italy. It tried to make the most of sending medical aid to Italy in the early phases of the Covid-19 crisis. Moscow also worked hard to create a new security relationship with Turkey (notwithstanding that Turkey remains a NATO ally), and it intervened at many levels, legally and illegally, in the politics of the Western Balkans.

For Moscow, there are some high-value diplomatic and strategic cards that can be played against the Western powers from north to south in Europe; military pressure in northwest Europe, inducements or energy blackmail in central and south eastern Europe; and a robust military presence in the Eastern Mediterranean with the air and naval bases Russia established in Syria after 2015, new understandings with Israel, growing economic influence in Cyprus and a new involvement in the civil war in Libya.

From the perspective of most Western leaders this amounts to a catalogue of opportunities for Russia to undermine the already shaky strategic consensus between the Western powers and particularly in Europe. Even though the cards could never have been predicted to play out this way, their presence on the table suggested a form of Russian grand strategy that has been foreshadowed in President Putin's 2014 Duma speech. The speech showed that Putin was determined to recover as much influence, or even outright control, of the former Soviet space as possible, while working assiduously to create the permissive political environment among the NATO/EU powers who would be unable to counter any of this, and keep them diplomatically off-balance to prevent the encouragement of any more 'colour revolutions' inside or around Russia. Not least, it was a strategy designed to leverage the United States away from its European allies and seek out those in Europe who might become susceptible to Moscow's economic or military pressure. It represented a half-formed, but potent, version of the old Soviet Union's 'Finlandisation' policy, but applied now to a number of possible countries nominally within the enlarged Western alliance. The Rossiyskaya Gazeta of 2015 embodied a public version of Russia's most recent National Security Strategy and it made these intentions very clear.[25]

So, while Russia loses power in relative terms both to China and India in the coming decade, its antagonism towards the United States and the West is likely to continue: increasingly assertive in Middle East politics, through its new bases in Syria, seeking also to displace Western influence in the Mediterranean – manipulating the Libya crisis – and parts of Africa. Most significantly from a British viewpoint, Russia aims to create a permissive political environment in Western Europe through an opportunistic policy that seeks to exploit the growing fissures in Western consensus wherever possible and create new ones where it can. This is an approach, it should be noted, that is driven by strategic weakness as much as President Putin's own tactical cunning.[26] This is noted in Washington. In reality, the US–Russia relationship no longer sets the tone for other relations between the United States and other powers. The United States explicitly scales its strategy against what it thinks China will achieve in the 2020s.[27] For US leaders, Russia's 'revanchist challenge' is not trivial, but nor is it central to their strategic thinking. If they can deal with China's emergence as a global power, they reason, they will also have the capacity to contain Russian revanchist tendencies.

None of this would matter too much to Britain if the relationship between Europe and the United States – and in particular that between Washington and London – had remained reasonably stable over the last twenty years, but it has not. Whether the United States is seriously detaching itself from its previous levels of political commitment to European security is the single biggest determinant of Europe's future prospects in peace and war. If the Atlantic Alliance, in its broadest sense, continues to be based on proactive US leadership, then the strategic aspirations of Putin's Russia are unlikely to amount to more than a persistent nuisance to the core Western powers as they face new security problems in the 2020s. But if US leadership is effectively absent, for whatever reasons, then President Putin's Russia will increasingly set the agendas surrounding new security issues, as well as the range of responses available to the European powers. And for Britain, given its erstwhile self-image as a political and military bridge across the Atlantic, responding to new moods in the United States looms as the greatest judgement call of all; how much should Britain rely on, and invest in, its close security relationship with the United States for the next decade or so?

Too much is normally read into the personal chemistry between Washington and London. Personal relationships have an impact on the political atmosphere, but greater questions are at issue. The US/British relationship, skilfully handled for the most part by diplomats and officials on both sides, has shown itself well capable of managing personality differences at the top. It has also shown itself to be fairly robust in its ability to weather individual policy disagreements, even over issues as central to the United States as Britain's refusal to support the Vietnam War. The key structural question, instead, is whether the current relationship could really withstand a genuine and long-term divergence of *strategic vision* underpinning Western policy.

In this respect, the challenge that US strategy really poses for Britain suggests some sobering realities. American security thinking since the 1990s shows a steady divergence from European thinking as it has interpreted its own visions of world order. The Trump presidency was not as eccentric or atypical as it often appeared to non-Americans. It was the culmination of some strong long-term domestic trends as well as the frustrations of dealing with a fast-changing global order.[28] The 'Trumpism' phenomenon is better seen as 'Jacksonian nationalism', harking back to a United States that believes principally in the power and legitimacy of the nation-state over any international institutions and the futility of any foreign entanglements unless in direct defence of the US homeland.[29] As Walter Russell Mead put it:

> For Jacksonians – who formed the core of Trump's passionately supportive base – the United States is not a political entity created and defined by a set of intellectual

> propositions rooted in the Enlightenment and oriented toward the fulfilment of a universal mission. Rather, it is the nation-state of the American people, and its chief business lies at home. Jacksonians see American exceptionalism not as a function of the universal appeal of American ideas, or even as a function of a unique American vocation to transform the world, but rather as rooted in the country's singular commitment to the equality and dignity of individual American citizens.[30]

Jacksonian nationalism remains a strong underlying element in US thinking, despite the avowed internationalism of the Biden administration. It expresses 'nationalist, sovereigntist instincts' and a rejection of an 'international systems' approach to doing business.[31] It relies primarily on bilateral approaches, and in this view, the straightforward duty of US leaders is to battle for fellow Americans against evident threats to their security, trade and money. Jacksonian nationalists are comfortable with a minimalist 'balance of power' approach to world order. It is a plausible thought that the Trump phenomenon may have represented the most prominent crest of the first breaking wave of global, anti-establishment populism which might last for some years yet.[32]

In truth, Britain has been on something of a roller-coaster ride in the last two decades, trying to work alongside the strategic visions of the United States across five presidencies. Britain had made the most of its military and intelligence relationships with the United States during the Clinton years of the 1990s. After the 9/11 attacks Tony Blair got very close to President Bush and Britain embarked on far more difficult and controversial foreign interventions from 2001 to 2011 in Afghanistan, Iraq, Afghanistan again and then – unintentionally as Obama tried to 'lead from behind' – also in Libya.[33] In fact, Britain was barely holding onto the strategic coat-tails of the United States during these years, contributing for most of the period to a right-wing, neo-con 'global-change agenda' in the United States, whilst arguing in Europe that it was somehow exerting influence on Washington to remain a liberal-internationalist power. There is little evidence that it was.[34] And now, Britain must assess a Democrat administration that still struggles with a society deeply polarized between 'Jacksonians' and 'internationalists'.

And, after 2017, in particular, important policy differences between the US and the European allies became more fundamental, leaving London greatly exposed. Britain struggled somehow to massage them to make such differences acceptable to European partners. They included US renunciation of the Iran nuclear deal, to which European powers remained committed; official renunciation of the 1987 Intermediate Nuclear Forces (INF) Treaty in Europe; withdrawal from the Paris Accord on climate change; the White House's unilateral decision to recognize Jerusalem as the capital of Israel and Israeli sovereignty over the annexed Golan Heights; its vacillating policy over Saudi Arabia and Qatar in the Gulf; inconsistent responses towards Russian policy in Europe; threatened trade war with China; and quixotic announcements of troop withdrawals from NATO, Iraq and Afghanistan.[35] There was constant angst over the depth of US transatlantic commitments. Disagreements over specific issues will pass, but genuinely new strategic assumptions in Washington – whichever political party holds the presidency – may not.

Britain carved out its global role largely on the natural identity of its essential interests with those of the United States. It could argue simultaneously that it was both morally right and self-interestedly prudent to champion an America-led rules-based approach to international order. It works hard to maintain faith in multinational and regime arrangements to deal with global problems, particularly as most of them have been based on liberal internationalism – that blend of raw power and liberal democratic ethics – that Britain and the United States largely created themselves. The prospect that successive US leaders may, in effect, have been falling back on a simpler balance of power approach to international politics – or even the jungle rules of mere coexistence – is both ethically and politically challenging for Britain.

The global economic landscape

As a globalized power that has operated a successful neoliberal economy since the mid-1980s, Britain's foreign policy landscape is influenced by the systemic evolution of the world economy as much as by the less systematic developments among the great powers. The 2008 global financial crisis and the 'great recession' that followed it for most of the decade changed Britain's future economic context in two essential ways.

Firstly, it accelerated the degree to which the Asian economies are driving global markets. In an extensive analysis in 2012 the University of Groningen and McKinsey Global Institute tracked the world's 'economic centre of gravity' to analyse how, after two millennia, the growth of the Asian economies now represents far and away the most *rapid* shift of economic power – back to Asia – in human history.[36] The phenomenon is also driven by the relative decline of the European economies. The European Union is the world's single biggest and most integrated international market of over 500 million people. Even so, after Brexit it will be less than a third the size of the integrated national market of China at almost 1.4 billion. Over the ten years, 2012–22 the *average* annual growth rate in China is estimated at 6.7 per cent; in India 7.3 per cent; in Vietnam 6.2 per cent and in Indonesia 5.3 per cent. By contrast, the average GDP growth over the same period for the EU is estimated at 1.6 per cent and for the broader European Area at 1.4 per cent.[37] Not surprising, then, that in 2015 Chinese investment in Europe almost doubled, mainly from Beijing's state-backed firms and investment funds. And China tries to operate bilaterally when it invests abroad, rather than working through organizations like the EU.[38] All of this emphasizes the fact that European countries as a whole – even the EU – can no longer act as a central pillar of the global economic system. There are clear opportunities here, as well as grave dangers, for Brexit Britain. As Adam Tooze puts it, 'rather than an autonomous actor, Europe risks becoming the object of other people's capitalist corporatism … Europe is out of the race. The future will be decided between the survivors of the crisis in the United States and the newcomers of Asia'.[39]

Secondly, it is not clear that the economic crisis is over. The 2017 recovery featured synchronous economic cycles but it was tepid and sluggish. A sense of fragility surrounds the global economic system. Governments across the world, banks, industries and citizens went into the Covid-19 economic recession still carrying historically unprecedented amounts of debt – albeit in an era of equally historic low interest rates. But still, total debt was close to a staggering 400 per cent of total GDP mainly among the mature economies.[40] The emerging market economies, already over-leveraged – mainly with expensive Chinese loans – are particularly vulnerable to the effects of the Covid-19 recession and a series of new debt crises. But even in the face of this debt mountain, little else has changed since 2008 beyond a raft of greater restrictions on the banking sector. The key actors who averted complete disaster in 2008 now have little room for further manoeuvre. Central banks have less ability to stimulate their economies to fend off the immediate effects of the new recession; there are few fiscal and monetary tools left unused in their armouries that would pack a sufficient global punch. And democratic governments are under greater pressure with extremist and protectionist parties closer to power, or even in office. Ratcheting up renewed long-term economic pain in the crisis is more than most liberal Western governments can contemplate.

The British economy – large and relatively strong – is highly sensitive to any movements in this volatile global economy. Britain's impressive economic growth before 2008 rested heavily on deregulation and free capital movements, low taxation and vigorous consumer spending – all driven by extensive credit and a buoyant housing market. It rapidly became an 80 per cent service economy. In some key respects it turned into an hourglass-shaped economy with a high-end manufacturing sector, where a third of all employment is now in foreign-owned companies. At the other end, there are more start-up businesses (and more failures) than in other European countries and greater labour flexibility in almost all sectors. Traditionally, there was unmet demand for more skilled labour at the top of the hourglass and a glut of low-skilled jobs being created at the bottom. Somewhere between 25 per cent and 40 per cent of all British jobs are classified as low-skilled.[41] Britain has a few big, successful companies and a great many small ones. There are comparatively few middle-sized enterprises.[42] Britain's service industries are ever dependent on importing skilled labour, while productivity – the real Achilles heel of the British economy – remains stubbornly low, precisely because (low-skilled) employment is so high.

In short, Britain's economy – successfully globalized in the previous period – faces the immediate future with an estimated drop of somewhere between 11.5 per cent and 14 per cent in its GNP as a result of the Covid-19 recession – marginally higher than in France or Italy, but considerably higher than in Germany, the Netherlands, Poland, Sweden, Norway or the United States.[43] The challenge will be all the greater in addressing the economy's unbalanced structure – patchily but not effectively devolved, over-centralized but subject to quixotic foreign ownership, dynamic but not sustained by its own skills or workforce. It is prone to uneven and inequitable success, overheating during the good times and exaggerating the economic pain during the bad.

The post-Brexit landscape

Whatever the outcome of the early years of Brexit, the country crossed a Rubicon in 2016. It created a massive undercurrent of change in relation to its European future on every level that will have to be managed during the 2020s. There is no hiding and no turning back from the position Britain adopted in 2016. And for this reason, Brexit has become the lens through which Britain's foreign policy future must be viewed. But it is also facing a series of new challenges in foreign and security policy that, in any case, require a fresh perspective.

The challenges are both conceptual and empirical. A return of great power competition, but in the post-Cold War context of a globalized world, with its networking, high interdependence and transformational global economy, is more dissimilar than it may look to most observers in Britain. The constellation of great powers does not line up so neatly that second-rank players like Britain can conveniently position themselves. Being the closest ally of the United States is not as easy, or maybe as advantageous, as it was a decade ago. From Britain's point of view, China is a different type of world power on the global scene. And Russia, for all its structural weaknesses, will continue to act assertively, especially where it can isolate a country from the political mainstream of its neighbours and partners. Britain must navigate its strategic objectives through whatever space it can find between the turning geopolitical wheels of the great powers. And, it must do so in an environment where all globalized modern economies are vulnerable to international economic trends and, in Britain's case, where economic penetration from both the United States and China is high and still likely to increase.

Britain's foreign and security policy concerns, therefore, range from protecting and enhancing its critical national infrastructure to safeguard its economic performance and attractiveness to foreign investment: through to countering terrorism and international organized crime – partly for the same reasons – in addition to dealing with the manifestation of great power competition to try to secure the greatest peace and prosperity available in a troubled international environment. The spectrum of foreign policy and security concerns that British governments have to address has never been so extensive. These concerns apply equally to Britain's relations across the greater Middle East – a potent mixture of positioning between new great power manoeuvrings and the evident rise of more potent regional players in the region, economic interdependence that goes far beyond the energy markets and genuine mutual security interests in dealing with terrorism, political fragmentation and all the ripple effects of it.

Such trends and challenges await Britain quite independently of Brexit. But they can now only be addressed through an understanding of the different relationships the country will henceforth have with its European partners, and by the economic effects of the 'Brexit decade' as it unfolds. Brexit doesn't change any of the strategic questions, but it changes literally all of the answers.

Exercising power in world politics is grounded on a country's economic performance and the economic effects of Brexit are therefore critical to British foreign policy. A short-term boost from withheld investment and consumer spending may be expected, once the immediate effects of the Covid-19 recession have passed, though the medium-term economic outlook over the next five or six years now looks less buoyant than in 2019 when Britain formally left the EU.[44] Britain's erstwhile reputation as an international actor has taken severe blows since 2010, and its standing in world politics and its image as a proactive, pragmatic and useful member of the international community will have somehow to be revived in the Brexit decade.[45] And while it addresses essentially traditional challenges in Europe from Russia and reacts to multi-layered relations in

Europe with China, Britain must still reconcile the fact that its relationships with its most important European partners and also with the United States are *both* changing rapidly, and perhaps radically. The constellation of international stars all moved against the Brexit assumptions that were made around 2015. Great power antagonism has increased, protectionism has grown, international institutions are under fire from all sides and it is not clear how Britain might avoid international isolation and achieve the trick of being economically decoupled but still strategically integrated with its most important European allies. Not least, the Covid-19 crisis and its attendant recession confirm the arrival of a perfect politico-economic storm for the early 2020s.

As Malcolm Chalmers points out, it would be prudent for a post-Brexit Britain to concentrate its attention on European security matters in the immediate future, not only to counter Russian pressure but also to demonstrate and emphasize the importance of European security and cohesion to its partners despite the Brexit outcome.[46] British diplomacy has not figured highly in the Greater Middle East over the last decade. It achieved at least its military objectives in destroying the Islamic State 'caliphate' but was effectively expelled alongside the United States from influence over the outcome of the Syrian civil war. Like other European states, it needs to keep some sort of new Iran nuclear deal in prospect; it treads a thankless diplomatic line between Europe and the United States in relations with Saudi Arabia and over the war in Yemen. And it tries to shore up deteriorating relations among the Gulf states. It has little influence with Turkey in the Eastern Mediterranean or over events in Libya that matter so much to the EU's southern members.

This is a depressing catalogue but, in fact, there are opportunities for Britain to demonstrate its post-Brexit European credentials precisely through a more proactive approach to issues across the Middle East region. There may be good reasons for Britain to concentrate its security resources on its own international neighbourhood during the 2020s, even as it tries to manage more diplomatic and economic relationships across the Asian economies. But Britain's security neighbourhood certainly extends to the Middle East, in terms of its intrinsic strategic importance, the ripple effects of any instability on Europe and the region's potential to be a bigger part of China's 'belt and road'. The Middle East remains a region where British policy can still be congruent with that of most of its European partners, albeit there is a natural Franco-British strategic competition. Above all, British policy in the region will still try to anchor itself, as far as possible, to changing US thinking about the region. There will be some subtle balances to be struck.

4

Still special? The UK and United States in the Middle East

Michael Stephens

The term 'special relationship' is a cumbersome phrase that appears to have meant more to the UK over the years than it has to the United States, and for a wide variety of reasons is unpopular among the many British policy practitioners who have served its cause.[1] It implies a unique intimacy that surpasses all other relationships held by both nations, and for Britain this is certainly the case. The National Security Capability Review of 2018 notes unequivocally that 'the United States continues to be our single most important international partner'.[2] But whether the same is true for the United States is questionable, given that Washington shares many intimate international relationships with states by virtue of its global role. A special relationship exists with Israel (even though it is not referred to as such), and Washington's relationship with Jerusalem has long been a sensitive topic that has been debated by those who sought to explain and understand Israeli influence on US politics.[3] Another special relationship exists with Japan,[4] with whom the United States shares an intimate defence and security relationship which has formed the cornerstone of American Pacific interests post-Second World War. Given Washington's broad set of global concerns, to label its relationship with the UK alone as 'special' might seem at odds with the facts. From the British point of view, there is little doubt that Britain's global influence and power projection are amplified by a close relationship with Washington (as it would be for any state); such is the dominant role that Washington has played and continues to play in the international system.

But the relationship is a more complex alliance than one-sided utilitarian benefit for London. US diplomat Eric Edelman noted that the Special Relationship rested on four pillars: (1) cultural ties and a belief in a shared destiny for English speaking peoples, (2) a willingness to wage war in support of shared goals, (3) nuclear weapons cooperation and (4) a deep intelligence relationship.[5] Cultural and linguistic ties aside, there is an intangible element to UK–US relations, which is characterized by personal relationships that stretch back decades, engendering trust and cooperation between the two nations. Forged in the Second World War and maintained after, it is these relationships that provide the bedrock upon which shared assumptions and policy preferences are expressed. The US–UK special relationship as it exists today is best characterized by a political and ideological superstructure, and an embedded military and intelligence substructure.[6] Indeed it is this substructure that is far more important to the health and maintenance of the relationship than the more frequently commented-upon political dynamic, which is prone to fluctuation and subject to the political fashions of the day. The real connections between the UK and the United States are formed by daily interactions between thousands of officials and military personnel who work closely together 'in person or electronically',[7] and such connections form an emotional link that 'has always been there'.[8] These close working links insulate longer-term shared goals against short-term distractions or challenges.[9] As a result, the special relationship is less the result of policy choices made by either the British or the Americans than it is the cause of the similar choices the two countries so frequently make.[10] And so, while US–UK relations have had their ups and downs, Washington – with London as a junior partner – has overseen nearly seven decades of a liberal world order that has encouraged relative global prosperity, and more importantly ensured that another world war has not come to pass.[11]

Britain's fall, Washington's rise

Britain's global role since the Second World War rested on a strong transatlantic relationship but this was not its only pillar. Outlined in Winston Churchill's 'three circles speech',[12] Britain's balancing role relied on the leadership of its commonwealth, the sustenance of an Anglo-Saxon global order underpinned by a special relationship with the United States, and strong support for a united Europe at peace with itself. In Churchill's view the United States was a critical component of this architecture that saw its interests advanced (particularly vis-à-vis the expansionist designs of the Soviet Union) by being part of this order, and not apart from it. The United States' rise to primacy in the post-Second World War era was marked by a concerted effort to roll back the colonial world built by Britain and France, and drive towards self-determination of states that the Europeans had once ruled. Although this took some time to materialize in the Middle East, America's supremacy over Great Britain was most forcefully demonstrated following the Suez Crisis of October 1956 where British and American interests could not have been more distinct. Britain's waning status as a global power was ignominiously highlighted after being forced into a hasty withdrawal from the Suez Canal following the threat of US sanctions.[13]

In 1962 another blow to British prestige was dealt by the great American statesman Dean Acheson, whose now infamous speech at Westpoint made it clear that Britain had lost an Empire but had yet to find a role, noting that Britain stood little chance of prospering on the edge of Europe unless it sought further integration.[14] The unwitting Acheson caused far more offence to London than intended, partly because his remarks contained within them a kernel of truth that Britain had sought to either downplay or indeed ignore.[15] Influence in the Middle East region remained strong, and the United States largely relied upon Britain to maintain order in the Gulf states until the latter determined in 1967 that it could no longer afford to maintain its custodial authority, leading to a total withdrawal from East of Suez by 1971.[16] Since then Washington's influence has been virtually hegemonic, the exception being a proxy war of sorts with the Soviet Union primarily viewed through the lens of the Arab–Israeli conflict. The emergence of the Nixon Doctrine in 1969 which extended US security guarantees to partners and allies intimately tied the United States into the security of its allies in the Middle East region. Both the Shah of Iran and the emerging Gulf states (especially Saudi Arabia) received large volumes of military aid and extended security guarantees from Washington. The collapse of the Shah forced the United States into a yet more assertive role, adopting an aggressive posture against Ayatollah Khomeini, and explicitly providing security guarantees to Gulf partners. The so-called Carter doctrine, which emerged in January 1980, stated that 'an attempt by any outside force to gain control of the Persian Gulf region will be regarded as an assault on the vital interests of the United States of America, and such an assault will be repelled by any means necessary, including military force'. Although the speech was written with the Soviet Union chiefly in mind, the commitment to the security of the Gulf states remained and extended to any power that sought to interfere in the Gulf region, which since the collapse of the USSR has meant Saddam's Iraq, and the Islamic Republic of Iran.

Britain played its part in supporting this US hegemonic role, bolstering Saddam Hussein as he fought a brutal eight-year war against Khomeini's Iran, before supporting US operations to remove Saddam's forces from Kuwait in 1991, following the Iraqi dictator's decision to invade. Britain also returned to fight in the US-led 'coalition of the willing' to oust Saddam in 2003, whilst simultaneously making a significant military contribution to NATO operations in Afghanistan in a fight that has been ongoing since 2001. Both Britain and the United States returned to war against Muammar Gaddafi in Libya in 2011 (this time at Britain's behest), and to Syria and Iraq following a blitzkrieg across both countries by ISIS in 2014. The second-order consequences of the counter ISIS campaign will be long running, and the United States, UK and France will likely be operating side by side in hostile terrain for many years to come.

But many years of conflict in the Middle East region have undoubtedly led to a war fatigue in both countries, and created a reluctance to intervene militarily in a region beset by instability. In recent times there have been no shortage of commentaries from across the Atlantic bemoaning the Middle East's lack of stability, and urging the United States to draw back from the region.[17] Military-focused scholarship has similarly viewed 'aspirational changes, such as catalyzing democracy and halting intrastate conflict' as falling 'outside the scope of change that the United States can readily bring about in a region that is beset by authoritarian legacies and seemingly chronic conflict'.[18] Questioning the Middle East's strategic priority to the United States is certainly not a new phenomenon. In 2007 a damning indictment of US policy was summed up by Edward Luttwak who bitterly complained, 'We devote far too much attention to the Middle East, a mostly stagnant region where almost nothing is created in science or the arts … its biggest industries are extravagant consumption and the venting of resentment.'[19] Luttwak's comments may not have been politically correct, and at the time of writing were certainly not mainstream opinion, but a kernel of truth lay behind the sentiment which is that the United States is less interested in the Middle East than it used to be. This has doubtless been accelerated by the United

States' re-emergence as an oil producing giant, resulting in a vastly decreased reliance on Middle East oil for its automobile reliant economy.[20] With the exception of its deep and lasting relationship with Israel, whose security the United States is sure to guarantee for many years to come, and an ongoing hostile relationship with Iran, it is no longer clear what strategic benefit results from maintaining a hegemonic influence in the Middle East.

Driven by the United States' increasing energy independence, presidents Obama and Trump made no secret of their desire to draw down US military presence in the region, preferring a lighter footprint that committed far less US manpower and resources but which achieved similar objectives to that which President Carter set out in 1980. But reality has proven rather more sobering. Both Obama and Trump found the Middle East far harder to walk away from than initially anticipated. Regional instability and conflict have frustrated US aspirations to pivot away from the burdens of military involvement in the Middle East in order to shift resources to other priorities or to parts of the world where the United States has more vital interests.[21] Military operations against Colonel Gaddafi in Libya were the catalyst. The United States tried and failed to lead from behind, gradually and reluctantly taking on the lion's share of operational activity. US reticence to undertake military action in Syria in August 2013 seemed prudent to Obama at the time; it wasn't America's war, and the United States historically held little interest in Syria.[22] But the administration found itself being sucked into the conflict as Syria began to disintegrate.[23]

As it turned out the Obama White House's desire to disengage from the region was a catastrophic mistake leading to the very opposite of what Obama had intended. In 2014, less than four years after drawing down troops from Iraq, the United States once again found itself the head of a military coalition headed to war, as Obama committed military assets and human resources in substantial numbers to Iraq and Syria to fight ISIS.[24] Having militarily defeated ISIS using his predecessor's strategy, President Trump's attempts to reverse course and pull out of a region that contained nothing more than 'bloodstained sand'[25] were haphazard and damaged global perceptions of America as a responsible security actor. Lacking any clear strategic purpose, US security forces now operate under a muddled vision that places US troops not only as counter-terrorism operators, but also as reminders to Iran not to push its weight around in the region. As a result, US troops remain in Syria and Iraq albeit in vastly reduced numbers. But with no strategic end state to work towards, and no clear definition of success the United States looks set to retain this footprint for years to come.

The United States and the UK have also paid the price for myopically focusing on counter-terrorism at the expense of larger regional security questions. As Yemen descended into yet another round of civil conflict in late 2014, the Gulf states led by Saudi Arabia piled in to stop the Ansar Allah (Houthi) movement from taking over the country. With strong ties to Iran, the Saudis saw the Houthis as a forward staging point for Iran on their southern flank. Already angry over the Obama administration's decision to negotiate the JCPOA with Tehran, and feeling alienated by the almost total focus of Western forces on the threat of ISIS rather than Iran, Riyadh launched a war that dragged resources away from Syria and Iraq, and refocused almost all the attention of the Gulf states on the defeat of the Houthis and their Iranian backers. The result has been a catastrophic conflict that has achieved very little of benefit for Saudi Arabia, and certainly not for local Yemenis who have suffered grievously in subsequent years.[26] Accordingly both Britain and the United States (who saw their support for Riyadh as effectively the price to pay for Saudi acquiescence to the JCPOA) have been the largest backers of the Saudi-led coalition. But they have overseen a failed war which has opened both nations up to accusations of war crimes and complicity in human rights abuses through arms sales.[27] In both countries, ties with Saudi Arabia have become strained as repeated efforts to end the war have failed. This is an embarrassing strategic anvil around their necks and a deep stain on their moral consciences. Yemen is perhaps the most serious cost of a lack of regional leadership from the United States, and one that Washington and London look set to keep paying for years to come.

Shared policy assumptions in the Middle East

Ironically the more the United States has found itself dragged back into the Middle East, the more its policy choices have had to take into account other military partners, most notably the UK and France. For all its military might the United States has only fought alone in the Middle East once, in Lebanon in 1958, and is by no means keen to repeat that action any time soon. Militarily there is no great need for the United States to fight alongside partners. In the complex long-running operations in Libya, Syria and Iraq, the United States could have conducted these alone; the same is true for the ongoing International Maritime Mission in the Gulf. However, even in the Trump era, where signs of US unilateralism occasionally reared their head (such as in the targeted killing of Iranian General Qasim Soleaimani in January 2020, and in a series of airstrikes conducted against the Assad regime in April 2017), the overwhelming preference has been, and continues to be traditional European partners. This runs in tandem with bolstering local actors such as Israel, the UAE and Saudi Arabia, three actors which the United States has expended a huge amount of effort to successfully bring closer together diplomatically and in the security space.

While the UK is occasionally forced to sit back as Uncle Sam bludgeons his way around the region (assassinating a top Iranian General without warning, or unilaterally taking measures on the Israeli–Palestinian conflict), the vast majority of the time the two countries can and will share ideas and try to shape each other's regional policy preferences. With the notable exceptions of the Iran nuclear deal, and the Israeli–Palestinian conflict, London lies in broad agreement with Washington on many of the major contours that define regional politics. Regional stability and the absence of interstate war is a desire of both nations, and since Saddam's invasion of Kuwait in 1990 this has largely been achieved. Overwhelming US firepower, forward deployed and used offensively (as in the case of 1990), has ensured that regional states cannot simply occupy or annex territory at will,[28] and in the case of 2003 and 2011 has reinforced Western military hegemony, albeit with significant political costs. Despite the high level of tension between states in the region, there has been no major military conflict among any of them since the time of Saddam. This is a principle of the international order that until recently was a key pillar of what Malcolm Chalmers has termed the 'Universal Security System' that both the UK and United States have been centrally involved in upholding across the world.[29]

Secondly, the UK and the United States prefer to deal with states rather than non-state actors. Both countries seek a strong foothold in the Gulf states, with whom they possess intimate security and economic relationships that are uncharacteristically close, and whose continued existence they strongly back. Key regional pillars such as Egypt and Iraq are considered too big to fail, and the ever fragile Hashemite Kingdom of Jordan is a crucial ally and lynchpin of regional stability that receives extensive US and British security assistance. However, it is certainly not the case that either nation (or indeed Western nations more broadly) has applied this principle universally across the region. Indeed, a selective pragmatism is employed in order to counter threats emanating from the region that reveals both Washington and London's highly selective approach to supporting state sovereignty. Conflicts in Syria, Libya and Iraq have foisted tough choices upon Western capitals. Since 2011 the policy of containment of Iran has caused Western states to abandon a singular approach to sovereignty. Reinforcing the power of the state has been a selective tool used to undermine the influence of Iran and its preference for backing sectarianized non-state actors across the region. But when it suited Washington, London and Paris, backing non-state actors to block Iran has also been desirable, as was the case in Syria where various opposition groupings, including the infamous Division 30,[30] and the New Syrian Army (now referred to as the Revolutionary Commando Army) have received strong backing and support. Both London and Washington display a similar pragmatism when confronting Sunni jihadist terrorist organizations. Having been burned by the experience of the 2003 war in Iraq and its aftermath, as well as the deployment to Afghanistan, both the United States and the UK have shown an increasing preference to deploy a light military footprint in the region. Such has been the case with the five-year war against the forces of the Islamic State, where both Britain and the United States have left the vast bulk of on-the-ground fighting to local actors such as the Kurdish-led Syrian Democratic Forces (SDF) in Syria, or the Peshmerga and the Golden Division in Iraq.[31]

Since the 1980s London and Washington's regional outlook has also been shaped by a belief that democratic norms and values are morally right and should be promoted. This policy is of course subject to the whims of political actors of the day. At times Britain and the United States have aligned closely, seeing a highly moral dimension to foreign policy, excoriating Middle East actors who ignored basic principles and rights, and even using protection of human rights as a pretext for military intervention.[32] At other times however British politicians, particularly from the Labour Party, have found themselves struggling to accept Washington's more hard-headed and realist approach towards regional strongmen, and broader human rights concerns.[33] But regardless of how important human rights may or may not be to a particular government, both Washington and London must contend with domestic public opinion. Egregious examples of rights violations such as the murder of Saudi journalist Jamal Khashoggi in the Saudi consulate in Istanbul drive media and public outcry and cannot be ignored by political elites in either nation. Such episodes have very real consequences for policy and the behaviour of political elites. Saudi Crown Prince Mohammed bin Salman has been largely shunned by political leaders in both countries;[34] the Houses of Congress have overwhelmingly voted to sanction individuals involved in the murder while publicly pointing the finger at the crown prince. As if to illustrate the difference, while Western countries amped up their rhetoric against Saudi Arabia, neither Russia nor China said a word about the killing, with Vladimir Putin's most notable contribution being to hi-five MBS at a G20 summit.[35] In contrast, Britain released a picture from the same summit in which then Prime Minister Theresa May looked gloomy and distinctly uncomfortable.[36] Nevertheless the issue of human rights violations is a line delicately trod, particularly in a region where regimes are by and large autocratic, and human rights records are extremely poor. For both the United States and the UK in the age-old tussle between economic benefit and human rights concerns, the former usually wins out.

American Poodle or Athens to America's Rome?

So dominant is Washington's regional role that any coherent UK Middle East policy since 1945 has been constructed with reference to the position of the United States. However, the UK can and does pursue its own goals across a gamut of issues in the Middle East; it has always been this way and will surely continue to be so in the future. For instance, in areas of the region where security is assured by an overwhelming US and Western military presence, such as in the Arabian Gulf states, the UK and the United States cooperate, but in a manner which is highly competitive. While neither works to undermine the broader security preferences of the other, both seek influence in the region for economic and domestic benefit in a manner which is zero sum. Washington aims for primacy in its relationship with Saudi Arabia, as London does for Oman leaving the other to scrap for second place, usually with Paris. While there is still plenty of business in the Gulf to go around, winning business and securing influence at the expense of the United States is both a welcome and indeed tacit goal of British policy. For example, Britain's Al Yamamah arms deal with Saudi Arabia, still the largest arms deal in history, was conducted in 1985 when relations between Margaret Thatcher and Ronald Reagan were uniquely close. London pounced on an opportunity to sell to the Saudis after the United States had been slow to follow up an initial tranche of sales of F-15 aircraft. Despite her friendly relationship with President Regan, Thatcher didn't compromise when it came to securing business for Britain at Washington's expense.

Under both Labour and Conservative governments this desire for an ever-larger slice of the Gulf pie is a strong undercurrent that drives policy, and has much to do with the formulation of Britain's 2015 Gulf strategy, termed by some as 'the return to East of Suez'.[37] There is little doubt that vestiges of Britain's pre-1971 outlook remain in British Gulf policy, and that this naturally drives a sense of competition with the United States (amongst others), particularly in the security and defence realm. This is not to say that the UK does not take into account US preferences, but that the UK must openly acknowledge that its goals and policy preferences are not the same as Washington's, and it should be prepared to stand by those policy choices. Washington may be tiring of the Middle East, but the UK does not have such strategic luxuries.

At the time The Gulf Strategy was written London's impression that Washington was pivoting to Asia under the Obama administration meant that British policymakers foresaw the vacating of a strategic space, which not only allowed for greater British military influence, but required it.[38] British concern about strategic vacuums being filled by Russian and Chinese actors was a crucial driver in pushing a more active British presence in the Gulf, which is largely viewed as being in Britain's economic and strategic interest. The Gulf strategy is a good formula on which to build a British policy of strategic hedging that acknowledges Washington's importance, but should re-emphasize Britain's unique interests. After all, losing business to the Chinese or the Russians is a bad outcome for Britain, regardless of what the United States thinks.

This competitive Realist world, in which UK diplomats and trade officials might get one over on their American counterparts in the service of national interest (and more frequently vice versa), is counterbalanced in areas of the Middle East where security is poor, and where the unstable nature of politics means that the need for the UK and the United States to operate together is crucial. In countries such as Iraq, Syria and Yemen, Washington is a far more influential player, and London tacks from polite rivalry towards a position of near total cooperation. The result being that British and American forces work alongside each other with a uniquely high level of integration and interoperability and are focused on nearly identical political goals and end states. Much of Britain's ability to influence Washington relies heavily on its military and defence posture, which affords London status as a leading military power. To this end the UK's usefulness is perhaps understood as that of a US force multiplier across the world, through basing infrastructure both on the UK homeland and further afield in British sovereign and overseas territories such as Ascension Island, Diego Garcia and Cyprus. These facilities provide the US logistical basing for operations globally (albeit with a particular focus on operations in the US CENTCOM region) as well as for joint intelligence work, allowing the two nations to conduct intelligence gathering operations against regional foes, but also allies like Turkey and Israel.[39] In these instances the UK can have leverage over the United States by the simple virtue of its cooperation. By 'being in the room' when an operational decision is made, the UK is at least afforded a voice where none might otherwise exist. Whether this is listened to by US policymakers is another matter; nevertheless, it is apparent that the UK's military and security capabilities are perhaps its greatest lever in dealing with Washington. This will continue to be the case given that the UK's political influence over the European Union has now diminished, placing ever greater weight on the UK's security apparatuses to carry the lion's share of its overseas power projection.

There are problems with this position, which lay the UK open to accusations that its security preferences are largely subsumed to that of the United States. And that London's only real influence in the Middle East comes at the implementation stage of any given US whim, while forfeiting almost all of its influence at the policy formulation stage. This is reminiscent of the Poodle accusations that were made of Tony Blair and his government during the lead up to the war with Iraq,[40] in which it became clear that Blair's position was to leverage the strength of the UK as an intimate security partner of the United States in order to persuade the United States to adopt some of London's own policy preferences. Quite apart from being unpopular with the British public, this requires disproportionate focus on defence and security spending in order for the UK to prove itself relevant to the United States and thereby influence its thinking. Much of this insecurity stems back to the removal of the UK from Washington's nuclear club following the Atomic Energy Act of 1946 that forced the UK to establish its own atomic bomb programme, before then concluding in 1954 that it must pursue the Hydrogen bomb.[41] So it is not exactly a new problem, and both the UK and the United States have danced around the issue of defence expenditure for many years. A recent example came in the form of a friendly, but firm request that the UK should retain 'the full combat spectrum, particularly the high end.' Because 'it is in the best interest of both our nations for the UK to remain the US partner of choice ... In that spirit, the UK will need to invest and maintain robust military capability'.[42] Such polite prods have been a consistent theme in the special relationship and mean that the UK needs to constantly evaluate Washington's military priorities in the region and adjust its own thinking accordingly.

The underlying assumption of this dynamic is that the UK seeks US approval, and in return is afforded the chance to feed its own policy preferences into the US debate. The hope being that this will make any given US policy more palatable to British tastes. John Bolton, moustachioed hawk of the Bush II and Trump administrations, summed up his distaste for the British approach. 'Many Brits believed that their role in life was to play Athens to America's Rome, lending us the benefit of their superior suaveness, and smoothing off our regrettable colonial rough edges.'[43] If this is truly the case, then the Trump administration long wore out Britain's supply of diplomatic sandpaper. Four years of a topsy-turvy Trumpian approach to the Middle East made it impossible to know whether the United States was engaging or disengaging from the region, which was further complicated by the sudden rush of Middle East peace deals that team Trump orchestrated in the middle of a re-election campaign. Walter Russell Mead termed the Trump approach to the world as Jacksonian, reflecting that the United States now only goes into conflicts if there is a directly observable benefit, but can and will use force if necessary.[44] True, there were elements of Jacksonian self-interest and realpolitik in Trump's worldview, but much of that was lost amid the endless barrage of chaotic tweets emanating from Trump's Twitter account. If there is any lesson to be learned from the Trump years it is surely this, the United States alone must define its role and how it behaves in the international system, and it should not be the role of suave talking Brits to sell the United States' policy positions to the rest of the world.

Despite the difficulties of the Trump era, there always remained a significant US military presence across the Middle East, affording the United States the ability to be Jacksonian and conduct military operations at will, while maintaining a commitment to maximum pressure strategies against Iran. In many ways the underlying sentiment that drove Trump's administration was curiously similar to that of Obama administration officials, many of whom now serve in the Biden administration. In that the Middle East was important particularly in terms of security, but clearly not at the top of the foreign policy agenda. And so, outside of imminent security threats there is no reason to think that any future president would be keen to continuously meddle with an area as politically complex and insecure as the Middle East which provides so little obvious economic incentives outside of security and defence sales.

This is especially the case since Israel signed a slew of peace deals with its Arab neighbours, thereby lessening the diplomatic burden on the United States in future years. Whether Joe Biden (or any other president) decrees by Twitter or not, there are some fundamental truths that London needs to absorb if it is to play a useful role alongside the United States in the years ahead. The 9/11 era is coming to an end,[45] and Washington has no desire to occupy or invade countries as it once did. Light footprint interventions such as Operation Inherent Resolve, Operation Freedom's Sentinel and Operation Enduring Freedom-Philippines are the new norm.[46] The UK will certainly play a role alongside the United States here, being a force multiplier, a good ally and offering counsel when required. In many ways limited displays of Britain's hard power will be the most effective way to serve alongside the United States, ensuring continued interoperability and friendship between the two when it comes to policy in the Middle East.

Balancing between the United States and Europe in an era of global rivalry

Biden administration officials have made it clear that the US rivalry with China will become the main focus for US policy in the years ahead,[47] and it is not an exaggeration to state that in the coming years US Middle East policy may be primarily driven by Washington's competition with Beijing. The coronavirus pandemic only seems to have accelerated what looks to be shaping into a Cold War between the two sides, and if a Cold War between the great powers does unfold, then the UK will need to consider how it should construct its policy with reference to the struggle. A policy of balancing between the two sides looks to be unlikely as the UK becomes increasingly reliant on the United States for economic and strategic support post-Brexit. As Borck and Stephens discuss later in this volume, there could be significant ramifications for Britain depending on how it incorporates this rivalry into its own thinking. British business interests in the MENA region will be affected if London adopts an approach to China which is competitive and zero sum.[48] And so, what is needed is a more precise calculation of US appetite for regional engagement, and to what extent the UK wishes to be a part of this strategy if it means adhering to a strongly anti-China line. Although this alignment by Washington is also broadly in alignment with Britain's own Indo-Pacific tilt, it requires a hard-headed acknowledgement in London of what the UK can achieve alongside the United States, as opposed to what it can achieve by itself, or in concert with other powers.

Given that there is very little the UK can achieve alone in the Middle East, a balanced conception of how and under what circumstances to form these concerts is essential. These could take the form of ad hoc collections of states seeing common cause on a given issue, or a more tried and tested formula such as the E3. But what is crucial is that the UK adopts a flexible approach to pursuing its interests. The E3 is a good example of such a concert where the UK can and does exert influence on regional questions, which place constraints upon the United States, and perhaps more importantly on Russia and China. The E3 is not an alternative mechanism to the Special Relationship, but it has proven a useful tool at times when the UK may want to beef up the message on any issue with which there is divergence with the United States. In recent times the British have made use of the E3 on three notable issues: The Israeli–Palestinian Conflict, the Iran Nuclear Deal (JCPOA) and the condemnation of Saudi Arabia following the murder of Jamal Khashoggi. On all three occasions the combined weight of London, Paris and Berlin proved a useful bulwark against Trump's inconsistencies. Again, it is important to state that the E3 cannot force the United States to change its mind. No amount of E3 pressure could have stopped Trump's decision to move the US Embassy in Israel to Jerusalem, or reword Jared Kushner's 'deal of the century'. Similarly, the E3 could not stop Trump from walking back from the JCPOA. But in all these instances the E3 showed it was able to mitigate the fallout of decisions taken in Washington, and present alternative options for regional actors.

On the most pressing regional question of Iran and its nuclear enrichment programme, it is important to remember that the Europeans' disagreement with the United States over the JCPOA was primarily a disagreement with the Trump administration's position, and not the United States, which was the primary proponent of the deal in the first place. The UK is not (nor indeed is Germany or France) in principle opposed to a new deal with Iran if it serves the same arms control purposes as the old one. Given that the Biden administration is keen to reinvigorate the terms of the existing deal, then it is very obvious that London would sincerely back and support any effort.[49] However, this would need to be contingent on Iran's regional activities, which have become increasingly difficult, if not impossible to divorce from its stance on the nuclear deal. Although the United States does not seek war with Iran, a US- or Israeli-led war with Iran remains a possibility, and should be considered a medium- to long-term risk that Britain must remain prepared for, and prepare mitigating strategies to counter. Whether London would be obliged to join any US-led operation against Iran would depend significantly on the circumstances that led to that escalation.

As previously stated, the UK will certainly rely more on its US relationship than in years gone by, and this will require keeping a constant balance between Washington and European capitals. Should the UK pivot too far towards Washington it would undermine the strength of the E3, and should the UK pivot too far towards the E3 then London jeopardizes its post-Brexit global position, particularly with regard to trade policy. Given that the E3 and the United States are all NATO allies, making too much use of the E3 risks undermining NATO solidarity if there are very public rifts between Europe and the United States over Middle East security policy. Any E3 military pact is also complicated by the fact that all three countries prefer to operate as separate entities in the Gulf states. The UK has never been committed to a European position in the Gulf above its own interest, and the strong commitments made by the UK in its Gulf Strategy mean that the UK often tacks towards the United States on Gulf security operations, thereby creating a rift between itself and other Europeans.[50] A good example of this confusion is the manner in which France has tried to lead Operation Agenor, a maritime security mission in the Persian Gulf, when an already-existing US-led International Maritime Security Mission known as Operation Sentinel has been patrolling the area for some time. Quite apart from creating unnecessary (and expensive) redundancies and capacity replications,[51] the two missions blur the lines of politics and military affairs. As a result, the British contribute to Operation Sentinel and not Operation Agenor, which the French view as being indicative of support for a US max pressure strategy on Iran. The result is a scrambled message which does little to calm tensions with Iran, but that costs more and, for all this confusion, is still heavily reliant on the United States for regional leadership and logistical assistance. This is not effective policymaking, and such needless replication and division of labour between the United States and Europe should be avoided in future years. London should of course try to be a friend to all, which has been made easier now that the United States displays a more engaging attitude towards Europe, and the current Biden administration values integrating US and EU interests under a more classic transatlantic footing. But the complexities posed by diverging US and European priorities will not disappear completely. For now at least the best utility of the E3 mechanism in the Middle East should be to create leverage on diplomatic questions where London, Paris and Berlin see eye to eye, and to leave any military coordination well alone.

Conclusion

Being a junior partner in any relationship (no matter how special it is) is always going to lead to frustrations and thwarted opportunities. For the UK this is particularly acute given the United States' changing global role, and the scars caused by the Trump years. Understanding where the UK should continue to act in partnership with the United States and bolster its capabilities and where London should be extremely clear and unapologetic about its own unique set of interests has never been more crucial. A more flexible approach to Middle East affairs is needed in which the UK moves in and out of ad hoc coalitions of states to guarantee its interests, but at no point should the UK undermine US strategic interests. Being a uniquely close security partner to Washington does not equal unqualified obedience, and the UK maintains long-term interests in the Middle East that will last for many years to come, possibly outlasting any US interest there. This should underpin any UK thinking about the region, particularly as the United States begins to withdraw from its global role. However, the United States remains a superpower with enormous military capacity that it continues to use in the Middle East region. Although the United States' reluctance to wade back into regional conflicts means that a widespread regional conflagration is unlikely, Britain should remain wary of the possibility of conflict and retain the option of not standing with the United States if it chooses to launch a war against Iran. Furthermore, the Middle East region is still highly unstable and will become even more so as the long-term effects of coronavirus leave severe impacts upon the already-weak economies of the region. The chronic lack of security in the region will no doubt keep the United States tied into a regional politics in a way that it does not wish to be tied, but the UK should nonetheless remain wary of Washington's desire to leave such problems behind, because the myriad of security challenges that remain cannot be solved without some form of US leadership. To this end slowing down a US retreat, while looking for collections of states to fill gaps in US leadership, is the most advantageous position for Britain to take in the coming years.

Part Two

Principles and pragmatism – The debates over the UK's Middle East priorities

5

Values

James Lynch

Human rights and values in UK foreign policy

For the last decade, the UK's stated foreign policy goals have largely been shaped around three priorities. The first is economic and commercial promotion, packaged under the banner of the 'prosperity agenda': increasing exports and investment and opening markets. The second focuses on contributing to the UK's national security through foreign policy: 'safeguarding the UK's national security by countering terrorism and weapons proliferation, and working to reduce conflict'.[1] The third is a basket of issues this chapter terms as 'values'. This theme has changed identity under successive governments more than the other two priorities, reflecting perhaps the challenge of capturing the British state's interactions with various norms and international regimes under one banner.[2] While the term might include work around governance, strengthening international institutions or climate change, this chapter uses 'values' to refer broadly to the promotion and defence of human rights and democratic institutions, the most politically charged elements of the 'values' package.

The Middle East has proved a key testing ground for questions about the relationship between the UK's pursuit and promotion of prosperity, security and values. This chapter explores how British politicians and diplomats have explained the role of values in their interactions with the region and examines whether the commitments they make to universal (or sometimes 'British') values ever trump security and prosperity goals.

Within this framework, the chapter considers a series of touchstone events since the 2010 election of the Cameron government: the 'Arab spring' uprisings; the overthrow of Mohamad Morsi by the Egyptian military; the use of sarin gas by the Syrian government and the conflict in Yemen. It looks at the impact of the Brexit vote and the current government's vision of a 'Global Britain'. It argues that within British strategy in the Middle East, values have a well-established position as the 'third wheel',[3] prioritized in policymaking only when doing so supports – or at least does not threaten – one or both of the two core goals of security and prosperity. Policymakers' insistence that there is no tension between pursuing these hard interests and defending values has been repeatedly challenged, including even in court. In practice, this generally means values can be pursued more freely in countries that are not British allies, generating division over whether military force should be used in support of the values agenda. The advent of Brexit and a Conservative government elected on a mandate to 'use our new post-Brexit freedoms to transform the UK', including through striking new trade deals with regional partners and the United States, seems likely to reinforce the third wheel status of values in Middle East policy.[4] The Covid-19 pandemic, which caused the biggest quarterly contraction of UK GDP since records began and has consumed the attention of policymakers and the public, will further strengthen the trend.[5] Within this restrictive framework, it will nonetheless remain important to British politicians, for electoral and ideological reasons, that the UK projects itself as a 'force for good' in the Middle East and elsewhere.

The driving force of prosperity

The Conservative-led coalition government that took power in 2010, in the wake of the global financial crisis, told parliament that the 'restoration of our economic fortune is essential to our foreign policy'.[6] New Foreign Secretary William Hague bemoaned the fact that the UK exported more to Ireland than to India, China and Russia combined.[7] The FCO was tasked to improve links with emerging markets to help drive the export-led recovery promised by the Tory manifesto.[8]

Hague also said he wanted human rights to be at the 'irreducible core' of the country's foreign policy.[9] Values, Hague said, would serve British interests rather than being in tension with them: 'It is not in our character as a nation to have a foreign policy without a conscience, and neither is it in our interests.'[10] He set up and chaired a Human Rights Advisory Group that included adversarial NGOs.[11] He maintained the FCO's annual Human Rights and Democracy report – established by Robin Cook to assess the state of human rights around the world – defying expectations that he might scrap it.[12]

Nonetheless, campaigners feared the push to intensify trade ties with emerging powers would mean doubling down on support for repressive governments, in particular those also perceived to provide security.[13] This policy had been central to Western strategy in the Middle East for decades – including under Blair and Brown's Labour governments, irrespective of Robin Cook's call for an 'ethical dimension to foreign policy'[14] – with authoritarian partners providing 'a forward military posture, access to energy resources and security for the state of Israel', in return for diplomatic and military backing.[15]

The 'Arab Spring' seems to shake things up

The events of 2011 challenged these long-held tenets of Western policy. It was only in 2009 that Barack Obama had called Egypt's Hosni Mubarak 'a force for stability [and] good in the region'.[16] Now, after the fall of Ben Ali in Tunisia, Mubarak came under unprecedented pressure, his corrupt and repressive government hugely unpopular. He turned to his backers in the West for support. After some uncertainty Obama sided with the demonstrators and David Cameron quickly followed his lead.[17]

Dropping Mubarak was a pivotal decision that framed the response of Western powers to the subsequent uprisings across the region, with leaders keen to be seen on the right side of history and play a leading role. Cameron paid an early visit to Tahrir square, calling the protests 'inspiring'.[18] Days later, he told parliament the UK 'must not tolerate [the Libyan] regime using military force against its own people' and presented a values-based case for military intervention. He secured overwhelming, cross-party parliamentary support for the UK to take military action, under a UN Security Council resolution deploying the Responsibility to Protect doctrine, aimed at the protection of civilians from the Libyan government. But Cameron made clear that Muammar Gaddafi needed to go – 'this is an illegitimate regime that has lost the consent of its people'[19] – and the mission rapidly developed into support for the rebel forces that would overthrow him.

Even in Bahrain, a close ally where the UK had most assets at stake and was most cautious, the British response to a bloody crackdown on protests – criticized for its relative meekness in comparison to the UK's reaction in other parts of the region – appears striking in hindsight. Arms export licences were revoked and London called on Bahrain to 'meet legitimate aspirations for greater social and political freedoms'.[20]

All the while, Cameron and Hague faced charges of opportunism and hypocrisy, as they continued to promote defence exports across the region.[21] The Arab spring was never going to put the brakes on the prosperity agenda. But in Whitehall there was some re-evaluation of what policies might serve British interests.[22] The 2011 uprisings challenged the assumption that to deliver on security objectives, it was necessary – or useful – to work with regimes that did not display respect for the values of human rights, democracy or good governance. Mubarak, Ben Ali and Co, who had seemed to offer a basic promise of stability and partnership in the fight against terrorism, had become the causes of instability. Declining living standards, perceived inequality and corruption, and restricted channels to express legitimate grievances had combined in a combustible mix.[23] Cameron addressed this directly in February 2011:

> For decades, some have argued that stability required highly controlling regimes, and that reform and openness would put that stability at risk. So, the argument went, countries like Britain faced a choice between our interests and our values … that is a false choice … Our interests lie in upholding our values.[24]

The question was whether these redefined aspirations would be followed by meaningfully distinct policymaking.

Reality bites: Sisi's coup, pressure from Abu Dhabi

The UAE, a priority for Britain's prosperity agenda, would directly challenge Cameron's assertion that Britain had no choices to make between pursuing its interests and promoting values. Alarmed by the West's abandonment of Mubarak and by new openings for Islamist political actors, Abu Dhabi and Riyadh reacted. In the Gulf, they deployed troops into Bahrain to shore up the government as it was rocked by protests, as well as tightening the screws on sources of challenge at home, ruthlessly squashing any signs of activism or free media.[25]

Outside the Gulf, Mohammed bin Zayed, the crown prince of Abu Dhabi, worked with Saudi Arabia and Israel to besiege the United States and other Western powers with complaints about Egyptian President Mohamed Morsi, elected as the Muslim Brotherhood-backed candidate in 2012.[26] He allegedly funded the anti-Morsi Tamarod protest movement, and promised Military Chief Abdel Fattah el-Sisi billions in economic aid if Morsi were deposed.[27] A week after Sisi overthrew Morsi in a July 2013 coup, Saudi Arabia and the UAE pledged $8 billion to Egypt.[28] When Sisi made his move, Hague cautiously called it a 'dangerous thing'.[29] Two years later, Sisi was welcomed to London by Cameron, signing an MOU on security cooperation.[30] In the intervening period, security forces had massacred 900 of Morsi's supporters at Nahdaa and Rabaa squares, 'one of the world's largest killings of demonstrators in a single day in recent history'.[31] What had changed since Hague's declaration in 2012 that 'greater freedom and democracy in the Middle East is an idea whose time has come'?[32] One factor was that the United States fell in behind Sisi after the coup.[33] But the UK also came under pressure from Abu Dhabi.

The Gulf had taken centre stage in the UK's global prosperity agenda. A cross-government 'Gulf initiative' had been set up in 2010 to deepen links with the six GCC states. Among other goals, the British wanted to reinvigorate defence sales to the UAE and promote BP's interests. But the crown prince of Abu Dhabi, Mohammed bin Zayed, felt the UK was too sympathetic to the Muslim Brotherhood. The day after Morsi's election victory, he appears to have told Cameron that progress on BP, a proposed £6bn Typhoon fighter jet deal and new investment in Britain would depend on how it engaged with the Muslim Brotherhood at home and across the Middle East.[34] The UK's failure to respond adequately, not least its outreach to the new Morsi government, frustrated Abu Dhabi and it 'signalled its displeasure with the UK through commercial and political pressure'.[35] By late 2012 the BP deal was off the table,[36] and by late 2013 so too was Typhoon.[37] By 2014, Mohamed bin Zayed was said to be 'steaming' with anger at London.[38] A month after he met Cameron, Downing Street announced a review of the Muslim Brotherhood's UK activity, and the review began with a visit to Abu Dhabi nine days later.[39] The next year Cameron welcomed Sisi – by then recognized as an even worse human rights abuser than Mubarak – to London. While other factors – the UK's goals in Egypt, the US position – also played a role, it is clear that London struggled vainly to reconcile pursuit of the government's prosperity goals in the Gulf with upholding the values they had espoused in Egypt after Mubarak's fall. The message from Abu Dhabi was clear: deeper trade and investment cooperation would need closer political and security alignment.

Conflict and crisis

For countries that were not British allies, the picture was different. The values agenda could be pursued as a priority without disrupting other goals. Syria had descended into a terrible civil war, with 90,000 people killed by 2013.[40] Syria was not strategically aligned with Western powers and Assad was drawing on Iranian and Russian support to fight its war, giving the UK free rein to align its espoused values with its security priorities: in this case, the two reinforced and supported each other with little tension. Britain publicly condemned atrocities by the Assad government, supported UN investigations into war crimes and pushed for sanctions and ICC investigations – efforts that were largely frustrated by Russia and China at the Security Council.[41] When hundreds of people in opposition-controlled suburbs of Damascus were killed by sarin gas attacks in 2013, a breach of the international prohibition on the use of chemical weapons,[42] Cameron argued for a swift US/UK military response to the attacks but failed to make the case at home.

As with Libya, he presented a values-based case, telling parliament that 'the question before the House today … is about the large-scale use of chemical weapons and our response to a war crime—nothing else'.[43] But opposition parties flagged the risks to regional stability and security and the Labour Party, which had made the case for military intervention in Kosovo, Sierra Leone and to some degree Iraq in humanitarian terms, refused to support the strikes. Rebel Tory and Liberal Democrat MPs joined Labour in refusing to support strikes, meaning that for the first time since 1782 a British prime minister failed to gain parliamentary backing for military action.[44]

In one reading, the political establishment, reflecting public opinion,[45] imposed a 'corrective, shifting the country away from an unpopular willingness to follow the United States into war zones, and back towards a less forceful approach to upholding international order based on law, the UN and diplomacy'.[46] Forceful defence of values (in this case the prohibition of war crimes) could undermine security, parliamentarians said, as well as endangering other values including the rights of those affected by airstrikes and respect for the United Nations.

When ISIS took control of swathes of Iraqi territory in 2014, displacing hundreds of thousands of people and committing widespread atrocities against the Yazidi and other minorities, MPs looked at the situation differently. ISIS was a non-state actor threatening an elected government, challenging the sanctity of established state sovereignty in the region and actively recruiting British nationals to its cause. All of this was topped off with a signature brutality carefully curated for the global public audience. Security priorities and values aligned, and parliament supported military action, albeit with the UK playing a limited supporting role as part of a wider coalition. This strong alignment, which generated an overwhelming consensus among the British public and political establishment on the need to confront ISIS,[47] meant that there was limited public scrutiny of the UK's membership of a loose coalition that included actors whose behaviour fell far short of Britain's espoused values, such as Iraq's Popular Mobilisation Unit (Hashd Al-Shaabi) militias, associated with atrocities against Sunni communities.[48] The following year, parliament backed airstrikes against ISIS in Syria following terror attacks in Paris. This time, perhaps mindful of his 2013 failure, Cameron was crystal clear that national security – not upholding values or norms – was the goal: 'The House has taken the right decision to keep the UK safe'.[49] When in 2018 Theresa May elected to join Donald Trump and Emmanuel Macron in striking Syrian targets after another gas attack by Assad forces, she did so in parliament's Easter recess and so avoided having a vote for unpopular strikes, prompting uproar among MPs on both sides of the house.[50]

A tilt towards security

As high-profile ISIS attacks in Europe brought security priorities into sharp focus, the summer of 2015 saw the issue of migration rise to the fore across Europe, with conflict raging in Syria, Iraq and Libya and large movements of people across the Mediterranean. With the promised Brexit referendum now on the horizon and under continuous pressure from the right over immigration, Cameron's reaction was to prioritize security – 'we need to protect our borders'[51] – and resist calls to resettle greater numbers of Syrian refugees from camps in Lebanon and Jordan.[52] The general (though not universal, see Germany) reluctance of European states to host refugees except through limited UN resettlement programmes increased the leverage of key transit countries such as Egypt, Turkey and Sudan, as Europe depended on them to control the flow of people[53] and further reduced the incentives for European states to engage them on difficult human rights issues.

The sense that events were spiralling out of control in the Middle East, with effects being felt in Europe, increased the priority that UK policymakers placed on security goals. In parallel, at a less macro-level, a change of leadership was shifting the policy emphasis of the Foreign Office. William Hague, a cabinet heavyweight who had said human rights would form the 'irreducible core' of British foreign policy, stood down in 2014. His replacement Philip Hammond showed less enthusiasm and emphasized that human rights promotion would be primarily a private enterprise. 'Lecturing people in public doesn't always work',[54] he said, a position that was becoming a 'mantra' among British diplomats in the Middle East.[55] In 2015 the FCO told the Foreign Affairs Committee that human rights was not one of its priorities,[56] while in that year's National Security Strategy, 'British' (rather than universal) values such as democracy and human rights were described as 'conditions that lead to security and prosperity', rather than as goals in their own right.[57]

British arms and Yemen

Perhaps no issue better exemplifies the tensions between security and prosperity goals and Britain's stated commitments to values than the Yemen conflict. Whilst it was not a member of the Saudi-led coalition that launched airstrikes in 2015 in an attempt to dislodge the Houthis' grip on power, the UK – alongside the United States – provided arms, intelligence and logistical support to Riyadh and its partners.[58] The UK's defence sales relationship with Saudi Arabia was well-established – between 2010 and 2017 it imported more arms from Britain than any other country, around 46 per cent of total volume[59]– and the Yemen conflict drove a surge in business. Almost as soon as the bombing began, evidence of disproportionate and indiscriminate airstrikes began to emerge.[60] The UN found evidence of war crimes[61] and called the humanitarian crisis caused by the conflict 'the worst in the world'.[62] The Saudi coalition dropped British cluster bombs, banned by the UK because of their devastating impact on civilians, particularly children.[63] The UK was accused of complicity in Saudi war crimes by former cabinet ministers, a possibility also raised by a UN report.[64] Labour argued that support for Saudi Arabia in Yemen was undermining the UK's ability to uphold values in other contexts such as Syria where it had called for accountability over Aleppo.[65] Britain rejected strident calls, and private advice from officials,[66] to halt arms sales to Saudi Arabia, arguing that it risk-assessed arms licences in 'robust' fashion and was working with the Saudis on avoiding civilian casualties.[67] This arguably reflected in large part the importance of defence sales to Saudi Arabia for the UK defence industry. BAE Systems is highly vulnerable to fluctuations in the defence sales relationship with Saudi Arabia, which generated 16 per cent of its total sales in 2017.[68] Supporting a national defence industry is a central pillar of defence policy, but the UK cannot sustain one on its own – since the mid-1980s, defence spending as a proportion of national income has fallen 60 per cent.[69] Promotion of defence exports has become a priority for every British government. Under the 2015 National Security Strategy, defence sales 'are essential for our security and prosperity'.[70]

Campaigners went to court over the sales, and in 2019 the Court of Appeal found that the government had not properly followed its rules when assessing the risk these arms could be used in the commission of war crimes.[71] Licensing was suspended and didn't resume until July 2020, with the government claiming its new methods allowed it to be certain the sales were safe.[72] For the country which had led the global campaign to establish an Arms Trade Treaty, the legal process had been humiliating. Successive Conservative governments believed they could thread the needle, pursuing the UK's security and commercial goals of supporting its national defence industry, while complying with legal obligations on human rights. In other words any tensions between values and interests could be resolved. On Yemen at least, the courts disagreed.

The Brexit effect

By 2016 the prosperity agenda was fully entrenched at the heart of foreign policy, crowding out other more sensitive conversations with emerging power partners in the Middle East such as the Gulf and Egypt. Meanwhile, the slender possibility of a re-evaluation of whether strongmen really offered security, raised by the Arab spring, was snuffed out by the twin factors of the Gulf backlash and the descent of parts of the region into conflict and mass displacement. The inclination of the UK to intervene militarily in support of values was dampened, with policymakers and the public scarred by failures and perhaps more conscious of the complexity and risk. It was, nevertheless, arming partners to fight a bloody war in Yemen, seemingly to safeguard its national defence industry. The effect of Brexit on this policy environment was not to change the direction of travel, but in some respects to accelerate it. It did this in three ways.

Firstly, the capacity of the government to focus on difficult foreign policy questions was reduced as the Brexit agenda took precedence. Cameron was replaced by May, who showed little interest in foreign policy beyond EU relations. Britain turned inwards. The FCO – which has responsibility for international human rights – was reduced in scope, losing functions to the new Brexit department DEXEU and the Department for International Trade (DIT).[73] Serious engagement on contentious questions of values requires investment of time by high-level officials and politicians as well as the spending of political capital. All of this has been in shorter supply since Brexit.

Secondly, Brexit intensified the domestic political debate around human rights law and standards, including whether the government would scrap or update the Human Rights Act (HRA), as respectively promised by the 2015 and 2019 Conservative manifestos, and the related issue of Britain's commitment to the European Convention on Human Rights (ECHR). Since 2016, politicians hostile to these instruments have gained influence and authority. In 2020, EU negotiators expressed concern when Britain refused to formally commit to continuing to apply the ECHR.[74] While the British government says that its commitment to human rights remains, these discussions, which are being conducted very publicly, will undoubtedly affect the UK's international credibility on these issues.

Finally, Brexit meant Britain leaving the single market under the Withdrawal Agreement, hastening the need for alternative trading partners. With a need to demonstrate a hopeful post-single market future and the prospect of new trade deals, the FCO and DIT doubled down on the prosperity agenda as the driving force for British foreign policy. By 2018 there were thirty-one trade envoys, compared to three human rights envoys or special representatives.[75]

EU trade agreements include human rights requirements, which can in principle if seriously breached trigger suspension of the trade measures.[76] Trade Secretary Liam Fox insisted to parliament in 2019 that he was not planning to sacrifice human rights standards in trade deals, despite being pressured by partners,[77] but evidence from early deals suggests that parliament's concern is legitimate and that some deals are going through without any human rights terms, and others with scant detail that could be enforced.[78] This likely reflects the difficulty of inserting contentious terms into trade agreements where Britain as a sole actor lacks the leverage the larger EU market holds, as well as the challenging wider climate for human rights and democracy. These negotiations are taking place as the rise of strongmen leaders has severely undermined what international consensus there was on the promotion of open societies and the so-called rules-based international order.

Trade deals and security partners: Saudi Arabia and Israel

In this new world for Britain, the Gulf has unsurprisingly been a priority. Just months after the 2016 referendum, Theresa May promised to 'turbo-charge' commercial trade relations with the region in order to 'lock in a new level of prosperity for our people for generations to come'.[79] Seeking a free trade agreement with the region, the government said it had identified new opportunities worth £30 billion.[80] In 2017 the government set up a trade working group with the GCC to identify 'barriers to trade and [forge] an ever-closer commercial relationship between the UK and the GCC'. Three Prime Ministerial Trade Envoys were dedicated to the GCC.[81] A UK Export Finance team dedicated to the GCC was established in the UAE in 2018.[82] In 2020, as Britain formally left the EU, Abu Dhabi said an early UK/GCC free trade deal was 'extremely important' for the UAE. The Emiratis also hinted at a political dimension to this mooted deal: 'We need a confident, active Britain that is closely involved in Gulf security and Middle East issues.'[83] In October 2020, the UK and the GCC announced a Joint Trade and Investment Review 'to assess the current state of our trade and investment relationship, as well as identify opportunities to enhance cooperation for the future'.[84] While it is yet to be seen what new form of trading partnerships may be pursued with the Gulf states, there is clear potential for the UK to be even more reluctant to confront difficult values issues with these partners, given the priority attached to expanding the UK's access to export markets in the region.

It is inconceivable that there will not be more difficult issues in the pipeline, given the rise to power of Mohammad bin Salman Al Saud, the crown prince of Saudi Arabia. Elements of Mohammad bin Salman's modernizing social and economic agenda, including giving women the right to drive and providing space for cultural events, have appealed to Western partners. But a pattern of thuggery and violation of accepted norms of behaviour has also been on show. The 'shakedown' of wealthy Saudis in the Riyadh Ritz-Carlton pleased some citizens frustrated by corruption but concerned investors who saw an absence of rule of law.[85] Hopes for a freer society have been dashed, with a sweeping crackdown that has caught up even the mildest of critics. Women who campaigned for the end of the driving ban – one of the crown prince's signature policies – have reported gruesome torture in detention.[86] International partners have been put on notice that debate on Saudi Arabia's human rights record is not up for discussion. When Canada called for the release of political prisoners in 2018, Saudi Arabia reacted forcefully, expelling Canada's ambassador, suspending new trade and investment and removing thousands of Saudi students and medical patients from Canada.[87]

Outside formal UN mechanisms, Britain steered clear of direct criticism of Saudi Arabia – regardless of who was Foreign Secretary or Prime Minister – until 2018, when journalist Jamal Khashoggi was murdered in the Saudi consulate in Istanbul. The shocking and high-profile nature of the case provided an unusually robust response from Foreign Secretary Jeremy Hunt who promised to 'treat the incident seriously – friendships depend on shared values'.[88] Remarkably, Hunt was suggesting that Britain's relationship with Saudi Arabia was in some way *contingent* on values, and that a breach of these values could potentially trump security and prosperity interests – a position arguably not supported by the evidence of history. With Saudi Arabia's international standing at rock bottom, it was in no position to react with its usual force to the various condemnatory statements from around the world. The following year, a UN investigation found that 'every expert consulted finds it inconceivable that an operation of this scale could be implemented without the Crown Prince being aware'.[89] But this did not have the impact on the bilateral relationship Hunt had promised. Instead, the UK called on Germany to drop the ban on arms exports that it had imposed, as it was disrupting the UK's production of Tornado and Typhoon.[90] Hunt justified Britain's reversion to the status quo with reference to those two key drivers of British foreign policy, prosperity and security,[91] seemingly demonstrating that in some cases, the tension between interests and values simply cannot be resolved. As Peter Oborne put it starkly:

> Britain regards Saudi Arabia as its closest ally in the Middle East, apart from Israel. On the other hand, it is the central contention of British foreign policy that it supports human rights. The two positions contradict one another; it is impossible to stand up for Saudi Arabia and human rights at the same time.[92]

This raises a question that goes beyond the relationship with Saudi Arabia: Is there a path to be found where the UK post-Brexit deepens trade arrangements with its Middle East partners and at the same time feels able to take actions that align with its professed values: halting arms sales where the risk is too great, or adjusting bilateral relationships in response to actions that breach accepted norms? The past decade suggests that finding that path will be highly challenging. Decisions in the Gulf are as a rule taken by individuals who may retain control for decades and who are highly sensitive to criticism. Interactions across a bilateral relationship are linked rather than seen as separate transactions. It may be that Raab's decision in July 2020 to include Saudi nationals connected with the Khashoggi killings in the first designations under the Global Human Rights Sanctions reflected an attempt to solve this conundrum. While some interpreted the move as putting London on a collision course with Riyadh,[93] arguably Raab was in fact choosing to restrict the UK's response to measures against private individuals, rather than adjusting bilateral ties with the Saudi Arabian state.[94] The fact that licences for arms exports to Saudi Arabia were resumed the day after this designation lends some credence to this interpretation.

Outside the Gulf, Israel has signed a continuity trade agreement with the UK, rolling over the EU–Israel deal. Both countries are committed to reviewing the agreement 'with a view to upgrading it'.[95] Talks began in 2020, with reports suggesting that Israel was pushing for Britain to extend a renewed agreement to the West Bank, Golan Heights and Jerusalem.[96] Britain's position on the occupied territories has until now been explicitly grounded in international law – including opposing new settlement activity. Its steps in support of that position have however generally been limited to statements, much to the frustration of advocates. In the face of expanded settlement construction, it has meanwhile pushed forward a broad programme of trade and security cooperation with Israel. At the heart of this relationship are defence and security sales, with Britain approving £221 million of licences to Israel in 2017, making it the UK's eighth largest partner for arms sales.[97] The government has consistently resisted calls to halt this trade in light of the manner of their use in Gaza, even during 2014's Operation Protective Edge, when Cameron said the UN was right to speak out about the Israeli shelling of schools and warned Israel that 'civilians should not be targeted'.[98]

In October 2020 the government said it was 'scoping and probing for talks for a new higher-ambition trade agreement with Israel'.[99] These talks may provide an early opportunity to assess how the Johnson government will handle what could end up being a choice between defending commitments to international humanitarian law and further deepening its commercial and security relationship with a key ally.

US influence on British policy

The UK's attempt to pivot from the EU towards the United States affected its approach to handling difficult questions, involving values, in the Middle East. The UK government has since the Brexit vote targeted a US/UK trade deal as a cornerstone of its Global Britain vision and a demonstration of the possibilities outside of the EU trading block. While there have been questions raised about the significance of such a deal for the British economy, its political symbolism has remained important.[100] Talks began in May 2020 and by the end of the year substantial progress had reportedly been made on some areas.[101] To get there, however, British leaders had to court President Donald Trump, including on foreign policy in the Middle East. Like the Gulf monarchies, Trump explicitly linked foreign, security and trade policies, and was 'unapologetic about making one conditional on the other'.[102] His administration could not be relied on to support allies over the defence of values, as Canada found out when it spoke out on human rights in Saudi Arabia.[103] After the United States killed Iranian Military Chief Qassim Soleimani in a drone strike in early 2020 and Trump threatened to attack Iranian cultural sites,[104] British spokespeople contorted themselves in an attempt to show support for Trump while simultaneously affirming the UK's commitment to international law.[105] A Trump ally warned the UK that its Iran policy would affect the prospects of a free trade agreement:

> It's absolutely in [Johnson's] interests and the people of Great Britain's interests to join with President Trump, with the United States, to realign your foreign policy away from Brussels.[106]

When the United States released its Middle East peace plan in early 2020, it was rejected immediately by Palestinian leaders, as well as by the EU, which said it departed from 'internationally agreed parameters'.[107] The plan, strongly supported by Israel, proposed among other things to 'incorporate the vast majority of Israeli settlements into contiguous Israeli territory'.[108] Netanyahu announced, with Trump's blessing, that Israel would immediately apply sovereignty to settlements in the West Bank as well as the Jordan valley.[109] The EU said it was 'especially concerned' by this development, referencing international law and UN Security Council resolutions, and warning that 'steps towards annexation, if implemented, could not pass unchallenged'.[110]

In contrast, the UK gave a warm welcome to the plan, which it said was a 'serious proposal, reflecting extensive time and effort'.[111] Johnson called on Mahmoud Abbas, who had said that plan would be thrown into 'the garbage can of history' to engage.[112] Initial British reactions did not mention international law. The episode opened clear blue water between Britain and the EU, with Trump delighted about the support from 'Boris' for the plan.[113] Pressed in Parliament on whether the UK had changed its position on Israeli annexation, the Middle East minister was forced to clarify that 'I have to underscore and reiterate the fact that our position has not changed'.[114] When the prospect of annexation appeared to recede with the US-backed UAE–Israel normalization later in 2020, Johnson said it had been his 'profound hope that annexation did not go ahead'.[115]

The UK strategy to manage Trump by bending in the wind and seeking to avoid confrontation – with supportive messaging in high-level public statements, burying formal commitments to international law in the small print – risked degrading the importance of values and as a result encouraging approaches by partners that disregard them. But the election of Joe Biden, who tied the prospect of a trade deal to the Northern Irish border question,[116] and said before taking office that he would not enter into any new trade agreement with anybody 'until we have made major investments here at home and in our workers', raised major questions about the future of a US/UK trade deal.[117]

Politics and values

The future relationship between security, prosperity and values in the UK's posture in the Middle East will of course be shaped by political developments in Britain. Reading the tea leaves is challenging, because there has been little air time for these issues in a political landscape dominated by domestic priorities and Covid-19. Foreign policy beyond relations with the EU and the United States did not feature prominently in the 2019 election or the two main parties' leadership battles in 2019 and 2020.

One key assumption in much of this chapter is that while British politicians' personal commitment to human rights and related norms varies, most consider it electorally important to be seen to promote values. Cameron's repositioning of the Conservatives as human rights-friendly was a recognition of how damaging it had been for the Tories to be portrayed as the counterpoint of Cook's foreign policy with an 'ethical dimension'.[118] But, notwithstanding his 2020 defeat, the example of Donald Trump, who openly scorned normally sacrosanct values and had electoral success, could potentially change that calculus. Perhaps there is no political need to be seen to promote rights overseas. Within the Conservative Party, the right is ascendant and there are fewer influential 'one-nation' or 'rule of law' Tories. British public opinion seems ambivalent about the importance of values in defining foreign policy, with a survey published in 2019 finding that only 14 per cent of respondents thought they should take precedence over strategic defence and economic interests – though the largest number of respondents thought there should be a balance between the two.[119] If Boris Johnson's government takes a more recognizably Trumpian approach to foreign policy, then one could imagine a more dramatic departure in which the pursuit of values lost even the status of third wheel, and became a policy add-on purely deployed in order to criticize adversaries, in the manner of authoritarian states.

The need to work with the Biden administration suggests this is not the likeliest pathway for this government, but there are also domestic political reasons why values are not likely to be discarded. The fact that Home Secretary Priti Patel felt obliged to disavow her previously expressed support for the death penalty shortly before the 2019 election suggests that the Conservatives still consider human rights to be politically salient.[120] Among the Brexiteer wing of the party, there is also an attachment to the civil liberties and individual rights packaged as 'core British values' in the 2019 manifesto – indeed, there is arguably some association between these values and the origins of Brexit.[121] Even as the Johnson government pressed ahead with the merger of the Foreign Office and DFID in 2020, a central plank of its argument in doing so was that 'we need a new all-of-government approach if we are to *secure our values* and interests in a changing world' [emphasis added].[122] Even should the right further strengthen their control within the Johnson government, there will remain a desire to demonstrate that Britain's role in the world extends beyond trade and that, as the party's manifesto asserts, it remains a 'force for good'.[123] In July 2020, introducing a Global Human Rights Sanctions regime to 'target people who have committed the gravest human rights violations',[124] Raab told parliament that the new measures 'underpin Global Britain's role as a force for good in the world'.[125] Until this point the UK had largely implemented EU and UN sanctions designations. In its impact assessment for the new measures, the FCO noted that the regime would demonstrate 'leadership and ambition on human rights values after we leave the EU'.[126]

Whether being a 'force for good' entails military force is open to question. Appetite for direct military intervention in support of values seems low on both sides of the house, with the centre of British politics, traditionally the constituency favouring use of force to defend values, hollowed out. The 2019 Conservative manifesto promised to 'put our national security first' and made no mention of interventions.[127] It is difficult to see this government – so focused on Brexit and recovery from the coronavirus – embarking on any major new values-driven military operation in the Middle East. That said, unlike Cameron and May, Johnson enjoys a large majority giving him more flexibility to gain authorization, for example, for limited airstrikes. He could anyway follow May's approach and ignore the convention of consulting parliament.

Labour under Starmer seems unlikely to back military action without strong legal arguments in favour. Starmer told party members there would be 'no more illegal wars' and promised a 'prevention of military intervention act'.[128] Were Starmer to bring Labour back to power in the next election, his foreign policy would be considerably more traditional than a Corbyn government might have been, though as a human rights lawyer, opponent of the Iraq war and conscious of the Labour membership, he would give values a more prominent role in policymaking than it enjoys under Johnson.[129] A Starmer government might aim to revive the spirit of Robin Cook's aspirations for an ethical dimension to foreign policy, perhaps without the military adventurism favoured by the Blair government. If this risked affecting defence relationships, it could cool relations with allies in the Gulf and Israel. More broadly, one would expect a preference for multilateral, institutional approaches to promoting values.

Looking forward

There is no indication that the Middle East and North Africa are entering a period of stability. After a period in which mass anti-government protests became rarer, recent years have seen a resurgence across the region, in Iran, Palestine, Sudan, Lebanon, Algeria, Egypt and Iraq. In Sudan and Algeria protesters brought down longstanding presidents and the Iraqi prime minister stood down. The underlying causes of the 2011 uprisings have not gone away, and some argue that 'the old Arab order, characterized by authoritarian political systems and oil-based economies, appears to be passing away'.[130] The 'dramatic economic cost' of Covid-19 – which as well as creating a demand/supply shock, collapsed oil prices – across the region could hasten this process.[131] Based on the evidence of the past, any such transitions are unlikely to be free of violence, as elites seek to protect their power bases. In Iraq, Amnesty called security forces' treatment of protesters in 2019 'nothing short of a bloodbath'.[132] Difficult questions about whether Western partner governments in the region share 'core British values' will not be going anywhere.

Ten years ago, one would have expected the UK to play an active role in wrestling with these scenarios, for good or ill. Yet as a general rule, its voice has been quiet. This reflects the shift in British politics over the past decade, accentuated by Brexit, away from the ambitious liberal vision of Blair that was largely maintained by Cameron and Hague, towards a narrower, more inward-looking conception of the UK's place in the world and its relations both with its friends and adversaries. Depending on your perspective, this may not be a bad development, given the results of these more ambitious policies in Iraq and Libya. As one analyst puts it, commenting on the creation of a Foreign Office human rights ambassador post in 2019, 'to say that Britain lacks the credibility to promote human rights to others would be to state the case very gently indeed'.[133] To simply assume that Britain 'doing more' on human rights in the Middle East is always an unambiguously good thing, is to ignore the context of its colonial history and the legacy of Western interventions in the region. That said, British withdrawal from engagement on human rights issues in the Middle East would not be welcomed by many of the region's activists: notwithstanding inconsistency and policy failures of the past, the UK's voice is still held in high regard in many contexts and its positions on values issues retain a weight – to the extent that its regional partners lobby intensely to stop it using that voice.

Could anything reverse the direction of travel? The presence of a US president likely to pursue more traditional and predictable policies in the Middle East could potentially create a more amenable environment for the UK to follow a more values-based agenda. But that would mean the British being interested in pursuing that agenda, as it seeks to boost a post-Brexit, Covid-affected economy. There is no evidence to suggest that Johnson's government will alter the third wheel status of values in dealing with its partners in the region. The pressure to deliver on security and particularly prosperity objectives is simply too high and the UK lacks confidence that it can insert values into this mix in any meaningful way without imperilling its other goals. Whether or not this sense of diminished influence is really justified – Britain after all remains the sixth largest economy in the world with a permanent seat on the Security Council – it will take a lot to restore the UK's confidence to the point where it looks far beyond its tangible interests in the Middle East.

6

Prosperity

David Butter

The UK's deep historical connections with the Middle East have provided some advantages in the development of trade and investment relations in the modern era, although these have been mainly confined to the Gulf Arab states. The region accounts for a relatively small portion of the UK's global trade and investment, and British commercial activity is concentrated in half a dozen countries – notably Turkey, the UAE, Saudi Arabia, Qatar, Israel, Egypt and Oman – and is heavily skewed towards weapons exports, financial services and oil and gas. The UK has tended to run trade surpluses with most of its major trading partners in the region, except for Turkey (which is the UK's second-largest partner in trade of goods, after the UAE, and which is, by some margin, the largest exporter to the UK from the region).[1] The UAE and Saudi Arabia are major destinations for UK services exports, and these two countries, together with Qatar and Kuwait, account for the bulk of inward investment into the UK from the MENA region.

As the UK government and British businesses seek to build up their commercial relationships with countries outside the EU, the MENA region will offer a mix of opportunities and challenges. One such opportunity would be free trade agreements (FTAs) with either the Gulf Co-operation Council (GCC) or the six member states individually. The EU has been in discussions with the GCC about an FTA for more than twenty years, but with little prospect of this being concluded. Once the UK establishes a new framework for its trade relations with the EU, there might be an opportunity to negotiate an FTA with the GCC or some of the member states in relatively short order, particularly if the UK were to drop any reference to political issues such as human rights. The 2008 FTA between the GCC and Singapore could serve as a model. However, the tensions among GCC member states may be an obstacle to either a collective deal or separate accords. If the UK were to opt for individual FTAs rather than a deal with the GCC, given the tensions within that bloc in the wake of the imposition of sanctions on Qatar by the UAE, Saudi Arabia, Bahrain and Egypt, the UK could find that each of its Gulf negotiating partners would demand terms that are more advantageous than (or at least equal to) those being offered to their neighbours. Taking into account the depth of the existing trading relationships between the UK and the GCC member states, the British government and its Gulf counterparts may conclude that there is no need for an FTA.

The process of forging post-Brexit trade relationships could be simpler in the cases of countries that have existing trade accords with the EU. This applies to the Economic Association Agreements that the EU has with most of the countries around the Mediterranean (plus Jordan), although different considerations apply to Turkey, as it has a customs union with the EU. The UK is seeking to replicate the association agreements and has made some progress in setting out how this might work. As of January 2021, the UK had agreed terms for post-Brexit trade agreements with seven MENA countries – Israel, Jordan, Lebanon, Morocco, the Palestinian Authority, Tunisia and Turkey – and was in discussions about trade deals with Algeria, Egypt.[2] The association agreements provide for tariff-free and quota-free access of EU-sourced goods to the partner markets, but some restrictions apply to the export of agricultural produce to the EU. As a form of compensation for these restrictions the EU is committed to providing finance and technical assistance for the upgrade of industries in the partner countries. Once the UK and the EU have decided on what kind of trading relationship they will have in the future, there will be an opportunity for the UK and the association agreement signatories to review their respective arrangements. Some of these countries may wish to negotiate full-fledged FTAs, allowing unfettered access of their agricultural produce to the UK market, rather than stick with a replica of the association agreement.

Another challenge that British exporters will face relates to the EU-sourced components in goods sold in the Middle East, although this will be affected by whatever trading and regulatory arrangements the UK and the EU eventually reach. This will be a particular issue for the aerospace sector, which plays an important part in UK exports to the Gulf, both in the form of sections of Airbus airliners and in military aircraft such as the Typhoon, as well as the next-generation Tempest, which the UK-based BAE Systems is developing with Italian and Swedish partners.[3] European arms export companies can be expected to highlight complications in British supply chains as they tout their wares in the MENA region. One factor that could yield advantages for the UK would be the exchange rate. A weaker sterling would benefit some exporters, while making UK assets cheaper for MENA investors. The role that the UK plays as a global services centre, in particular for finance, has been a crucial element in the country's attraction for Gulf Arab investors. There is a risk that this attraction might be diminished if barriers go up in front of the export of services from the UK to the EU. However, many Gulf investors have made a deep and long-term commitment to the UK, and would not necessarily be inclined to shift their focus to mainland Europe as a result of some regulatory complications. A tally of outward investment by UAE entities between 2003 and 2015, for example, shows the UK as the top destination, outside India and the Middle East, with projects and company stakes worth $12.7 billion in total, ahead of China ($9.1 billion) and the United States ($5.4 billion). Only two EU member states figure among the top thirty: Spain and Germany, in twenty-fifth and twenty-sixth place, respectively, with investments of just over $1.9 billion each.[4] These include high-profile assets such as the DP World London Gateway port and logistics hub east of London, Qatar's stakes in the British Airports Authority and in iconic real-estate assets such as the London Shard, Abu Dhabi's ownership of Manchester City Football Club, and Saudi Arabia's stake in UK-based semi-conductor venture, ARM Holdings, via the $45 billion share held by the Public Investment Fund in the Soft Bank

Vision Fund. The UK also ranked third as a source of investment in the UAE over this period, behind India and the United States, with interests worth $11.7 billion.

Trade by numbers

According to the UK's Office for National Statistics (ONS), two countries in the MENA region – the UAE and Saudi Arabia – make it into the top twenty destinations for exports of British goods and services, and Turkey and the UAE are included among the top twenty sources for imports. In 2018 UK exports to the MENA totalled £42.2 billion, making up about 6 per cent of the UK's total exports. The six member states of the GCC made up about half of the regional total, with Turkey, Israel, Egypt and Morocco accounting for most of the remainder. The MENA region accounted for about 4 per cent of the UK's total imports of £686 billion, with Turkey (£10.6 billion), the UAE (£6.7 billion), Saudi Arabia (£3.9 billion) and Algeria (£2.3 billion) making up about two-thirds of the total. Among the leading destinations for UK exports in the MENA region, services make a significant contribution to the total. For Saudi Arabia, for example, services made up just over half of the UK's total exports of £7.7 billion in 2018, and in the UAE and Qatar the proportion was about 40 per cent and 30 per cent, respectively. In the Saudi case, this reflects major long-term military service contracts undertaken by BAE Systems, as well as oil and gas sector engineering services and finance. In the UAE, the strength of the services component of UK exports arises from the strong involvement of British companies in sectors such as property, tourism, retail, sport and entertainment.

The breakdown of the UK's merchandise trade with the MENA region shows heavy reliance on a few categories, in particular aircraft (mainly military), power generation equipment, cars, medical equipment and pharmaceuticals, and jewellery. Petroleum products and gas dominate the import slate from the Gulf Arab trading partners, while Turkey exports significant volumes of household goods, electronic equipment and food to the UK.

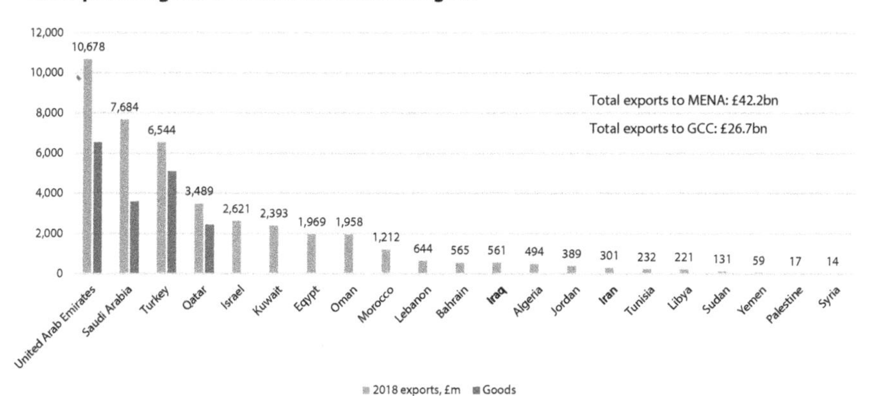

UK's leading export markets

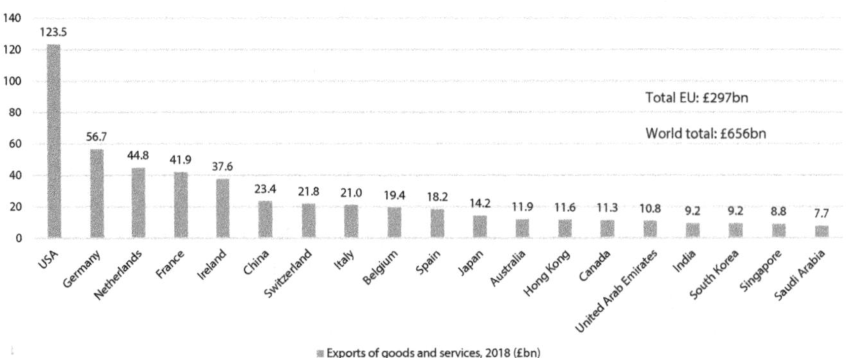

The UK typically runs a substantial deficit in its merchandise trade, which is partially offset by a surplus in its trade in services. During 2018, the UK's services exports totalled £307 billion, of which finance, insurance and consultancy were leading categories, along with tourism and air travel; services imports totalled £197 billion. The surplus on the services account was not sufficient to cover the shortfall on the UK's merchandise trade, and the current-account deficit in 2018 was £82.8 billion, equivalent to 4.3 per cent of GDP.[5] In order to finance this persistently high current deficit, the UK relies heavily on capital and financial inflows, to which Gulf Arab countries make a significant contribution through investments in UK securities and property.[6]

The MENA region does not figure in the top ten destinations for UK services exports, although Saudi Arabia and the UAE are close to being in this group. The EU accounts for just over one-third of the UK's total services exports, and the United States is the largest single market, with a share of about 22 per cent. Switzerland, Japan and Australia are also important markets. The MENA region accounts for less than 4 per cent of the UK's total services exports. UK services exports to the MENA region embrace a wide range of activities, including defence, oil and gas engineering, finance and insurance, consultancy, architecture, property management, marketing, retail and public relations.

UK's leading services export destinations

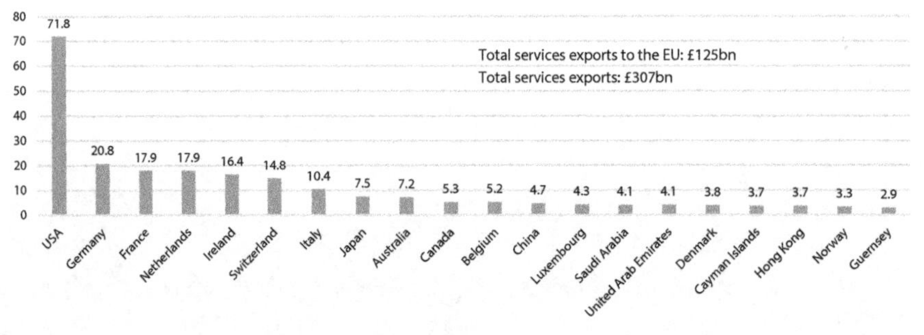

Playing to the UK's strengths

Prospects for developing the UK's trade relation with the MENA region will depend to a large extent on the economic priorities and performance of the target countries themselves. The British government and business groups will also have to decide on their own priorities – whether to try to build on previous achievements or whether to focus on new sectors.

One of the core strengths of the UK's export performance is the arms trade, and the MENA region has been an important element in this. The UK was the world's sixth-largest arms exporter during 2014–18, according to rankings compiled by the Stockholm International Peace Research Institute (SIPRI), after the United States, Russia, France, Germany and China.[7] The reliance on the Middle East was reflected in the fact that 59 per cent of the UK's arms exports during this period went to the MENA region, mainly consisting of aircraft sales to Saudi Arabia and Oman. This highlights a potential vulnerability for the UK, in respect of over-reliance on a few key markets, in a highly competitive industry.

According to SIPRI, there were nine MENA countries in the list of the top twenty global arms importers in 2014–18: Saudi Arabia (1st), Egypt (3rd), Algeria (5th), the UAE (7th), Iraq (8th), Turkey (13th), Qatar (14th), Israel (15th) and Oman (18th). In only two of these countries did the UK figure among the top three suppliers: Saudi Arabia, for which it was in second place with a 16 per cent share, and Oman, in first place with 39 per cent. France and Germany have had notable success in penetrating new regional markets in recent years, in particular Egypt, which has made major investments in upgrading its navy with French and German surface vessels and German submarines. Germany also figured among the top three suppliers to Qatar, Algeria and Israel. Even in Jordan, a country with which the UK has a strong defence relationship, the UK did not figure among the top three suppliers, which were the Netherlands (37 per cent), the United States (30 per cent) and Italy (5.8 per cent). In approaching the MENA arms market the UK also has to reckon with the strong marketing push of Russia, which has yielded some major deals in Egypt and Iraq, as well as in its largest regional market, Algeria.

The chances of the UK breaking into new MENA arms markets appear slim, given the recent advances of its competitors. It will also be hard for the UK to extend its record in Saudi Arabia, where the two Al-Yamamah programmes and the Eurofighter/ Al-Salam deals provided a sustained source of revenue for BAE Systems from the mid-1980s onwards, both in terms of procurement and operations and maintenance services. Saudi Arabia is now looking to develop its own local basis for arms procurement. UK companies could have an important role to play in this area, but will face formidable competition, in particular from US corporations.

Focusing on the arms business would also entail developing increasingly close contractual relationships with the security establishments of MENA governments whose human rights records have come under close scrutiny. This is a particular concern in relation to Saudi Arabia and the UAE, with reference both to the Yemen war and to the treatment of their own citizens (and in the UAE's case, British citizens). The human rights policies of Bahrain, Oman and Egypt are also matters of concern. However, the resounding defeat of the Labour Party, under the leadership of Jeremy Corbyn, in the December 2019 general election has changed the political context, broadly in favour of unfettered trade with the Gulf Arab states. The Labour Party had been strongly critical of Saudi Arabia in particular.[8] However, the United Trade Union, an important power broker within the Labour Party, is a strong supporter of the UK's military industries, given the large numbers of the union's members who are employed in this sector.

Another traditional strength for the UK has been in the provision of services to countries with strong historical ties to Britain, such as the UAE, Oman, Qatar and Bahrain. UK consultants, financiers, architects, management companies, landscapers and retail specialists played important roles in the development of the modern urban centres of the Gulf. In the UAE, for example, the UK ranked third, after India and the United States, among foreign investors in greenfield during the period between 2003 and 2015, according to a tally published by Dhaman, the state export and investment guarantee agency, citing the *Financial Times FDI Intelligence*.[9] The total value of these investments was $11.7 billion, spread between 551 companies and 644 projects, indicating a relatively small scale for the majority of the ventures concerned.

Some of this business will continue, as Qatar gears up for the 2022 World Cup and attempts to maintain a legacy from this event, and Dubai seeks a new relaunch with the 2020 Expo Dubai. However, this mode of development is closely tied to the financial surpluses arising from Middle East oil and gas. These industries will continue to generate important revenue for the region, but the boom conditions of some earlier periods are unlikely to return. Nevertheless, the diversification efforts of Gulf Arab governments, in particular Saudi Arabia, do offer opportunities for UK businesses to develop new kinds of markets in this region and to expand existing ventures.

Saudi Arabia's Crown Prince Mohammed bin Salman has brought fresh energy to Saudi Arabia's drive for diversification, notably through opening up sectors such as sport, leisure, tourism and entertainment. UK companies are already active in these areas in other parts of the Gulf, notably Dubai, Qatar and Oman. Saudi Arabia offers an opportunity to apply that experience in the considerably larger potential market of Saudi Arabia. The staging of a world heavyweight boxing bout in a purpose-built area in Diriyah, outside Riyadh, in December 2019, was a recent example of a new form of UK–Saudi venture. The event was promoted by UK-based Eddie Hearn and won by Anthony Joshua, a British boxer, who beat his American opponent, Andy Ruiz Junior, on points. It attracted thousands of British supporters, and Joshua was backed by sponsorship deals from prominent brands, including Jaguar LandRover, British Airways and Beats by Dre. Hearn said that more bouts were planned, as Saudi Arabia was looking to become the 'home of boxing'.[10] Saudi Arabia is also seeking to put itself on the global map for motor racing, following the examples of Abu Dhabi and Bahrain, a sport in which UK drivers, car developers and fans play a prominent role. The opening up of the entertainment sector has prompted a surge of investment by Saudi business people in cinemas, and a similar response is likely with the promotion of tourism. These are sectors in which UK services companies have proven strengths.

One of the side effects of the changes in Saudi Arabia has been a drop-off in Saudi visitors to other regional entertainment and leisure centres such as Dubai and Bahrain. This has prompted the authorities in Dubai to cast around for ways to attract new visitors, with China on the main target markets. One activity that is being seriously considered is gambling, again a business in which the UK has plenty of major players.

The reputational risk of deeper engagement with Saudi Arabia is not confined to weapons suppliers, however. Mohammed bin Salman started to make his mark on the world stage in early 2016, announcing in the course of an extensive interview with *The Economist* his revolutionary plan to sell part of the equity in Saudi Aramco, the national oil company, in order to finance a domestic and international investment drive. Over the next three years, initiatives designed to attract and impress investors and major global corporations were punctuated by actions suggesting that there was a high degree of risk in becoming associated with Saudi Arabia's effective ruler, known as MBS. In July 2017, he consolidated his political position through a ruthless, though bloodless, coup in which he supplanted Mohammed bin Nayef as crown prince. In October that year he hosted a lavish investment conference, at which the $500 billion NEOM mega-city project was unveiled to an audience including corporate titans such as Masayoshi Son, head of SoftBank, Blackstone CEO Stephen Schwartzman, and Richard Branson of Virgin Group. These investors were apparently unfazed by the incarceration of many of Saudi Arabia's best-known businessmen in the Riyadh Ritz Carlton the following month as part of a supposed crackdown on corruption, and MBS sought to firm up a series of major investment deals during an extended tour of Europe and United States in early 2018. However, the mood turned sour later that year, after details emerged of the gruesome murder of Jamal Khashoggi, a prominent Saudi journalist, in the kingdom's consulate in Istanbul. The eventual flotation of a 1.5 per cent stake in Aramco to domestic investors at the end of 2019, yielding $25 billion to be used to boost the Public Investment Fund, helped to rekindle investor interest. However, investment flows into Saudi Arabia remain subdued, compared with earlier periods, and it will take some time to rebuild momentum.[11]

Egypt: A prime target?

As the UK was preparing for its formal exit from the EU at the end of January 2020, the government of Prime Minister Boris Johnson provided an indication of where it envisages new opportunities by holding an Africa-focused investment conference in London. There was a particularly strong turnout of Egyptian officials, including President Abdel-Fattah el-Sisi and the Planning and Economic Development Minister, Hala el-Said, who also chairs the recently created Egyptian Sovereign Wealth Fund. During the preceding months, there had been a stream of high-level Egyptian officials to the UK, including the ministers of health, investment, transport and finance, reflecting the intensive engagement between the two governments in trade and investment affairs. Egypt has sought to position itself as a gateway for UK companies seeking business in the rest of Africa, as well as a significant market in its own right. Among MENA countries, Morocco has made a similar pitch, underpinned by a strong track record for Moroccan companies around Africa. UK companies have a stronger presence in Egypt than in the Moroccan market, but British exports to Morocco have been on a rising trend over the past few years, whereas sales to Egypt have been flat (partly reflecting the contrasting political and economic conditions since the 2011 Arab uprisings). UK exports of goods and services to Morocco rose from £440 million in 2009 to £1.7 billion in 2017 (although they slipped back to £1.2 billion in 2018), whereas in Egypt they fell from a record of £2.2 billion in 2009 to £1.5 billion in 2013, before recovering to just below £2 billion a year in 2016–18.[12]

According to Egyptian government figures, the UK is the largest foreign investor in Egypt, with a total portfolio worth $48 billion.[13] Recent annual data show a consistent pattern of UK investment flows. In the breakdown of FDI by country recorded by the Central Bank of Egypt, the UK was the clear leader in the ranking of gross inflows between 2014/15 and 2018/19 (July–June fiscal years), with total investment of $27.5 billion, followed by the United States ($17.3 billion), Belgium ($7.9 billion) and the UAE ($5.7 billion).[14] Much of that UK investment relates to the activities of oil and gas companies, as BP and Shell are among the leading producers. Other major investors include HSBC, GSK and Vodafone (although the latter is now in the process of divesting its 55 per cent stake in the country's leading mobile-phone operator). The UK has also recently secured one of its largest regional export orders, through Bombardier being selected in August 2019 for a contract valued at €3.72 billion in total for the construction of a monorail system linking Cairo to the 6 October satellite city, to the southwest, and to the new administrative capital, to the southeast. The contract includes the supply of rolling stock that would be produced at Bombardier's plant in Derby, in Northern England.[15] The Egyptian government is now looking for the project to include a localization element, with the creation of a plant in the East Port Said industrial zone to produce some of the trains for the monorail, as well as rolling stock for future rail and metro projects in Egypt and around Africa. As Egypt is ramping up its plans for investment in rail transport, the UK has an opportunity through the Bombardier deal to claim a significant share in this sector, although it faces stiff competition from French, Japanese, South Korean and Chinese companies that have already established a strong position. One of the critical factors will be finance. Egypt is a major beneficiary of multilateral development finance, from the World Bank, the European Investment Bank and the European Bank for Reconstruction and Development, and transport projects have also been supported by preferential financial packages, notably from France, Japan, South Korea and China. One potential advantage for the UK could be the Egyptian government's strategy of turning to its own sovereign wealth fund as a source of finance for new infrastructure projects, to be structured as public–private partnerships. This is an area in which the role of London as a centre for financial and corporate legal services could be turned to the UK's advantage. That, of course, depends on how the UK's financial services sector is affected by whatever future arrangements are reached with the EU.

Mixing ambition and realism

The UK's departure from the EU is unlikely to have a dramatic impact on British economic ties to the MENA region. In most of the major markets in the region, the UK has a long-established presence, and links are maintained through active engagement

undertaken by chambers of commerce, trade and investment associations and embassies. In an indication of the government's recognition of the Gulf in particular as a crucial element in the UK's post-Brexit commerce, UK Export Finance chose to highlight a deal in Dubai in an advertisement placed in newspapers in early 2020.

The example cited by UK Trade Finance in its advertisement is a relatively small, £7 million, contract for a British company to supply furniture for a luxury development on the Palm Jumeirah, supported by a £1.2 million guarantee from the UK government agency. The choice of this deal provides some important clues as to the kind of opportunities that the UK authorities envisage for British companies in the MENA region. The hospitality and real-estate sectors in the Gulf have generated substantial business for UK firms, and the government is clearly intent on helping to ensure that this continues. Another important message lies in the focus on small- and medium-sized enterprises (SMEs). The value-added generated by export orders by SMEs in terms of employment, diverse regional development and sustainability is as important in wider economic terms as a few high-profile arms deals or infrastructure contracts. The UK's ability to enhance the competitiveness of SMEs through the support of government agencies may be greater than in the case of large contracts, where rivals could be backed by governments with greater strategic weight than a post-Brexit UK.

The UK's stock of investments in the region and its commercial record provide a platform for seeking to achieve continued expansion in exports of goods and services to the region. Based on past performance, it makes sense to continue to focus on core GCC markets. The stand-out performer has been the UAE, the UK's largest market in the region, which has seen the fivefold exports increase over the past twenty years, with a generally steady upward trajectory. Sales to Saudi Arabia rose steadily between 2006 and 2016, but have since started to decline. The value of exports to Qatar has increased tenfold since 1999. Whether the UK will be able to achieve similar rates of growth in exports to these markets over the next ten years will depend on a number of

Growth in UK exports to top Gulf markets

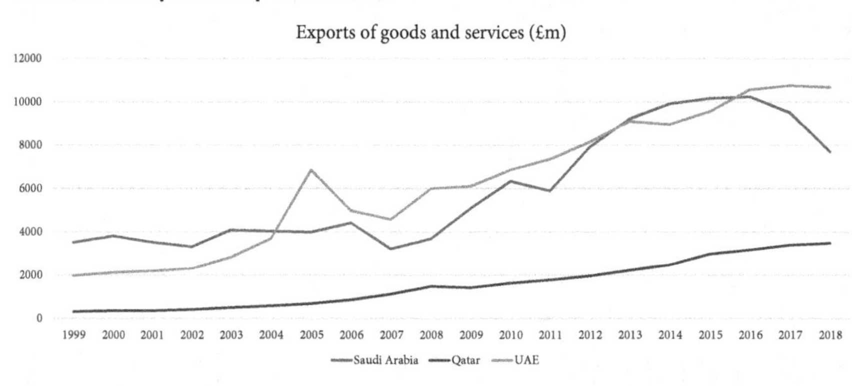

variables. Some of these will be in areas over which the UK will be able to wield little influence, in particular the effects on the Gulf economies of global decarbonization. However, if UK companies can adapt to changes in these markets, they should at least be able to sustain their current share. At the same time, there is much untapped potential in the region in the higher-population countries, both those where the UK has yet to make much of a mark in commercial terms, for example, Iran, Iraq, Morocco and Algeria, and in countries such as Egypt, where the UK can build on a solid existing presence.

The coronavirus pandemic has had a profound impact on the global economy, and UK-MENA economic relations will inevitably be affected as well. In the Gulf Arab states, the spread of Covid-19 has not been as severe as in Europe, in terms of cases, hospitalization and deaths, but the knock-on effects on the economy have been considerable. The collapse in oil and gas export revenue has forced governments to rein in spending and develop new domestic revenue streams – for example, through the trebling of the value-added tax (VAT) rate in Saudi Arabia to 15 per cent. Hundreds of thousands of expatriate workers have also left the Gulf states as their jobs have disappeared. Most of these workers are from the Indian subcontinent, but UK nationals have also been affected, particularly those involved in services such as real estate, leisure, tourism and retail. The authorities in the UAE and Saudi Arabia have sought to offset these negative effects through offering incentives for wealthier expatriates to stay, and for new companies to invest in projects with longer-term potential.[16]

In conclusion, the future of the UK's economic interaction with the Middle East and North Africa will depend more on developments within the region than on factors related directly to Brexit. British companies and expatriates have established a strong platform for continued trade with and investment in the Gulf Arab states. UK companies will have to be alert to changes in their target markets, but this is a process that has been in train for some time. Saudi Arabia, the UAE and Qatar will continue to be the main attractions, by virtue of their market size and their dominant positions in the oil and gas sector, which should enable them to augment their market share even as decarbonization advances. UK investors have played their part in supporting these governments' efforts to develop the non-hydrocarbon economy through expanding the services sector and building up local industries, including in the defence sector. Another critical element in the Gulf's diversification strategy is outward investment. As a global centre for financial, legal and consultancy services, the UK will be in a position to take full advantage of the ramping up of activities by agencies such as the Public Investment Fund in Saudi Arabia and the UAE's Mubadala, provided Brexit does not seriously impair the UK's financial services sector.

7

Security

Louise Kettle

The protection of British political, commercial and trade interests in the Middle East has long led to UK concerns over regional security issues. In the last two decades British security activity in the area has increased further in response to humanitarian crises to fulfil international and ally responsibilities and in recognition that regional terrorism, extremism and war have international reverberations. At the same time, the UK has faced an increasing political battle over whether to leave the European Union (EU). The EU has had an interest in defence and security matters for some time, with cooperation stated as an aim since the 1992 Maastricht Treaty and a Common Security and Defence policy (CSDP – originally named the European Security and Defence Policy) in place since 1999. However, security has remained an intergovernmental – rather than a federal or functional – matter. Consequently, when Britain voted to leave the EU in 2016, there was little initial disruption to existing military operations – especially in the Middle East. Instead, this chapter argues, the most significant impact of Brexit on Britain's security relations is the local perception that Britain's international importance has reduced. As a result, it is recommended that British policies be reconsidered to counteract this concern. To assist, this chapter provides an overview and assessment of British security efforts in the region in the last two decades. It highlights three key policies – counterterrorism (CT), promoting regional stability and an increasingly remote warfare approach – and evaluates their success before considering policy options and offering recommendations for the future.

Brexit and security

The EU has long considered defence and security issues an integral part of its common foreign and security policy. However, the European Council and the Council of the European Union have always taken decisions on CSDP by unanimity, effectively providing Britain with a veto over policy proposals. More significantly, security has remained a sovereign issue with no specific EU force (only voluntary secondments from the forces of member states) or a permanent military structure.[1] The UK has also never pushed for further EU security integration, instead preferring to work with EU partners through the framework of NATO and viewing the EU as a complementary power focused on collective diplomatic and economic pressure, crisis prevention and management and post-conflict stabilization. In fact, the British government has consistently heralded NATO as the cornerstone of its defence strategy; Britain is the second largest contributor to the defence organization and the government has committed to the NATO target of spending 2 per cent of GDP on defence and security each year. The 2015 Strategic Defence and Security Review (SDSR) also agreed to increase the defence budget by 0.5 per cent a year above inflation until 2020–1, whilst in November 2020 the prime minister pledged to increase spending by £24.1 billion and investment by £190 billion over the following four years – bringing Britain's share of GDP to at least 2.2 per cent.[2] As a result, Brexit had little direct impact on UK security activities in the Middle East and NATO will continue to provide the opportunity for Britain to work with many of its former EU colleagues, including France and Germany.

From an intelligence perspective post-Brexit Britain will lose access to important EU databases holding details of terrorists and criminals (both the Schengen Information System and the European Criminal Records Information System) and the EU's cross-border law enforcement agency Europol as well as the European Counter Terrorism and Cybercrime Centres that coordinate responses to activities across Europe. However, there is precedence for membership and access to these facilities by non-EU nations and therefore the UK may be able to re-negotiate access in the future. In addition, much of UK intelligence sharing has traditionally been conducted through bilateral relations, based on long-standing relationships which will remain intact, and supported by the Five Eyes alliance where trust has been built over decades. Whilst the UK will have to balance these relations with European ones, moving forward the UK has strong, entrenched bilateral intelligence relations with most EU nations and is highly regarded in the intelligence sphere, therefore making a desirable ally and ensuring little will be affected by Brexit.

Instead, where Britain will find the greatest impact of Brexit on security relations is through the perception of its importance in the international arena. While there may be some concerns about the reliability of the UK – given the government's attempts to overwrite some parts of the agreed EU withdrawal agreement – regional allies in the Middle East are more focused on the UK losing its powerful function as an interlocutor between the United States (and other nations) and Europe on security matters, as well as between the EU and NATO – a role that is likely to now fall to France. This damage is likely to be felt even further during a Biden administration as the President Biden is known to be supportive of the EU whilst at the same time having little regard for Prime Minister Johnson. As a result, the UK will need to compensate for this loss in order to persuade Middle East regional players that it remains a partner of value.

Nonetheless, Arab governments have traditionally preferred to focus on bilateral relations over relations with the EU. In addition, the December 2019 election success of the Conservative government – which is considered to be strong, pro-Gulf and hawkish – has likewise left leaders optimistic about working with a post-Brexit Britain compounded by a welcomed commitment to an increase in UK defence spending.

Furthermore, Britain has a timely opportunity in this region as the US 'pivot' towards Asia – likely to be continued under President Biden – has provided a particular opening for Britain to capitalize on its history of experience to fill (although not like-for-like replace) the American vacuum.[3]

Much of the groundwork to achieve this has already been laid; the UK has tried to secure its defence influence in the region through diplomacy (including biannual bilateral steering or joint working groups with a number of countries), defence engagement (through training sessions, exercises, meetings and personnel exchanges), intelligence sharing (which has included Saudi Arabia and the Gulf states sharing intelligence that has helped prevent terrorist attacks on UK citizens),[4] defence contracts and the gifting of equipment. In 2016 the UK gifted Iraq's Ministry of Peshmerga Affairs over £1.1 million worth of heavy machine guns and sniper ammunition, the Lebanese Armed Forces £5.8 million worth of equipment to support their border control and Oman's Ministry of Defence £1.2 million worth of Challenger tank spare parts.[5]

In addition, despite the lack of active combat for the British Army in more recent years, the UK has expanded its permanent presence in the region to support the continuing role of the Special Forces, Royal Navy and Royal Air Force and to pursue defence engagement activities, with around 1,500 personnel in the region at any one time. A permanent British naval base (HMS Jufair) opened in Bahrain in April 2018 as the first UK Naval base East of Suez since 1971, and this presence is supported by the memorandum of understanding signed in 2017 between the UK and Oman to allow the Royal Navy to use the facilities at Al Duqm port. In addition, British forces have access to al-Minhad airbase in the UAE, just south of Dubai, so that the base can be operationalized quickly for UK use, whilst Bahrain is set to become the base for one of the two new Littoral Response Groups of the UK's Future Commando Force, designed specifically to be deployed East of Suez.[6] There are also defence advisers or attachés across thirteen countries and the 2015 SDSR established Defence Engagement as a funded Ministry of Defence task, leading to the establishment of a defence staff in Dubai specifically focused upon retaining a level of influence in the Gulf and wider region.[7]

As a result, the UK is poised to increase its influence in the Middle East if it can overcome the perception of decreased importance in the international arena post-Brexit. To achieve such an ambition effort must be prioritized and existing policies re-evaluated through the prism of prestige. Consequently, while the security of British interests and people will always be paramount, prestige must become a crucial secondary consideration in policy debate and selection for the future. The question to be asked of policy must be: 'Will it increase the perception of British strength?' To answer affirmatively it must be concluded that the policy will provide a significant, visible or tangible difference to UK–Middle East security relations. Policies which fall short of this should, therefore, be disregarded. To commence this process three core policies of UK–Middle East security relations – CT, promoting regional stability and an increasingly remote warfare approach – have been briefly examined. In each case the policy has been assessed for success, policy options provided and recommendations for the future selected using the prism of prestige.

Counterterrorism

Iraq

Much of the last two decades of British Middle East security policy has stemmed from the fallout of 9/11. After the 2001 terrorist attacks Britain supported its American ally in the 'global war on terror' and was the second largest contributor to the 'coalition of the willing' that launched the Iraq War in 2003 – codenamed Operation Telic in the UK. After successfully removing Iraq's president from power, British forces remained in the country to combat an insurgency which rose up against the Western occupation and its installed democratic structures. After six years of fighting Britain withdrew troops before stabilization had been achieved; the 2010 Iraqi elections saw the country without an administration for 249 days and by 2012 attacks on Shia Muslims sparked new fears of sectarian violence. The political vacuum that ensued provided the environment for anti-government, anti-Western and extremist groups to thrive. By July 2013, levels of violence had returned to that of 2008 and opposition fighter groups were growing in strength. In January 2014, one group, known as the Islamic State of Iraq and the Levant (ISIL), infiltrated the cities of Ramadi and Fallujah, less than fifty miles west of the capital. By June 2014, ISIL had seized Iraq's second city, Mosul – in the north of Iraq, and had begun advancing towards Baghdad, taking other key cities and towns along the way. It declared the creation of a caliphate and changed its name to Islamic State (IS now known as Daesh).

British policy post-Telic quickly became focused on fighting Daesh. This meant shifting from a counter-insurgency approach to CT operations, which has since become the core of Britain–Middle East security relations. The 2015 SDSR committed an additional £1.4 billion to Britain's security and intelligence agencies, with a doubling of investment into Special Forces (amounting to an additional £2 billion), specifically to deal with the ongoing terrorism threat from Islamic groups. By 2017–18 £541 million of the £855 million spent on British military operations was spent specifically on operations against Daesh.[8]

The shift in national policy was compounded by the UK joining an international coalition of – now eighty-two – partners acting to fight against Daesh.[9] The Global Coalition's approach was to focus on regaining control of Daesh captured territory, cut off sources of finances, degrade its media and communications capabilities, prevent the flow of terrorist fighters, support stabilization efforts and disrupt key leaders and networks, all of which required multinational efforts, with Britain providing support in each area. More specifically, UK military operations in support of the Global Coalition – codenamed Operation Shader – began in Iraq in August 2014 when the British provided humanitarian air drops on the Sinjar mountains to deliver relief to fleeing Yazidis who were under genocidal attack.

Following a request for military support from the Iraqi government, the UK extended its efforts in September 2014 and began conducting strike operations against Daesh, subsequently deploying more than 4,300 precision ground attack weapons against targets, including missiles, laser and GPS-guided bombs and long-range cruise missiles.[10] In November 2014 the UK also began training and providing advisory support to Iraqi Security Forces in specific capabilities including countering improvised explosive devices, infantry skills, engineering, urban operations, bridge building, logistics and medical training. Today there are 400 British soldiers providing this training and, in total, over 94,000 members of the Iraqi Security Forces (including the Peshmerga) have been trained in preparation for counter-Daesh operations.[11] These activities are further supported by an ongoing partnership to build capacity within the Iraqi Armed Forces and to deliver Security Sector Reform.

Syria

In the meantime, across the border from Iraq, in Syria, an uprising against the Assad government began in the first half of 2011, off the back of the Arab Spring. By August the UK had called for the Syrian president to step down from power and by 2012 all diplomatic personnel had been withdrawn from the country. Although there were reports of British Special Forces operating in the area, and the UK had begun to provide non-lethal equipment (such as medical supplies and radio and satellite equipment) to Syrian opposition groups, Parliament rejected any direct military action against the Assad regime.[12]

However, the unrest provided a further fertile breeding ground for Daesh (then known as the Islamic State of Iraq and Syria (ISIS)) and in 2013 the group mounted a concerted effort to acquire territory. By 2015 it had gained control of a number of assets including oil reserves, dams, roads and cities and declared them to be part of the Islamic State. After turning the focus in Syria away from Assad and towards fighting Daesh, Parliament voted in favour of extending military action to Syria.[13] Air offensive operations against Daesh began in December 2015, and the Royal Air Force continued to conduct daily armed reconnaissance missions over both Iraq and Eastern Syria.[14] Since then, the UK has had around 800–900 personnel in the Middle East, making up the majority of the approximately 1,350 British service men and women committed to defeating Daesh based in Cyprus and the region.

Policy success, options and recommendations

The success of Britain's CT policy has been mixed. In the fight against Daesh it is difficult to assign specific success to Britain as it has acted as part of, and in line with, the policies of the broader Global Coalition. Nonetheless, the Global Coalition has made significant progress. While Daesh used to control territory approximately the size of the UK, Global Coalition operations have helped to liberate more than 7.7 million people and 100,000 square kilometres in Syria and Iraq, leaving no occupied territory remaining. Much of Daesh's funding has been cut, by denying access to its primary source of income – revenue from captured oil fields – and the UK contributed to precision airstrikes against Daesh-controlled infrastructure (oil fields, refineries and tankers) to facilitate this process. The Global Terrorism Index also reveals that deaths from terrorism have been on the decline since 2014 (down 50 per cent from 2014 to 2019), corresponding to the campaign against Daesh, with Iraq seeing 3,217 fewer deaths in 2018 from 2017 (a 75 per cent decrease) and a decrease in the number of terrorist attacks by 53 per cent from 2018 to 2019.[15] In addition, the number of deaths attributed to Daesh across the globe decreased in 2018 by 63 per cent, and 2019 by 37 per cent, a decline for the third year in row, with no deaths at all attributed to the group in 2018 from terrorist attacks in Europe. Overall, Europe and the Middle East North Africa regions were the two that recorded the biggest improvement from the impact of terrorism in 2018, with deaths falling by 70 and 65 per cent respectively. At that time only two Middle Eastern countries saw an increase in deaths – Iran and Jordan – whilst the number of deaths from terrorism in the region was 83 per cent less than its peak in 2014.[16]

However, despite these successes, terrorism remains a significant issue in the region. In 2019, terrorist attacks in Syria were up 25 per cent and in the same year 8 per cent of all terrorist attacks globally took place in Iraq, with 9 per cent in Yemen. In fact, the war in Yemen has resulted in a significant upsurge in terrorist violence in the last few years, with Houthi extremists responsible for a 55 per cent increase in attacks and 54 per cent increase in deaths from 2018 to 2019. In addition, whilst there has been CT success within the Middle East against Daesh, the Global Terrorism Database reveals that the group's influence has expanded outside of the region with attacks carried out by operatives, affiliates or individuals pledging allegiance in thirty-one different countries in 2019. In addition, affiliate groups have recorded an increased level of terrorist activity with the Khorasan Chapter of the Islamic State listed as the fourth deadliest terrorist group in 2018.[17]

Consequently, it is clear that terrorism will continue to be a significant problem in the region for many years to come. For British security CT in the Middle East will remain on the agenda to protect regional interests and because of its direct impact on Britain's domestic security. However, the scale of the problem and response means that prestige and ability to make a significant difference are limited. The options for the UK moving forward are to extend British efforts to focus on Daesh and its affiliates globally, but this would stretch limited resources and therefore be unlikely to result in providing a significant difference; shift to tackling new and emerging terrorist threats within the region more broadly (including Yemen) in which the UK could take a leadership role, therefore providing a visible difference; focus specifically on terrorist activity in Iraq and Syria alone (Daesh or otherwise), which has thus far proven to be challenging and is unlikely to change; or reduce CT altogether in order to focus on other security activities which may offer more opportunities to increase prestige. Whilst CT has dominated Britain's experience in the region for the last twenty years, its prioritization has often been a distraction from larger regional security challenges. The tectonic plates that exist in the Middle East of secularism, nationalism and Sunni and Shia Islam are continuously shifting to reveal new crises and, as terrorism decreases across the region, state conflict has already begun to rise, with tensions involving Turkey, Syria, Saudi Arabia, Iran and Israel ongoing in conventional and unconventional spheres. These are areas in which the UK may be able to act more independently – or offer coalition leadership – in support of its allies, but doing so will require a return from CT to a focus on conventional warfare and deterrence.

As a result, it is recommended that the UK does not focus upon the global fight against Daesh. While some provision to the Global Coalition will continue to be important, Britain should reconsider the extent of its support generally and instead cogitate on how it could have a greater impact, such as taking a leading role in adapting the coalition to the swift combating of new terrorist organizations that emerge, especially in the Middle East. In the meantime, the majority of UK forces should be redirected and retrained in conventional deterrence and warfare in readiness to support regional allies who are grappling with hard power crises.

Promoting regional stability

Refugee crises

After CT, the second priority for the UK in the Middle East over the last decade has been the promotion of regional stability, or at least the management or counteraction of regional instability. This has proved to be incredibly challenging due to the fallout from the Iraq War and the series of anti-government protests, which spread across the region from December 2010. The Arab Spring saw the end of existing regimes in Tunisia, Egypt, Yemen and Libya, but there were also outbreaks of protests and violence in Algeria, Jordan, Oman, Djibouti, Sudan, Bahrain, Kuwait, Morocco and Saudi Arabia – each ending in political concessions to the opposition. It also led to the civil wars in Syria, Libya and Yemen which remain today and, along with Iraq, have had a huge impact in the countries themselves and a heavy burden for surrounding countries as they struggle to deal with the subsequent refugee crisis. The UN Refugee Agency estimates that over 5.6 million people have fled Syria since 2011 with a further 6.6 million internally displaced.[18] Turkey currently has 3.5 million registered refugees whilst one in four of the Lebanese population are now Syrian refugees.[19] The bombing by Russia and President Assad in the south of Syria around Daraa has also pushed many refugees into Jordan and Israel, placing additional pressure on an already challenging area of the region.

To aid in counteracting this instability, the UK has pledged more than £2.81 billion to support those affected by the Syrian conflict, including refugees in Turkey, Lebanon and Jordan. This includes more than £1,102 million going directly to Syria, making Britain the third largest bilateral humanitarian donor to the Syrian crisis and the UK's largest ever donation to a single humanitarian situation.[20] In Yemen, Britain has committed £770 million of aid since the start of the conflict in 2015 with Britain being the fifth largest donor to the UN's humanitarian plan for the country,[21] whilst in Iraq the UK has pledged more than £103 million since 2015 to try to address the underlying drivers of conflict and radicalization, including the provision of schools, hospitals and infrastructure.[22]

Weapons of mass destruction

In addition to dealing with the refugee and humanitarian crises resulting from civil wars, the UK has attempted to maintain regional stability by managing weapons of mass destruction in the Middle East during this time. Much of the rationale for the

Iraq War was based upon claims of Saddam Hussein's possession of such weapons and Britain has been, and remains, committed to the Nuclear Non-Proliferation Treaty, the G7 Global Partnership against the Spread of Weapons and Materials of Mass Destruction and a nuclear weapons free zone in the Middle East. The government supports the Wassenaar Arrangement, Australia Group, Nuclear Suppliers Group and Missile Technology Control Regime with expertise and hosting meetings, but also leads and participates in verification missions for compliance with Conventional Arms Control agreements. In addition, the Ministry of Defence provides scientific and technical expertise to help strengthen the Chemical Weapons Convention (CWC) and the Biological and Toxins Weapons Convention.

The particular priority for the region has been managing Iran's growing nuclear capability (see Chapter 10 by Sanam Vakil for more details) but also addressing the concerns over President Assad's use of chemical weapons in Syria, which has been further complicated by Russian support. Despite Assad signing the CWC in September 2013, agreeing to destroy the country's stockpiles and declaring 1,300 tonnes of chemicals to the Organisation for the Prohibition of Chemical Weapons (OPCW), there have been over 100 reported sites of attacks using chemical weapons in Syria. OPCW has also investigated and determined thirty-seven incidents of chemicals used as weapons up to April 2018, while the UN Human Rights Council's Independent International Commission of Inquiry concluded there to be reasonable grounds to conclude the use of chemical weapons in eighteen other cases, with the Syrian government believed to be responsible in most instances.[23] Following the use of chemical weapons in the city of Duma, just outside of Damascus, the UK, United States and France conducted airstrikes against Syrian chemical weapons facilities in the hope of destroying Syrian capability and deterring future use.

Iran

Beyond the management of its growing nuclear capability Iran has continued to be an ongoing threat in the last two decades to regional stability. For the UK, even though some diplomatic success has been achieved through the Joint Comprehensive Plan of Action (JCPOA), Britain has continued to have a difficult relationship with Iran; in the last ten years the Iranian parliament has voted to expel the UK ambassador, protestors have stormed the British embassy in Tehran and the UK temporarily closed the Iranian embassy in London. Much of the continuing distrust between Tehran and London is due to the UK owing Iran nearly £400 million for the cancelled sale of Chieftain tanks after the Iranian Revolution but refusing to repay the amount. At the same time Tehran has detained a number of British nationals, who are thought to be being held hostage as leverage over the ongoing debt dispute, including the high-profile case of Nazanin Zaghari-Ratcliffe. In addition, in 2017, intelligence agencies blamed Iran for a major cyber-attack on Parliament, with hackers attempting to access Parliamentary emails, including those of ministers. There have also been concerns around Iranian hostile activities in Europe, including a planned bombing in France in June 2018, two assassinations in the Netherlands and a thwarted assassination plot in Denmark.[24]

UK–Iranian tensions rose further in the Summer of 2019 when, on 4 July, the UK seized the Iranian tanker, *Grace 1*, off the coast of Gibraltar, reportedly based on American intelligence that it was breaking EU sanctions by transporting oil to Syria.[25] In response, on 19 July, the Iranian Revolutionary Guard seized the British flagged tanker *Stena Impero* in the Strait of Hormuz, claiming that the tanker had broken maritime rules. As a result, the UK agreed to join the United States in stepping up its maritime presence in the area in an effort to protect commercial shipping and act as a deterrent for any further Iranian aggression. Whilst Britain did try to create a European-led taskforce to support maritime security in the region, initial European hesitation resulted in a turn towards the UK's transatlantic partner.

Policy success, options and recommendations

Despite a significant amount of money, time and resources, regional stability is far from achieved in the Middle East. Conflict continues in Iraq, Syria, Libya and Yemen, with little end in sight and there are ongoing protests in Iraq and Lebanon, akin to those during the Arab Spring, crackdowns on protests in Iran, more arrests of dissenters in Saudi Arabia and sectarian rumblings in a number of countries across the region, including Bahrain and Kuwait. Many refugees remain in large camps across the region which are now under further threat economically and healthwise from Covid-19. British humanitarian donations to support regional stability have also been criticized in the face of more than £4.7 billion worth of arms being sold to Saudi Arabia (almost half of the UK's total arms exports), which have reportedly launched indiscriminate bombing campaigns against the Houthis in Yemen leading to the deaths of thousands of civilians.

At the same time there has been limited success in managing weapons of mass destruction in the Middle East. As well as Iran taking a number of steps to reduce its commitment to the JCPOA, following America's withdrawal from the agreement in 2018 – including removing its limit on its stockpile of nuclear fuel, enriching uranium to a higher purity and injecting uranium gas into centrifuges – chemical weapons have continued to be used in Syria; the United States confirmed that an attack in Idlib, in the northwest of the country, in May 2019, used chlorine as a chemical weapon.

Similarly, there has been little attainment in the endeavour to curb Iranian destabilization. The overreliance on the JCPOA as a tool to both restrain Tehran and provide embryonic regional and international relations backfired when US President Trump introduced the policy of 'maximum pressure'. In response, Iran escalated its activities in the Gulf and against Saudi Arabia, with further accusations of involvement in Houthi claiming drone and missile strikes on Saudi infrastructure. Furthermore, the UK has been particularly concerned about Iranian ballistic missile activities, transfer of missiles and technical knowledge to armed groups in the area, attacks on maritime traffic and continued support of Hezbollah and its destabilizing activities in Israel. The UK has argued that Iran continues to conduct ballistic missile activity,[26] with missiles fired from Syria into the Golan Heights and that Tehran has transferred expertise on UAV production to Iraq in violation of arms transfer restrictions. However, little has been achieved to counteract any of these concerns.

As a result, it is clear that policies supporting regional stability need to be reconsidered. In each case the UK has the option to commit to doing more or less, but the current policies have not made a significant, visible or tangible difference and therefore do not further prestige. In the wake of the Covid-19 pandemic, the Conservative government has already announced a reduction in aid spending, despite its manifesto commitment to maintain the budget. Consequently, it is unlikely to increase financial support for the refugee crisis. Critics of the cut have argued that falling below the UN aid target of 0.7 per cent of national income reduces Britain's position in the international community, and there is likely to be some fallout from partners who had been promised funding which has now been reallocated. As a result, to retain prestige, it is recommended that the aid budget return to 0.7 per cent as soon as possible. Even still, the underlying cause of the refugee crises of civil conflicts and ungoverned spaces is likely to persist and the UK can choose to offer military or political solutions in response. Militarily, intervention is difficult, prolonged, thankless and has limited domestic support for UK involvement and therefore is not recommended. Politically, the UK does not have significant international clout to make a difference on its own, and therefore the government will need to consider whether it wishes to play a supporting role to a leading power in any diplomacy.

The same is true in regard to the issue of WMDs. Whilst it will be important for the UK to continue its commitment to preventing the use and spread of WMDs, much of the leadership on this topic will have to be left to the United States. America's input on this issue is crucial because of its power in the region, as demonstrated by the collapse of the JCPOA when the United States decided to withdraw its influence with Israel and its ability to counteract Russia on the international stage over Syria. For the UK, it is recommended that the government continues to encourage US leadership in these areas. Doing so will allow Britain to take a step back to create space to direct efforts to where it can create a more significant, immediate and tangible difference. One exception here is on negotiating with Iran. Although the Biden administration is likely to want to return to an Iranian nuclear deal, it will not be possible to simply reinstate the previous agreement, due to the progress that Iran has made on its nuclear programme during President Trump's term in office. For the UK, involvement in renegotiating terms with Iran will offer significant prestige internationally, allow an opportunity to reconnect UK–US relations in the region and pave the way for improving UK–Iranian relations more broadly.

The remote warfare approach

Throughout this time, whilst prioritizing CT and promoting regional stability, Britain's approach to intervention has changed. The experience in Iraq and Afghanistan led to nervousness amongst politicians and the public about sending regular land forces to directly engage with combatants. This loss of appetite, combined with increasing developments in technology, shift towards CT and recognition over the limitations of British military size, stretch and subsequent capability, has led to post-Iraq policy following a trend that has become known as 'remote warfare'.[27] Remote warfare is characterized by a hands-off approach, where the focus is on indirect action. Through this policy UK intention is achieved by increasing military capability of allied local groups – in order that they can conduct the required kinetic activity themselves – and by building the resilience of friendly nations. The UK has taken this approach in Iraq, Syria and Yemen, supporting the Iraqi government, Syrian Democratic Forces and the Saudi-led coalition, respectively.

The primary method of support for local forces has been through training, with the UK taking part in 411 bespoke training activities across the Middle East and North Africa in 2018–19.[28] As well as the training of Iraqi Security Forces, the UK has deployed personnel to support US-led training programmes for Syrian rebels and provided training in the wider region. In Lebanon, for example, the UK has helped to support the Lebanese Armed Forces training programme to secure its borders, whilst in Jordan there has been training of the Jordanian Quick Response Force.[29] In Oman, maritime training teams have helped improve security by focusing on improving capabilities to prevent the transit of illicit people and goods and to protect maritime traffic. In addition, in 2018, UK forces conducted Exercise Saif Sareea 3 in Oman with the Omani military – the largest joint exercise of its kind in seventeen years, with 5,500 service personnel involved – leading to the UK-Oman Joint Defence Agreement.[30]

Training has been supported with other security strengthening activities in the region, enabling the UK to take less of an active fighting role whilst also solidifying defence relationships. For example, in Kuwait, British amphibious teams have helped to restructure and train partner tactical level capabilities to improve the protection of waterways and to promote regional security, whilst in Lebanon, training has been supported by funding and advice for the building of towers to protect its border with Syria. In Iraq, stabilization efforts include supporting the creation of local government structures to ensure that previously persecuted sectors of society can return home, and contributions to explosive clearance efforts.[31] Jordan and the UK have also just renewed their security cooperation, putting together a programme to provide support in key areas including CT and policing.

Policy success, options and recommendations

Although the remote warfare approach has been more palatable for a war-weary British public, it has also provided its own set of challenges. The UK's initial reluctance to intervene directly in Syria – and failure to respond to President Assad's use of chemical weapons in 2013 – arguably led to the escalation of the conflict in terms of the number of fatalities, injuries and refugees. Once Britain decided to apply a remote warfare approach, there was a challenge to find a suitable local partner; it took until mid-2016 to be confident that the selected coalition of groups – umbrellaed under the name the Free Syrian Army – was suitable for Western backing.[32] In addition, the UK and other Western nations eventually came to support the Kurdish-led Syrian Democratic Forces (SDF) which was established in 2015 to fight Islamic and Arab nationalist groups in Syria in an effort to protect secularism and democracy. Whilst the ambitions of the SDF aligned with those of Western nations, the decision to support the group was mired with controversy as most of the SDF forces were militants from the YPG (People's Protection Unit) – an offshoot of the Kurdistan Worker's Party (PKK) which has been deemed a terrorist organization by the United States and EU because of its ongoing activities against the Turkish state. However, the success of the SDF in fighting Daesh, and the need for its assistance in May 2017 to retake Raqqa, led to an increase in support for the group, including the provision of weapons and much to the outrage of Ankara.

Beyond partner selection, remote warfare has the obvious challenge of having less control over regional military activities and the direction of fighting. Furthermore, without simultaneous political reforms much of the effort of local partners can be in vain. In many cases the progress of military efforts has outstripped the progress of the political campaign, therefore leaving instability in the wake of successful military operations, as seen most significantly in the 2011 intervention in Libya, Operation Ellamy.[33]

In support of this consideration, it is important to note that the UK's current remote warfare approach is increasingly not conducive with the needs of many of the Gulf states, which are struggling with hard power crises internally and externally. If Britain does intend to deepen its relationship with the region in coming years, there will be mounting pressure and expectation of support in dealing with these security issues. This will involve increasing conventional deterrence and being aware that if state-on-state conflict returns to the region the UK may have to abandon its remote warfare approach and support its allies on the ground. Any change in this approach will also have to be carefully managed abroad (by working with, or in response to a request by, local allies) and at home, including persuading the UN, Parliament and the public that all lessons from the Iraq Inquiry have been embedded in operational planning to avoid repeating any mistakes from the past.[34] Groundwork for this can be laid early, with greater public transparency and further communication around the changes that have been made in response to the Chilcot report and some recognition of the challenges that have been faced as a result of pursuing a remote warfare approach in Libya and Syria.[35]

However, where the remote warfare approach has been particularly successful for British prestige has been where the UK has been able to offer support for state allies in terms of training and joint exercises. This has been hugely beneficial in strengthening trust, bilateral security relations, creating goodwill and reinforcing British leadership capabilities, as well as resulting in more permanent defence agreements and contracts. Consequently, it is recommended that such opportunities are maximized further in the future but for efficiency should be primarily based on specific and limited training or advisory sessions rather than providing any form of ongoing commitment.

Conclusion

The decision to leave the EU has had little impact on British security operations in the Middle East. Britain's preference for working through a NATO framework has meant that disentanglement from the EU on security issues in the Middle East has been relatively straightforward. However, more broadly, Brexit has left Middle Eastern allies with the perception that Britain has lost power and influence in the international arena. To counteract this concern, the UK needs to actively pursue policies that provide a significant, visible or tangible difference in order to increase British prestige in the region.[36] This chapter has begun this process by examining Britain's three key security policies for the last two decades – CT, promoting regional stability and an increasing remote warfare programme – and offering recommendations for the future based upon the requirement to increase prestige. By assessing policies in this manner, and by building on Britain's existing regional relationships and defence presence, the UK has a timely opportunity to entrench its security presence in the region even after Brexit.

Part Three

Britain and the non-Arab powers

8

Turkey

Bill Park

Even before the prospect of exiting the EU had seriously appeared on the British political agenda, the UK was committed to cultivating a close relationship with Turkey. One manifestation of this was the UK's unwavering championing of Turkey's accession to the EU. David Cameron, in an address to the Turkish parliament in 2010, powerfully expressed the UK's stance. 'I'm here to make the case for Turkey's membership of the EU. And to fight for it', he said. With perhaps more prescience than he anticipated, he also proclaimed that the UK knows 'what it's like to be shut out of the club. But we also know that these things can change'.[1] Labour Prime Minister Tony Blair was no less committed to Turkey's EU accession. He pushed for accession talks to begin, argued for rapid progress once they commenced in 2005 and also lobbied against any EU isolation of the Turkish Republic of Northern Cyprus (TRNC) in the event of Cypriot accession to the EU.[2] On the other hand, Blair's government did not veto Cypriot entry in 2004, an issue that has since bedevilled Turkey's relationship with Brussels.

Cameron's 2010 visit to Turkey was accompanied by the signing of a bilateral UK–Turkish 'Strategic Partnership', which aimed at expanded cooperation on trade and investment, energy, defence and security. A similar rhetoric and frequent high-level visits followed, notwithstanding the erosion in Turkey of the rule of law, democratic conventions, media independence, judicial autonomy and of human rights.[3] This had commenced in the wake of the 2013 Gezi Park protests, if not before, and intensified with the crackdown following the July 2016 failed coup attempt. Alan Duncan, then the UK's minister for Europe, was the first Western politician to visit Turkey after the failed July 2016 coup, offering a degree of sympathy with the Turkish government and people that no other Western government matched. Prime Minister Theresa May's January 2017 visit to Turkey was the first post-coup visit by any Western leader. Yet the ongoing crackdown, which worsened following the April 2017 constitutional referendum that sped up Turkey's slide towards autocratic government, reached far beyond the Gulenist circles alleged to have plotted the coup. It incorporated elected Kurdish politicians, human rights activists, and critical journalists and academics. Although the UK Foreign and Commonwealth Office (FCDO) insists it raises such transgressions with the Turkish authorities, neither the Turkish government's behaviour nor UK–Turkey relations have been impacted, and there has been little overt criticism.

May's visit also saw Britain and Turkey sign a defence deal worth more than £100 million pounds to develop Turkish fighter jets. The deal involved BAE Systems and TAI (Turkish Aerospace Industries) cooperating on the TF-X Turkish fighter programme.[4] However, hopes that Rolls Royce would win the contract to develop the engine fell flat.[5] The UK was reported to have sold $1 billion worth of defence equipment to Turkey in the two years following the failed coup.[6] The aspiration to further increase arms sales to Turkey, and UK–Turkey trade more generally, is very much part of the UK's post-Brexit agenda. During Recep Tayyip Erdogan's second presidential visit to the UK in May 2018, billed by May as 'an opportunity for the UK and Turkey to demonstrate our close bilateral relationship', he was controversially afforded a meeting with the Queen.[7] It wasn't surprising that Erdogan described the UK as a 'true friend' and a 'strategic partner' and that 'cooperation between Turkey and the UK in the fight against terrorism is at a much more advanced stage than mechanisms we have with other partners'.[8]

Erdogan's visit coincided with a rising tide of American anger with Turkey. This animosity was driven by a number of factors: the holding of the American pastor Andrew Brunson as 'hostage' on false charges; Turkey's planned purchase of S-400 air defence missiles from Russia and its improving relationship with Moscow; its murky relationship with Islamist groups in Syria; differences over Iran and with US sanctions against it; the conduct of Erdogan's bodyguards during a 2017 trip to Washington; the treatment of US embassy staff in Ankara; and the anti-Western and stridently Islamist rhetoric spilling out from Ankara on an almost daily basis.[9] This anger eventually resulted in Turkey's expulsion from the F-35 fighter jet programme and US–Turkey relations remain troubled on a number of fronts.

The UK's EU partners were also inclined to be more critical of Turkey's democratic failings than the UK. At the end of 2016, the EU froze accession negotiations pending Turkey's return to a reforming path. There was also a series of – often bilateral – tensions between Turkey and EU members. German relations with Turkey remained tense in the aftermath of a flood of Syrian refugees, via Turkey, to Europe in 2015. In February 2020, the Turkish government again began encouraging refugees to head into Europe. During this crisis, UK Foreign Minister Dominic Raab visited Turkey, offered no criticism of Ankara's behaviour and mirrored Turkey's attempt to link the crisis with events in Idlib, even though none of the refugees were from Idlib and many were not even Syrian.[10] In March 2020, UK Defence Secretary Ben Wallace, who had previously shocked NATO allies by expressing support for Turkey's October 2019 intervention in Northeast Syria, visited the Turkey–Syrian border and echoed Raab's position.[11] On the other hand, the visit was accompanied by another UK delivery of aid to Syrian refugees, to be dispensed by the Turkish Red Cross. The uncritical UK stance overlooked the contribution to extending the war that Turkey has made as well as Ankara's separate incursions into Northern Syria against Kurdish fighters, causing a separate, internal Syrian refugee crisis.[12]

The UK is something of an outlier in its cultivation of Turkey. There are a number of general explanations for this. They include the UK prioritizing hard security issues, with Turkey important to the security of both Europe and the Middle East. Among EU states, only France is driven by similar considerations. Additionally, recent Conservative governments have in practice tended to marginalize human rights as a foreign policy issue. For example, they barely featured during May's visit to China in early 2018, while Saudi Arabia's Crown Prince Mohammed bin Salman was uncritically lionized as a modernizer during his March 2018 UK visit. The UK's search for alternative trading partners and diplomatic allies in the wake of its EU departure has only intensified its commitment to friendship with Ankara, which in any case has been largely conducted hitherto not via the EU but on a bilateral basis or via NATO and other US-led multilateral formations.

The UK's friendless friend?

However, any post-Brexit enhancement of the UK–Turkey relationship, especially with respect to the Middle East, will not be without problems. When Turkey's EU accession negotiations began in 2005, there was much speculation about the gradual 'Europeanisation' of Turkish foreign policy, featuring the adoption of a more norms-based, cooperative, consensual and collective approach to foreign policy.[13] Yet Turkey's political and security culture, characterized by an intense nationalism and prickly mistrust even of its closest allies, and its geostrategic location, proximate to the instabilities of the Balkans and the Caucasus as well as the Middle East, were always likely to bedevil such a process.[14] Additionally, the end of the Cold War and the increasing instability of Turkey's Middle Eastern neighbourhood also challenged Turkey's transatlantic relationship.[15] Added to these considerations are the ideological leanings of the ruling AKP, and Erdogan in particular. Turkish foreign policy has in recent years been described as 'neo-Ottoman',[16] 'Turkish Gaullism',[17] 'pan-Islamist',[18] 'Eurasianist'[19] and as nationalist and anti-Western – not least as a reflection of the government's sinister association with Dogu Perincek and his Patriotic Party, which is anti-Gulenist and pro-Russian.[20] The AKP's alliance with the arch-nationalist Nationalist Movement Party (Milliyetci Hareket Partisi, or MHP), dating back to the April 2017 constitutional referendum, has added to this nationalistic tendency. The Turkish government's thinking remains coloured too by the 'strategic depth' doctrine of the now discredited former Foreign Minister and Prime Minister Ahmet Davutoglu.[21] Erdogan's sometimes impulsive, angry, confrontational and autocratic personality is a factor too.

In fact, each of these strands shapes Turkish foreign policy towards the Middle East region, and indeed towards the West and Russia too. Unlike its Kemalist predecessors, who were inclined to regard the Middle East as a quagmire best avoided and preferred to forget the Ottoman past, the AKP government regards Turkey as a Middle Eastern as well as a European country, and as a regional power and successor to the Ottoman Empire. In this spirit, Turkey took the lead in backing the opposition to Bashar al-Assad's regime that emerged in 2011. This stance was soon supplanted by Turkey's growing concerns with the progress of the Kurdistan Workers Party's (Partiya Karkeren Kurdistane or PKK) Syrian sister militia, the People's Protection Units (Yekineyen Parastina Gel or YPG). The self-governing zones that the YPG established along Syria's border with Turkey were seen by Ankara as an existential threat.[22] The US-led coalition had militarily assisted the YPG in its defence of the largely Kurdish town of Kobane alongside the border with Turkey against an Islamic State (IS) siege while Turkish forces looked on. Erdogan loudly objected to the US-led support for Kobane's Kurdish defenders, and access to the NATO base at Incirlik in Turkey was denied.

As IS became identified as the main threat in Syria, an alliance emerged between the United States, its allies, including the UK, and the YPG-led and US-sponsored Syrian Democratic Forces (SDF). Erdogan's anger at this was illustrated by his observation that the PKK and IS were as bad as each other.[23] Turkey subsequently launched unilateral incursions into Syria on four separate occasions, alongside often jihadi-inclined proxy forces. Although Turkey contributed to the anti-IS campaign, most of its activities and those of some of its proxies in Syria have been against the Kurds.[24] Indeed, many suspected Turkey of assisting IS. French president Emmanuel Macron accused Turkey of 'ambiguity' towards IS, asserting that 'sometimes they work with ISIS proxies'.[25] Others share these suspicions, relating to Turkey's treatment of IS suspects domestically, its relationship with IS in Syria and its apparent passivity as the so-called 'jihadi highway' of militants travelling to Syria via Turkey emerged.[26]

Ankara's regional activism is not confined to Syria. Turkey also maintains dozens of military bases in Northern Iraq, contrary to the wishes of Baghdad. The primary role of these forces is to combat the PKK there, which they regularly target. Turkey's passivity in the face of IS's capture of Mosul caused Iraqi Kurdish leaders to question Ankara's commitment to the struggle against IS. Iraqi Kurdish leaders also noted that Turkey's military campaign against the PKK in Northern Iraq, which was itself engaged in a struggle against IS, further set back the struggle against it.[27] Elsewhere in the Middle East Turkey has fallen out with the Egyptian regime of Abdel Fatteh el-Sisi over Ankara's backing of his Muslim Brotherhood predecessor Mohammed Morsi.[28] Turkey has also backed Qatar in its dispute with a Saudi-led coalition of the United Arab Emirates (UAE), Bahrain and Egypt, over Qatar's support for MB activities in the region. Turkey's acquisition of 'formal expeditionary bases' overseas in recent years – in Qatar, Somalia and Sudan – and the expansion of its blue water navy capability testify to Turkey's expanded role as a regional power and are widely interpreted as counters to its Arab rivals.[29]

Again in coalition with Qatar, Turkey has shipped armaments, its own military personnel and even some of its Syrian proxies into Libya to back the often Islamist and MB factions of the UN-recognized but heavily factionalized Government of National Accord (GNA). This is in conflict with the so-called Libyan National Army (LNA) of General Khalifa Haftar, which in turn has the support of Egypt and the Gulf states (again), Jordan, Russia and a broadly sympathetic France. The LNA, which controls swathes of Libya's territory, has banned commercial flights between Turkey and Libya, prohibited Turkish ships from docking on the Libyan coast and threatened to arrest Turkish citizens. In February 2020, a number of Turkish soldiers lost their lives in both Syria – at the hands of Syrian government forces and perhaps Russia – and in Libya, at the hands of Haftar's forces. Greek, Italian and Libyan authorities have detained a number of vessels carrying Turkish-supplied weapons to its Libyan proxies in contravention of a UN resolution banning such activities. The UN resolution is openly breached by external actors backing all sides of the Libya struggle.[30] In February 2020 the EU, of which the UK was no longer a member, decided to deploy warships to enforce the embargo on arms to Libya.

In the energy exploration race in the Eastern Mediterranean, Turkey again finds itself at odds with Egypt, but also France, Italy, Cyprus, Greece (all EU members, whose position is backed by the EU as a whole) and in effect the United States and Israel too. Its energy exploration and drilling activities in disputed waters and the aggressive behaviour of its warships, including towards a vessel chartered by the Italian energy company ENI, have raised the temperature.[31] The delivery of a UK-provided drilling vessel in February 2020, augmented Turkey's capacity.[32] In January 2019, Cairo hosted a wider regional Eastern Mediterranean gas forum at which the countries in attendance – Cyprus, Greece, Israel, Egypt, Jordan, Italy and the Palestinian Authority – founded the Eastern Mediterranean Gas Forum. Turkey has been excluded from it. This issue overlaps with the perennial territorial sea dispute between Turkey and EU member Greece, both NATO members. Ankara has signed a bilateral maritime demarcation agreement with the GNA that conflicts with Greek maritime claims, further inflaming the issue.

Turkey also maintains an estimated 30,000 strong force in the so-called Turkish Republic of Northern Cyprus (TRNC), a legacy of its 1974 intervention against a coup engineered by the Greek military junta in Athens. The UK, as a guarantor power along with Turkey and Greece, chose not to act. The subsequent division of the island of Cyprus has since been a serious obstacle to improved Turkish relations with the EU, Greece and Cyprus itself. London has been actively engaged in the search for a solution to the island's division, but in practice it has handed formal responsibility to the UN and the EU, while behind the scenes the United States has been central to any diplomatic efforts. The US interest has largely been related to UK bases on the island. The UK's two sovereign base areas (SBAs) in Cyprus are essential assets in support of the UK's military and intelligence missions in the Middle East and beyond, and are used as staging post for military aircraft, for troop and air force rotation, including basing of fighter and transporter aircraft especially at RAF base at Akrotiri, and for training and exercises. Intelligence facilities on the island are no less important. The UK's intelligence agency, the Government Communications Headquarters (GCHQ), runs the Ayios Nikolaos station and other facilities on the island. These are largely funded by the United States, as the intelligence they gather is shared with Washington and is central to the role the United States plays in the region. The Cyprus issue has not generated major difficulties in the UK's relationship with Turkey, but if tensions in the Eastern Mediterranean heat up further, the UK's position could come under closer scrutiny, not least because the SBAs are located within Greek Cyprus.

UK–Turkey bilateral relations post-Brexit

With the UK's exit from the EU, the remote prospect of Turkey's accession to the EU and the queue of other countries for accession, the outlier status of these two countries in Europe is highlighted. The UK is the only country to have departed the

EU, and Turkey is the only non-EU member of the EU's customs union and its most longstanding and frustrated applicant.[33] With the UK's departure, Ankara will lose its most persistent champion in Brussels.

With EU–Turkey tensions over Syria, refugees, Cyprus, Eastern Mediterranean energy, Aegean maritime demarcation, Libya, Ankara's involvement with Europe's Turkish community, the customs union, Islamic radicalism and 'Islamophobia', Turkey's human rights record, and a host of other issues, and with a comparable list of threats to US–Turkey relations, the UK's uncritical approach to its relationship with Ankara in its desire to stay on good terms could pose challenges. No longer an 'insider', the UK might struggle to have influence over EU deliberations on Turkey. The UK government might also struggle to keep Turkey's human rights record off its own agenda given growing asylum requests from Turks and of extradition requests by Ankara, the refugee issue, and pressures generated by the UK's own civil society and its Turkish and Kurdish communities. Difficulties in the US–Turkey relationship could also drag in the UK. It is unlikely that the Biden administration will be as accommodating towards Turkey as was that of Trump, which even so introduced moderate sanctions against Turkey just prior to its departure from office as a response to Ankara's S-400 acquisition. EU unhappiness with Ankara's behaviour in the Eastern Mediterranean could similarly result in sanctions against Turkey. In any case United States–EU relations are likely to become more cooperative in the wake of Trump's departure. Were this to incorporate an alignment on sanctions against Turkey, the UK's isolation could be harshly exposed.

Additionally, although they back opposite sides in both Syria and Libya, and more recently in the Nagorno-Karabakh conflict between Azerbaijan and Armenia, Turkey and Russia have emerged as the two key external actors in all three conflicts. Between them they negotiated ceasefires in Syria and Libya, while Turkey is to monitor the Moscow-sponsored ceasefire in Nagorno-Karabakh forged in late 2020, which in any case handed victory to Azerbaijan, heavily assisted militarily by Turkey. Overall, Turkey is not only far less rhetorically critical of Russia than it is of the West; it also appears less confrontational in practice. This unnerves Washington but the UK appears more relaxed, interpreting the Turkey–Russia relationship as transactional.[34] Should this difference also emerge as a more overt source of tension between the UK and the Biden administration, again the UK might find itself under pressure to change tack.

One point that can be made, however, is that the UK could glean from the Turkish experience how difficult it can be to sit outside the EU but remain intertwined with it. This is largely because the EU is loath to allow external third-party actors to sully its policymaking autonomy, both in the economic and in the security spheres. As a member of both the EU customs union and NATO, Turkey has had little choice but to operate under rules determined in Brussels.[35] In the security field, this has also been so in cases where the EU pursued missions as part of its Common Security and Defence Policy (CSDP) and not backed by NATO, where the Berlin-Plus agreement softens the exclusionary effect.[36] On the other hand, US president Donald Trump's erratic behaviour, his unfriendly attitude towards the EU and his criticism of European contributions to defence and security shook faith in the American commitment to Europe. This might encourage the EU to be more accommodating towards third parties such as the UK and Turkey. This is perhaps made more likely by the fact that the UK and Turkey are significant actors in the military and security fields. Whether London and Ankara would be able to develop a coordinated security approach to the EU is an interesting question.

In economic terms, having pursued a so-called hard Brexit, the UK is free to make its own trade arrangements with non-EU countries, but is also obliged to trade with the EU on less favourable terms than those Turkey enjoys. Then again, the EU's internal economic and political stresses, and the fact that two countries as important as the UK and Turkey sit outside it, might encourage Brussels to soften its approach to third-party partners. Only time will tell, but at the moment that seems over-optimistic. Post-Brexit, the UK sees Turkey as a potentially more significant market for its arms exports. However, although the arms industry is important to the UK economy, it lies only around sixth in the world as an arms exporter – France and Germany are bigger arms exporters. Furthermore, arms dealings can fluctuate considerably from year to year. However, it should be noted that in 2017 Italy and Spain, trading under the same terms as the UK, exported more military equipment by value to Turkey than the UK. Around 60 per cent of Turkish arms exports emanate from the United States. The UK's biggest arms markets are in the Gulf.[37] Should Turkey's relationships in the Gulf seriously worsen, the aspiration to increase UK–Turkey trade in arms could become problematic.

Furthermore, Turkey is determined to maximize its self-sufficiency in arms production, not least because it has in the past been stung by trade embargoes placed upon it by allies such as the United States and Germany. Since 2002 domestic military procurement has risen from 24 per cent to 64 per cent of the country's needs, and Turkey has become a significant arms exporter in its own right. Ankara also negotiates with potential partners for maximum licensed domestic production and technology transfer. In 2017 Turkey's armaments industry was placed under presidential control.[38] Turkey is also more willing to look beyond its NATO partners in its search for armament purchases. Russia and South Korea have been beneficiaries of this. It could be a tall order for the UK to penetrate the Turkish arms market further.

It should be noted that while the UK is Turkey's second biggest export market after Germany, Turkey is less important as a UK export market, ranking seventeenth and accounting for around 6 per cent of UK exports, with a trade imbalance in Turkey's favour.[39] France, Italy and Spain – trading under the same EU customs union terms as the UK – as well as China and the United States, all export more to Turkey. Should Turkey remain a member of the customs union, and should the UK depart it, then obstacles to their bilateral trade will be erected. Turkey would enjoy very limited scope to negotiate a separate trade agreement with the UK, as its trade with third parties is also largely covered by its membership of the customs union.[40] Financial and other services constitute the most niche sector of the UK economy, but this is already excluded from Turkey's customs union arrangements with the EU. Furthermore, Turkey's financial sector is notoriously difficult to negotiate.

Turkey's economy is also prone to periodic crises, often induced by domestic political turmoil. Thus in 2018 Turkey's overall trade with the EU declined. There may be scope for the already considerable UK Foreign Direct Investment into Turkey to be augmented, although there is no reason to assume that the UK's EU membership somehow restricted these flows or that its departure would necessarily offer fresh opportunities. Since 1990 the UK has fluctuated between second and fifth in terms of global outward investment, with the United States accounting for almost 90 per cent of the UK totals.[41] Thus even an improvement in UK outward investment into Turkey would add little to the UK totals, but might impact on UK domestic investment and employment.

Even if UK–Turkish trade does increase, this would not guarantee closer relationships in the security and political sphere. Turkey's relations with the United States, Germany and the UAE are fraught notwithstanding the considerable trade they conduct with Turkey. Israel's Turkish trade has even prospered as its diplomatic relationship with Ankara plummeted. Thus it might be helpful to regard UK–Turkey security relations as being largely independent of their economic interaction. However, beyond arms trading, what does their security relationship consist of, and how might it develop in the post-Brexit era? As a House of Commons Foreign Affairs Committee expressed it in 2017, 'both the UK and Turkish governments used the word "strategic" to describe the relationship between the two countries. Both sides emphasised trade, security, and defence co-operation as being at the heart of the relationship'.[42] However, security and defence cooperation is generally conducted in the context of their joint membership of NATO, or as an accompaniment to the activities of the United States. Clearly as NATO members, there is a degree of routine interaction between the two countries, but that doesn't distinguish them from any other pairing of NATO members. What else is there to this relationship?

As noted, Erdogan has stressed that UK–Turkey cooperation against terrorism is at an 'advanced stage' relative to that with Turkey's other partners. Erdogan regards all members of the Gulen movement, elected Kurdish politicians, many journalists, academics, human rights activists and many political opponents generally, as well as the PKK and IS, as terrorists or in support of terrorism. Security cooperation is by its nature opaque but it is not unheard of that security agencies pass on information about the activities of dissident communities to friendly countries. It may also be worth noting that the United States ended its programme of providing Turkey with intelligence on PKK activities only after Turkey's military incursion against the SDF into Northeast Syria in October 2019.[43] Sir Alan Duncan told a parliamentary committee that the UK and Turkey work closely together in the struggle against IS, but we have already noted the widespread scepticism about and disappointment with Turkey's counter-IS activities.

With respect to Syria, Turkey is widely known to have cooperated and even trained, armed, cooperated with and funded a number of rebel groups that many would regard as jihadi. As early as 2012 UK special forces may have been providing assistance to the Syrian Al-Qaeda-affiliated group known as Jabhat al Nusra,[44] possibly entering Syria from Turkey.[45] The UK also provided communications and other equipment to Syrian rebels, and passed on intelligence gleaned from its listening posts in Cyprus via Turkey.[46] The UK is also believed to have been instrumental in channelling fighters and arms from Libya, where they had been trained by the British in the bid to overthrow Gaddafi, to Syria and to have conducted training of rebels in Qatar.[47]

It isn't clear to what extent the UK was involved in the Pentagon's poorly supervised Train and Equip Programme for Syrian rebels. Much of the equipment provided ended up in the hands of IS and Al-Qaeda-affiliated groups, some of which were sponsored by or in alliance with Turkey.[48] The UK's involvement in the four-year-long CIA programme to aid Syrian rebels is similarly unclear. Codenamed Timber Sycamore, and mainly operated from Turkey and Jordan, it was wound up by President Trump in summer 2017, partly because many of the weapons provided ended up in the hands of the Al-Qaeda-affiliated al-Nusra Front and other groups in Idlib.[49] Each of these US-led programmes were coordinated with Turkey. UK forces have operated alongside the SDF of course, but Turkey would hardly regard this as cooperative behaviour with respect to terrorism. However, UK-trained and -supplied elements of the FSA may also have fought against the SDF.

In short and in the absence of detailed official information, it is hard to be sure what exactly the UK's much-vaunted security relationship with Turkey consists of. In this context, it is worth noting that in February 2020 the UK declared its recognition that the Kurdistan Freedom Hawks (Teyrebazen Azadiya Kurdistan or TAK) and the People's Defence Forces (Hezen Parastina Gel or HPG) should be regarded as extensions of the proscribed Kurdistan Workers Party (Partiya Karkeren Kurdistane or PKK). Turkey's Ministry of Foreign Affairs (MFA) welcomed the UK's move, in a statement that called on Turkey's other Western allies to follow suit.[50] Whatever the UK–Turkey security relationship comprises, it is important to note that it has not been channelled via the EU, but has been bilateral or, if multilateral, through NATO or other US-led arrangements. In this respect, the UK's exit from the EU will change little.

The UK, Turkey and the EU

So, what aspects of the UK's relations with Turkey will change in light of the UK's withdrawal from the EU, if any? Clearly, with respect to issues that directly involve the EU, such as Cyprus or Syrian refugees, the UK will no longer be automatically consulted. With respect to the tensions over energy exploration in the Eastern Mediterranean too, the UK might find itself on the outside looking in. The UK's main stake in Cyprus relates to the SBAs there, and this issue is more likely to be addressed either bilaterally with Cyprus, or trilaterally with the United States. As a guarantor power, the UK would find itself closely involved in any broader effort to settle the island's division, although there has hitherto been little indication that the stances adopted by either Turkey or the EU would be greatly influenced by the UK. With respect to the Syrian refugee issue, the EU was in disarray in 2015. Some members closed their doors altogether, Germany agreed to take in 1 million, while the UK committed to take just 20,000 and preferred to prioritize in-theatre humanitarian assistance. Again, it isn't clear that the UK's EU withdrawal impacts much on the UK–Turkey–EU handling of this problem.

Although the UK joined with France in assisting the 2011 overthrow of Libya's Gaddafi, again there was little overall EU consensus. In any case, the UK has subsequently largely conducted its Libyan policy via the UN. Its former EU partners are again not as one on Libya, so here too the UK's EU exit would carry little consequence. With respect to tensions between the Gulf and other Arab countries on the one hand, and Turkey and Qatar on the other, there is no substantive EU or UK position. London has good relationships with Turkey's Qatari ally, but also with Saudi Arabia, the UAE and others. This appears not to have been an issue between London and Ankara.

However, London's inclination to sympathize with Turkey's actions might pit the UK against other EU states. The UK was one of just a handful of Turkey's European allies to offer substantive support to Turkey, in the form of anti-missile defences and electronic warfare capabilities, in response to a NATO meeting held at Turkey's request under Article 4.[51] The meeting, in February 2020, came in the wake of an escalation of clashes in Idlib in Syria between the forces of the Assad government and Turkish and Turkey-backed opposition groups. However, many EU countries have been more critical of Turkey's involvement in Syria, and most have not assisted. Then again, the UK joined with other EU states to express 'concern' over Turkey's October 2019 incursion into Northeastern Syria, dubbed 'Operation Peace Spring', and joined many of them in suspending new arms export licenses to Turkey.[52] In short, even as a member of the EU, the UK's positions on Syria and other Middle Eastern crises sometimes aligned with and sometimes diverged from what in any case were typically weak and often divided EU positions. This seems unlikely to change.

A post-Brexit UK in the Middle East: Spot the difference

At the time of writing the UK has around 1,300 armed personnel contributing to the US-led struggle against IS in the Middle East. A newly opened base in Oman will be able to support a UK carrier and there are also maritime facilities in Bahrain. The RAF's regional operational headquarters is in Qatar, and it also has access to facilities in Oman and the UAE. UK personnel are also present in Saudi Arabia and offer assistance in the Saudi-led campaign against Yemeni rebels. Along with the over 3,000 UK personnel stationed in Cyprus, this is a not inconsiderable regional presence. Figures for deployed special forces are unavailable.[53] Although it might be taken to reflect a post-Brexit 'global Britain', the deployed forces long predate the UK's exit from the EU or even the debate about it, as does procurement of the carriers and other capabilities.[54] Most of the UK's military presence in the region results from bilateral agreements with host countries. The force size and vulnerabilities suggest that the UK could not fight a Middle East war on its own, but it could make a contribution to a US-led operation, with Iran as the most plausible adversary. Turkey's relationship with Iran is ambivalent. It has been unhappy with Iranian support for Shia factions in Iraq's sectarian divide and with its backing for Assad. But they are in closer agreement on the region's Kurdish issues, and Turkey has sought to get around US-imposed sanctions against Tehran, not least because of its considerable energy dependence on Iran. It is not likely that Turkey would align with any serious anti-Iranian campaign in the region. The UK stance in the region could be seriously compromised should Turkey's confrontational relationship with almost every UK friend in the region escalate further.

After Brexit the UK government proposed a review of Security, Defence, Development and Foreign Policy, with many leading politicians favouring the idea of a UK with global reach and influence.[55] However, past British governments, even that of the pro-EU Tony Blair, have been drawn to the idea of the UK as a global power. EU membership did not obstruct the sentiment, the policies or the procurement of capabilities necessary to pursue such an aspiration. It has generally been more likely that the UK would act in a NATO- or US-led than in an EU-led force. It is now perhaps a little more likely. However, the Trump administration's transactional approach to allies, its self-centredness and its unpredictability made Brexit a particularly bad moment for the UK to contemplate forging 'independence' from its European allies. Although the Biden administration has signalled a return to a more business-as-usual approach to its allies, it is far from clear that it will be better disposed towards the UK than towards its other European friends. Moreover, there are and have always been doubts that the UK possesses or could possess the capabilities to play an independent 'global' role.[56] The Covid-19 pandemic is likely to further undermine the UK's global capacity. The unprecedented peacetime pressure on public spending that the pandemic has generated is likely in due course to impact on UK defence spending. Along with Brexit, it has and will continue to preoccupy the British government, possibly at the expense of a focus on the UK's wider global role. The risks of transmission will complicate any military missions abroad, and there is a general global shift towards greater national and regional insularity. In short, it is not self-evidently a good moment for the UK to be contemplating an enhanced global reach, in the Middle East or elsewhere.

Furthermore, much of the UK's pro-Brexit talk of a 'global Britain' has emphasized support for a rules-based international order, championing human rights and encouraging free trade.[57] However, the UK's relationship with Turkey does not at all exhibit much British commitment to human rights abroad. Pinning down the substance of the UK–Turkey relationship, and identifying the scope for enhancing it, is less easy than identifying the UK's rhetorical commitment to it. Has the UK simply internalized Washington's traditional commitment to Turkey's importance as a security partner – a commitment that still exists in some quarters notwithstanding the current tensions – and been slow to notice the potential for a US–Turkey parting of the ways? Does London believe it is playing a long game, keeping the relationship on the road for when Erdogan finally departs the scene? In the post-Brexit era, it might also reflect either a desperate search for alternative partners or misplaced optimism.

9

Israel

Ian Black

Hopes for a negotiated settlement of the Israel–Palestine conflict may be at an all-time low, but any British government looking at the Middle East in the coming years has little choice but to pursue policies designed to contribute to that elusive goal. Even after Brexit, prospects for ending the long impasse still depend to some extent on European and wider international involvement, more so in the age of 'America first' and the growing perception that the United States is simultaneously pursuing disruptive policies while disengaging from the region. And looking ahead, of course, requires a clear understanding of what has come before, especially in recent times.

The UK has a specific interest and arguably a duty dictated by historical responsibility. That was highlighted in November 2017 when the centenary of the Balfour Declaration served as a reminder of the strong and divisive feelings aroused by the issue and the demand that the rights of those, who were once infamously defined only as Palestine's 'non-Jewish communities', finally receive the recognition they deserve.[1] The legacy and consequences of three decades of British rule still attract infinitely more attention than, for example, France's far longer presence in colonial Algeria.

It is important, nevertheless, to acknowledge that Palestine/Israel or what is often referred to as the Middle East Peace Process (MEPP) has slipped down British and international agendas. The issue attracts less attention from governments than it did until the early 2000s. That is because of deadlock and mistrust, fatigue, lack of interest and the sense that there are more urgent crises to tackle. These include the aftermath of the Arab Spring, conflicts in Syria and Yemen, refugee flows into Europe and the threat posed by the Islamic State. Related trends include the confrontation between Saudi Arabia and Iran and the convergence of views between the Gulf states and Israel. All have contributed to the weakening of pan-Arab solidarity and the marginalization of the divided Palestinians. That peaked in September 2020 with the signing of the US-brokered Abraham Accords between Israel, the UAE and Bahrain, which were then followed by similar agreements with Sudan and Morocco.

It is also necessary to note that the status quo continues to extract a heavy price: Palestinian rights in the occupied territories are permanently breached. Economic opportunities and freedom of movement are restricted by Israeli checkpoints and settlements. In all, 60 per cent of the West Bank is under full Israeli control, leaving

2.9 million Palestinians in 169 fragmented 'islands' in Areas A and B (constituting 40 per cent of the total). The limited powers of the Palestinian authority (PA) in Ramallah do not extend to Israeli-annexed East Jerusalem or to the Hamas-ruled Gaza Strip, where Israel's blockade and deteriorating economic and humanitarian conditions for 2 million people sustain a culture of resistance. In the year from March 2018, when weekly 'Marches of Return' began, more than 190 Palestinians were killed by Israeli forces and nearly 29,000 injured. Israeli territory has been targeted by rocket and mortar fire and incendiary kites launched from inside Gaza. In the course of 2020 the outbreak of Covid-19 in the occupied territories, and Gaza specifically, highlighted the effect of the ongoing blockade on public health at a time of unprecedented crisis.

Popular awareness is increasing in the UK and internationally. The growth of the Boycott, Disinvestment and Sanctions (BDS) movement in Britain, Europe and the United States, inspired by the anti-apartheid struggle in South Africa, is evidence of the cost to Israel – though that has so far been more reputational than substantive. Accusations about anti-Semitism in the UK Labour Party are also relevant. Of all the correspondence received from members of the public by the Foreign and Commonwealth Office (FCO), a quarter is about Israel/Palestine – from supporters of both sides.

Recognition is growing that Israel will not survive as a Jewish-majority but democratic state if it continues to rule over millions of stateless Palestinians in the OPTs while denying them citizenship and other rights. The notion of it being transformed into an apartheid state is part of liberal political discourse in Israel and no longer confined to foreign or Arab critics. Israel's controversial nation-state law, passed in July 2018, fuelled that argument and blurred the lingering distinction between the pre- and post-1967 borders. What is often described as a 'one-state reality' is by no stretch of the imagination a solution to the conflict. Seeking to 'manage' it rather than working to end it involves long-term risks.

The Palestinian issue deserves to be resolved for its own sake in line with the right to self-determination. It is also a matter of self-interest for Israelis. Popular sympathy constrains Arab governments that are ready to improve relations with Israel, though Abu Dhabi and Manama ignored that factor when they agreed to normalize relations with Israel. Its wider resonance means tensions can escalate regionally. It can be exploited by Iran, Hezbollah or Islamic extremists. It is only necessary to imagine a replay of the Gaza crisis of 2006, followed by the second Lebanon war – but next time with Hezbollah armed with a far larger arsenal of missiles that could reach anywhere in Israel and would be targeted by the infinitely superior Israeli military. That is a future scenario. Current reality is bad enough.

Stick to two states?

The strategic priority for British governments must continue to be to sustain the notion of a viable two-state solution to the Israel–Palestine conflict, with Jerusalem as a shared capital. Rooted in international law and UN resolutions, that approach has not been bettered since it achieved a broad consensus in the early 1990s. The PLO, which recognized Israel at the time of the Oslo accords in 1993, continues to do so while demanding an independent Palestinian state within the 1967 borders with East Jerusalem as its capital. The position of Hamas (the Islamic Resistance Movement), controlling the Gaza Strip, is that it will support a long-term ceasefire and refers to the 1967 borders. It refuses, however, to recognize Israel.

The Arab Peace Initiative (API) of 2002, reiterated in 2007 and many times since, remains the formal commitment of the Arab League and the Organisation of the Islamic Conference. In 2013 the API was significantly modified to include the concept of land swaps taken from the Clinton Parameters of 2001. A workable regional plan for ending the conflict is therefore still available even if it is not currently on any negotiating table. And there is no alternative plan. Supporters of what is described as a 'one-state solution' under which Israelis and Palestinians would somehow enjoy equal rights in a unitary democratic state do not have a coherent strategy, although belief in the idea is growing amongst younger Palestinians.[2]

UK policy towards an Israeli–Palestinian peace agreement was formulated as follows in 2018:

> It should be based on the lines as they stood on 4 June 1967 with equal land swaps to reflect the national, security, and religious interests of the Jewish and Palestinian peoples. Jerusalem should be the shared capital of the Israeli and Palestinian states, and its status must be determined through a final status agreement. A just, fair, agreed and realistic settlement for refugees is needed that is demographically compatible with the principle of two states for two peoples.[3]

Israel's commitment to two states became far less clear during the rule of the Likud leader, Binyamin Netanyahu, prime minister continuously from 2009 to 2021.[4] Key figures further right on the political spectrum call for the annexation of what is defined under Oslo as Area C – 62 per cent of the West Bank. Netanyahu resisted that but did speak of 'a state-minus' in which Israel would retain overall security control. On the eve of his fifth election victory in April 2019 he pledged to start annexing settlements, a potentially fatal blow to already slim hopes for reviving negotiations. Borders, settlements, the status of Jerusalem and the Palestinian refugee question all remain thorny issues.[5]

The policies pursued during the first two years of Donald Trump's term in office were welcome to Netanyahu and damaging to Palestinian national aspirations – even though effective US involvement in any active peace process had ended long before he arrived in the White House in January 2017. John Kerry, secretary of state in the second Obama administration, gave up his mediating efforts in April 2014.

Successive Trump administration decisions displayed open bias towards Israel and hostility to the Palestinians. The biggest was the transfer of the US embassy from Tel Aviv to Jerusalem, announced in December 2017 and implemented with deliberately symbolic timing on the seventieth anniversary of Israel's independence in May 2018. Others involved slashing US aid to UNRWA, the closure of the PLO mission in Washington and the suspension of aid to PA security forces.[6] All were damaging to the international consensus of many years and the – to some, already outlandish – idea that the United States could play the role of honest broker.

President Mahmoud Abbas's decision to sever ties with Washington was little short of inevitable. Expectations for Trump's long-trailed 'deal of the century', drawn up by his son-in-law Jared Kushner and Middle East envoy Jason Greenblatt, were low long before it was unveiled in January 2020 (see below). Trump's announcement in March 2019 that the United States recognizes Israel's annexation of the Golan Heights was seen as another example of the president's reckless and transactional foreign policy and a harbinger of what might eventually happen with the West Bank. The UK position is that occupation is 'unacceptable' and 'unsustainable.' Its stance should be designed to prevent unilateral changes implemented by Israel and supported by the United States.

Resisting Trump

The formal UK position was made clear before Trump became president. In November 2016, after the US election, Britain voted to back UN Security Council Resolution 2334, while the US abstention was widely interpreted as Obama's attempt to 'Trump-proof' decades of US policy. The UK played a key role in drafting the resolution, coordinating with Egypt, the Palestinians and France.[7] Its main purpose was to reaffirm the illegality of Israel's settlement enterprise and re-emphasize the need to differentiate between Israel and the territories occupied in 1967. Netanyahu condemned the US position as 'shameful'.

Earlier US plans to draw up a broader 'terms of reference' resolution updating and clarifying UNSCR 242 of 1967, and which were also backed by the UK, were abandoned.[8] Resolution 2334 was seen in London as 'more modest and marketable'. Shortly afterwards, Kerry warned that a two-state solution was in jeopardy because of what he characterized as 'the most right-wing government' in Israel's history, in which the 'settler agenda' was defining the future. 'If the choice is one state', he said, 'Israel can either be Jewish or democratic, it cannot be both, and it won't ever really be at peace'.

Theresa May's response to Kerry appeared to distance her Conservative government from the UN vote by expressing support for 'a more broad-ranging approach to encourage peace'. Settlements, her statement said, 'are far from the only problem in this conflict. In particular, the people of Israel deserve to live free from the threat of terrorism, with which they have had to cope for too long'. In what was seen as a rebuke to the outgoing US secretary of state, May said Britain did not believe 'that it is appropriate to attack the composition of the democratically-elected government of an ally'. The UK, she continued, 'believes that negotiations will only succeed when they are conducted between the two parties, supported by the international community'. The prime minister's remarks were widely attributed to fears about the uncertain aftermath of the Brexit referendum in June 2016 and to concerns about future relations with the incoming US administration, as well as with Israel. It was seen too as Downing Street re-asserting itself over the Foreign Office, encouraged by lobby groups like the influential Conservative Friends of Israel.

Speculation mounted about a 'Brexit effect' in which the UK would abandon or modify fundamental and long-standing foreign policy stances because of the need to strengthen bilateral trade relations in the age of what was called 'Global Britain' outside the EU.[9] In January 2017 Britain blocked EU support for a Paris conference designed to advance a two-state solution that was boycotted by Israel and the PA. The UK position was that the conference 'risked hardening positions just before the transition to a new US President'.[10] It was also striking that when Netanyahu met May in London, their talks focused almost exclusively on bilateral relations – trade, intelligence sharing and the threat from Iran – with only perfunctory reference to UK support for two states and opposition to settlements.[11]

Subsequent events however, once Trump was installed in the Oval Office, showed that assumption of a 'Brexit effect'[12] to be exaggerated, though pro-Israel lobbyists still welcomed the potential for enhanced UK trade once Britain had left the EU.[13] In the course of 2017, however, London distanced itself from Washington on other Israel/Palestine issues. The most important was supporting a UN Security Council resolution condemning the announcement of the move of the US embassy to Jerusalem.[14] British responses went further: when the United States cut off contributions to UNRWA, the Department for International Development (DFID) announced an additional £7 million to keep schools open and provide medical care in the West Bank, Gaza, Lebanon and Jordan. Alistair Burt, minister of state for the Middle East at the Foreign Office and DfID (until March 2019), made clear that Britain would continue to support UNRWA. On other issues, however, critics still complained that the UK was not only deferring to Washington but also following it far too closely. It was a familiar line.

Mitigating the impact of occupation

Financial support for UNRWA represents continuity of UK policy towards the Palestinians, of which a central plank is working to mitigate the impact of the occupation. Another element is to help develop the institutions of a future Palestinian state to ensure it can effectively deliver services and act as a partner for a two-state solution with Israel. The activities of UK diplomatic missions on the ground reflect that. The British embassy in Tel Aviv is matched by a consulate-general in East Jerusalem. The assumption is that the consulate would become an embassy if/when a Palestinian state is created. The Tel Aviv embassy would then move to West Jerusalem.

The Palestinian Authority is the largest recipient per capita of international aid in the world.[15] UK contributions were £75 million in 2016.[16] British ministers are often called upon to defend the PA from complaints made by Israel and its supporters, including the issue of payments made to prisoners and the families of 'martyrs' or those convicted of acts of terrorism by Israel. Accusations of Palestinian 'incitement' and the content of textbooks are a related issue.

In July 2018, the UK announced that it was to provide up to £38 million over five years (2018–23) to support economic activity in Gaza and the West Bank – more than double the amount of support previously allotted for development in the OPTs in the preceding five years. In 2017/18 the UK also provided £20 million to the PA to help pay the salaries of up to 30,000 teachers, doctors, nurses, midwives and other health and education public servants on a vetted list.

Critics, however, warned repeatedly that the government's approach was perpetuating the status quo and doing nothing to stop creeping annexation by Israel. That suggests the need to examine whether UK aid is supporting Palestinian sovereignty or helping to sustain Israeli rule. Britain 'should explore how aid can be shifted away from PA budgetary support and the promotion of an aid-dependent economy, in favour of Palestinian economic independence', recommended the European Council on Foreign Relations (ECFR).[17] Simply cutting aid, however, would, more than anything else, cause misery for ordinary Palestinians.

British officials are aware that the PA is unpopular because it lacks new thinking and crushes dissent. A drift towards authoritarianism has become a hallmark of Abbas's long rule, fourteen years into his four-year term. Palestinian opponents call regularly for an end to security coordination with Israel, the withdrawal of the PLO's recognition of Israel and the end of the Oslo arrangements. The existence, however, of the PA, is a different matter. 'If dissolving the PA means giving the Israelis back control of education and health I would say no', said Mustafa Barghouti, founder of al-mubadara al-wataniya (the 'national initiative') 'If you mean ending security coordination with Israel I would say yes. We need to preserve our institutions.' For a former UK official the picture is clear: 'Even though it's not working very well the Palestinians do have a degree of autonomy in the West Bank and Gaza, which is a starting point for statehood. Turkeys don't vote for Christmas. What they say is: "we've got something and we are not going to give it up."'

The PA's complicity in the situation in Gaza – by cutting employees' salaries and restricting electricity supplies – is seen as factional and vindictive. It was the subject of a demarche by the EU on the eve of the UN General Assembly in September 2018. The PA has also opposed the multi-million dollar financial contributions made by Qatar to provide relief to Gazans, accusing it of bolstering Hamas. In December 2018 the PA was unhappy with a conference convened in London to examine options for relieving Gaza's humanitarian crisis.[18] The position of the PA is that it needs to maintain both the territorial integrity and the political leadership of the OPTs. Efforts to deal with Gaza as a separate entity are regarded with suspicion in Ramallah. 'Israel's agenda', warned Husam Zomlot, the Palestinian ambassador to London, 'has always been Gaza first and Gaza last'.[19] The bottom line, as far as the UK is concerned, remains that if the PA was not there, 'the situation in the West Bank would be even more precarious'.[20] It is hard to see that argument changing in the near future.

Looking ahead

British policy needs to anticipate future developments. The biggest, indeed overarching question is about the irreversibility of the status quo/continued viability of a two-state solution given everything that has happened in recent years – whether that is the number of Israeli settlers (600,000) now living beyond the green line, the permanent separation barrier, debilitating Palestinian divisions or the steady erosion of the belief on both sides that such a solution is achievable.

Many UK and other diplomats admit privately that a two-state solution is not likely to happen but believe that in the absence of any other it cannot be taken off the table. 'International reluctance to discuss alternatives ... is less a refusal to recognize the trends that have undermined it and more a fear of abetting those trends', as Nathan Brown and Marwan Muasher have argued. 'Open embrace of an alternative approach threatens to legitimate Israeli settlement activity, acquiesce in the Israeli annexation of Jerusalem and perhaps parts of the West Bank, abandon the tremendous international investment in the PA, and encourage rejectionist actors (including Hamas) on the Palestinian side.' [21] Formal abandonment of the idea of occupation, in the words of another expert, would risk 'accelerating a one state outcome in which a Jewish minority benefits from greater rights than a Palestinian majority'.[22]

Nevertheless, that big question is unlikely to go away. Some have called for acquiescence in (future) Israeli annexation of the West Bank and the creation of a 'unitary state'.[23] Eran Etzion, a former Israeli deputy national security adviser, proposes the EU declare it will abandon the two-state formula within a given timeframe if an agreement is not reached, to be replaced by a demand for equal rights for all Palestinians within a single state.[24] It seems more reasonable to assume, however, that a one-state solution would only make it onto the policy agenda if the Palestinians themselves put it there. Palestinian civil society activists doubt that their demands are likely to be adopted by a PA with an overwhelming interest in maintaining its own elite status, privileges and power and in securing national independence. Israeli government officials share that assumption.

Such scenarios have been looked at by think tanks and government analysts but have rarely reached ministers' desks. Still, a realistic option for the UK and other governments is adopting what has been described as a more 'rights-based' approach as opposed to a peace process/two-state-based approach.[25] That, it is said, would shift the burden of proof onto the Israeli side to offer an alternative end state rather than taking refuge and comfort from what one analyst describes as 'no solutionism'.

The Ecfr argues succinctly:

> A new UK policy should take into account the emerging one state reality on the ground, acknowledging that while a two state solution may remain the desired outcome, negotiations alone will be insufficient to achieve this, absent efforts to create the political conditions necessary for their success. While continuing to defend the long term viability of the two state solution, HMG must put greater emphasis on de-occupation while tackling those factors that prevent the success of peace talks, and undermine the two state solution.[26]

Equal rights, suggests the Oxford Research Group, is not an alternative to a Palestinian state, but a strategy that applies pressure to bring it about.[27] Put differently, the trick will be to keep that solution on life support rather than declare the patient dead.

Focusing on de-occupation and Palestinian rights should not prevent governments from responding to illegal acts by Israel. The UK and other EU member states displayed rare determination in 2018 when they confronted Israel over the Bedouin village of Khan al-Ahmar because of its strategic location – connecting the north and south of the West Bank. The UN said proposed demolitions could amount to 'forcible transfer' in violation of international humanitarian law. That succeeded in staving off Israeli plans despite the approval of the High Court. A similarly robust response would be required if, for example, an Israeli government decided, as right-wingers advocate, to annex all or part of area C, where all settlements are located.

Zooming out, another highly relevant question is about the role of the United States and the value of London's relationship with Washington. 'Given the United States' special role as guarantor of Israel's security, any real progress towards a peace settlement is bound to involve the Americans', in the words of the FCO submission to the Foreign Affairs Committee in 2017. 'We therefore make use of our close relationship with Washington to support and encourage progress on the MEPP' under the Trump administration, however, that became much harder. Boris Johnson, foreign secretary from 2016–18, offered to consult with the United States over the president's peace plan, but Kushner is described as having listened to UK representations in a 'studiously neutral way'. Diplomatic sources report more strongly worded complaints. In the Trump era Britain has become 'more mealy-mouthed', said one former official. The UK is simply a 'nodding donkey' for US policy, 'according to Clare Short, the often outspoken secretary of state for international development from 1997 to 2003'. This is embarrassing and humiliating and means we are part of the problem and not part of the solution.[28] British diplomats are hoping that cooperation on Israel–Palestine will be smoother under Joe Biden's administration.

Recognizing Palestine?

The most common specific demand for a change in UK policy is that it recognizes the State of Palestine, first declared by Yasser Arafat in November 1988. In September 2011 Britain said it would recognize Palestine but only with non-member observer status, rather than full membership, at the United Nations. In November 2012 – on the anniversary of the UN partition resolution of 1947 – Britain notably abstained while other EU member states voted for it and thus missed an opportunity to send an important signal.[29]

In October 2014, after that summer's conflict in Gaza, the House of Commons passed a motion which called on the government to recognize Palestine as an independent state by 276 to 14.[30] The devolved government of Scotland called for recognition of Palestine and for the UK to open an embassy. The Labour leader Jeremy Corbyn, a long-time advocate for the Palestinian cause, repeatedly pledged to recognize the state if elected. It was in the party's manifesto in the 2017 and 2019 elections. 'It is', as one commentator put it, 'a swiftly deliverable act of symbolic significance for party activists, on an issue which almost no-one else – save perhaps British Jews and Muslims – cares much about'.[31]

Current UK government policy is that it 'reserves the right to recognise a Palestinian state bilaterally at the moment of our choosing and when it can best help bring about peace'. Arguments against recognition include the view that by doing so, governments have reduced their influence with Israel. The Commons vote came in the wake of Sweden's decision to become the first EU member (and the 136th country worldwide) to recognize Palestine. (Malta and Cyprus recognized it prior to joining the EU, as did several Central European member states when they were allied with the Soviet Union). Parliaments in Ireland, France, Portugal, Spain and Italy adopted resolutions supporting Palestinian statehood after Sweden's decision. Israel's response to that was furious and designed to deter others from following suit. Sweden's foreign minister was declared persona non grata when she called for Israel to end 'extrajudicial killings' of Palestinians.[32] Britain, it is assumed, would be less vulnerable to pressure than Sweden was.

The Balfour Project, set up to focus attention on Britain's role in Palestine, argues that UK recognition would contribute to a two-state solution and help redress a historic injustice that was described succinctly as 'unfinished business' in 2017. The demand was supported in September 2018, on the twenty-fifth anniversary of Oslo by an impressively heavyweight list of former British ministers, diplomats and MPs from all parties, along with prominent Palestinians as well as dovish Israeli academics and intellectuals.[33] British recognition would result in 'slightly levelling the very unequal playfield between the Israelis and Palestinians', according to Liberal Democrat Friends of Palestine.[34]

Arguments against recognition would be stronger if credible peace talks were under way as there would be a case for claiming that acting prematurely might prove disruptive by encouraging Palestinian unilateralism and undermining bilateral negotiations. Recognition, it is conventionally argued, would have symbolic power in granting Palestinians 'parity of esteem' though little in the way of practical consequences apart from the 'feelgood' factor of having done something. If the UK were to act on recognition together with France, four of the five permanent members of the UN Security Council (in addition to Russia and China) would then have recognized Palestine, adding considerably to its impact.[35] The PLO complained in 2017, however, that British officials had begun to mention conditions for recognition such as the need for the PA to address incitement against Israel, or reconciliation between Fatah and Hamas. These were perceived to be 'excuses for not recognising the State of Palestine'.[36] It looks likely, nevertheless, to remain an option for future governments, perhaps as a response to Israeli annexationist moves.

Terrorists or partners?

Britain's long-standing position is to emphasize the PLOs recognition of Israel and condemn violence even when defined by Palestinians as legitimate resistance to occupation and to urge proportional responses by Israel. The UK proscribes the Izz al-Din al-Qassam brigades, the military wing of Hamas, because of their 'aims to end Israeli occupation in Palestine and establish an Islamic State'. Its policy is 'no contact with Hamas in its entirety'. Under the conditions laid down by the Quartet (the UN,

United States, EU and Russia) in 2006, before any engagement Hamas must first accept Israel, renounce violence and agree to abide by previous agreements. Opponents argue that those demands should not be a barrier to diplomatic engagement. 'Ruling out any contacts may well be counterproductive', according to the Council for Arab-British Understanding. 'Isolating Hamas has allowed more hard-line elements within the movement to dominate and for Hamas to portray itself as a victim.' Initial contacts could be made at a lower level, progressing to more senior representatives if certain benchmarks are met.[37] Norway and Switzerland, outside the EU, both talk to Hamas.

Tony Blair, prime minister when Hamas won the 2006 elections, admitted later that he regretted the decision to boycott the movement, though he noted that to have done otherwise would have met strong resistance from Israel.[38] In 2015, he held talks with Khaled Mashal, the head of Hamas's politburo, on ending the blockade of Gaza. Jack Straw, British foreign secretary from 2001 to 2006, believed his private support for dialogue with Hamas had been a factor in his being sacked by Blair.[39] Hamas argues that it is a legally elected government and has the right to conduct military operations against Israel.[40] In 2017, it amended its charter to include a reference for the first time to the 1967 borders but there was no lessening of its opposition to recognition of Israel. Resistance to occupation was defined as a legitimate right guaranteed by divine laws and international norms and 'the strategic choice for protecting the principles and the rights of the Palestinian people'.[41] Israel and its supporters have always lobbied hard on this issue. In 2017, the Palestine Expo in London – the largest such event in Europe – was threatened with a ban because its organizer, the Friends of Al-Aqsa, was linked to Hamas, but it went ahead in the end following threats of legal action.[42]

At the EU level there is widespread recognition that the no-contact policy has failed and probably needs to be re-thought but there has been no agreement on how to move forward. In November 2018, the European Court of Justice dismissed an appeal by Hamas against the freezing of its funds because of involvement in terrorism.[43] Hamas still appears central to intra-Palestinian reconciliation and, by extension, to the slim possibility of reviving negotiations with Israel. The issue of British contacts with it may well be re-visited in future.

Not saying 'boo!'

Critics of UK policy complain that official protests about Israeli actions in the OPTs are not accompanied by real pressure, let alone punitive action. 'There is condemnation fatigue in the FCO because the automatic response of the complainant is that "it's fantastic that you condemned this, but what are you going to do"', sighs one former official. 'To which there is no answer. There is never an answer. They never want to say boo to Israel.'[44] Nadia Hijab, founder of the Palestine policy network Al-Shabaka, puts it like this: 'Everything is issuing statements which Israel can sweep under the rug and is not held accountable.'[45]

Israel's view is that its relations with the UK have never been better, whether measured in record levels of trade, military and intelligence cooperation,[46] and a growing appreciation of its 'start-up nation' tech sector, especially in cyber-security.[47]

UK officials share that assessment. The first-ever official visit by a British royal, Prince William, to Israel (and the OPTs) in June 2018 is cited as an important indicator.[48] 'Over the past several years, the close but often complicated relations between Israel and the United Kingdom have grown much closer', the liberal daily *Haaretz* reported before the royal visit. 'Experts point to rising trade figures, stronger economic ties, increasingly transparent military cooperation and even the hope of a creeping shift in Britain's voting patterns in international institutions.'[49] In January 2020, the Prince of Wales visited Israel (and the OPTs) to mark the seventy-fifth anniversary of the liberation of Auschwitz.

UK criticism is made, it seems, more in sorrow than in anger. So when Hunt condemned US support for Israel's annexation of the Golan Heights in April 2019 as unacceptable under international law, he immediately qualified it: 'I do that with a very heavy heart, because Israel is an ally and a shining example of democracy in a part of the world where that is not common. We want Israel to be a success, and we consider it to be a great friend, but on this we do not agree.'[50]

In recent years there has been a focus on the UN Human Rights Council (UNHRC) in Geneva, which the Trump administration quit in June 2018. Britain issued a warning at that time.[51] In March 2019, it followed the United States partially. It explained that it would in future vote against any item raised under the council's item 7, devoted exclusively to Israel, on the basis that its human rights abuses should not be elevated to a special status above other global abuses. 'Instead of promoting reconciliation and compromise, Item 7 strengthens the narrative that one side alone holds a monopoly on fault', wrote Hunt, lamenting 'disproportionate and discriminatory focus on Israel'.[52]

At the same time, a group of UK charities protested about a 'dereliction of responsibility' when the government refused to endorse a UN-mandated commission of enquiry report into 187 deaths in Gaza (during 'March of Return' protests) that placed responsibility in almost all cases on Israel forces. At a meeting of the UNHRC the UK abstained, saying it could not back an investigation or a resolution that failed to investigate the role of non-state actors, and in particular Hamas. The charities urged the government to show what they intend to do to prevent impunity in the OPTs in future.[53] The abstention decision was made though the issue was not raised under item 7. Hamas, said the UK ambassador to Israel, had 'cynically exploited the protests' while Israel had the right to self-defence. The UK had however 'publicly and privately expressed our longstanding concerns about the use of live ammunition and excessive force by the Israel Defence Forces'. In the words of the Conservative Middle East Council, 'British quiet diplomacy is practised assiduously – and ignored'. The response showed, in microcosm, the limitations of the British attempt to remain even-handed in an extremely uneven situation.

Another area highlighted by critics is the UNHRC database of companies doing business with settlements in the OPTs. 'The database is a unique transparency tool and soft power enforcement mechanism that could provide a service to states and their corporate nationals who may become involved in illegal business activities', explained one expert.[54] The issue is sensitive because companies listed could be targeted for boycotts or divestment. Britain refused to go along with this, officials admitting that they had come under pressure from the United States and Israel.

It is not a new issue. Pro-Palestinian voices have long wanted a tougher approach to the EU's labelling of settlement products – moving from simply informing consumers so they can make a choice to a mandatory ban.[55] Comparisons are made with the total ban on imports from Russian-occupied Crimea. In 2015, the FCO published a warning under the heading 'Overseas Business Risk – the Occupied Palestinian Territories', which stated: 'Settlements are illegal under international law … There are therefore clear risks related to economic and financial activities in the settlements, and we do not encourage or offer support to such activity.' A related idea is for the UK to require Israeli settlers living in the OPTs to apply for visas – unlike Israelis living within the green line.

UK policy has been to resist boycotts of any kind. It thus rejects the argument that Israel must be made to bear the cost of maintaining the status quo. 'We oppose boycotts. We oppose attempts to delegitimize Israel – they do not further progress towards peace', as FCO minister Tobias Ellwood told a conference organized by the pro-Israel organization Bicom in 2015. In February 2016, the government banned public boycotts of Israeli goods because the practice 'can damage integration and community cohesion within the United Kingdom, hinder Britain's export trade, and harm foreign relations to the detriment of Britain's economic and international security'. A legal challenge by the Palestine Solidarity Campaign failed.

The UK sticks to clear differentiation between Israel and the OPTs but it does not apply any sanction for illegal actions across the green line. The differentiation was maintained in early 2019 when the government announced that the Brexit-related 'continuity agreement' with Israel 'applies only to sovereign Israeli territory and not to the occupied Palestinian territory' – thus excluding illegal settlements from preferential trade access.[56] UK officials agree that the blurring of boundaries – for different reasons by both Israel and BDS – is problematic. Politically it is an extremely sensitive issue – 'too much pain for not much gain' in the words of one senior figure.

Contradictory British reactions to Trump's 'deal of the century' reflected much of the above. Boris Johnson praised the plan as having 'the merits of a two-state solution'. Corbyn, Labour's outgoing leader, characterized the US approach as legitimizing Israel's annexation of Palestinian territory and denying Palestinian rights. He called on the prime minister to tell Trump 'frankly and candidly that on this you are wrong'. Johnson replied: 'No peace plan is perfect, but this has the merit of a two-state solution. It would ensure Jerusalem is both the capital of Israel and the Palestinian people.' Dominic Raab, the foreign secretary, initially praised Trump's deal but two days later expressed concern about reports of moves towards annexation of parts of the West Bank by Israel. Britain also reiterated its commitment to UN resolutions but described the US plan as a 'potential first step' while urging the Palestinians to 'offer (their) own vision for a settlement'. Four EU members of the Security Council (Belgium, Estonia, France and Germany), by contrast, warned that the US initiative 'departed from internationally agreed parameters'. Labour's shadow Foreign Secretary, Emily Thornberry, responded: 'This is not a peace plan, it is a monstrosity and a guarantee that the next generation of Palestinian and Israeli children, like so many generations before them, will grow up knowing nothing but fear, violence and division.' In summer 2020, Johnson's government, distracted by the coronavirus pandemic, was urged by a coalition of UK charities and human rights groups to commit to concrete measures and not just 'lacklustre' verbal condemnation if Netanyahu went ahead with annexation plans.[57]

Conclusion

If there is a single lesson to be drawn it is that the UK, which remains a permanent member of the UN Security Council, attaches far greater importance to relations with the United States and Israel than it does to the still stateless Palestinians. By and large, the Palestine question is less central in UK relations with Arab states, especially in the Gulf, than in the past with the partial exception of Jordan, in part because of Israel's own visibly intensifying links with Saudi Arabia, the UAE, Bahrain and Oman.[58] The same is true of Egypt. In August 2020, when the Abraham Accords were announced between Israel and the UAE, Johnson welcomed this 'hugely good news' and emphasized his 'profound hope' that annexation would not now go ahead. Dominic Raab called for direct talks between Israel and the Palestinians – 'the only route to a lasting peace.'[59]

It is hard to avoid the conclusion that Britain should in future act more decisively and urgently in pursuit of the goals it has long enunciated, and make them more central to its relations with Israel. 'We repeat the mantra of support for the two-state solution', complained an FCO veteran, 'but the reality is that our government has so much on its own agenda that it is perfectly happy to leave it to the Americans'.[60] That had long been the view of the Palestinian authority. 'I think the British Government are trying their best to help but I can see … pressures coming from the Israeli and American side', as the Palestinian ambassador to the UK, Manuel Hassassian, told MPs in 2013. 'The British are there not as full partners in the political process. They are much more involved in paying the cheques rather than in playing an important role in the peace process itself politically.'[61] Four years later, that view had not changed: 'The UK government has chosen to sit on the fence and has fallen short in translating its support into concrete action on the ground', the Palestinian mission told the FAC enquiry.[62] No formal changes have taken place in regard to UK positions, observed the Israeli peace activist Daniel Seidemann, but the British government increasingly focuses on the bilateral relationship and 'avoids adversarial engagement with Israel regarding policies and acts that are in violation of long-standing UK positions'. That, he suggests, constitutes a 'pivotal change'.[63]

The view from Israel, although not publicly articulated by government officials, is that in spite of good and indeed deepening bilateral relations, and notwithstanding its principled opposition to settlements in the OPTs, Britain is a less significant player than in the past when it comes to the MEPP.[64] John Jenkins, UK consul-general in Jerusalem from 2004 to 2006 and then FCO director for the Middle East and North Africa, insists that there is virtue in expressing support for a two-state solution if that keeps it alive. 'But the policies are supposed to be more than declaratory', he continues. 'They are supposed to have a practical underpinning. Yet no one has really applied international law. What we have is a succession of fig leaves covering the absence of policies.'[65]

Tom Phillips, former British ambassador to both Israel and Saudi Arabia, has argued that the EU failed 'to translate declaratory clarity into operational strategy and tactics, or to use its potential weight as Israel's most important export market and economic partner'.[66] The Ecfr takes a similar view: 'While European governments have offered Israel generous positive incentives contingent on making steps towards de-occupation, they have largely been reluctant to establish negative incentives for Israeli violations of international norms.'[67] The same arguments apply to Britain. Whatever else happens, addressing that failure, or reluctance, remains the principal challenge in seeking to help end the Middle East's oldest and most intractable conflict.

10

Iran

Sanam Vakil

Britain's decision to leave the European Union (EU) will have a meaningful impact on UK's global economic and political relations for decades to come. But questions abound regarding Britain's future trade and security relationships including the UK's foreign policy priorities after Brexit. Most importantly, it remains unclear if the UK will be able to shape international outcomes or influence wider challenges relating to the global order. In the case of Iran, due to limited economic ties and tepid political relations, Brexit will not have a meaningful impact on bilateral Anglo-Iranian relations. Ironically though, to manage continued challenges stemming from Iran's regional role and ballistic missile and nuclear programmes, the UK must continue to work multilaterally with European and American partners.

In 1892, British politician Lord George Nathanial Curzon, who would then become Viceroy of India and foreign secretary, published his two volumes of *Persia and the Persian Question*[1] providing one of the first detailed studies of Iranian politics, society and culture. After travelling through Iran, Curzon saw Persia as geographically and strategically important for the UK's defence of India and containment of Russia. His contribution argued for developing a more engaged British policy in Iran setting in motion Britain's growing political and economic involvement in Iranian politics. At the same time though, Curzon was acutely aware of the limitations of foreign political investment in Persia presciently warning that 'colossal schemes for the swift regeneration of Persia ... will only end in fiasco'.[2] Over 100 years on from Curzon's advice Anglo-Iranian relations continue to be defined by similar tests. As the UK considers its post-Brexit foreign policy, relations with Iran remain a strategic challenge.

The impact of Great Britain's political and economic presence in Iran, which dates back centuries, and its interference in Iranian politics has undoubtedly negatively influenced relations from the Iranian side. Principally, Britain's hand in a number of Iranian domestic turning points, including in the 1953 coup against Iran's Prime Minister Mohammad Mossadegh, has not been forgotten. The outcome of the 1979 Iranian Revolution and the policies of the new revolutionary Islamic government have had equally detrimental consequences for the UK side. For four decades, relations have been repeatedly hampered by crises related to Iran's domestic and regional policies and over its nuclear programme. In reaction, the UK has downgraded relations with the

Islamic Republic three times over a forty-year period with the most recent incident taking place in 2011 after the storming of the UK embassy in Iran. These differences alongside contemporary domestic developments in the UK and Iran and the spillover effects of wider international and Middle Eastern politics have also constrained nascent opportunities for improved relations. The UK's participation and support for the Iran nuclear agreement or Joint Comprehensive Plan of Action (JCPOA) signed in 2015 was once such recent opportunity to build upon. Yet, ties between London and Tehran remain lukewarm and have been constrained by Brexit politics, Iran's foreign policy in the Middle East and exogenous factors on both sides.

While the UK does have bilateral ties with the Islamic Republic of Iran, these ties have been limited by diverging UK–Iranian regional interests and policies in the Middle East, contending international alliances, the lack of trust on both sides and the arc of their long history has since 1979 been punctuated by numerous crises. In response to these challenges, the UK has managed its Iran relationship in coordination with its allies. Here, the UK has maintained a bridging role implementing Iran policy in tandem with the United States and EU. Most recently, this was evidenced in the multilateral decade-long negotiations and sanctions policy that resulted in the JCPOA. It has also been visible since President Trump's withdrawal from the nuclear agreement where in tandem with its European partners, the UK has worked alongside France and Germany (together known as the E3) to protect the agreement. Maintaining this unique position could allow Britain to carve out a future bridging role for itself on Iran policy.

For the UK, Iran and the Iranian question are also intimately tied to the challenge of regional security and stability. Tehran's presence is visible in the conflict resolution and stabilization of Yemen, Syria, Lebanon and Iraq, relevant to the Middle East Peace Process and concerns over nuclear non-proliferation. Gulf security and threats from migration, humanitarian crises, counter terrorism and the regional spread of Covid-19 also share an Iranian dimension. Bearing in mind the Iranian nexus in these aforementioned issues, strategic opportunities for engagement focusing primarily on security and regional cooperation with Iran can also promote a wider strategic role for the UK in the Middle East. To be prepared for the impact of Brexit, the UK should craft an Iran policy that builds on its bilateral ties while also leveraging its multilateral coordination and shared policy interests with Europe and the United States. This position would enable Britain to balance economic opportunities against regional and security concerns towards Iran and the Middle East. Without such a policy in place, it is unclear if the UK will have the leverage and influence to engage in a meaningful way on regional issues.

A troubled history

British–Iranian relations have been coloured by a long history dating back as far as the thirteenth century. Reviewing some highlights of this history contextualizes the opportunities and challenges of the relationship amid the important shifts resulting in the decline of British influence within the Iranian sphere and the emergence of the

Iranian Revolution. What becomes clear from this review is the growth of indigenous nationalism against continued patterns of foreign interference. Important to this history is that as relations with Iran became strained, Britain's growing relationship and support of the Arab Gulf states grew in importance, adding to the current imbalance and challenges.

Early exploratory ties did not amount to meaningful diplomacy between Britain and Persia, but during the early Safavid dynasty (1501–1722) ties developed again as both sides sought alliances to curtail threats from the expansionist Ottoman Empire. The Qajar period (1789–1925) saw the development of commercial ties amid growing international rivalry between Great Britain and Russia.[3] Iran's borders were defined by military losses with both powers in this period fuelling anti-foreign sentiment. It signed the Treaty of Golestan in 1813 and Treaty of Turkomanchy in 1828 with Russia losing northern territory. After the Anglo-Persian war over Afghanistan, Tehran settled its eastern border in the 1857 Treaty of Paris.[4] The loss of territory to foreign powers was the first of many negative experiences that would come to determine Iran's defensive worldview that is relevant still today.

During this time, Britain's dominance was not limited to Persia, but extended throughout the Persian Gulf. Seeking to protect its trade routes and commercial interests, British policy was also focused on the Trucial states of the Arab Gulf.[5]

During the second half of the nineteenth century, the British strengthened their economic links to Persia by taking advantage of financial weaknesses of the Qajar kings. The discovery of vast quantities of oil in 1908 resulted in increased British involvement and interest in Persia as it acquired a majority of shares in the Anglo Persian Oil Company that would later become the Anglo-Iranian Oil Company (AIOC).[6] Growing political activism led to the 1905–11 Constitutional Revolution that sought to curtail monarchical influence through the creation of a constitution and a parliament.[7] Through this period, Britain continued to interfere in domestic Iranian politics, including supporting the coup that ended the Qajar dynasty, and saw Reza Shah institutionalize Pahlavi rule. Oil politics would become a defining theme of tensions leading to the renegotiation of Iran's oil concession and eventually the removal of Reza Shah from the throne.

Under the leadership of Mohammad Reza Shah and his nationalist Prime Minister Mohammad Mossadegh, oil politics would resurface as an important inflection point. Iran's parliament voted to nationalize its oil industry in 1950 setting in motion a direct Anglo-Iranian conflict.[8] Britain's refusal to negotiate resulted in an oil blockade and a growing fear that the crisis would impact Britain's foreign relations. British politicians, stoking fears of a Communist influence in Iran, began lobbying the newly elected Republican Eisenhower administration against Mossadegh. The result of this pressure was seen in the joint MI6-CIA executed plan, named Operation Ajax, that resulted in the overthrow of Mossadegh in 1953. The impact of the coup had dramatic consequences for political life in Iran. Mohammad Reza Shah saw the coup as an opportunity to claim authority in a more autocratic manner.[9] Despite re-establishing influence in Iran after the outcome of the coup, Britain did not emerge unscathed from the Mossadegh era. Within Iran, while Britain resumed its ties with Mohammad Reza Shah there was a widespread perception that the British were behind the coup. As reported, 'Britain is believed by all classes, down to the peasants, to support the shah and the government, and therefore, is held responsible for the ills of the country'.[10]

Over a decade later in 1968, Britain would announce its withdrawal of all troops East of Suez to take effect in 1971.[11] The decision was primarily economic as the British cabinet in the wake of a domestic crisis at home decided to cut military spending. While the British departure effectively ended Britain's role as 'arbiter and guardian of the Gulf', British influence did not diminish.[12] The immediate impact of this withdrawal policy did require Britain to balance its interests on both sides of the Persian Gulf. Britain had long implemented a policy that sought to maintain a balance of power between the regional heavyweights Iran and Saudi Arabia while protecting the region from Soviet encroachment.[13]

Revolutionary reverberations

The Iranian Revolution and the radical ideology of the new Islamic government drastically altered the dynamics of Anglo-Iranian relations. Because of past British history and support of the Shah, Ayatollah Khomeini saw the 'residual influence of Britain' as a threat to the revolution. The new government drawing from the historical precedent of past US and UK interventions in Iranian affairs feared the possibility of another Mossadegh-like coup. In revolutionary chants, the United States referred to as the 'Great Satan' was considered a primary threat for the new revolutionary government. Britain was afforded the secondary status of 'little Satan'. Seeking to maintain its independence and protect itself from foreign interference, Iran's foreign policy was defined by the concept of 'neither East nor West'.[14]

From this period onwards event-driven crises seen in a number of bilateral and multilateral conflicts would come to limit the contours of the UK–Iranian relationship. Tensions with the West over Iran's expansionist regional foreign policy would constrain relations between Iran and the UK. Alongside the repeated crises, thematic issues relating to Iran's policy of exporting the revolution, human rights, support for non-state actors beyond its borders and its ballistic and nuclear programme would further hinder the development of meaningful ties.

Iran's post-revolutionary system is managed by the Supreme Leader who has a mix of direct and indirect authority over the judiciary, executive branch, legislature, the armed forces, media and economic foundations. Under him, the political system is balanced between elected and unelected bodies of revolutionary elite that have contending views and political leanings. While no political parties exist in Iran, groups can be broken down into factions of conservatives, pragmatists and reformists – all of whom support the system of the Islamic Republic but have differing views on domestic and foreign policy. Conservatives remain steadfast in their commitment to the values and policies of the Iranian Revolution fearing that political compromise on social and domestic issues will erode their power. They too are deeply suspicious of Western powers believing that Western governments ultimately seek to change the regime in Tehran. On the other end of the spectrum, reformists aim to transform policies from within while pragmatic politicians have sought to pursue economic liberalization as a means of domestic and foreign policy reform. As opposed to conservatives, the latter groups have favoured stronger ties with Western governments and have led more open engagement initiatives.[15]

Electoral shifts between hard line and reformist governments have created political openings for engagement with Iran. Reformist Muhammad Khatami's tenure from 1997 to 2005 led to greater moderation of international ties while conversely hardliner conservative Mahmood Ahmadinejad's 2005 election gave rise to more confrontational policies. The 2009 Green Movement protests and government crackdown following the contested presidential elections also marred international tensions. Most notably, after eight years of rising international tensions over Iran's nuclear programme and the imposition of sanctions on Iran for its nuclear violations, the 2013 election of centrist Hassan Rouhani, who was widely supported by the population, gave rise to greater multilateral engagement and cooperation. The JCPOA was the most successful of such diplomatic initiatives.

As part of its policy, Iran has supported non-state actors and proxy groups such as Hezbollah and various militias in Iraq as a means to advance its interests and create leverage outside of its borders. This policy has brought Iran into direct and indirect confrontation with the US and European actors including the UK, Israel and the Arab Gulf states who see Iran has a destabilizing regional actor.[16]

To confront repeated regional security challenges, the UK developed its Iran policy in tandem with its European and American partners. Since 1979, US policy towards Iran has been based on a policy of containment. Europe's strategy however has been predicated on engagement and pressure. The UK has swung in between the two poles and worked with Europe and the United States to formulate a coordinated policy.[17] A first example of this was seen in 1979 when in reaction to the hostage taking and seizure of the US embassy, the UK closed its embassy in Tehran. Alongside its French and American allies, the UK supported Saddam Hussein, supplying him with military hardware in his eight-year war against Iran. The impact of the war left a defensive imprint on Tehran's worldview.[18]

Upon conclusion of the war in 1988, Britain reopened its Tehran embassy but relations were yet again ruptured by the Salman Rushdie affair and *fatwa* or ruling issued by Ayatollah Khomeini, ordering Muslims to kill Rushdie for blasphemy.[19] European allies also followed British suit withdrawing their ambassadors yet again. Despite attempts at resolving the crisis, tensions on both sides over the Rushdie affair effectively simmered until 1998 when Tehran agreed to no longer support the fatwa. For Britain and Europe, who coordinated closely, the Rushdie affair exposed their divide with Tehran over freedom of speech and liberal values. The group saw the issue of human rights violations as an area where they could collectively pressure Tehran. This extended to include Iran's violations in Europe where its intelligence operatives had been implicated for assassinations of Iranian dissidents.[20] The defence of these principles however hindered the growth of diplomatic and trade relations. Britain, because of its past patterns of interference in Iranian domestic politics, was impacted more so than its European counterparts.

Relations began to gradually improve after the 1997 election of Iranian Reformist President Muhammad Khatami. Khatami called for a dialogue of civilizations and gradual social and economic liberalizations in Iran. This shift in tone in Tehran was welcomed by the UK and many in the West hoped that Khatami would alter the dynamics in Iran's regional relations. Following 11 September and the US invasion of Afghanistan, British Foreign Secretary Jack Straw also visited Tehran in 2001 hoping that Iran would be a constructive partner. Trade between the two countries also improved, doubling from $305 million in 1999 to $734 million in 2006.[21] While Tehran proved to be instrumental in the war effort, promises of better ties soured when Tehran rejected the credentials of Ambassador David Reddaway in 2001 believing him to be a spy. Prince Charles also visited the Iranian city of Bam after the devastating 2004 earthquake. The US invasion of Iraq in 2003 coupled with British support for the United States brought the presence of US and UK forces in close proximity to Iran creating new sources of tension that would result in accusations of destabilizing Iranian activity.[22]

During the presidency of hardliner Mahmoud Ahmadinejad a number of crises stalled the limited progress made under Khatami's tenure. Ahmadinejad's tone and policies were more populist and conservative relative to his pro-engagement predecessor. Western policymakers' hopes that Iranian policy would moderate were equally dampened when Ahmadinejad resurrected Holocaust denial policies and called for 'Israel to be wiped off the map'.[23] The most important of the crises to emerge was the issue of Iran's nuclear programme, but a number of additional issues further compounded tensions between Tehran and Whitehall. In 2007, British sailors that inadvertently strayed into Iranian waters in the Aravand River were arrested by Tehran, although they were eventually released after an embarrassing public ceremony presided over by the president. The controversy of the 2009 presidential elections that saw massive protests throughout the country against government fraud proved another challenge for UK policymakers. Iran's Supreme Leader Ali Khamenei blamed 'arrogant powers' in the West for the unrest and even called the UK out as the 'most evil of those powers'.[24]

A further strain on ties since Brexit has been Iran's detainment policy of UK–Iranian dual nationals such as Nazanin Zaghari Ratcliffe who has been held in Iran since 2016. An estimated five other similar cases such as Anousheh Ashouri, Aras Amini, Kameel Ahmady, Morad Tahbaz and Kamal Foroughi have also been documented. Iran has, since 2007, systematically arrested dual nationals from many countries around the world. Tehran does not recognize dual nationality and does not allow for claims or consular support made by the other nationality. In November 2017, it was reported that over thirty dual nationals had been detained in Iran.[25] Human Rights Watch believes these are part of 'politically motivated arrests', in order to pressure foreign governments and use these individuals as leverage in wider negotiations.[26] Most of these individuals have been accused of espionage by IRGC-affiliated intelligence agencies resulting in lengthy prison sentences. Efforts by Boris Johnson and Jeremy Hunt to secure Zaghari-Ratcliffe's release, among others, have yet to yield results. In fact, in May 2019, the FCO warned Iranian British dual nationals against travel to Iran. Despite repeated Iranian government denials, some speculation suggests that the UK repayment of the 1971 Chieftain tanks case could help facilitate movement on the cases. The previous Iranian government purchased UK tanks without receipt of the bulk of the order and through the decades the Islamic Republic has been pursuing the case through the judicial process.[27] Repayment of the debt has been hampered by economic sanctions imposed by the Trump administration and wrangling over interest payments.

A growing pattern of Iranian-backed cyber-attacks has also strained ties. Cyber warfare has increased as Iran has been both a victim and an aggressor in cyber activities with the most prominent attack being the Stuxnet computer virus designed to stall operations at Iran's Natanz nuclear facility.[28] As part of its asymmetric leverage building, Tehran has stepped up cyber-attacks in response led by its IRGC-controlled cyber army since 2010. A 2019 postal service and local government attack and the 2017 parliamentary network attack are two examples where UK organizations have been exposed to the stealing of personal details of thousands of personnel.

The nuclear dossier, the JCPOA and maximum pressure

As stated above, during the presidencies of Khatami, Ahmadinejad and Rouhani, Iran's nuclear programme became the most critical issue defining Iran's relations with the UK, Europe and the United States. The background to the JCPOA, the content of the agreement itself and the current impasse with the United States and remaining signatories of the agreement provide a good case study in the potential opportunity and challenges facing the UK and Iran. Going forward, the fate of the nuclear deal will define future relations between Iran and the wider international community. These issues range from Iran's economic stability, trade potential, regional and maritime security challenges and prospects for counter-terrorism cooperation. However, despite these prospects, the Trump administration's maximum pressure campaign has negatively impacted Iran's regional posturing. It has also helped facilitate a conservative resurgence within Iran's political system. The outcome of both could forebode further nuclear and regional challenges. For post-Brexit Britain, the case of the JCPOA can enshrine Britain's bridging relationship between the European and American poles. In fact, Boris Johnson's government has considered this approach as an opportunity to incentivize all sides to come back to the negotiating table.

Despite active UK participation and investment in the Iran nuclear negotiations and the UK's commitment as a signatory to the JCPOA, the growth of UK–Iranian relations has been constrained by wider regional security challenges involving Iran and relations with the Arab Gulf. Iran's support for regional non-state actors such as Hezbollah in Lebanon, popular mobilization units (PMF) in Iraq, the Houthis in Yemen and assisting Bashar al-Assad in the Syrian civil war has long resulted in international criticism. Despite the expectation that the JCPOA would lead to the gradual moderation of Iran's 'malign' regional interference, Tehran became more regionally activist providing financial and military support to Assad in 2012, in the fight against ISIS in Iraq in 2014 and in the 2015 Yemen war. These activities heightened regional tensions particularly with Arab Gulf states who were not only incensed that they were not a party to the

JCPOA discussions, but also angered that regional issues were not included in the deal. President Obama's remark that 'our friends as well as … the Iranians … need to find an effective way to share the neighbourhood' added anxiety to the already complex security dynamics and competition between Tehran and Riyadh.[29]

Widespread Arab Gulf concern over the nuclear deal particularly from Saudi Arabia and the UAE has left the UK toeing a cautious line between supporting the JCPOA and contesting Iran's negative regional behaviour.[30] The UAE and Saudi's explicit support for President Trump's maximum pressure campaign has resulted in concerted lobbying efforts to sway Britain and European countries in their favour. The smaller GCC states of Kuwait, Qatar and Oman who have a history of pragmatic relations with Tehran however have favoured multilateral engagement. Here, the UK has sought to insulate and protect its relationship with the Arab Gulf by supporting the 2015 Saudi/Emirati war in Yemen, through arms sales to the Gulf states and bilateral ties in the hope that it can benefit from post-Brexit trade deals.

While balancing Gulf relationships has been a priority, bilateral trade between Britain and Iran has languished. The ongoing feelings of mistrust, the challenges of conducting business in Iran and the impact of US sanctions are all to blame for the limited commercial ties. In contrast to its E3 partners, France or Germany that had £3.8 billion and £3.5 billion worth of trade with Tehran, the UK's trade with Iran was estimated only at £860 million.[31] Unlike its French or German counterparts, British businesses had not returned to post-revolutionary Iran once diplomatic ties were restored after the war years. That said, transport, aviation, financial services, technology, telecommunication, pharmaceutical and retail sectors all made entries into the Iranian economy after the signing of the JCPOA. British Airways restored direct flights to and from Tehran in August 2016 as a signal of rising British commercial interest in the Iranian market.

British companies, however, struggled to finalize contracts with local partners in Iran due to sanctions compliance. The long due diligence process required businesses to avoid commercial engagement with Iranian companies affiliated with groups and entities, such as the IRGC, that were still subject to US non-nuclear sanctions. At the same time, the residual impact of snapback sanctions alongside US non-nuclear sanctions also led to limited financing opportunities and the reluctance of banks, who feared penalties and fines, to process transactions. Moreover, Theresa May's government, while rhetorically supportive of British commercial engagement, did not provide the political and financial backing, such as comfort letters to UK banks, that could have facilitated the growth of economic ties. Taken together, these issues placed the UK at a disadvantage relative to its European partners.

The decision by President Trump to pull out of the JCPOA in May 2018 – despite the E3's last-minute efforts to persuade the Trump administration to the contrary – left the UK government at odds with the United States and in the ironic position of working with the EU27 and Russia and China to save the agreement. The stated goal of the Trump administration has been to bring Iran back to the negotiating table.[32] Some analysts suspect that some members of the administration such as former National Security Advisor John Bolton and Secretary of State Mike Pompeo sought regime change or regime instability. European and British officials, fearing a repeat of the 2003 Iraq War, also expressed concerns over the lack of clarity of US objectives.

In November of 2018, US nuclear sanctions were re-imposed impacting Iran's energy sector as well as placing blocks on Iran's ability to connect to international banking. In turn, European and British companies withdrew from the Iranian market. British Airways indefinitely suspended its flights and business travel collapsed under the expectation that tensions would escalate and business interests could not be insulated or sustained. Subsequent sanctions were gradually imposed on Iran's petrochemical, mining, textile, copper and aluminium sectors as well as on individuals such as Iran's Foreign Minister Mohammad Javad Zarif and institutions such as the IRGC that were designated a foreign terrorist organization.[33]

Despite US pressure to follow suit in withdrawing from the JCPOA and efforts by the Trump administration to break E3 unity, the E3 has remained committed to the JCPOA. The British government has also not faltered in its adherence to the nuclear agreement. First, the European Union passed a blocking statute to allow companies to recover damages from the extraterritoriality of US sanctions. This move was purely symbolic though because the bloc could also not compel the private sector to continue to conduct business in Iran. The creation of INSTEX, a special-purpose vehicle, to facilitate trade between Iran and the EU is one important effort created to defend the deal.[34] INSTEX, however, took over a year to become operational leading to tensions and pressure tactics between Tehran and Europe. Iran, through this period, began to incrementally breach its nuclear commitments placing the burden of saving the JCPOA on the E3 by demanding incentives in exchange for its compliance. French president Emanuel Macron led E3 efforts in September 2019 to facilitate negotiations between Tehran and Washington. Throughout this period, Tehran insisted that it would only return to the negotiating table when the United States offered sanctions relief. The failure of that initiative resulted in further nuclear breaches, including Iran's resumption of enrichment processing at its Fordow facility.[35]

In January 2020, the E3 triggered the JCPOA's dispute resolution mechanism – a process designed to resolve compliance and implementation issues. Despite further threats and pressure from the Trump administration that was seeking Iran's referral to the United Nations Security Council (UNSC) and the return of snapback sanctions, the E3 issued a statement affirming that they were 'not joining a campaign to implement maximum pressure against Iran' and that they remained committed to the JCPOA.[36] Furthermore, the three countries agreed to continue to postpone dates and time limits to delay the UNSC process. Should Iran refrain from further breaches, it is expected that this postponement strategy will continue until the outcome of the 3 November 2020 US election is determined.

At the same time, the US decision placed the UK, who was seeking to build stronger post-Brexit trading relationships, in a particularly cautious position in its courting of Washington and Riyadh. The British prime minister Theresa May during her visit to the Gulf in December 2016, sought 'to assure … that I am clear-eyed about the threat that Iran poses to the Gulf and the wider Middle East; and the UK is fully committed to our strategic partnership with the Gulf and working with you to counter that threat'.[37]

To compensate, the UK has supported the 2015 Saudi-Emirati war in Yemen and continued to overlook Saudi human rights violations for the benefit of the commercial and security-based relations.[38]

During the summer months of 2019 though, the UK bridging strategy was under pressure when Iran began to escalate in a number of regional theatres. These escalations were designed to push back against the Trump administration's decision to halt oil waivers that allowed Iran to export limited oil to a number of designated countries. As such, in May 2019, Iran began to seize, attack and disrupt the transit of tankers through the Straits of Hormuz. In June, Iran downed an American drone raising fears of direct kinetic action between the two sides. In response to these events, the United States and the UK increased their military presence in the Persian Gulf. The British government also responded to an American request to detain an Iranian tanker, the Grace 1, off the coast of Gibraltar that was believed to be delivering oil to EU-sanctioned Syria. This event resulted in Iran's seizure of a British maritime ship, the *Stena Impero*, in the Straits. After weeks of negotiation, both ships were eventually released but the British government was heavily criticized for aiding American Iran policy. Nevertheless, the UK began to collaborate with the United States over maritime security issues and joined the US naval security mission in the Persian Gulf to protect shipping.[39] European countries, however, in an effort to protect the JCPOA, chose to distance themselves from the US mission and instead have organized their own EU maritime security initiative.[40]

Iran's aggression through its support for non-state actors also continued to increase through this period. Because Tehran was not directly involved in these strikes, it could operate under the shield of plausible deniability. The Houthis in Yemen persisted in their military campaign against the Saudi–Emirati coalition and continued firing ballistic missiles at Saudi targets. Events escalated further when Saudi oil facilities Abqaiq and Khurais were attacked on 14 September using drone and cruise missiles. Although the Houthis claimed responsibility for these attacks, it was widely believed that Iran was responsible for this brazen operation. Boris Johnson ahead of his trip to the United Nations stated, 'I can tell you that the UK is attributing responsibility with a very high degree of probability to Iran for the Aramco attacks. We think it very likely indeed that Iran was indeed responsible, using both drones and cruise missiles.'[41] While directly implicating Tehran, Johnson also stressed his desire to avoid any escalation, stating he believed the UK's role would be 'serving as a bridge between our European friends and the Americans' on the issue.[42]

Iranian-backed militias in Iraq also pursued similar strategies that escalated in December 2019 when attacks on a US base resulted in the death of an American contractor. The Trump administration, which had yet to militarily respond to Iranian indirect and direct provocations, had long stated that the loss of American life was its clear red line. In response, Washington hit back against the PMU group Khataib Hezbollah's depots and command centre in Iraq and Syria, a move that led PMU groups to attack the US embassy in Baghdad. Events spiralled further when on 3 January 2020 President Trump issued an order resulting in the killing of Iran's influential Qods force commander Qassem Soleimani. Iraqi PMU leader Abu Mahdi al Muhandis was killed alongside Soleimani. The strike caused much anxiety about the prospect of direct war between Iran and the United States. European countries and the UK, who were not informed of the operation and have long felt frustrated that maximum pressure would pose direct challenges for their own security presence in the Middle East, issued muted statements expressing concern for regional stability alongside calls for de-escalation. While vowing to seek revenge for Soleimani's death, Tehran responded by attacking a US military base in Iraq also giving advance warning to prevent further loss of American life. In choosing this path, Tehran signalled that it was de-escalating in this instance, but that further strikes would continue.

The outbreak of Covid-19 in Iran has posed additional domestic challenges for the Iranian government and its ability to stem the spread of the virus. It has not however altered Tehran's regional strategy or effort to resist the Trump administration's policies. Under pressure from the impact of sanctions, the government response was belated and subject to domestic infighting. At the same time, the Rouhani administration argued that US sanctions have impeded their ability to respond quickly and effectively. To manage the economic challenges, Iran requested $5 billion from the IMF.[43] This is Iran's first such request since 1962. Because of the fiscal constraints brought on by declining revenue from exports, Iran was not able to provide economic relief packages similar to those provided by European or Arab Gulf states. Additionally, unable to access its foreign reserves to purchase additional medical equipment, the Rouhani administration lobbied the E3 for sanctions relief on the basis of humanitarian concerns. Regional countries such as the UAE, Qatar and Turkey provided Iran with support.[44] The E3, unlike the Trump administration, did send Iran $5 million in financial and material relief to assist the internal effort to fight Covid highlighting their distinct strategy designed to protect the JCPOA and facilitate engagement. Here again, Britain has remained a committed partner to this agenda. Going forward, health diplomacy and humanitarian support for Covid can be an important part of the UK's Iran strategy.

Post-Brexit recommendations: Balancing and bridging

The uncertain future of the JCPOA presents an opportunity to develop a UK-led long-term wider engagement strategy that includes both Tehran and the region. The November 2020 US presidential election of Joe Biden offers an off-ramp and reset of the trajectory of tensions with Tehran. Biden has declared his intent to re-enter the JCPOA and build wider regional discussions to address Iran's regional role and missile programme alongside wider regional stability. For this process to succeed the support of the E3 is critical. Future nuclear negotiations with Iran could also facilitate a bilateral UK–Iranian dialogue that would be important to address mutual political, economic, security concerns. Going forward, the UK should consider the opportunities and relevance of bridging the gaps and facilitating talks between all sides. As President Macron's initiative to jumpstart talks failed, there remains an opportunity for Boris Johnson to display his leadership, and strong personal ties with the United States to bridge the divides.

Since the US withdrawal from the JCPOA, the UK's strong defence of the nuclear agreement alongside its EU partners opens the door to wider engagement efforts with

Tehran. While it is unclear if the UK or EU will be able to prevent the collapse of the JCPOA, the UK's symbolic political support is seen as an important signal in Tehran, allowing the UK to maintain dialogue with the Iranian political establishment. The issue of nuclear non-proliferation and the creation of a nuclear-free Middle East is one area where Tehran will be eager to continue discussions. All parties including the UK have suggested that a new version of the Iran nuclear agreement could be the outcome of such future discussions. Important for the UK, alongside France and Germany, though is the protection of non-proliferation principles, controlling Iran's nuclear enrichment programme, and maintaining IAEA access and monitoring. Beyond these elements, a new deal could try and address Iran's ballistic missile programme and regional interference. These later issues would require a multilateral regional solution that would extend beyond the case of Iran and require other regional players to make similar concessions. There is an opportunity for the UK to leverage its regional ties to Gulf states in these discussions.

Simultaneously, the UK could continue its work in partnership with its E3 partners, Germany and France, to engage Iran multilaterally to address the challenges of regional security in the Middle East. In the context of the JCPOA and regional de-escalation, the UK can continue to seek out political solutions serving as a bridge between Washington, Israel, Gulf states and Tehran. Including Iran in conflict de-escalation and post-conflict de-militarization plans in Iraq, Syria and Yemen would be an important strategy to avoid Iran playing its traditional role as the regional spoiler. Covid-19 is also an important entry point for regional discussions. Enlisting Iranian assistance and cooperation on ongoing counter terror issues with the potential resurgence of ISIS is also necessary.

Through the prism of regional security dialogue, the UK should work alongside its EU partners to promote solutions to regional wars in Yemen and Syria and build multilateral discussions around maritime security alongside other common areas of regional importance such as health cooperation, climate change and human rights. Iranian participation and acceptance of negotiated solutions in these discussions are essential for long-term stability. A longer-term strategy would focus regional partners including Iran to build a sustainable regional security architecture shepherded by the UK and EU.

Within the context of US nuclear sanctions, it has been very difficult for the UK to build on its current levels of investment in any meaningful way. Nevertheless, the UK should consider Iran, with its population of 82 million and middle-class-dominated consumer market, as a long-term investment opportunity. The economic damage from Covid and from sanctions could herald more commercial engagement. A diverse array of UK companies ranging from pharmaceutical, auto, retail, to the telecom sector and energy has expressed interest in the Iranian market. The potential to capitalize on a future bilateral trading relationship would benefit post-Brexit Britain. Doing so, however, would require a political commitment from the UK government to support the development of business ties. A bilateral dialogue between Tehran and Whitehall to discuss and address wider political and security issues would be a first step to resolving mistrust, addressing Iranian detainment of dual nationals and finding common ground in areas of economic development and regional security.

Due to its tenuous history with Tehran, there are indeed limitations to consider. Above all, it is unlikely that the UK will be able to build a robust relationship with the Islamic Republic of Iran (IRI) in the short term. Moreover, as an outcome of maximum pressure, Iranian conservatives have been gaining political ground at the expense of reformists. A conservative presidential victory in 2021 would result in a conservative monopoly of formal and informal institutions in the country. That outcome would fortify Iran's resistance worldview and harden the tone and tenor of Iranian policy vis-à-vis the international community. However, to create a thriving 'Global Britain', the UK should pursue a policy of engagement with the Tehran on issues of mutual concern such as regional security, counter-terrorism, nuclear security, investment and domestic governance. Moreover, regional stability and challenges stemming from terrorism, development, governance and human rights can serve as consistent themes for wider regional engagement. Leading discussions and elevating these issues could provide the UK a new platform to take a larger role in solving regional security issues, while also advancing its own interests and overturning the years of crisis-driven history between both countries.

Part Four

Britain and the Middle Eastern Arab states

11

Syria and the Levant

Christopher Phillips

With the outbreak of civil war in Syria in 2011, Britain significantly increased its interest and activity in the Levant.[1] The conflict and its regional consequences, notably the refugee crisis and the rise of ISIS, prompted the UK to significantly step up the money, resources and personnel dedicated to the region. However, this increased attention did not translate into increased influence. Indeed, events in the Levant combined with wider regional and global trends saw Britain's importance diminish. Moreover, despite this investment, the UK did not accomplish its primary goal in Syria – the toppling of President Bashar al-Assad – although a later goal of defeating ISIS was achieved. This chapter explores the reasons for the UK's failures in Syria. It considers how Britain's other Levantine relationships, with Jordan and Lebanon, were impacted by the conflict, before looking at the coming challenges the UK is likely to face in the region in the future. In doing so, it suggests that Britain might benefit from accepting its limited leverage in Syria, and instead focus on areas it has more influence: Lebanon and, particularly its long-standing ally, Jordan.

Broad goals, limited capacity

One of the ironies of Syria's conflict is that it reversed Britain's traditional focus in the Levant. Historically, Britain had far less interest, influence or involvement with Syria than with either Jordan or Lebanon. On the eve of Syria's uprising, Britain approached the Levant with limited capacity. The austerity of the 2010–15 Coalition government combined with war weariness after the UK's involvement in Iraq and Afghanistan limited Britain's military capability, which was already reluctant to act independently of the United States. Its diplomats were capable but similarly tended to echo Washington's policies in the Levant. Meanwhile its economic footprint, especially in Syria, was negligible – in 2010 it imported $142 million from Syria, exporting $229 million.[2] Unsurprisingly the UK's interests were limited to the core goals of security and trade, although the Levant fell behind other MENA regions in terms of priority. Secondary goals included how Syria, Jordan and Lebanon fitted into wider strategic calculations, notably supporting Israel and containing Iran, and promoting values such as human rights, state-building and democracy, though these were declining in importance.

Britain, along with its Western allies, was conscious of the potential security threats emerging from Syria when unrest broke out there in March 2011. Diplomats in Damascus warned of the risk that sectarian conflict, Jihadism, chemical weapons usage and proliferation and regional instability could also all be triggered.[3] Nevertheless, after a few months of caution, London switched to a more hawkish tone in response to Assad's brutal crackdown. In August 2011, the UK, along with the United States, France, Germany and Canada, formally declared regime change in Damascus as their policy, calling on Assad to 'stand aside'. Such a statement suggested that values – human rights and democracy promotion – were taking precedence over the potential security threats flagged. Yet Britain's capacity to act remained limited: it was militarily ineffective without the United States, as seen in the strikes on Libya a few months earlier – Washington having to take charge despite hoping to 'lead from behind' France and Britain. Similarly, the UK had limited economic levers to pull in Syria. Economic sanctions against Assad, partly initiated by London, were not as effective as hoped because Syria was not well integrated into Western economies.

So why did Britain set out a policy in August 2011, potentially against its security interests that it had limited capacity to achieve? Firstly Britain, like its Western allies, misjudged the situation in Syria. Cameron, like Obama and other Western leaders, believed that Assad's fall was inevitable and that he would fall quickly – long before any of the potential security threats came about. Having been slow in recent popular revolutions in Tunisia and Egypt, calling for Assad's departure would put them on the 'right side of history' without requiring a significant military intervention. Secondly, Cameron specifically misjudged Barack Obama, believing that, in the event Assad did not fall quickly and the killing continued, the US president would eventually authorize military intervention as he had done in Libya. Thirdly, Cameron and his government appeared to prioritize short-term domestic and international pressure to act, especially from Gulf allies, over long-term strategic consideration. This was what one British diplomat called 'the escalator of pressure': for politicians to be seen to be doing something in the face of Assad's brutality, while at the same time being unwilling or unable to actually prevent him.[4] This led to an incremental set of diplomatic, economic and eventually military actions, of which announcing regime change as policy was one measure. However, this was primarily to ward off domestic and foreign criticism and wasn't accompanied by a set of measures to actually bring it about.

Failing in Syria

In many ways Britain was trapped by its own hawkish rhetoric in Syria: it was committed to overthrowing Assad but incapable of doing so. In the early years of the conflict, Britain was a leader of the Western international community's diplomatic opposition to Assad: leading EU economic sanctions; pursuing resolutions at the UNSC; pushing for chemical weapons inspectors to enter Syria; supporting peace negotiations at Geneva; and, on several occasions, Cameron urging Obama personally to do more. It also dedicated funds to backing Syria's political opposition and supplied non-lethal support to the 'moderate' armed rebels. By 2016, the UK had spent over £100 million on non-humanitarian support to Syria, Jordan and Lebanon, with the Syrian segment directed to opposition forces. This included training and equipment for rebel fighters based in Jordan at the Moderate Armed Opposition (MAO) command centre, and rebel civilian initiatives such as the Syria Civil Defence rescue service and the Free Syrian Police.[5] The UK also took the lead among Western diplomats in training and supporting the Syrian Opposition Coalition (SOC), which it recognized as the 'sole legitimate representative of the Syrian people' in November 2012, soon after it was formed.

Yet these efforts failed. Assad and his regime proved to be able to withstand Western sanctions and they prompted neither economic collapse nor an internal coup as Britain had hoped.[6] Russia protected Damascus at the UN, vetoing all Security Council resolutions that threatened Assad. Britain also failed to persuade Obama to act unilaterally. Cameron saw his personal appeals to Obama repeatedly be rebuffed and, by Autumn 2012, told advisers that he had raised the point but couldn't see the president moving forward.[7] To his frustration, on the one occasion when Obama did seriously entertain direct attacks on Assad after he allegedly used chemical weapons in August 2013, the prime minister mismanaged the related vote in parliament, who opted not to join any strikes. Obama then decided to delay and ultimately agreed a peaceful means with Russia to remove Assad's chemical weapons stockpile.

At the same time, the opposition inside Syria fractured and radicalized. The UK, United States and France had informally agreed that their regional allies, Saudi Arabia, Turkey and Qatar, would lead the provision of lethal aid to rebel forces, while they would offer only non-lethal means.[8] Yet these regional powers backed multiple groups, including some radicals, contributing to divisions. This was possibly inevitable given the ideological and geographical differences among the rebels. However, by the time the United States reversed its position and began to send weapons, with British logistical support, the palatable 'moderate' rebels were too weak to realistically overcome either the radical Jihadist rebels or Assad. Arguably, however, earlier Western support would have still been insufficient as Assad's own external allies, Russia and Iran, ultimately offered him far more military and economic support than any friend of the opposition, enabling his survival.

As it became clear that Assad's departure was not guaranteed and Syria was descending into a long and brutal civil war, the consequences shifted Britain's priorities. While toppling Assad remained official policy, resources were directed more towards core security concerns. Two arguably foreseeable worries came to dominate: the humanitarian crisis and the rise of Jihadism in Syria. Refugees had been pouring out of Syria into neighbouring countries since 2012, but the British public became alerted to the crisis when hundreds of thousands of migrants headed to Europe. By late 2018, the UN stated that 13.1 million people inside Syria were in need, while a further 5.6 million had fled as refugees – making over 80 per cent of the pre-war population combined. At the time the UK was one of only six countries that met the UN target of giving 0.7 per cent of national income to overseas development aid, and already a major donor to Syrian refugees, but the 2015 European refugee crisis increased pressure to do more. From 2012 to 2018 it committed £2.46 billion to the humanitarian crisis, the second largest donor behind the United States. According to DFID in 2018, £897 million of this went to projects inside Syria or across its borders, while £543 million went to Lebanon, £441 million to Jordan, £319 million to Turkey and £19 million to Iraq.[9] That said, London was also criticized for being willing to take only 20,000 Syrian refugees into the UK by 2020, compared to more accommodating European neighbours Germany and Sweden, which took 600,000 and 110,000 respectively.

The other emerging threat was Jihadism. After ISIS captured Mosul in 2014 and declared its 'Caliphate', the UK was quick to join the US-led anti-ISIS coalition, Operation Inherent Resolve. While Britain's involvement was initially limited to Iraq, it joined operations in Syria in late 2015 in response to an ISIS-inspired terror attack in Paris, this time benefitting from Cameron's new majority in Parliament. The UK claimed in early 2019 to have launched over 1,600 airstrikes against ISIS in Iraq and Syria, second only to the United States within the coalition – although still representing under 5 per cent of all attacks.[10] As well as taking part in airstrikes, the UK deployed military personnel, over 600 in total, to train anti-ISIS forces on the ground. While the majority of these went to train the Iraqi military, some special forces were deployed to Syria to aid the Kurdish-dominated Syrian Democratic Forces (SDF) coalition that the United States developed as its principal anti-ISIS Syrian ally. The total cost of this was relatively modest: £200 million in 2014/15, rising to a peak of £500 million in 2017–18, considerably less than military operations in the past, notably the £4.8 billion spent in 2009–10 at the peak of the Afghanistan campaign.[11] However, it is notable that the money the UK committed to the anti-Assad rebels (£100 million by 2016) was barely a fraction of the huge sums spent on the consequences of the Syria war – £2.46 billion on humanitarian aid and £200–300 million per year on counter-ISIS activities.

Herein perhaps lies the irony of the UK's Syria policy since 2011. Based on a combination of miscalculation and domestic and international pressure, it set itself the goal of toppling Assad in 2011 yet lacked the capacity to achieve it alone and couldn't persuade the United States to act. Instead, London contributed to fuelling the conflict – giving the opposition sufficient resources to fight but not enough to win, especially when Assad's allies waded in to help him. Yet the consequences of the conflict – foreseeable shocks such as refugee crises and the rise of jihadism – have consumed even more UK resources. London and its allies have had some successes with these consequences. The anti-ISIS campaign was successful, and the so-called 'Caliphate' was destroyed by Western bombers and Kurdish forces, with its last formal territory captured in March 2019, and the 'Caliph' Abu-Bakr al-Baghdadi killed the following October. The refugee crisis, however, remained unresolved and, with Assad emerging from the war victorious, it seems likely that many won't return. On balance, the Syria conflict weakened the UK's overall security interests: ISIS was defeated but it or other Jihadists could yet re-emerge, and the refugee crisis is far from over. At the same time the values-based goals that initially drove UK policy, human rights and democracy have weakened. Its geopolitical position is also weaker, with its rivals Russia and Iran stronger after their involvement in Syria. Britain has little to show for its considerable involvement in Syria. If anything, the war helped accelerate Britain's (and its Western allies') diminishing regional influence.

Jordan and Lebanon

Jordan is Britain's oldest ally in the Levant. Independence in 1946 was not accompanied by hostility towards the former colonial ruler and, aside from occasional contretemps, London and Amman remained close. While the United States and Saudi Arabia are Jordan's most essential allies, providing vital economic and security support, the UK occupies a unique position of closeness compared to other European powers. At an elite level, the Hashemite and Windsor royal houses have been historically close, with King Abdullah of Jordan regularly emphasizing the common ties of monarchy and the personal links they have brought.[12] Institutionally this is supported by a close security relationship, particularly at the senior level with Jordanian military officers regularly training at Sandhurst, including King Abdullah and his son Crown Prince Hussein. Security has been at the centre of Britain's approach to Jordan in recent years, particularly the fallout from the Syria conflict. The UK gifted military vehicles worth nearly £400,000 in 2015, a further £600,000 in 2017 for training for the Jordanian Armed Forces and then £5 million in military equipment in 2018, all aimed at securing the Jordan–Syria border.[13] The UK dispatched further military trainers to Jordan as part of the anti-ISIS campaign, though the UK military has historically held several exercises in Jordan each year anyway, including four in 2017 alone.

Related to this, by far the UK's greatest concern in Jordan was the refugee crisis caused by Syria's war. The UK spent $750 million in Jordan alone. As well as deflecting international criticism for the small number of refugees taken in by Britain, there was also a security logic: improving conditions for refugees in neighbouring states to deter them from either turning to radicalism or fleeing to Europe. The Jordanian government was careful to minimize social tension caused by the large Syrian presence – over 670,000 registered refugees, more than 10 per cent of Jordan's population. The UK agreed along with other donors to the 2016 EU–Jordan compact and other measures that ensured considerable funding was diverted to provide jobs and opportunities for Jordanians as well as Syrian refugees in Jordan.

Beyond security and the related issue of refugees, the UK's other priorities have rarely driven policy towards Jordan. Trade is negligible. In 2017 the UK imported barely $45 million worth of goods from Jordan, mostly agricultural products and textiles, representing 0.56 per cent of Jordan's exports. Similarly, UK exports to Jordan were $426 million, 2.1 per cent of Jordan's imports, mostly a mixture of refined oil, cars and other manufactured goods.[14] Britain has shown enthusiasm for Jordanian state-building, committing £60 million in 2017 to support infrastructure building, skills training and education.[15] However, this is proportionally little more than the €335 million–€410 million promised by the EU over 2017–20 for similar projects and is unlikely to give Britain particular influence in this field.[16]

In terms of democracy and human rights, the UK repeatedly vocalizes its support for these principles, as it has for much of Jordan's history. However, while Jordan is less repressive than many of its neighbours, on many occasions when it has violated these norms, such as cracking down on public protest or utilizing torture, the UK has done little beyond statements of regret and not cancelled its close cooperation. Minor victories have been won, such as the Abu Qatada case when London obtained a guarantee from Amman to not use evidence obtained under torture to prosecute an alleged jihadi preacher being extradited from the UK.[17] However, such incidents have done little to nudge Jordan towards improved human rights and the UK shows little interest in cashing in its limited leverage for this issue.

The UK's relations with Lebanon are more complex as Lebanon falls less clearly into the Western orbit than Jordan. Western states and their Middle Eastern allies have long had to contend with Syria and Iran for influence over several players within Lebanon's confessional politics. At the same time, the confessional system and heavy influence of external powers have contributed to an inherently weak central government, further limiting the effectiveness of any British influence over Beirut anyway. Historically, Britain has been behind the United States and France in terms of Western influence in Lebanon, though it has still sought to be involved in several areas to maximize its limited power.

The UK's main avenue of support is via the military, the Lebanese Armed Forces (LAF), a weak force in regional terms but widely regarded as one of Lebanon's few functioning national institutions. Western support not only encourages state-building but also serves a geopolitical goal: though the LAF takes a neutral stance in national politics, it is widely considered the only plausible balance in Lebanon against the Iranian-backed militia, Hezbollah. Even before the Syria crisis, the UK had committed with the United States to train the LAF, spending £63 million since 2010 and claiming to have trained over 10,000 Lebanese soldiers by 2019. The outbreak of the Syria war amplified the LAF's importance to Western governments – firstly, in preventing the growing violence in Syria spilling into Lebanon, especially after Hezbollah sent fighters to help Assad, riling Lebanese Sunnis sympathetic to the Syrian opposition; secondly, in the anti-ISIS campaign: keeping ISIS and other Jihadists like *Jubhat al-Nusra* from crossing the porous mountain border from Syria into Lebanon. In this latter goal, Britain helped establish, mentor and fund the LAF's new Land Border Regiments.

The other major fallout from Syria in Lebanon, the refugee crisis, was complicated by the particularities of Lebanese politics. The UK and other EU states were able to negotiate the EU–Jordan compact to ensure that at least some Syrian refugees in Jordan could enter the Jordanian labour market and education system. Yet in Lebanon, which received over a million refugees, adding 25 per cent to the population, the weak government, confessional divisions and the unresolved position of earlier Palestinian refugees meant no such agreement was possible. Western governments were able to fund services for the refugees, but little progress was made on integration, bringing the risk that they will be the source of future security concerns.[18]

Beyond security and geostrategy, the UK's influence in Lebanon is marginal. The trade relationship is small. In 2017 the UK imported $45.5 million worth of goods from Lebanon, representing 1.2 per cent of Lebanon's exports, primarily agricultural products and clothing. The UK's exports to Lebanon were $474 million, 2.3 per cent of Lebanon's imports, the largest orders being cars, manufactured goods, food and medicine.[19] In terms of promoting state-building beyond the military, the UK has been active in post-conflict schemes such as de-mining south Lebanon and other areas. Similarly, it has sponsored economic development programmes, committing £40 million to one such scheme in 2018. Yet as with Jordan, this is no more pronounced than other Western states. The EU, for example, promised €186.5 million–€227.9 million for economic development schemes from 2017 to 2020.[20]

Democracy promotion and human rights are welcomed by the UK government, but seemingly as an afterthought rather than a driver. For example, UK ministers made a point of insisting the LAF forces it supported were 'in line with agreed international human rights standards'.[21] Similarly the UK welcomed the formation of a government in February 2019, nine months after Lebanon's first parliamentary elections since 2009, even though it included Hezbollah and was dominated by pro-Iranian groups.[22] Conversely a few weeks later, the then British Home Secretary Sajid Javid, endorsed by parliament, surprisingly decided to outlaw Hezbollah's political wing in the UK. This may complicate the UK's engagement with the government and seemed driven by Mr Javid's desire to appeal to domestic hardliners and the anti-Iran instincts of the Trump administration. These two seemingly contradictory episodes might suggest that while the desire for stability evidently trumped values, ultimately all are sacrificed for immediate domestic and geopolitics. Except when it is overruled by external priorities, security will likely remain the primary driver of UK–Lebanon policy. However, unlike in Jordan, where it occupies a unique position due to its history and deep institutional ties, in Lebanon the UK remains just one of many Western players who, as a bloc, are losing influence.

Future challenges

Looking forward, the Levant looks set for continued instability and possibly further conflict in the next decade. Lebanon, Jordan and Syria can all be considered weak states that suffer from some or all of the trends that led to the Arab uprisings: poverty, lack of employment, demographic bulges, autocratic government and poor governance. The ruling elites will no doubt try to mitigate and minimize instability caused by these issues but, based on their past record, it seems unlikely any will attempt wholesale reforms to seek a permanent solution. Of the three, Syria looks most unstable, with recovery from its civil war likely to take years, and a good possibility that fighting could return. Jordan looks the most stable, though just because it has avoided recent crises does not mean that problems will remain below the surface. Lebanon seems too war-weary to return to the civil strife of 1975–90 yet also too internally divided to properly move forward and could yet be destabilized by a new round of Hezbollah–Israeli conflict. The Lebanese protest movement that emerged in 2019–20 highlighted these problems. The state's incompetence and inability to deliver prompted unrest, galvanized by the negligence that led to a horrific explosion in Beirut port in August 2020 that destroyed much of the city's downtown. Despite this, the political leadership proved incapable of meaningful reform while the demonstrators appeared unable to translate grassroots activism into political outcomes. Spikes in the Covid-19 crisis interrupted these protests but the tensions remained and looked set to continue.

Though these problems seem familiar, the region has changed since 2011 and the UK must adjust its policies accordingly. Britain has less influence than in the past and policymakers must limit their ambitions, while also identifying particular areas where

London does have leverage and can reap rewards. Both the regional and international orders have changed from a US-dominated order to a one of multipolarity. Western power is weaker globally, and, specifically in the Levant, the UK's rivals have increased their influence. Russia and Iran are the dominant external players in Syria, with Turkey holding some sway near its border. The delicate balance of external influence in Lebanon has tilted more towards Tehran than UK allies like the United States and Saudi Arabia, while Russia is also becoming more influential. Jordan meanwhile remains firmly in the Western/Saudi orbit, though it too has increased contacts with Moscow since its involvement in Syria. Given their weakness all three states can expect to be an arena for competition between regional and international players. With the West weaker in general and Britain in particular due to Brexit, this high state of competition is likely to make it difficult for the UK to amplify its influence beyond broad support for its US and EU allies. Given this, the Levant might prove a good place to focus on depth rather than breadth: focusing attention in a few limited areas, with Jordan the most obvious candidate.

Security is likely to remain at the top of Britain's Levantine priority list. While ISIS's physical 'Caliphate' has been destroyed in Iraq and Syria, Jihadist ideology has not been defeated. As ISIS fell several hundred fighters melted away into the Iraqi and Syrian countryside and could return. Meanwhile a further Jihadist threat, *Hayat Tahrir as-Sham*, the latest incarnation of Al-Qaeda's *Jubhat al-Nusra* could similarly transform itself into a transnational cell-based actor if Assad and Russia eventually conquer its current Idlib base. Jihadist cells have launched multiple attacks across Syria for years and these will likely continue. Lone attacks might also be launched in Jordan and Lebanon, though it seems unlikely any will be able to construct significant levels of support and pose a major threat to the Lebanese, Jordanian or Syrian governments. A significant worry for the UK in the medium term is that former British ISIS recruits could find a way home undetected and launch or inspire attacks, and the UK has sought to detect and prevent this. A more long-term problem is the spectre of Jihadism re-emerging in the Levant, especially if the weak governments continue to neglect vulnerable and impressionable members of the population. Past precedents, such as the growth of the Taliban from Afghan refugees in Pakistan or Palestinian militants emerging from squalid camps in Lebanon and Jordan, suggest that Syria's refugees are particularly at risk of radicalization. While the UK has spent considerable resources on refugees, this has still been insufficient, especially in Lebanon, and preventing the emergence of a new generation of jihadists or other radicals among refugees will be a major challenge. There is a particular danger that, when the 'next' international crisis takes attention elsewhere, the UK and other donors cut funding to Syria's refugees. The Covid-19 crisis, for example, prompted cuts to international aid budgets, with the UK signalling in 2020 it will cut its aid from 0.7 per cent to 0.5 per cent of GDP. However, as was seen with the Syria crisis, prevention is often less costly than waiting for symptoms to emerge.

In contrast, UK trade to the Levant will probably remain low. While rebuilding post-war Syria will present opportunities for investment, Western states including the UK will likely be among the last of Assad's enemies to re-engage with the victorious regime, maintaining economic sanctions that restrict British companies doing business.

London could theoretically break ranks with its allies, as it is no longer beholden to EU sanctions after Brexit. However, the cost of such a move, the ire of America and the EU, is too great for very little gain. This is especially so given the UK has historically few commercial connections with Syria to reactivate and that Russia, Iran, China and probably the Gulf will be given preferential treatment over Britain in any investment. The UK therefore has little choice but to remain locked into US and EU policy on Assad. Sanctions may be slowly lifted, but probably more as a reflection of Western frustrations than any real concessions from Damascus. Any renewed engagement between the Biden administration and Iran may also lead to an easing of the harsh 'Caesar' Sanctions on Damascus, but this will not likely impact the UK's Syria trade. With Assad in charge, the UK will remain of marginal economic importance to Syria and vice versa for years to come.

It is difficult to see considerable expansion in Lebanon's economy either. London has identified infrastructure, energy, education and healthcare as particular areas its companies can deliver, but such capital projects require a level of funding and domestic political agreement that Lebanon has not seen for some time. With the domestic economy relatively stagnant, projects are normally funded externally and donors, notably the United States, prefer to contract their own companies to deliver. Further complicating matters are the Trump-era sanctions against Iran and Hezbollah and Britain's own prescription of the Shia militia, which will deter UK business, as will the risk that any construction projects risk destruction in a Hezbollah–Israel war. The twin crises of the protest movement and the Covid-19 pandemic made Lebanon even more unstable, but it is unclear whether Britain has the capacity to assist or the inclination, given Lebanon's generally low priority. Beyond companies linked to the UK Lebanese diaspora, a major increase in UK–Lebanon trade is not therefore expected, although continuing to channel aid to refugee-related areas remains a valuable route for some limited influence.

Jordan offers the greatest opportunity for UK business in the region, though almost by default given the low appeal of its neighbours. Jordan has a more stable government than Lebanon and is more pro-Western than Syria, meaning more opportunities. Business conditions are slowly improving, though Jordan still ranked only 104th in the world in the 2019 World Bank's Ease of Doing Business index – considerably behind other regional partners like Turkey (43rd), Israel (49th), Oman (78th) and Saudi Arabia (92nd), but ahead of Egypt (120th), Iran (128th), Lebanon (142nd) and Syria (179th).[23] Jordan does have some advantages to its neighbours alongside relative political stability, including a young, relatively well-educated population with many speaking English, although it is currently haemorrhaging many to Saudi Arabia and Turkey.[24] It has invested in technology and officials boast that 23 per cent of MENA tech entrepreneurs are Jordanian, meaning it has potential to mimic Kenya's emerging role as a regional tech hub.[25] The UK, however, has not made much effort to sponsor this sector, and it is a possible space for intensive British investment and partnership. Britain has sought to leverage its historical relationship to act as head cheerleader for the Jordanian economy, hosting a promotional conference 'Jordan: Growth and Opportunity – the London Initiative 2019' in London in February 2019, attended by King Abdullah and then Prime Minister Theresa May. However, the UK's departure from the EU may limit its ability to act as a bridge for Jordanian trade into Europe and its cheerleader role could easily be taken by another medium power such as Germany in the future. A challenge for post-Brexit Britain will be identifying ways it can maintain its special role with Jordan in the face of potential European competition.

Reduced influence in Syria and Lebanon will limit even further Britain's opportunity to promote values such as human rights and democracy. While public statements on these values are likely to, and should, remain part of the UK's discourse on the region, policymakers should also recognize that this is a more hopeful than realistic approach. In contrast in Jordan, the opportunities to promote values are higher, given the broader institutional links, not just in security but governance, media and education. While also being realistic that progress will be slow, the UK should beware the temptation to indulge the Jordanian elite's autocratic tendencies at the expense of its population's growing political engagement.[26] Alongside upping the UK's financial and diplomatic commitment to Amman, Jordan-specific plans could be explored as to how best to promote governance and democratic values. One option is to explore soft power methods such as education promotion. The UK currently offers scholarships to 1,500 foreign students a year through its Chevening scheme, twenty-four of which were awarded to Jordanians in 2018.[27] There is scope to either expand the provision for Jordanians in this scheme or develop a parallel Jordan-only scholarship that increases considerably the number of Jordanians studying in the UK, and helps build positive relations at a societal level.

Given the UK's limited resources in the Levant, exploring the value of soft power more broadly could reap benefits. Already the UK is leading European powers in support for refugees but could make more of its position as a humanitarian champion. This may require taking more refugees into the UK itself, but this could have long-term benefits for international relations. Many Iraqi Kurds that fled to the UK during the 1980s and 1990s built strong business relations with British companies when they returned to Iraq in 2003, for example. Similarly, Britain's other soft power tools such as the British Council and the BBC are a good means to build a positive image of the UK in the Levant, as are its universities. Britain has the second most successful university sector in the world, after the United States, but it is an underutilized tool of international relations. If more Levantine students study in the UK and then return home, they would bring with them (hopefully) a positive view of Britain and its political system, which could trickle down to their networks, while they themselves might end up in influential positions with a pro-British outlook. Likewise contacts and connections built in the UK might be utilized to build business and investment connections.

Security will not cease to be important for the UK in the Levant, and policymakers would do well to consider preventative action rather than waiting to deal with far more costly consequences. Poor economic and governance conditions raise the spectre of fresh public unrest across the region. The issue of water shortage, especially in Jordan, is likely to exacerbate this. Fresh fighting elsewhere, such as in Israel–Palestine, Iraq or Turkey, could spill into Syria, Jordan or Lebanon, prompting fresh conflict to erupt. Long-term UK security planners would do well to establish more clearly how Britain might react to renewed instability in this region. Were either Lebanon or Jordan to fall into civil conflict, how would the UK react and how might it best use the assets at its disposal to further Britain's interests? Were the Lebanese protest movement to escalate into violence, would the UK prefer a return to the status quo in the interests of stability, despite its evident failings, or be willing to invest energy in supporting those trying to reform the state, no matter how painful? Similarly, were the Jordanian regime to be challenged how would the UK react? An Islamist challenge would presumably be opposed by London, supporting its Hashemite allies, but what about a secular democratic challenge? The UK would not want to find itself backing repression of democratic activists, but that may end up being a prospect it faces. This underlines the need to urge some reforms of its Jordanian allies to avoid such an outcome.

Conclusion

In the medium term it is difficult to see how Britain can improve its position in Syria. The conflict is likely to continue for some time and Britain will struggle to change its position without losing face. In the long term, the UK will similarly struggle to influence Syria in the post-conflict era, and the war has illustrated how limited London can actually be. Focused policies on certain areas, most notably refugees over which it is relatively uniquely active, might be a wiser prospect. In the even longer term, policymakers should draw lessons from the Syria crisis to avoid making similar errors elsewhere in the future: in particular, recognizing what Britain's long-term strategic interests are and the dangers of miscalculations and short-term, domestic-driven escalatory pressure.

Ironically, Britain is probably now actually more influential in the countries in which it has invested less attention: Lebanon and Jordan. Both states continue to be at risk from short- and long-term spillover from the Syria crisis. However, unlike in Syria in 2011, the UK already has pre-existing institutional links with both states. In Lebanon the UK competes with several other foreign states, but retains good ties with security and development institutions, even if its economic links are minimal. Of the three states however, the UK is best placed in Jordan, having long-standing ties with the military, monarchy, educational facilities and new refugee institutions, and also has the advantage of being the most prominent European power. The UK might consider directing disproportionate resources towards Jordan (over that in Syria and Lebanon), exploring how it can maximize this influence to aid necessary stabilization in Jordan and best pursue the UK and Jordan's shared long-term interests.

12

Iraq

Jack Watling

Since the foundation of Iraq in 1920 Britain has played a pivotal role in the development of the state. Britain set Iraq on a course that saw a multi-ethnic, majority Shi'i region become a Sunni-dominated centre of Arab Nationalism, just as Britain played a leading role in upending that order in 2003. Despite Britain's deep involvement in Iraq, however, the drivers of Britain's policy have rarely been Iraq itself, and despite successive military deployments to the country the British government has usually been eager, even as it has struggled, to withdraw. A confluence of events in 2020 renders it difficult for the UK to simply maintain the status quo. The violent crackdown against the Iraqi Protest Movement, the assassination of Qassem Soleimani and Brexit mean that the political terrain is in flux, in Iraq and the UK. At the same time, coronavirus has dampened some of the immediate effect of these events. This provides an opportunity to think critically about what Britain's interests in Iraq are, and how they can best be supported. This chapter outlines what those interests might comprise, how they might be secured, and identifies the primary threats to them over the following decade. The chapter begins by establishing a baseline for where Iraq is headed in the next ten years. Only once this is established does it seek to identify the UK's core interests in the country.

The conclusions of this chapter are that Britain's foremost interests in Iraq concern regional security, both relating to Iranian activity threatening the Gulf and the continued risk from terrorism. In both cases intelligence and surveillance are of greater value than conducting strike operations, and the priority ought to be to develop long-term liaison posts with trusted Iraqi formations to develop sufficient situational awareness and facilitate the entry of forces if necessary. Economically the UK has limited interests in Iraq, and opportunities are inhibited by the client–patron system in Baghdad which underpins endemic corruption. The lack of jobs, owing to structural weaknesses in the economy, will also be the primary cause of ongoing instability. At the same time the dependency of much of the country upon key government ministries dampens the impetus for change. Britain should therefore push Iraq diplomatically to engage in economic reform. If this takes place Britain should aim to facilitate foreign investment. If it does not, then Iraq should not be an economic priority. Despite general strategic alignment with the United States, Britain gains a great deal by pursuing an independent – though not divergent – policy in the region and should leverage the relationships that this creates to maintain channels that Washington cannot, in order to facilitate negotiation and influence.

Iraq in the 2020s

By 2018 the Iraqi population surpassed 38 million, continuing a rate of growth undiminished by the fighting over the previous decade.[1] This is set to continue, leading to an expanding youth population. Iraq does not collect reliable unemployment statistics. Many Iraqis are best described as partially or informally employed, rather than unemployed. But anecdotal evidence from the protest movement shows that youth unemployment in particular is high. It is unlikely to improve, owing to structural problems with the economy. Because government-backed companies underpinned by oil revenues tend to aggressively compete with the private sector, while corruption deters foreign investment, the capacity for jobs growth in the private sector is limited, while available public sector jobs are dependent upon oil revenues. The oil sector, accounting for upwards of 60 per cent of Iraqi GDP, and generating over 90 per cent of government revenues, is not expected to significantly expand over the next decade.[2] It is also hard to see Iraq restructuring this damaging economic system. Iraq's oil market has created a client patronage system that allows government officials to receive and distribute money from state revenues. Private enterprise in Iraq is strangled by bureaucracy and held hostage by approval processes that facilitate corruption.[3] To liberalize this system would decentralize control of the economy and thereby disrupt existing patronage structures. Thus, there is very little interest in improving business legislation to enable foreign investment or economic diversification.

The failure to deliver economic reform, ensuring the perpetuation of high levels of corruption and unemployment, means that Iraq will remain a challenging environment for foreign investment outside of large state infrastructure projects. This must inhibit investment into reconstruction and the rejuvenation of industry in territories liberated from Daesh. The lack of investment, and bureaucratic barriers to trade, means that Iraq is likely to see a high level of smuggling across its borders. The growth of the informal economy means that the security environment will remain volatile, with low-level criminality and violence targeting legitimate businesses that threaten illicit trade routes.[4] Iraq's security environment faces a prolonged period of 'durable disorder'.[5] There has been much speculation about the 'return of Daesh'.[6] There remain active Daesh cells across Salah Ad-Din, Al Anbar, Diyala, Kirkuk and Ninevah provinces, and sympathizers have infiltrated the police and local institutions. Slow progress in the reconstruction of Falujah, Ramadi, Mosul and other towns that were extensively damaged during the campaign of liberation will entrench frustration with government. Internally displaced Iraqis complain that they have been prevented from returning home and face harassment from militias.[7] But the factors that enabled the fall of Mosul in 2014 are very unlikely to be repeated. The collapse of the Iraqi army around Mosul came after extensive clashes with a Sunni population that was empowered in the aftermath of the Sunni awakening. Daesh therefore entered Iraq to find a sympathetic populace, with robust networks to exploit. Furthermore, Daesh had a safe haven, and a considerable arsenal of weaponry in Syria. Today, by contrast, the Sunni population is fragmented and Shia paramilitary groups are keeping a tight hold on the territory. With the drawing down of the conflict in Syria, Daesh are likely to remain fragmented and weak, able to carry out damaging attacks in isolation.[8] This will deter foreign investment but is not likely to threaten Baghdad's hold on these provinces.

The Popular Mobilization Forces (PMF) are determined to maintain their position as a component of the Iraqi security forces under a separate chain of command from the military and police.[9] Given the political position of many PMF aligned MPs, and the number of power bases around the Prime Minister's Office enabled by the continuation of the PMF, it would be naïve to believe that armed militias are going to disappear over the following decade. If anything, as economic patronage is protected with force, the hold of PMF units on Iraq is liable to increase.[10] Since the PMF gives its commanders power in communities, while the offices they gain through political activity exert power over the army and police, the latter are in many respects increasingly subordinated to the former. This ensures that Iran will retain considerable influence in the country. Iran's influence spans the economic, cultural and political spheres. Tourism to Najaf and Karbala is growing, while for Iraq's low-income families the availability of cheap Iranian goods is largely welcomed. Approximately 70 per cent of Iran's non-oil exports went to Iraq in 2018,[11] and though this will fluctuate, Iraq is set to remain Iran's primary export market.[12] There are constraints to Iran's influence however, as Tehran must always benchmark its expectations against the force of Iraqi national sentiment. So long as US sanctions continue, Iraq and Iran remain economically interdependent. Given the volume of smuggling between Iran and Basra, and as Saudi Arabia's economy diversifies, the southern border may become an increasing focal point for illicit trade, which has security implications.

Nevertheless, Iraq will remain poised between Iran and the United States. Iran is a critical economic partner, and a serious political spoiler, while the United States remains a vital political partner and could be a catastrophic economic spoiler if it were to impose sanctions. Avoiding antagonizing these competing powers will remain the hardest foreign policy challenge for Baghdad.[13] This will be complicated when Baghdad faces the prospect of renewed relations with Damascus, as the civil war in Syria ebbs. Iraq has little choice in re-establishing links to Damascus. At a local level many tribes straddle the Iraqi–Syrian border, facilitating trade and smuggling, while PMF units have been eager to secure crossing points. Many PMF units have been operating in Syria for several years, and Iran has a strong interest in ensuring trade, both to stabilize Syria's economy and to recoup its own costs from the conflict. There is already a significant material flow across the border, and this will probably expand with or without the approval of Baghdad and Damascus. The Syrian government will struggle to exert direct control over much of the country given the patchwork of militias it has relied on to hold territory.[14] One peculiar example of this is the growing collaboration between Assad and the YPG. Given common cause against Turkey, the Kurdish region in Syria is unlikely to create trouble for Assad and will continue to facilitate trade with Iraq. The disorder of Eastern Syria however ensures that Iraq will continue to face security threats, facilitated by illicit trade routes over its western border.

The Kurdish question may well bring Baghdad closer to its regional neighbours over the next decade. Ambitions for independence remain firm within the Kurdistan Regional Government (KRG), though the likelihood of any successful attempt to break away is minimal. As a landlocked and economically vulnerable territory, the KRG would face severe economic pressure from Iran, Turkey and Baghdad if it attempted to separate from Iraq, and this would quickly be backed up with military action. For the international community maintaining good relations with Turkey, and stabilizing Iraq will trump any romantic sentiments regarding Kurdish autonomy. As in 2017 tensions between Baghdad and Erbil will simmer, and at points boil, but there is little prospect of the KRG achieving independence within the next decade.

Risks and uncertainty

There are a number of highly disruptive scenarios that would require a significant adjustment to British policy in Iraq. The greatest threat to Iraq stems from a sustained slump in the price of oil. Oil revenues are critical to the government for paying salaries, providing services, funding reconstruction, as well as underpinning the client–patron system. The crash in the oil price in 2014 exacerbated instability across Iraq, with public servants left unpaid for months. It was also a flashpoint in the perpetually uneasy relations between Erbil and Baghdad.[15] In 2020 the coronavirus pandemic saw an even more severe collapse in the price of oil that is putting Baghdad into an economically unsustainable position.[16] There is an expectation that as vaccines are distributed this will see an uptick in economic activity, a rise in demand for oil and a consequent rise in price, so that external support to get Iraq through the immediate gap in its budget might be sufficient. However, to look beyond the immediate rise and fall of commodity prices there are reasons to believe that the 2020s may see a structural change in the oil market. Firstly, the volume of shale available means that if the price rises above $60 per barrel, the market can draw upon more supply, which in turn reduces prices. At the same time demand may be in long-term decline as states take more drastic measures to cut carbon emissions.[17] The Iraqi government needs prices above $60 a barrel to have a sustainable budget. It is highly unlikely that prices will remain at that level over much of the next decade. This poses challenges for the UK's foreign policy in both the short and medium term. When Baghdad's finances fall, it leaves civil servants and military personnel unpaid. This often leads to an increase in crime and lower-level corruption and can create structural weaknesses in Iraqi security institutions. The non-payment of troops and police could quickly expand corrupt bookkeeping inside the force and hollow out units, which was a leading cause of the collapse of security forces in 2014.[18] Unlike in 2014 however, today Baghdad faces challenge from Shia majority areas in the South, arising from the country's financial difficulties, which would be exacerbated by a sustained reduction in oil revenues. Given the short-term consequences of a budget deficit in Baghdad, this may lead external powers to offer Iraq financial assistance.

The problem is that if the international community underwrites the Iraqi economy, there will be no incentive for the Iraqi elite to enact changes in the short term that in the long term are essential. The economic precipice on which Baghdad finds itself is one that could provide the necessary impetus for reform. Alleviating the pressure is likely to delay, rather than remedy, the malady.[19] But economic pressure is liable to be destabilizing. If this prompts Iraq to begin to restructure its economy, that would be highly desirable. But it could also simply precipitate the collapse of the state. On balance, it seems that the international community should be clear that assistance is conditional on reform. So long as those advocating reform continue to be murdered and disappeared with impunity,[20] it is unlikely that external financial assistance will do anything but perpetuate the current durable disorder. In many respects the best bell weather is the government's approach to the Protest Movement.

The Protest Movement represents a major potential disruptor to the status quo in Iraq.[21] Having organized over half a decade and with widespread support, the movement has clear demands and is willing to take risks over a prolonged period. The protests have an effective leadership structure and have been endorsed by the Marjai'yah,[22] so that its legitimacy is hard to attack. If the government gives ground to the protest movement, it could significantly reshape the institutions of the Iraqi state, not least by putting officials at risk in their posts if they fail to deliver. Unfortunately, the Iraqi government has a great deal of bureaucratic patience – using legal and political procedure to slow its reactions to protest demands. Iraq's elites do not have a shortage of thuggish malevolence and have used procedural delays to organize the murder of protesters, and the assassination of the movement's leadership.[23] This is likely to continue. The Federal Police and elements of the security forces have shown little restraint in shooting demonstrators, while the government – as with atrocities conducted by its forces in the campaign of liberation,[24] or the anti-corruption commission – has shown total apathy in punishing such behaviour. Despite Prime Minister al-Kadhimi's vow to prosecute those who murder protesters and listen to the movement's grievances, the system has proven effective at failing to implement his decrees. Precisely because the protest movement's goals threaten the client–patron system, it is unlikely that the government will moderate its approach, and unless the protest movement manages to deter attacks against it, it risks bleeding out. The movement is also vulnerable to being sold out by its allies, especially Muqtadr al Sadr. Sadr has used the movement to bolster his leverage, showcasing his ability to flood the streets, but he does not share the movement's goals. At the same time the structural issues that drive the movement persist, so that while the movement may be beaten back, protests are likely to continue in successive waves over the next decade. The Protest Movement presents a further dilemma for British policymakers. If the movement succeeds this would advance British interests, reducing corruption and potentially unlocking a route to economic reform, enabling foreign investment, job creation and stabilization. However, the British government, while sharing the movement's goals, cannot work against the existing government without rendering its current position in the country untenable. There is also a moral question. Given that Iraqi officials are responsible for the murder of protesters, Britain must work out how it engages with the large number of officials who already have a great deal of blood on their hands and remain undaunted by the prospect of shedding more.

The Protest Movement's capacity to sustain casualties is in part a reflection of the fervour generated by Ayatollah Sistani's endorsement of the protests. Sistani has been a unifying figure throughout the life of post-Baathist Iraq. His endorsement, or withdrawal of favour, has propelled Iraqis to the ballot and broken governments. His *fatwa* in 2014 brought the PMF into existence and bounded their conduct. Even Major General Qassem Soleimani went out of his way to acknowledge Sistani's authority in his public pronouncements during the war with Daesh.[25] Sistani has stood as a unique island of authority, recognized throughout the divided Shia community. He has also remained a bulwark against Iranian influence. When he dies the authority of the Marjai'yah will enter a period of flux. The institution will retain its authority, but the leadership of the Shia community is passed both by the recognition of scholarly peers and by the adherence of followers. Followers are not obliged to immediately declare who they will follow once an Ayatollah dies, and so there will be a period of transition in which authority within the Shia community will be less unified. Although Sistani's successor is likely to share many of his precepts regarding the relations between Marjai'yah and state, two of Sistani's colleagues in Najaf are supportive of *wialyet al-faqih*, the belief that clerics should wield executive authority. It cannot be guaranteed that Sistani's successor will offer his support to the institutions of the Iraqi state, as Sistani has chosen to do. If the Marjai'yah becomes more politically assertive, this will create an important question for British diplomats. Influence in Iraq would – under these conditions – require a presence in Najaf. However, in pursuing relations with the Marjai'yah the British government would also be empowering a non-state organization, which would necessitate appropriate permissions and procedures. Given that access would be dependent upon trust, and trust takes time to develop, the UK will need to build channels with the Marjai'yah before Sistani passes away, if they are to be in position to exercise influence when it is most relevant.

The final significant cause of uncertainty in Iraq over the next decade is the ongoing contest between the United States and Iran. At its most extreme this could lead to a direct military confrontation. There are several avenues that could lead to this eventuality, not least if Iran tries to break out for a nuclear weapon. The first issue for the UK would be that its diplomatic facilities, military personnel and nationals inside Iraq would be targets for Iranian strikes, or for attacks by Iranian proxies. The risk necessitates a robust contingency for carrying out Non-Combatant Evacuation Operations from Iraq. Although such planning exists, Britain would likely have to redraw its footprint in the area if US forces reduce their presence in country. Despite differences with the United States over its Iran policy, in the event of a war the UK could not avoid involvement. Given the location of bases the conflict would likely focus on the Gulf. Under these circumstances however US and UK forces could quickly be drawn to take the fight into Iraq, not least to deny Iran access to key areas, which could be used to launch shorter-range missiles at targets in the Gulf and Israel. Iran would lose this conflict but would inflict immense damage. The collapse of the Iranian government would drastically reshape the balance of power in Baghdad. Exactly how it would affect British interests is difficult to judge. In the aftermath it would be necessary to reappraise expectations and craft a new policy according to the reality on the ground.

There are many events short of war; however, that could significantly disrupt UK policy in Iraq. Given that the stakes for the United States are much higher in its dealings with Iran, Iraq policy will remain subordinate to the Iran file through the 2020s. The departure of President Trump is likely to see a shift in the tone of US diplomacy, and to curtail sudden threats to withdraw from the country, but there is also likely to be significant continuity. Although President Joe Biden has indicated a desire to re-enter negotiations over the JCPOA, there is a strong belief in US defence circles that 'maximum pressure' will pay off in the long run, and any initiative to bring Iran back to negotiations by the United States could be an arduous process, so that despite the shift in US objectives, the use of sanctions and other deterrent activity that could play out on Iraqi soil will continue. The issue of sanctions is of particular relevance. Under President Trump sanctions were largely applied against Iraqi officials to target Iranian interests. This is less likely under the new administration. However, sanctions may expand in Iraq owing to the culpability of many Iraqi lawmakers in the murder of protesters. The imposition of sanctions on Iraq would have a number of destabilizing effects. In the first instance Western companies would withdraw from the market, as occurred in Iran. This in turn would undermine work to modernize Iraq's gas turbines, electricity grid and other infrastructure, and limit the government's ability to modernize and secure revenues. Since the majority of UK business in Iraq is in the petrochemical sector, sanctions would pose a threat to UK economic activity in the country. The Iraqi government would almost certainly be forced closer to Iran by such a move, and would likely withdraw protections for US forces, which would increase the threat against UK personnel.

The effects of sanctions being imposed, a collapse in the price of oil, or the death of Sistani, may be understood as significant, but largely predictable. These therefore constitute risks that British policy must work to mitigate. The effects of economic collapse and the protest movement forcing reform of government, or war with Iran, are by contrast highly unpredictable. Policy cannot simply adjust to these changes. Instead it requires the ability to redraft the policy in light of new information. Nevertheless, British interests in Iraq are liable to remain fairly constant, even while the opportunities for advancing them could shift dramatically. To understand those interests it is necessary to consider the history of Britain's Iraq policy.

Britain in Iraq: A century of contradictions

Britain's occupation of Mesopotamia during the First World War stemmed from its contestation with the Ottoman Empire.[26] The military objective of denying the region to the Ottomans did not determine Britain's post-war policy, however. Instead, Britain's position was shaped by its commitment to the establishment of the League of Nations,[27] and by demands to reduce Britain's commitments abroad.[28] Thus the government settled upon Iraq as the proving ground of the Mandate system, in which imperial powers would support states to independence. Wishing to reward an ally, and unable to fulfil their wartime promises, the British government further settled upon Faisal bin Hussein as the prospective King of Iraq and the lynchpin of a constitutional monarchy which it was hoped could take over an increasing share of administrative responsibilities while remaining aligned with British interests. The foisting of Faisal on Iraq made the creation of an Iraqi identity difficult, because he was neither from the region, nor a member of the predominant sect. Furthermore, there were few institutions that could foster an Iraqi identity. This led officials to support the promotion of Arab Nationalism,[29] which was primarily advanced through the Iraqi education system under the leadership of Sati al-Husri.[30]

British policy in Iraq suffered from a contradiction. On the one hand, Britain proclaimed its objective to be the creation of an independent state. On the other hand, Britain retained military forces in the country and controlled most ministries through liaison officers and advisers, who would not allow Iraq to implement policy contrary to British interests. This critique was levelled at Britain by fellow imperial powers as the government sought to gain the League of Nation's approval for Iraq's independence. Despite the reservations of many British officials in Iraq, the government determined to convince the League, using Iraq as the proof of the Mandate process.[31] Iraq gained independence in 1932 to prove Britain's commitment to the international order it had authored in 1919. Britain's actual interests in the country were limited to minor economic concerns, the security of the port of Basra to ensure control of the Gulf, and the right to use airfields and lines of communication in the event of general war.[32] Britain did little to counteract the seizure of power in Iraq by military officers following the coronation of King Ghazi in September 1933, or the promotion of nationalist, and anti-British material from the royal court.

The build-up of nationalist and anti-British sentiment ultimately led to a pro-Axis coup in 1941, which prompted British forces to be deployed from India, and other parts of the Middle East, to reassert control.[33] Again Britain sought to wrestle with a contradiction. Iraq's turning away from the governmental structures set up by the British in the 1920s was thought to stem from the failure of Iraqis to understand democratic values. Belief in democracy was viewed as an antidote to Fascist sympathies and so the British government embarked upon an extensive propaganda campaign to promote democracy in Iraq.[34] At the same time Britain's hard interests in the country centred upon denying Iraq to the Axis. This necessitated control, and control was achieved through military occupation. Thus, Britain simultaneously exerted great efforts to convince Iraqis of the value of their national independence, and representative government, while standing as the foremost barrier to Iraqis expressing themselves politically.

At the end of the war, as a new contest emerged with the Soviet Union, the UK sought to cement access to Iraq, and prop up a government that was willing to arrest and suppress the Iraqi Communist Party. The Anglo-Iraqi Treaty of 1848 secured Britain further basing rights in Iraq used to establish a number of listening stations for signals intelligence.[35] The treaty was met with protests in Baghdad but would survive until the military coup of 1958. In the coup's aftermath Britain found its forces expelled and in consultations with the United States considered military intervention.[36] However Britain's Iraq policy was once again determined by regional considerations. The administration of Abd al-Karim Qasim reassured Britain by leaving arrangements in place with regards to Iraq's oil exports. Perhaps more importantly, as an Arab Nationalist counterweight to the newly formed Nasserite project of the United Arab Republic, Whitehall felt that the Iraqi government was more compatible with British interests than the reputational harm in the region of an intervention. The subsequent three decades saw a consistent British policy of balancing. While Iraqi relations with the

UAR, and the Soviet Union, fluctuated, the consensus remained that Iraqi governments were more consistently pro-independence than aligned to wider ideological commitments.[37] By the time of the Iranian Revolution, despite the nationalization of oil, claims against Kuwait and domestic repression, Whitehall maintained relations with Saddam Hussein. Britain could not see much chance of either side in the Iran–Iraq War winning outright by force, and sought to retain influence with both parties,[38] but covertly backed Saddam.

The era of balancing ended with the Iraqi invasion of Kuwait in 1990 and the collapse of the USSR. In the aftermath of the war Britain set about a policy of containment. Alongside the United States, Britain was concerned with the threat to regional security that a strong Iraq would represent, but also feared the consequences of the state's collapse. This led to a highly problematic sanctions policy. Under new labour Britain attempted to redraw the sanctions framework,[39] but as Tony Blair had made clear in 1999 Iraq was, to some extent, the test of the international community's ability to manage rogue states. As he explained in Chicago, 'many of our problems have been caused by two dangerous and ruthless men – Saddam Hussein and Slobodan Milosevic … If NATO fails in Kosovo, the next dictator to be threatened with military force may well not believe our resolve to carry the threat through'.[40] Britain's role in the 2003 invasion of Iraq was the result of a number of interests. The British government wished to support the United States. Tony Blair made clear that he saw Saddam as precisely the type of pariah that the international community was duty-bound to remove. Meanwhile established policy was perceived to be ineffective and morally compromised, given the humanitarian impact of sanctions. The determination to act however was, once again, driven by interests beyond Iraq. Iraq was simply the canvas upon which Britain was to demonstrate its commitment to its Atlantic ally, and as a warning to other 'rogue states'.

Britain's third occupation of Iraq returned to a persistent theme, with the aim of establishing democratic institutions that would foster a peaceful and toothless economic partner, enabling a rapid British withdrawal. Just as previous Iraqi institutions had been built around trusted allies, the politicians of post-2003 Iraq were initially those exiles with whom US and British officials were familiar and therefore comfortable. The withdrawal occurred, though as with previous iterations of the policy the effectiveness of the institutions was doubtful, and the ineptness of the Iraqi government of Nouri al Maliki led British forces to return to Iraq in 2014 to fight Daesh, following the fall of Mosul. Today we are once again faced with the prospect of diminishing Western engagement, stymied by concern that Iraq has entered an Iranian orbit.

Britain's enduring interests

As the incomplete survey of British relations with Iraq to date demonstrates, despite changes of direction there have been persistent interests that have shaped Britain's policy in Iraq. The first and foremost has been Britain's regional security concerns. Intervention during the First and Second Word Wars centred on the use of Iraq as a springboard for further operations into the Gulf. Today, there is a danger that Iranian proxies will position medium-range ballistic missiles in Iraq[41] and strike the Gulf. Britain's economic relations with the Gulf will strengthen over the next decade and are tied closely with security cooperation. Britain therefore has a strong interest in constraining Iranian exploitation of Southern Iraq for military purposes. This can only be achieved with sufficient intelligence and surveillance. Although Britain is unlikely to be the primary provider of the latter, it may make a significant contribution to the former.

The primacy of security interests also prevails in the north and west of Iraq. Britain maintains an interest in preventing Iraq becoming a haven for terrorist groups. On balance Iraq is unlikely to provide much room for groups to plan and operate internationally. Whether it be the Taliban in Afghanistan, Al-Qaeda in the Arabian Peninsula or Daesh in Raqqa, expeditionary attacks require a stable base of operations, and that expeditionary capacity declines as groups are forced to fight at home. Baghdad will not give Daesh the breathing space to use Iraq as a reliable base of operations for acting internationally. Britain's primary interest therefore is to maintain intelligence cooperation with Baghdad and the Kurdistan Regional Government (KRG) to allow the UK to understand whether the commitment of further capabilities is necessary. The best way to ensure intelligence cooperation is the provision of Intelligence, Surveillance and Reconnaissance (ISR) support to key partners, such as the Iraqi Counter Terrorism Service (CTS). The CTS is capable of striking terrorist cells but benefit from assistance in building target packages. Intelligence cooperation with the Kurdish security services is also valuable.

While ISR assets enable access, the measure of success for the UK's security posture is likely to be the number of long-term liaison officers it can maintain. When Daesh seized Mosul in 2014 the UK's response was slow, and there were deficiencies in expertise available on the ground.[42] The slowness of the build-up was noted by Iraqis, who for a critical period believed that Iran was the only country to provide immediate and immediately useful support. UK Special Forces deployed in response to the crisis recall that it took time to rebuild some of their relationships on the ground. The British government is highly susceptible to the fallacious belief that its long history of interaction in a country provides a depth of knowledge in government. What has given the UK a depth of insight in a number of countries across the region are the long-term liaison and loan service posts it maintains. If these can be established in Iraq then the UK could maintain a valuable early warning system and be more responsive should the situation deteriorate in the future. The targeted deployment of Specialised Infantry may also help to build the necessary relationships and skills to facilitate subsequent access.

The challenge the UK faces is in avoiding trying to do too much. Britain has funded and furnished expertise to play a leading role in clearing Iraq of improvised explosive devices following the defeat of Daesh.[43] This is an appropriate use of humanitarian aid and is something that Britain was well placed to do. But even in the cleared areas Internally Displaced Persons (IDPs) are slow to return. The UK attempting to deliver significant humanitarian assistance in this context is likely counterproductive until there is political determination in Baghdad to rebuild these communities. This does not mean that the UK should be unwilling to offer aid, but British support ought to follow Iraqi politicians investing political capital in the effort. That Baghdad not prioritizing reconstruction indicates that external resources will suffer from a lack of access or security. The priority therefore should be aimed diplomatically at Baghdad, with clear prerequisites before development aid is made available to the liberated territories.

The primacy of politics must also inform Britain's economic policy in Iraq. The UK exported approximately £338 million worth of goods to Iraq in 2018.[44] By far the largest export was in pharmaceuticals. Exports have grown in recent years, but it remains a small market. UK companies are active in the Iraqi oil and energy sector, but wider participation in the economy is limited, and there are few prospects for growth unless the Iraqi government engages in economic reform. In order to participate in the market British companies must engage in high levels of corruption, exposing them to legal risk, and introducing a level of unpredictability into transactions that deters smaller businesses. The UK's provision of £2 billion in export finance loans is unlikely to be fully utilized. Unless the business environment can be reformed, opportunities will remain scarce. The foremost business priority for the UK in Iraq therefore is diplomatic, and best achieved with cooperation across the diplomatic community, to urge the Iraqi government to implement economic reform. Delivering economic reform is equally critical in addressing Iraq's political and economic woes. But the sequence for pressure must focus on the political will in Baghdad.

British interests in Iraq, over the following decade, are, if not antithetical to, then certainly distinct from, those of the United States. The United States' foremost security concern is Iran, and its counterterrorism policy is likely to continue to emphasize strike operations. The United States has enough hard power to maintain its position irrespective of Iraqi sensibilities. For the UK advancing its interests is largely a question of persuasion in Baghdad: persuasion to enable liaison to continue; persuasion to make progress on economic reform and persuasion to facilitate humanitarian access. Being seen to be joined at the hip with the United States is a disadvantage if Britain wishes to be persuasive. This does not mean that the UK needs to pursue a divergent policy from Washington. In many respects, retaining better access and relationships adds value to the United States, since its personnel are increasingly restricted owing to force protection concerns. Over the preceding decade Washington has made extensive use of allies – including the UK – that are able to maintain channels, and deliver messages, that the United States cannot. Pursuing such a policy requires the UK to accept risks to its diplomatic personnel, in order to maintain access and relationships. To fully exploit such a posture the Foreign, Commonwealth and Development Office (FCDO) must accept a culture of courageous diplomacy.

The need to present an independent policy from Washington in Iraq must be balanced against the diplomatic weight that can be brought to bear by being seen to have strategic alignment with the United States across the region. The calibration of this relationship, and how it is messaged, must be shaped by how UK policy develops, but in principle the UK should aim to occupy an ambiguous position whereby it is clear that Britain is not directly advancing US interests, but remains a close-enough ally with the United States to deter attacks on British interests. Again, being perceived to be too close to Washington could make British targets more vulnerable, as the UK could be seen as the softer target. To some extent Britain's deterrence posture can be enhanced by also working closely with European allies, since attacks on joint operations may elicit economic or diplomatic retaliation that would be undesirable for

Iran. Furthermore, European diplomatic weight would be crucial in applying pressure in favour of economic reform. Such efforts however should be premised upon bilateral cooperation, whether through the Lancaster House framework with France, or via direct diplomatic collaboration with the European Commission, rather than through multilateral mechanisms and frameworks. Such frameworks tend to have high force protection requirements, are very restricted in scope and lack the flexibility within their mandate to remain diplomatically agile. For the UK continuity in the relationship of liaison officers, and the capacity to engage in courageous diplomacy – sacrificing force protection for access – is necessary if it is to maintain influence.

Another question that affects Britain's policy in Iraq, especially with regards to alignment with Washington, is Russian and Chinese engagement in the country. Fear of ceding influence as the world enters a renewed era of great power competition can be a major constraint on policy. In Iraq, however, this risk is limited. Russia does not have the resources to invest heavily in the country and is more likely to opportunistically exacerbate tensions between Baghdad and the United States and UK. For instance, if tensions flare with the KRG, and London and Washington back Baghdad, Russia may offer the KRG oil and arms deals. Such promises however are unlikely to materialize. Russia has limited stand-alone interests in the country. China is a different matter. It is likely that access and control of resources will become a key area of competition between the United States and China. Given Iraq's large oil reserves, and the demands of China's economy, access to Iraq may prove a growing Chinese interest. It does not follow, however, that the UK or United States should seek to limit Chinese access. On the contrary, Chinese reliance on oil from the Gulf represents a vulnerable supply chain, and the threat to disrupt it could provide a key lever in deterrence to prevent an outbreak of hostilities elsewhere. Nor does achieving this require a strong presence in Iraq, since oil would need to leave via the Straits of Hormuz. It does, however, underscore the need for a continued security presence in the Gulf.

Global Britain aims to enable the UK to maximize its trading relationships and diversify its economic and security partnerships. However, this is not best achieved by actively engaging everywhere. In Iraq, the UK has sufficient access to see that a strong bilateral relationship is possible. At present, however, it must be recognized that Iraq stands to gain much more from bilateral cooperation than the UK. Iraq is unlikely to become a viable market for major UK exports. Nor is the country likely to wield diplomatic influence in the UK's favour. As a security partner Iraq is likely to remain closely aligned with Iran, and if Iraq gains significant capabilities, it is as likely to threaten, as it is to support UK interests. Thus, the emphasis of UK policy should be to service its bilateral links, to maintain situational awareness in the country and make clear that under the right conditions Britain stands poised to engage with Iraq on either the security or economic file. But unless the right conditions are met the UK must avoid committing itself, expending valuable time and resources on a country that poses a great many risks and can offer few rewards.

The relations between states do not inexorably advance along linear progressions. The logic of politics often binds states into adversarial, transactional or dependent relationships for periods, interrupted at intervals by windows of opportunity in which the orientation of states can be altered. The capacity to predict, identify and prepare for those windows of opportunity is critical to a state's ability to advance its interests. One such window of opportunity may open in Iraq as the state emerges from the coronavirus pandemic. At present the country is being ravaged by Covid-19. The severity with which it is suffering is concealed by a lack of healthcare or effective monitoring. The impact may also be concealed by Iraq's large youth population. But there can be no doubt that the virus has stymied economic activity, dampened pilgrimages and cultural gatherings, undermined the government's finances and constrained security activity. The reduced presence of Western military forces has for a time limited clashes with the PMF, though harassment continues. The suppressive effect of the virus on Iraqi politics will eventually end, whether because the country has achieved herd immunity or by medical intervention. When it does the PMF will move rapidly to secure their economic and political position. The protest movement will attempt to revive. Whoever moves quickly and decisively in that period may set the conditions for the next decade. The UK faces an opportunity here. It could offer significant support to the Iraqi government. If the UK is successful in developing an effective vaccine, it could also – through medical aid – accelerate and influence the tempo at which Iraq emerges from the virus's shadow. This would constitute a major investment in Iraq's future, at a time when the UK is itself undergoing severe stress. Such a course is not necessarily advisable, but its merits should be considered. It could serve as an important demonstration of why tying development aid with foreign policy – embodied by the formation of the Foreign, Commonwealth and Development Office – can yield greater results than either activity in isolation. If the opportunity is not taken, then the UK will have to react to the conditions that emerge and accept the logic of the political environment in post-Covid Iraq as a constraint upon its policy ambitions.

13

The Gulf

Tobias Borck and Michael Stephens

The Arab Gulf states lie at the centre of British foreign policy towards the Middle East region. This has been the case for the past two centuries and will remain the case for the foreseeable future. British–Gulf relations are characterized by a degree of familiarity and shared history that sets them apart from many of the UK's other foreign relations with countries in the Middle East and beyond. There is a certain acceptance in British policy circles that the UK has long been relegated to the status of junior partner to the United States, which has been the region's undisputed hegemonic security guarantor for the past several decades. Nevertheless, it is also true that Britain has a unique understanding of the Gulf and a special bond with its rulers that cannot be matched by any other external power. The UK and the Gulf states' shared status as monarchies has often been emphasized by British diplomatic efforts in the region, and there are close and long-standing personal relationships between the British royal family and ruling families in the Gulf.[1] The royal family is a very powerful tool of British foreign policy in the Gulf and one that is used to great effect in order to maintain long-standing personal relationships that span decades, thereby building an intimacy and familiarity over years that no politician could ever hope to do. As a result, British royals are able to engage with their Gulf counterparts in a cordial and friendly manner that often allows for frank discussions about a range of topics, such as human rights concerns, and political intrigues that are sometimes difficult for ministers to broach.

But beyond this nominal commonality as fellow monarchies, the Gulf states have little in common with the UK, particularly with regards to their political systems, and it is clear that any feelings of mutual affection do not extend much beyond the strata of political, military and economic elites. Amongst the wider British public the Gulf states and the Arab world more broadly are not seen as natural partners for the UK, with the most recent survey on the Arab world revealing that gender roles, Islam and wealth dominated peoples' often negative perceptions of Arabs. This finds expression in British media coverage about the Gulf,[2] as well as in voices from across the political spectrum (though most consistently from the political left).[3] The Gulf states – and their rulers in particular – are regularly portrayed as anything from fabulously wealthy strangers that swoop in to buy up British football clubs, to religiously conservative autocrats who disregard human rights and bear, at least partial, responsibility for threats such as Islamist terrorism.

For some, maintaining and deepening these relationships are essential for Britain's economic prosperity, national security and standing in the world[4]; for others the ties with the Gulf's absolute monarchs represent the epitome of British values being cynically sold out in exchange for questionable benefits.[5] In short the Gulf is a textbook example of how interests and values are, should or can be balanced in Britain's foreign policy.

Over the past decade, successive British governments have sought to redefine, but ultimately strengthen and expand, Britain's engagement with the Gulf states. These efforts were set against a backdrop of seismic changes in the Gulf itself. In the context of a rapidly evolving regional environment, the Gulf monarchies have asserted themselves at home and abroad. They have sought to consolidate their political power and advance the diversification and transformation of their countries' hydrocarbon-dependent economies. In their foreign policies, the Gulf states – specifically Saudi Arabia, the UAE and Qatar – have adopted unprecedentedly activist postures, clashing with each other in the process.[6]

At the beginning of the 2020s, the Gulf remains an area of simultaneous insecurity and opportunity in which British interests are at stake. In terms of the wider Middle East, the Gulf states are very obvious partners needed to manage and resolve the region's various security crises. But this is not without cost, as each Gulf state's own interpretation of what drives these crises and strategic interests differs dramatically from that of their neighbours. Economically, the Gulf states remain attractive partners as Britain seeks to reposition itself as a global trading nation after Brexit. But ongoing transition towards a low(er)-carbon global economy and the economic fallout from the Covid-19 pandemic are sure to create ever-more difficult economic policy dilemmas for the region's monarchs. Consequently, Britain's engagement with the Gulf has reached a fork in the road: Britain can rely on the aspects of continuity that have bound it to the Gulf monarchies for decades and muddle through while trying to dodge or ignore mounting questions over the ongoing transformations in the region. Or it can confront the new realities that have emerged in the relationship, settle on policy positions accordingly and forge a more strategic and comprehensive approach.

Past: Evolving continuity

As the UK develops its post-Brexit foreign policy, there will be a temptation to regard the Gulf as a region in which existing relations can simply be expanded and deepened, which does not require much new intellectual input or strategic consideration. The notion of a natural, historic bond between the UK and the Gulf looms large, and it is not unreasonable to expect that future British governments will mostly default to implementing policies towards the region that were developed by their predecessors. Throughout the past decade, the governments led by Conservatives David Cameron and Theresa May have sought to reinvigorate Britain's relationships with the Gulf states, particularly under the rubric of the July 2015 Gulf Strategy.

Initially conceived and developed as a foreign policy centrepiece of the Cameron premiership, the strategy was supposed to set out the UK's priorities for the Gulf region over the next thirty years, but these plans were derailed by the outcome of the Brexit referendum in June 2016. Some of the strategy's elements were still carried forward, but no document was ever published. In December 2016, May attended a summit of the Gulf Cooperation Council (GCC) in Manama to 'open a new chapter in relations between the UK and the Gulf states'.[7] The declared ambition was 'to forge a strategic relationship',[8] to further develop and bring together a relatively diffuse set of existing bilateral economic, defence and security relations with the six GCC states under one dedicated umbrella. But in the years since little has happened in this direction, with all available bandwidth for questions around the direction of British foreign policy consumed by the Brexit process and subsequently the coronavirus. This does not mean that British–Gulf relations have been on hold during this time – quite the opposite. There have been a number of high-profile developments that have required much attention from London, such as the outbreak of the Gulf crisis between Qatar and its neighbours in 2017, the high-profile visit of Saudi Crown Prince MBS to London in March 2018,[9] the murder of Jamal Khashoggi in October 2018,[10] the conviction of British doctoral student Matthew Hedges as an alleged spy in the UAE in November 2018[11] and Iran's seizure of a British tanker in the Persian Gulf in July 2019.[12] But devoting attention to high-profile events is not an example of a British strategy. If anything, these events all reveal how unprepared the UK has been for the level of complexity and instability that has consumed the Gulf region over the past three years. Despite planning thirty years into the future, Britain has remained largely reactive to events, and a hostage to fortune.

At the heart of a British re-engagement with the Gulf has been the notion that the UK can activate historic leverage and recapture a position of influence it had relinquished only a few decades ago. Some observers have written about a British desire to return to 'East of Suez'.[13] This term resonates powerfully in any discussion about the UK's foreign policy towards the Middle East. The formal withdrawal from East of Suez in 1971, a process instigated by the Labour government of Harold Wilson and completed under Conservative Prime Minister Edward Heath, was a watershed moment for Britain's relationship with the region as a whole and the Gulf in particular.[14] The withdrawal marked the end of Britain's position as the dominant external power in the Gulf, and the United States assumed the mantle of the region's hegemonic security guarantor. Reconciling itself with Britain's post-Empire status as a middle power, London focused its attention elsewhere – especially on Europe. Bilateral ties with the Gulf monarchies moved down London's list of priorities, and Britain's Gulf policy became much more limited in scope, and generally less comprehensive and strategic in nature. Once all-encompassing and with the balance of power clearly tilted in favour of the UK, these relationships became more diffuse, less centrally coordinated in Whitehall and much more complex in terms of the distribution of power and dependency. In fact, in several areas – including trade, investments and even at the societal level – relations deepened significantly.

Despite its political decline, Britain maintained an almost uninterrupted military presence in the Gulf after the withdrawal from East of Suez. British special forces helped the Omani monarchy to defeat the Dhofar rebellion in the early 1970s; during the Iran–Iraq War of 1980–8, the Royal Navy's Armilla patrol supported the US Navy in policing Gulf sea lanes; and Britain was the largest coalition partner in both US-led wars against Saddam Hussein's Iraq in 1990/91 and 2003–7.[15] In addition, bilateral defence relationships with the Gulf states were bolstered by Britain becoming one of the region's primary arms suppliers. This has been enormously lucrative, even existential, for Britain's defence industry and its research and development capacity. The Al-Yamamah deal with Saudi Arabia particularly stands out. First signed in 1985, and encompassing the transfer of equipment and services worth around £40 billion over thirty years to Saudi Arabia, it remains the UK's largest ever export arrangement.[16] Yet, despite these substantial deployments and arms deals, in political and geostrategic terms Britain was relegated firmly to the role of the United States' junior partner in the Gulf. With the partial exception of Oman (and the military campaign in the 1970s that installed Sultan Qaboos as its ruler), the UK's presence in the Gulf, and its importance in the security calculations of the region's monarchs, was dwarfed by Washington's overwhelming military might and geopolitical interests.

Economically, relations between Britain and the Gulf states have developed significantly, creating interdependencies relevant to the prosperity of all. This has gone far beyond the activities of British energy companies in the hydrocarbon-fuelled economies of the Gulf states, or direct British imports of oil and gas from the Gulf. The dramatic rise in oil prices during the first decade of the twenty-first century enabled governments across the Gulf to rapidly grow their economies and ramp up spending, both at home and overseas. In the process, trade in goods and services between the UK and the six Gulf states more than doubled from £10.4 billion in 2000 to over £24 billion in 2010 – with the defence sector only accounting for a small portion. Bilateral trade with the UAE and Qatar grew particularly rapidly: from £3 billion to over £10 billion with the former, and from £421 million to £4.2 billion with the latter. This upward trend has continued since 2010, with the annual trade volume between Britain and the Gulf reaching nearly £33 billion in 2016.[17] At the same time, the UK has also become one of the principal destinations for investments from the Gulf. Through their sovereign wealth funds, estimated to hold assets in excess of 2 trillion US dollars,[18] the Gulf states have invested billions of pounds in British businesses, brands and infrastructure. As of 2019, Qatar alone had holdings worth over £35 billion in the UK,[19] including high-profile investments in Barclays, Heathrow Airport, Harrods, Sainsbury's, The Shard, Canary Wharf and other major real-estate developments in London.[20] One of the UAE's most famous purchases in the UK, the Manchester City football club, has won the Premier League four times in the last ten years. Many of these investments were not just headline-grabbing, but represented vital capital injections in some of the UK's most well-established companies. In the wake of the 2008 financial crisis, in particular, Gulf investments played an important role in saving major British businesses from collapse.[21]

Partly driven by these expanding economic ties, and partly as a continuation of long-established historic practices, UK–Gulf relations have been supported by deep and growing inter-elite relationships. This has set Britain apart from any other non-Arab country active in the Gulf. The most illustrative representation of this can be found in the résumés of various Gulf rulers. The Ruler of Dubai Sheikh Mohammed bin Rashid al Makhtoum and the King of Bahrain Hamad bin Issa Al-Khalifa are closely tied to the British royal family through a shared love and ownership of horses, and both rulers can be found annually in attendance at the UK's most prestigious horse-racing events. Amongst the thousands of military officers from across the Gulf who have been educated at the UK's military academies at Sandhurst, Shrivenham, and the Royal College of Defence Studies over the decades are Bahrain's King Hamad, Qatar's Emir Tamim bin Hamad Al-Thani, the UAE's de-facto ruler Mohammed bin Zayed Al-Nahyan as well as numerous other senior members of the royal families of all six Gulf monarchies. In fact, for tens of thousands of Gulf Arabs – not just princes and princesses – London and other British cities have become frequent travel destinations; many own property in the UK, seek healthcare in British hospitals and send their children to British private schools and universities.[22] At the same time, hundreds of thousands of British nationals have moved to live and work in the Gulf states (including many former British government and military officials taking lucrative consultancy positions, some directly within the Gulf states' own government institutions), and many more spend holidays in the region.

In sum, the UK's relationships with the Gulf states since the withdrawal from East of Suez have been characterized by both a degree of continuation and evolution. In the process, the nature of these relationships and the balance of power and influence have shifted significantly. Fifty years ago the UK was still directly involved in, and responsible for, the domestic politics of the Gulf states. In the decades since, as Britain's geostrategic position reduced in status, its ties to the region have actually become deeper and more complex, particularly with regards to trade, investment, and travel and migration patterns of British and Gulf nationals. Even after its formal withdrawal, the UK has remained engaged while welcoming the Gulf states' increased diplomatic and economic presence in the UK. Their phenomenal spending power has given the monarchs of the Gulf the means to buy themselves into the British economy and thereby achieve a degree of leverage that in some areas of the bilateral relationship makes them the more powerful party. It is also clear that between 1971 and the early 2010s, developments in British–Gulf relations have generally occurred without an overarching sense of strategic direction, certainly not one articulated by the British government. Throughout this time a shared sense of history and doubling down on pre-existing ties has played the central role in shaping UK–Gulf ties, giving them a different character than those between other European countries and the Gulf monarchies.

Addressing this lack of a strategic foundation and bringing together the (geo) political, economic and security strands of the six bilateral relationships with the Gulf states in order to strengthen all of them were the driving objective behind the Cameron government's initiative to develop a new Gulf strategy. It was also at the heart of Theresa May's pitch for the opening of a 'new chapter' in Manama in 2016, and it remains the challenge for the Johnson government at the beginning of the 2020s.

Between persistent interests and changing realities

Britain was initially drawn into the Gulf due to geography. At the time of the British Empire, the Gulf region was a vital strategic link on the route between the UK and India. The discovery of the Gulf's vast oil and gas resources in the early to mid-twentieth century then made the region pivotal to the industrial development of the UK and ultimately fuelled the creation of the globalized world economy of today. These days, the UK is no longer directly dependent on energy imports from the Gulf (with the partial exception of Qatari natural gas),[23] and the global movement away from hydrocarbons and towards renewable energy resources casts some doubt on the continued economic relevance of the Gulf.[24] However for the next several decades the Gulf's oil and gas resources will remain a key factor that ties up British economic and wider strategic interests in the region. As a trading nation with particular strengths in areas such as financial services, Britain's prosperity is inextricably linked to the health of the global economy, which will continue to depend on the uninterrupted flow of energy from the Gulf, even if most of that heads towards Asia. Furthermore, as the UK seeks to boost its trading relationships outside Europe after Brexit, it will become even more interested in benefitting from the revenues the Gulf states generate from their energy exports. As the Gulf states themselves are trying to diversify their economies, there are opportunities to further grow exports to the region and attract investment for British companies. The financial services industry and in particular areas such as new financial technologies (short fintech) and Islamic finance are likely to be areas of focus. In 2019, the British fintech industry grew by 38 per cent, faster than that of the United States or China, and the City of London was the most important hub for Islamic finance services outside the Muslim world, administering assets worth more than $5 billion.[25] Additionally, British expertise in helping the Gulf states to eliminate corruption and malpractice will be crucial towards integrating emerging Gulf economies into globalized markets.

The Covid-19 pandemic has thrown a spanner in the works of some of the Gulf states' economic plans. Some of the ambitious goals set out in Saudi Arabia's Vision 2030, already in doubt before the pandemic, now appear even less attainable. Oman and Bahrain's precarious economic situations have also become even more worrisome over the course of 2020. To a certain extent, the Gulf states will of course recover, just like the rest of the global economy. A global upturn could even result in a rise of hydrocarbon prices, which would be a boon for the monarchies' coffers. Yet, the pandemic has also served as a reminder of the vulnerability of Gulf economies. In addition to a collapse in global oil demand, and therefore state revenues for the Gulf states, it has laid bare once again the public health risks – and human rights concerns – of large migrant worker populations living in close quarters. Moreover, it has also underscored the brittleness of industries Saudi Arabia and others had identified as future areas of growth, such as tourism and entertainment. Britain will therefore have to be nimble to react to the new realities that could emerge, even once the pandemic is confined to the past.

The sale of British-made defence equipment to the Gulf states is both the most strategic and the most controversial aspect of Britain's trading relationship with the Gulf, even though it accounts for just a fraction of overall trade. The criticism of arms exports to the Gulf states is well established; they centre around the question of whether the UK should supply weapons to states that do not share its political values and may use them in a way that violates both British values and interests, as well as human rights more generally.[26] Despite this, defence sales to the Gulf states remain in Britain's economic and strategic interest. Exports to third countries are vital to the viability and profitability of the UK's domestic defence industry, and only by exporting a share of its products can the industry continue to develop new systems for Britain's own armed forces. Without exports, the British government would have to either heavily subsidize the UK's defence industry or accept that it has to rely on arms imports (primarily from the United States) in order to equip its military. Defence sales to the Gulf also function as a conduit for long-term political and military relationships because of the inclusion of training and maintenance arrangements. For the Gulf states this means that when they buy British equipment they are also 'buying' a continued British presence in their national security structures; likewise, for the UK, selling arms to the Gulf states means securing a foothold for Britain in their foreseeable futures.

This serves as a segue to Britain's persisting geopolitical and national security interests that bind it to the Middle East, and the Gulf in particular. The UK has a continued interest in the maintenance of freedom of navigation through the Gulf, both for its own ships and for the flow of energy resources to markets around the globe. But Britain's geopolitical and security interests in the region extend far beyond the protection of shipping lanes. Conflict and instability in the region, and its by-products such as terrorism, refugee and migration crises, and the potential proliferation of nuclear weapons (centred around Iran's nuclear programme) will continue to affect British interests at home and overseas. Maintaining relations with the Gulf states has been and will remain an important part of engaging with these geopolitical and security challenges. With the exception of Bahrain, the Gulf states have remained the most stable part of the Middle East, and working with Gulf governments has been essential in dealing with terrorist threats emanating from the region. There can also hardly be a conceivable strategy to counter the ideological aspects behind Islamist violent extremism without cooperating with the Gulf states, located as they are in the very heart of the Islamic world. Furthermore, as the cases of Afghanistan and Iraq have shown, the capacity of Western states to impose political solutions on crises in the Middle East region is inherently limited. Working with local partners – both bilaterally and multilaterally – who themselves have a stake in resolving conflicts in their immediate neighbourhood is the only plausible option.

Engaging with the region's six monarchies individually and collectively opens commercial opportunities for Britain's post-Brexit economy and remains vital for the protection of Britain's national security. Furthermore, the interrelated nature of these economic, security and geopolitical interests supports the intention of the British government to take a more comprehensive and strategic approach to its ties with the Gulf. Capitalizing on the economic opportunities in the Gulf is only possible if a modicum of stability exists in the region. Conversely, given that economic decision-making in the Gulf is highly centralized, productive political relationships, boosted by a clear British commitment to Gulf security, are necessary to expand commercial ties. It therefore made sense for Theresa May to tell GCC leaders in Manama in

December 2016 that for Britain 'Gulf security is our security' and 'your prosperity is our prosperity'.[27] Considering the depth and scope of British interests in the Gulf, it is understandable why so much of London's rhetoric has focused on continuity and a broadening and deepening of existing ties, rather than a wholly new approach.

The strategic conundrum

As tempting as this narrative of continuity may be, it would be careless and even counterproductive to devise British policy towards the Gulf in the 2020s on the assumption that the UK should continue as before, just with more determination. It is crucial that the UK is clear-eyed about the significant changes that have taken place in the Gulf, particularly over the past decade, and understands why these changes are occurring. The Gulf states may still be governed by men with the same family names as those who sat on their thrones in 1971, but they are behaving very differently today than at any point in their histories. In the wake of the Arab Uprisings of 2010/11, the Gulf states (Saudi Arabia, the UAE and Qatar in particular) have emerged as significant foreign policy actors in their own right with their own regional agendas. All three have bold and ambitious leaders eager to turn their countries' accumulated power projection capabilities (including Western-made defence equipment, and money, but also diplomatic relationships and media networks) into regional influence. At the same time, they have seen the regional order around them collapse, not least enabled by what they have perceived as dithering and increasingly unreliable US administrations keen to extricate themselves from the Middle East's problems.[28] To protect themselves and their regional interests, but also to pursue emerging opportunities, leaders in Riyadh, Abu Dhabi and Doha have felt compelled to act. In doing so, they understood and approached many of the strategic and security challenges in the region in ways that differ dramatically from one another, but also from the assessments and preferred courses of action of the UK.

This has been most obvious in Egypt, Libya and Yemen. In Egypt, Saudi Arabia and the UAE welcomed the 2013 overthrow of President Morsi against Qatar's opposition, and supported the subsequent authoritarian power consolidation of a regime under former Army General Abdulfatah Al-Sisi resembling that which ruled Egypt before 2011. In Libya, the UAE and Qatar have backed opposite sides in a civil war that started shortly after the removal of the Gaddafi regime in 2011 and continues at the time of writing, although Qatar has increasingly taken a backseat in Libya leaving its ally Turkey to take a more active role. In Yemen, Saudi Arabia and the UAE have led a coalition of states to intervene in an escalating civil war since 2015. At the beginning of the 2020s, the original goals of the operation to reinstate the elected government of President Rabu Mansour Hadi and diminish the military power of the Iranian-backed Houthi rebels appear impossible to achieve. The broken country now suffers from rampant outbreaks of disease and famine, and is one of the world's most severe humanitarian crises. Furthermore, Yemen's historically fragile polity is once again on the brink of fragmentation with southern secessionists, supported by the UAE, in the ascendancy. Regionally, the three Gulf states also disagree bitterly over the role that political Islam can and should play in the region's future. This has in turn shaped their perception and approach towards dealing with the challenge of radicalization and terrorism. The UAE believes that all forms of Islamism that are connected to the ideological foundations of the Muslim Brotherhood have to be rooted out without compromise. For Abu Dhabi, terrorist organizations such as ISIS and Al-Qaeda are inextricably linked to what others regard as more moderate Islamist groups, and the only effective strategy to defeat terrorism in the region is to close any political space that could be filled by Islamists. Qatar, meanwhile, has seen Islamist groups as potential allies and conduits for influence. It insists that even some violent groups such as Hamas or various elements within the Syrian opposition (though not ISIS) can be persuaded to moderate if they are allowed to participate in politics. In its view, radicalization and terrorism are the result of the kind of repression it accuses the UAE of fostering. Saudi Arabia, finally, has mostly come down on the side of the UAE, particularly since the rise to power of Crown Prince Mohammed bin Salman.

This competition for regional influence and disagreements about the region's political future culminated in the Gulf Crisis of 2017 which, although now ended, will have ramifications well into the 2020s. The political and economic embargo launched by Saudi Arabia and the UAE, together with Bahrain and Egypt, against Qatar has effectively upended the GCC, the Middle East's only real functioning regional body. The rivalry between the Gulf states has played out across the region via various forms of intervention, ranging from providing economic assistance in exchange for political fealty, standing up media operations to support one political faction over another and even deploying armed forces.[29] All of which have done nothing but to pull countries apart and increase political polarization across the region. This is not to say that the Gulf states were the initial cause of the instability, but their actions – whether in Egypt, Libya, Syria, Somalia or Yemen – have exacerbated crises and spurred developments in ways that have diverged from the UK's own preferences. The UK has studiously avoided taking sides in the intra-Gulf dispute, insisting that it wants to maintain and expand relations with all six Gulf monarchies, ideally within the context of a functioning GCC.[30] This position is consistent with the fact that the UK's own views of the region do not align with those of either side of the dispute – not with regards to the question of extremism and terrorism, nor with the Gulf states' differing positions towards Iran.

The UK has generally agreed with the Gulf states' joint assessment that Iran has acted in a way which destabilizes the Middle East, particularly over the past two decades.[31] There has also been a clear UK–Gulf consensus that Iran must be prevented from obtaining a nuclear weapon. But the substantial differences among the Gulf states mean that aligning UK interests with them is almost impossible. All six states (with the partial exception of Oman) very reluctantly endorsed the Joint Comprehensive Plan of Action (JCPOA) between Iran and P5+1, being upset that the deal only focused on Iran's nuclear programme, but did not include provisions to address Tehran's regional activities.[32] Saudi Arabia and the UAE in particular strongly opposed the diplomatic and economic rapprochement with Iran that European countries, including the UK, pursued in the deal's aftermath. Over the past three years, Riyadh and Abu Dhabi have enthusiastically welcomed the US withdrawal from the JCPOA and the Trump administration's subsequent 'maximum pressure' policy, while doves led by Doha and

Muscat have continued to engage directly with the leadership in Tehran. With regard to Tehran's destabilizing military activities, the UK has taken strong action against Iranian threats to maritime security in the Gulf, including joining a US-led naval protection mission in 2019. Nevertheless, it has maintained its commitment to the JCPOA, while closely monitoring Iranian enrichment activities that Tehran claims are a response to Washington's withdrawal from the agreement. This is enough to assuage frustrations of Gulf states at the tactical level, but does little to alter the strategic dynamic that Riyadh and Abu Dhabi especially fear, namely normalization of the Islamic Republic, and its integration into the wider region.

At the beginning of the 2020s, there is little clarity about how the UK's and the Gulf states' individual priorities with regards to Iran can be reconciled. All sides agree that a large-scale war between the USA and Iran would be catastrophic for the region and that Iranian military activity is highly destablizing. But beyond this there is little that can be agreed upon. To some extent UK–Gulf agreement on Iran policy may be a moot point as the United States is the ultimate arbiter of any nuclear deal with Iran and the dominant factor in any military escalation. This was demonstrably shown in the unilateral US decision to target and kill Iranian General Qassim Soleimani, which left the Gulf States, Britain, France and others scrambling to contain an escalation that could well have enveloped the region in wider conflict. The Biden administration, which contains a number of senior officials who were intimately involved in the negotiation process for the JCPOA, is keen to re-engage with Tehran, and potentially resume America's commitment to the agreement, although at the time of writing, there is no guarantee this will be successful. In any case, it is clear that the United States will remain the dominant actor with regard to Iranian regional and global policy for years to come, and so it should remain the foremost goal of the UK to mitigate any potential fallout (military and/or diplomatic) from strained US–Iranian relations. To this end it is acceptable to bifurcate Iran policy between tactical deployments that both constrain Iranian regional activity in the Gulf and reassure the Arab Gulf, from the strategic question of the JCPOA in which the UK needs to focus heavily on maintaining functioning relations with the United States and the Europeans. This may sound dismissive to Gulf concerns on the JCPOA, but ultimately the UK should not apologize that it views the JCPOA as the best possible vehicle for non-proliferation that currently exists. Holding to this policy might irritate partners in the Gulf, but given there is no unitary Gulf policy on Iran anyway, the negative consequences of holding to this line are minimal.

All of this confusion has only one outcome, which is that whatever policy path the UK chooses, it is bound to annoy at least one country in the GCC. The fundamental strategic shifts that have occurred, driven partly by the United States' reluctance to play the role of regional hegemon, which is likely to continue under the Biden administration, have led to a systemic political and security vacuum, which the Gulf states have rushed to fill. Qatar, Saudi Arabia and UAE in particular will no longer be quiet actors, passively buying armaments and watching the region's politics unfold around them. As the political and security order in the Middle East region changes beyond recognition, the Gulf states will do their utmost to ensure that it does not change in ways that harm their own stability, which means being active across the region. It is incumbent upon British policymakers therefore to ask whether these divisions in the Gulf are deleterious to Britain's wider economic and strategic goals, or whether these divisions preclude a more stable security order from emerging. None of this can be achieved without the support of the United States, alongside a concert of wider actors including France, China, Japan and India to name but a few. But given the relative reluctance of any of these external actors to sustainably engage to solve regional disputes, the possibility of a stable GCC region seems far off indeed.

Human rights

The poor standard of human rights and lack of accountable governance that exist across all of the Gulf states should not be ignored. It remains true that the promotion of British values is a core part of UK foreign policy, even if at times the topic can seem an afterthought. When confronted with the undeniable fact that the region's authoritarian regimes contradict liberal British values, the traditional argument goes that when it comes to matters of security cooperation and the geopolitics of the region, British and Gulf interests align. But given the developments of the past decade and the subsequent disruptions that have been caused by intra-Gulf squabbling, it is becoming increasingly difficult to argue this is true. Through the Gulf strategy, London hoped that with direct engagement and continued quiet messaging on human rights Britain could champion its own values and perhaps nudge its partners in the Gulf states towards positive reforms. Theresa May for example, argued that 'we don't uphold our values and human rights by turning our back' and that Britain could 'achieve far more by stepping up, engaging with these countries and working with them to encourage and support their plans for reform'.[33] But the notion that British engagement with the Gulf regimes has had or could have a liberalizing influence on their political systems is not supported by any evidence. The Gulf states may have embraced measures of social liberalization in the past decade, most notably in Saudi Arabia where women now drive and young Saudis flock to pop concerts. However, in terms of political freedoms the Gulf states have unquestionably gone into reverse. And when it comes to their own positions on maintaining political stability all six Gulf states have taken inspiration from the political model of China more than they have from the UK and the West. Until recently the Washington Consensus that sought to match economic liberalization with political reform appeared the only model that the Gulf states could follow. But with Beijing's rise to become a global superpower the Gulf states have an example par excellence of economic advancement that requires little to no political reform.

To this end the Gulf states have enthusiastically embraced the idea that they should reform economically (albeit it with mixed success). Yet, the political structures of the Gulf are nearly identical to how they were twenty years ago. The question is therefore not one of reform, because the Gulf states have reformed, just not in the way that London had hoped. Today's Gulf rulers are younger, more modern and tech savvy than their predecessors. Their governments have been moved increasingly to online services, and the general standard of government bureaucracy across all six countries has certainly improved from even ten years ago. But there is little doubt that technological innovation has led to increasingly more efficient tools of repression and enabled the Gulf states to simply be better authoritarians.[34] After years of cajoling and persuasion London needs to acknowledge a basic fact. The Gulf states have always been autocracies, and they will likely remain autocracies no matter what London says, or what political reform initiatives it tries to push forward. Acknowledging this uncomfortable truth will be hard for London, but it needs to be done.

British policymakers may think there are shades of grey in the values debate, and ministers will continue to deliver messages of Britain's concern about human rights, as they always have. But outwith consular issues, and individual cases of egregious human rights abuses, there is little that can be done to change the political direction of the Gulf. The Gulf states do not want to appear global pariahs, which affords a space for engagement on issues of concern to London, but there is a difference between window dressing gestures, which protect the Gulf's political elites, and deep structural reform, which fundamentally rebalances how the state-citizen contract is constructed. And so, when it comes to its relationship with the Gulf, London will need to more realistically balance economic benefits (which are admittedly substantial), against strategic benefits (which are increasingly less clear), and measure both alongside the promotion and propagation of British values in Foreign Policy, which the Gulf states pay little more than lip service towards, and even actively work against. The problem is eloquently stated elsewhere in this volume by James Lynch who notes that values will most likely be subordinated to economic and security interests when dealing with Britain's allies in the region.[35] No better has this trade-off been exemplified than by Britain's imposition of sanctions on individuals in Saudi Arabia for human rights abuses, while simultaneously communicating its apologies in private to the Saudi government so that arms sales could resume.[36]

While a realist policymaker might be comfortable with this new norm, the average British voter certainly will not be. For years to come politicians will be raising human rights concerns to ministers, especially if and when a Labour government returns to power. The stage is set for more uncomfortable years ahead, whereby UK Foreign Office officials will have little in the way of substantive answers to questions that penetrate deeply to the core of Britain's identity and values.

Calculating British interests in an era global competition

The balance of world power is shifting. Accelerated by the coronavirus pandemic and its aftermath, China has begun to solidify its presence on the world stage, chiefly at the expense of the United States. For London, this is becoming the central strategic issue it must urgently consider as it recalibrates its post-Brexit foreign policy, including in the Middle East.[37] It will be a challenging task to build a Gulf strategy that has longevity in the midst of a changing global order and that is able to sustain British economic and security interests in an era of great strategic uncertainty. The UK has certainly thought about the challenge of a rising China, which was partly addressed in the 2015 Gulf Strategy. But until recently London had no real need to face the reality of the Gulf region being pulled between the world's two preeminent powers. Economically the

Gulf has been turning eastwards since the beginning of the twenty-first century. This is hardly in dispute and, given China's thirst for energy, this trend can only continue regardless of the actions of Western states.[38] In the security realm the United States unquestionably remains the most important actor. However, the global role of the United States is subject to question, particularly as a result of taking a back seat in tackling the coronavirus. This in turn has led the Gulf states to consider how to position themselves in such a fragile and unstable global order.[39] What is clear however is that the United States is in no mood to allow China to capitalize from the coronavirus pandemic, and Washington is keen to face down the Chinese economic and diplomatic activity across the Middle East. Across the region, but especially in Israel and the Gulf, the United States has been encouraging local companies to decouple from China or face punitive consequences.[40] The Gulf states for their part have already signalled that they do not wish to be drawn into a great game between the two sides,[41] but this may become increasingly unavoidable if global tensions between China and Washington continue to rise. For now, the Gulf states can adopt a balancing act whereby the United States retains its domination of the security sphere, while Beijing increasingly becomes the main economic actor in the region. But much depends on events outside of their control.

Without careful thought the UK could become caught in a vice whereby the pursuit of British security interests in the region (which London mostly shares with Washington) secures the Gulf, allowing GCC states to pursue aggressive trade and economic policies that strengthen their relationship with Beijing. To avoid this problem, any Gulf policy must be considered within the wider rubric of Britain's policy on China and Britain's Indo-Pacific tilt. Should the Indo-Pacific tilt encourage the perception that London is in lockstep with Washington in resisting Chinese influence globally, then the trade and security relationships that Britain forges in the Gulf carry an additional zero-sum component to them. This is to say that any business won for Britain is business that Beijing is not winning, which prevents (or more likely delays) the point at which Beijing becomes the dominant actor in the Gulf region. This may all seem largely irrelevant at the micro-level, more British business in the Gulf is surely a good thing, and for sectors of the economy such as education, healthcare and hospitality, the notion that their day-to-day activities are somehow part of global competition with China will seem distant, if not irrelevant. However, given US pressure on Gulf companies that cooperate with China on medical testing facilities, and Washington's deep concerns about the activity of Huawei, telecommunications and security firms, the problems are very real. Washington's penchant for sanctions to constrain China may mean there are risks for those companies that empower Chinese activity in the region or that cooperate in any way with Chinese firms operating out of the Gulf.

The Gulf states will undoubtedly mitigate such concerns by pointing to the fact that their growing economies mean that there is more trade and economic benefit for everyone who wishes to trade with them. There is no doubt that, under the right circumstances, the Gulf states and in particular Saudi Arabia could emerge from the coronavirus pandemic in a strong position, increasing market share in the global oil market and taking advantage of steadily increasing oil prices to place themselves in a strong position financially in the medium term.[42] But whether the UK chooses to view this through the lens of narrow economic benefit, gladly accepting Gulf cash to help boost Britain's post-Brexit coffers, or as a warning light for the increasing presence of China in the region, largely depends on how it chooses to view Chinese political and economic activity at the macro-level. It would certainly be an attractive option for the UK to strike out on its own with a Gulf policy that pursues economic self-interest in the Gulf regardless of what Washington and Beijing think. But given London's deep military integration with the United States in the Gulf this would be a difficult balancing act. Simply muddling through and relying on the UK's traditional strengths and relationships in the region will not be enough and is liable to create serious long-term problems for British businesses and political headaches for Whitehall. To avoid this and the inevitable further diminishing of British influence in the Gulf that would come with it, the government will have to make clear strategic decisions about how it wants Britain to navigate the looming US–China competition, both at the global and the regional level.

As with the Iranian nuclear deal, both the UK and the Gulf states are hostage to forces beyond their control. Much will depend on how and in what ways the Biden administration decides it wishes to confront China, and what diplomatic capital it is willing to expend to do so. The UK must be mindful that the Gulf is now an arena of competition between Washington and Beijing and will become ever more so in the future. London may be able to avoid picking a side economically, but in the security realm no such choice exists. As previously stated any future Gulf strategy must now consider the geostrategic implications of engagement with the Gulf far more carefully than in years gone by. The days in which the UK could focus narrowly on regional security concerns, while increasing its economic share in the Gulf look to be coming to an end.

Conclusion

The Gulf states have played and will continue to play a central part in the UK's foreign policy towards the Middle East. Over the coming decade, the six Gulf monarchies are likely to be important trading partners and sources of investment for the UK's post-Brexit economy. Existing relationships are strong and multifaceted and have the potential to grow further – including, for example, Gulf interest to invest in UK-based research and development efforts to find treatments for the coronavirus, in the growing British fintech and Islamic finance industries, and in London's real-estate market that has long been a favourite destination for Gulf capital. It would be foolhardy for the UK not to welcome and seek to deepen these commercial ties in the years ahead.

Nevertheless, the 2020s will not be business as usual and much has changed since the UK first launched its Gulf Strategy in 2015. Global shifts in the distribution of power, both economically and geopolitically, coupled with inconsistencies in US regional policy in the Middle East, have fundamentally altered the way in which the Gulf states view both their prosperity and security. The UK must evaluate how its political, economic and security interests in the Middle East have been and will be affected by these changing dynamics. As the Gulf states see China as an increasingly important strategic partner, building on hydrocarbon exports that remain the lifeblood of their own economies and societies, the UK has to contend with the fact that both its and Washington's voice will increasingly count for less. Governments in London and in capitals across the Arabian Peninsula will have to find a way to navigate a post-coronavirus world that is being shaped by an increasingly adversarial relationship between the United States and China.

Additionally, the activist turn in the Gulf states' own foreign policies during the 2010s has opened up deep divisions between them that have undermined their own prosperity and wider regional security and stability and that are unlikely to disappear anytime soon. The UK therefore faces a balancing act in the region: it cannot engage with the GCC as a whole as the organization has become paralyzed by divisions; instead, it has to construct its Gulf policy around six separate bilateral relationships that do not promote the political or strategic objectives of one Gulf state over another. Accordingly, any highfalutin goals of creating a regional security architecture amongst the Gulf states, much less between them and Iran, will be out of London's reach. Only by focusing solely on maximizing the bilateral engagement with each state is the UK likely to reap substantial benefits in the short to medium term. The UK will also need to come to terms with the uncomfortable fact that the model of political and economic reform espoused by Western states is unlikely to happen in the Gulf. China's model of authoritarian state-led economic development presents a genuine alternative for the Gulf monarchs. They are keen to reform, but in the pursuit of more centralized power, rather than towards the political liberalization the UK has long sought to promote. The long-standing debate about if and how the UK should weigh prosperity and security interests and values in its engagement with the Gulf is likely to become even more fraught.

The pursuit of economic benefit will ultimately be the main driver in Gulf policy for many years to come, the fallout from the Covid-19 pandemic notwithstanding. But the risks of narrow-minded economic engagement will lead to significant challenges for London, and possibly be deleterious to wider British strategic concerns regionally and indeed globally. A clear-headed assessment of the increased risks of Gulf engagement is required for the UK to successfully make the most out of its most important partnerships in the region, and to reinforce the logic behind the decision to return East of Suez.

14

Egypt

Emman El-Badawy

Events in Cairo formed a significant part of the past 150 years of British foreign policy and were once a centrepiece of Britain's policy in the Middle East. Seen as the pinnacle of the Islamic world and the heart of the Arab Middle East, Egypt carried influence greater than its relative size and wealth. Though attention to Cairo has subsided as Gulf and Levantine countries dominate today's regional affairs, the importance of this historic relationship has not diminished. The political future of Egypt matters, not only because of the size of its fast-growing population (now at over 100 million) and its geographical proximity to Europe and the UK, but also because any changes within its borders will undoubtedly impact its immediate neighbourhood.

How the next era for Egypt is managed at the political and diplomatic levels could lead to a critical partnership in handling many of the contemporary problems facing the wider region. But the challenges ahead are great. Not least because the only relatively fixed course appears to be towards the consolidation of a controversial military power following the period of political instability from 2011. Alternatives, should they emerge, will most likely come through the military or as the result of significant upheaval.

Attempting to place Britain's long-term role and British interests within such challenging contexts can feel like battling between two minds: that of a realist on the one hand, recognizing that sometimes you have to work with what you have for the sake of influence and engagement and that of an idealist on the other, convinced of the prospects for a different and more prosperous future, and a sense of duty to enable it at any cost.

To examine the future of the relationship between Britain and Egypt in the context of a post-Brexit 'Global Britain' is to reflect first on a controversial legacy of British presence in Egypt, and to acknowledge both Britain's limitations today and Egypt's resistance to reform. It is through these considerations that Britain's approach towards Egypt should now be shaped.

When it has come to shaping Britain's policy on Egypt, contemporary Britain has tended more towards a realist agenda. It has done so, however, for reasons of circumstance rather than profound calculation. Even the staunchest of realists within Whitehall would prefer allies that were internally stable and politically predictable.

With regards to Egypt, any attempt at managing the trade-off between strategic interest and moral imperative will be a long-term craft, with an ally that is neither stable nor predictable.

Historical baggage

Britain's colonial legacy in Egypt may well be, for those in Whitehall, a ghost of Britain's past, but for Egyptians, the memory of imperial Britain is residual. To find an Egyptian who is not intimately familiar with the story of Egypt's struggle for independence would be near impossible. The history of Britain in Egypt has been systematically drummed into every generation of Egyptians since 1952 for the purpose of sustaining a sense of collective memory and national unity, if nothing else. Through the formal education system, Britain's imperial grip on Egypt still lies at the heart of the story for self-determination, with history and civic study textbooks each recounting Egypt's quest to define its own destiny and overcome British interference. Beyond this, Egyptians are daily exposed to the street names, post-stamps, statues, currency and imposing buildings that feature relics and icons of nationalist agitators and the enemies of imperial Britain. From Ahmed Urabi who led a (failed) military revolt against British rule in 1882 to Saad Zaghloul who spearheaded negotiations for Egyptian independence after the First World War, Egyptians have become accustomed to daily references of nationalist heroes from President Gamal Abdel Nasser to Ahmed Shawqi, Taha Hussein, Mohammed Abdel Wahab and Um Kulthoum. History, for Egyptians, is not confined to the past.

Few bilateral relations in Britain's modern history are laden with more historical baggage than that with Egypt. Most educated Britons would feel they knew the main outlines of their country's involvement with, for example, the sub-continent. Very few would hazard a guess about Britain's involvement with Egypt. What little they might come up with would concern the Suez Canal: its building, its vital role in maintaining sea communication with British India, the battles fought in the Western Desert to defend it in 1942–3 and the humiliating final act of the Suez Crisis of 1956. The focus on the Canal is entirely justified, from an imperial perspective. It also suggests a lack of acknowledgement of the significance of Egypt in its own right: an ancient land with one of the earliest great settled civilizations, and a strong sense of national identity. Such depth of historical identity is rare in the modern world of nation-states, perhaps especially so in the Middle East and Africa. It continues to play a determining role in how Egypt regards itself as a polity and its resistance to foreign assistance. Political reflexes in the governing circles, above all in those made up of the military, derive strongly from this common and almost now subconscious recollection of Britain's and Egypt's contentious past.

The origins of Britain's modern relations with Egypt were skewed from the start in a relationship of coercion as well as ambiguity. Egypt was nominally independent but in practice in a semi-colonial state of dependency for decades. It was not part of Britain's formal empire, but informally was regarded almost as a possession, though one in which the welfare of the ordinary people was conveniently left to the national authorities.[1] British rule cut off the consolidation of an Egyptian military and administrative elite, and placed landowners, merchants, officials and intelligentsia into a secondary elite. Still hampered by British occupation, these elites eventually came to power in 1922 and governed until 1952. Unable to overcome the dilemmas of governing under foreign rule, and divided by nationalist and Islamist political leanings, the divided elites of the constitutional monarchy were eventually deposed and replaced by a new generation of Arab nationalist military officers who instituted the military regime that governs Egypt to the present day.

This then was the heavy negative baggage that has weighed on Britain's image among the Egyptian ruling class, as well as among the ordinary people. It was offset to a small degree by British involvement in higher education, including the founding of Cairo University. The narrative of the independence movement however had discounted even this: British policy was alleged to have been to keep Egypt in a state of educational disadvantage as part of its imperial strategy. There were cordial and respectful personal links with British professionals living in Egypt, but these tended to be in the wider cosmopolitan circles that had grown since the early nineteenth century.

A notable exception of such cordial interactions concerns the military. Resentment of the 1882 suppression of the military uprising persisted and formed an enduring grudge. In contrast to how the late period of British rule in India saw close and mutually respectful relations develop between the British and Indian officer classes, no such contact occurred in Egypt. Instead, mutual hostility and distrust prevailed. When the Free Officers mounted their coup against the decadent and discredited constitutional monarchy in 1952, the views and historical perspective of the close-knit military class suddenly counted for more than anything else.

The Suez Crisis of 1956 was of course a disaster for Britain as it hastened the collapse of its imperial status in the wider world. But it was a triumph for Egypt's military president, Gamal Abdel Nasser, and his fellow officers, as Nasser's popularity soared among the region's Arabs. As Nasser's popularity grew, so did the mandate for the military to rule the country. During those years the new regime had expelled almost the entire population of non-Egyptians: British, French, Greeks, Jews, Italians, Syro-Lebanese and Maltese. This was to have catastrophic results on the quality of urban life, just as the expropriation of large estates and Egyptian businesses was to have on the economy. At the time, it provided a windfall of funds and patronage that the new ruling military clique could use to strengthen their hold on the country. Egypt has been trapped by the consequences ever since, but so too has Britain.

Since the birth of the Republic of Egypt in 1952 and its independence from British rule, Britain has sought to maintain diplomatic ties with Egypt under six presidents: Mohammed Naguib (1952–4), Gamal Abdel Nasser (1954–70), Anwar al-Sadat (1970–81), Hosni Mubarak (1981–2011), Muhammad Morsi (2012–13) and Abdel Fatah al-Sisi (2014–present). However, establishing and sustaining new relations via army cadres (easily the most deeply nationalistic and by extension anti-British cohort of Egyptian society) have taken years of diplomatic effort. It was during the Mubarak era where the British–Egyptian relationship became most cordial and constructive. Since the early 1980s, relations have steadily progressed past the tense decades of the 1950s and the 1960s. Britain has achieved this while having to circumvent the sensitivities of ever appearing to overly intervene in Egyptian affairs.

Today, the relationship is bound by mutually convenient cooperation agreements and partnerships from security to trade and economic reform. For the last two decades, Britain's relationship with Egypt has been secured via the EU–Egypt Association Agreement, now due to end for Britain as it exits the bloc.[2] Britain played a critical role in 2001, supporting Egypt's demands before the EU member states during the negotiation over the agreement, and this helped to secure a positive bilateral partnership.[3] The two countries in this period shared interests and cooperated on critical issues, from the Palestinian question, to Sudan, Somalia, Iraq, disarmament and non-proliferation; with much of this channelled through the framework for political dialogue provided by the EU–Egypt Association Agreement. Discussions to establish a new UK–Egypt Association Agreement were underway since the decision to leave the EU. The new bilateral agreement, signed in December 2020, provides continuity on the trading relationship and replicates many elements of the old one, but with removal and replacement of references to the EU.

British cooperation with Cairo, beyond the framework of the new bilateral agreement in trade and investment, has never been stronger. The UK remains one of the largest investors in Egypt to date, investing $48 billion across all sectors.[4] The relationship boasts eighty partnerships between British and Egyptian higher education institutions, and through the UK's Chevening Scholarships Programme; fifty fully funded professional scholarships are awarded to young Egyptians every year. This is all part of a broader economic partnership between the UK and Egypt towards its 2030 national agenda, in line with the UN Sustainable Development Goals. On the horizon is even more potential, with the UK looking to deepen financial links in Egypt and boost trade and investment through the British–Egypt Investors Forum, and the structural assistance it continues to provide on education and healthcare. Despite distractions from Covid-19 in 2020, Egypt went ahead with listing its first sovereign Green Bond on the London Stock Exchange before the year ended.[5] The move – the first of its kind from the Middle East and North Africa – was a bold gesture, designed to increase both the environmental rating of Egypt and the confidence of foreign investors in the Egyptian market, and goes further to setting the agenda for a partnership between the UK and Egypt on climate issues.

Likewise, in defence and security the relationship continues to deepen through crafted agreements and methods for cooperation. Flight restrictions imposed by the UK on Sharm el-Sheikh since the terrorist attack on a Russian civilian aircraft in 2015 had left a bitter taste for UK–Egypt diplomatic relations, but in March 2019, Britain and Egypt engaged in the first bilateral military training in thirty years, with more joint exercises to come.[6] As well as historically serving as an important regional interlocutor, Egypt has been one of the largest contributors to peacekeeping forces in Africa and so remains a critically important defence partner for Britain. Both countries remain deeply committed to confronting the threat of international terrorism and this shared enemy forms the basis of a firm partnership. As the Egyptian army continues its longest and largest operation to date to overturn Islamic State's affiliate in the Northeastern

Sinai Peninsula and the Western Desert that borders Libya, this partnership has never been more warmly received. To formalize the strategic partnership, Britain and Egypt signed the first Memorandum of Understanding (MoU) in 2018, with commitments to conduct joint military exercises on counterterrorism warfare. In a show of joint British and Egyptian commitment to this MoU, Britain's Chief of Secret Intelligence Service (MI6), Richard Moore, travelled to meet with President el-Sisi in Cairo in the midst of the unfolding pandemic in November 2020. The exchange reportedly focused on boosting security and intelligence between the UK and Egypt.[7] Moore praised Egypt for its 'stabilising role' in the region – both in countering terrorism and in the Libya crisis.

On the surface then, the relationship between Britain and Egypt is thriving – pragmatic and mutually beneficial. Yet, the question is, beyond immediate shared interests, does Britain have the relationship or leverage to deviate past the point where immediate interests meet? For every partnership and area for cooperation between Britain and Egypt today, there is a short-termism and realism running throughout. Is this the best Britain can hope for, or is there room to craft some space for idealistic, long-term thinking?

Conservation of power or reform?

Ten years on from the popular uprisings that deposed President Mubarak, Egypt's potential for failure has been its greatest leverage. The determination to keep Egypt politically stable and maintain peace in an otherwise chaotic region has seen Cairo receive funds under the auspices of upstream prevention of conflict and instability via programmes administered by the UK Foreign Office (FCO) and Departments for International Development (DfID) – now FCDO or Foreign, Commonwealth and Development Office – and Business, Energy and Industrial Strategy (DfBEIS). From energy, governance, technology and innovation, to education, migration, conflict and security, British development assistance to Egypt in the last decade has seemingly been in line with broader UK objectives abroad: to help build prosperous and democratic countries, tackle the drivers of instability and insecurity, and address global challenges. Yet the formation of a progressive and coherent bilateral policy with Britain towards Egypt has proved enigmatically difficult. Success stories on single-issue joint agreements in defence or economic reform carry the risk of ignoring the bigger picture. It is, in the end, all dimensions of economic, political and social realities that will determine Egypt's stability.

The events from 2011 confirmed much of what had already been well-documented in FCO and DfID reports concerning MENA up to 2010: Security-based regimes with weak civil society and unaccountable governance were sleep-walking into daunting times, and it was in Britain's interest to support political, economic and social reform. A FCO Strategy Unit paper, published in Spring 2010, concluded that a positive enabling environment for UK interests was best secured by a Middle East that was stable, well-governed and prosperous, and that actions on the Arab Human Development agenda were key to breaking the cycle, including action on political and social participation.[8]

The recommendations put forward were too broad and multifaceted to be actioned, but they recognized then the need, before the uprisings began, for greater central coordination and oversight, clearer strategic direction and policy goals, and firm allocation of resources to address a daunting list of challenges that could threaten UK interests in the region. Conflict prevention, energy security, counterterrorism and anti-radicalization, migration, and securing defence interests, commitments and commercial opportunities were noted as central to UK concerns related to the region broadly, and these remain priorities today. Under Mubarak, Egypt more specifically had become central to some of the UK's foreign policy goals, including the Middle East Peace Process, conflict in Sudan and in supporting the establishment of a Middle East Nuclear Weapon Free Zone.[9] Egypt's leading religious authority, al-Azhar, was also regarded across the FCO as a powerful counterweight 'to radical forces in the region and a valuable partner in countering extremism'.[10] While signs of brewing internal tensions in Cairo were flagged by research analysts by 2010, it was not clear how important a stable Egypt was to UK policy until a credible threat had materialized that risked unravelling decades of bilateral cooperation on priority concerns in the region. Before 2011, by no means was Egypt a focal country for the Arab Human Development department, which would later be named the Arab Partnership Unit. Instead, its remit clearly stated Iraq, Lebanon, Yemen, Israel and the Occupied Palestinian Territories to be priority areas for tri-departmental (FCO, Ministry of Defense, and DfID) funds and initiatives.

Yet Egypt became the largest and most significant country to be affected by the popular uprisings that ricocheted across the region. The Egyptian protestors' achievements in deposing one of the longest-serving and deeply rooted leaders in the Middle East undoubtedly galvanized protestors in Syria against Bashar al-Assad and in Libya against Colonel Gaddafi. But unlike Libya and Syria, the overall picture in Cairo after all the upheaval remains largely unchanged. Egypt's figurehead is still a quasi-military man, consistent with every president before him since 1954; the military still maintains a monopoly over economic, political and social affairs of the country; emergency law is still the daily norm for Egyptians as it has been almost consistently since 1967, justified largely by the threat of Islamist insurgency and political insecurity that is now a war of attrition in the Sinai; the same accusations of corruption and clientelist networks that long plagued Egypt's political and economic systems have also been levelled against today's regime by al-Sisi's critics, with poor distribution of wealth a living consequence; and the same security-over-rights-pact that has underpinned the social contract for Egyptians for decades and led to the uprisings in 2011 in the first place continues – newly packaged but otherwise identical.

Whether the UK's engagement thus far has been in the best interests of the Egyptian people depends on the unanswerable question of who speaks on behalf of the Egyptian people, and on a fine judgement of whether it is the conservation of power, or reform – or a combination – that can provide the most stability and least catastrophic future from Britain's perspective. This is the defining principle through which Britain's policy with Egypt must now be shaped. But such a view must be based on (a) an informed, multi-disciplinary and critical analysis of competing power dynamics and emerging political and security risks across the country – focusing on those that would simultaneously pose a risk to Britain and (b) an assessment of Britain's degree of influence in helping to mitigate those risks. All good risk assessors know that a risk assessment is ongoing, and that some risks lead to 'no action'. But it is the process of acknowledging the risk that is essential to managing it.

As far as the conditions still exist, the 'Arab spring' cannot be dismissed as over, and the threat of further popular dissent and political instability for Egypt remains a distinct possibility. Despite the assessments and reports written before and since 2011, no policies today have built in the scope and flexibility to assess and respond to any emerging threat should it evolve again across Egypt, and then prepare for it politically. Political preparedness needs an established and informed conviction that the route to building prosperity for the Egyptian people requires a decision in the end – to work with and support Egypt's current leadership or instead back revolutionary forces. As the latter is impossible given that those revolutionary forces of 2011 are no longer organized or united, Britain currently has one clear route – to formulate a policy that consolidates support for the existing regime.

Critics will argue that this approach sees a return to the Machiavellian Realpolitik that made Western allies of autocratic regimes unpopular on the Arab streets. Yet Realpolitik does not have to be cunning and self-serving. It can, by its original conception as put by its pioneer, German liberal theorist Ludwig von Rochau, simply mean a rejection of liberal utopianism whilst still putting forward liberal ideals.[11] In such a theory, Britain can work to assist a comprehensive reform agenda – paving a vision for the future and guiding Egypt through a realistic path.

This means that Britain will need to exert its full diplomatic skills to improve and maintain trust from the military regime for the sake of cooperating on urgent, short-term but likely ongoing priorities, such as regional security and counterterrorism, while simultaneously staying true to the values Britain hopes to represent over the long term. Alienating the regime and making public threats will not incentivize the Egyptian regime to open up the political space and relieve the stranglehold on public life. Instead, trust-building is paramount for any policy in Egypt to be workable. The Egyptians remain one of the hardest governments to penetrate, fiercely resistant to receiving international assistance or technical support unless invited on their terms.

Though al-Sisi has engaged in long overdue economic reforms, it has not been a silver bullet by any means. Deeper and more structural reform is needed to raise the standards of living for the average Egyptian, more so now with the arrival of a global public health crisis that has forced unprecedented long-term economic damage. Despite recent World Bank reporting on Egypt suggesting healthy economic growth as a result of reforms, the dividends were yet to be felt on the streets. The recent economic improvements that saw Egypt's Gross Domestic Product (GDP) expand by a reported 5.6 per cent were at the time still just abstract figures to the average Egyptian, but any positive trajectory will most certainly now be disrupted by the Covid-19 pandemic, placing greater pressure on the regime to secure public funds and channel them more strategically.

Numbers of Egyptian families struggling to make ends meet had grown since uncertainty hit in 2011, with the number of Egyptians relying on food subsidies reaching 22 million by 2013. With Covid-19 limiting tourism like never before, as well as the disruption of payments received from the Suez Canal and remittances from Egyptians working abroad affected by the slowdown of economies worldwide, the economic downturn could become severe, with little to cushion the impact. Egypt's GDP was expected in March 2020 to decline by almost 1 per cent for each month that the global crisis continues.[12] The impact on the Egyptian people already struggling before Covid-19 could become untenable, with household consumption and expenditure forecast to decline by around 10 per cent on average at the start of the pandemic, and unemployment rising by a reported 7.7 per cent as of August 2020 due to the initial Covid-19 mitigation measures.[13] For now, the government insists that its costly national construction megaprojects, including the development of the New Administrative Capital, has been the 'pillar of growth during the partial lockdown'. Yet the latest wave of protests has been triggered not by Covid-19 measures, but by al-Sisi's construction plans that now see homes demolished and fines administered in some of Egypt's most deprived quarters amidst growing economic instability.

National confidence in the government's long-term reform agenda was weakened long before the pandemic. A wave of serious accusations hit the regime in 2019, from low-level corruption and wasting of public funds to accusations made against al-Sisi for exacerbating the conflict in North Sinai for business interests, and the deliberate targeting of civilians during counterterrorism operations in the Sinai. This triggered small-scale but coordinated protests in Egypt's major cities and was a sign of more flare-ups to come. The challenging road ahead with interruption to economic growth may well precipitate the next wave of instability and political protest against the regime and put pressure on the regime's allies and supporters to secure vital stability. Yet accusations by activists that Britain remained silent amidst the regime's wave of arrests and its heavy crackdown on protestors in 2019[14] miss the central most important point when devising the future policy with Egypt: do not overestimate Britain's leverage.

Some strategic patience towards Egypt now recognizes the long journey ahead and the need to build trust between Britain and Egypt. It resists temptations for reflex, short-term decision-making and acknowledges both Egypt's sensitivities to reform and Britain's limited leverage. It allows for principled engagement to continue with commitments on both sides, whilst investing in relationships and building expertise that can pay dividends towards a step change when future opportunities and political openings may reveal themselves. This can and must be done all while still upholding the universal values, rights and freedoms that Britain once identified as key to breaking the cycle of discontent in countries of the Middle East.

The realities of the Iraq War, and later the failings of the Arab Spring, show that evolution and agreed processes of change are better than revolution or regime change, especially in the absence of a discernible alternative that could unite the people of a country. No matter how abhorrent a dictatorship, once the dictator is removed, elements of extremism can and will move into the void to create chaos and instability. The lessons of the West's past in the Middle East are clear, but the conclusions are flawed. A fallacy that stability and reform are somehow in competition, and that we must choose between reform at the expense of stability (read: security), or stability at the expense of reform (read: insecurity), has seemed to entrench itself deep within Western foreign policy circles. This false trade-off has crippled the region and constrained Western policymakers. No doubt in the last twenty years, since 9/11, containment and security alliances have become the priority agenda with regards to the Middle East, which has obscured any possibility that there could be another way – a hybrid of the two options, realistic and yet optimistic.

The Arab Spring and subsequent Egyptian protests showed that there was a desire for change. Whatever their political ideology, protestors were demanding an alternative to the status quo. But what began in 2010 was far more complex than the simple Western paradigm of progress equals democracy. It was instead an emerging narrative for modernization, accountable government and solutions to address the deep economic hardship against the flagrant corruption that existed in the country. In 2019, protests in Lebanon, Iraq and Iran also showed a rejection of the politicization of Islam in everyday life and day-to-day politics. A post-Arab Spring generation is emerging and with it an increasing demand for change. 'Reform', therefore, in any conception of a British–Egypt policy that combines realism with optimism can focus on how Britain can assist in accelerating a programme for social and economic reforms beyond security cooperation and trade agreements. This means working to secure a way forward for Egypt and the region built on modern societies that are religiously and culturally tolerant, and where matters of religious belief and the state are actively separated. This should be accompanied by modern economies based on diversification programmes, the embrace of technology and high standards of education. This type of message resonates with a new generation that is technologically advanced, entrepreneurial, and hostile to the misuse and politicization of religious and cultural identities that resulted in opportunities lost for previous generations of the region.[15] This is precisely where Britain's interests and the current regime's interests can naturally align when it comes to reform, and can form part of a wider strategy that complements reforms elsewhere in the region, as pressures rise to diversify economies and modernize societies towards a brighter future.

Walking the tight rope

Courting the current Egyptian government carries reputational risk for Britain, as does any relationship with an authoritarian regime in a polarized society with a failed attempt at revolution. A UK policy in Egypt that intends to maintain a workable partnership on shared interests in the region must do so in the knowledge that the dominance of the military in Egypt's political, social and economic future is here to stay. Should there be any serious political challenge to al-Sisi, it will not directly affect the military's hold on power in the country, and any alternative candidates for the presidency will be almost certainly put forward by the army itself.

While al-Sisi remains the figurehead with executive powers, he does not yet have the unwavering support and authority across the military establishment that Mubarak once had. His control over state institutions was not directly inherited by Mubarak, contrary to allusions. Al-Sisi has instead had to earn it or formulate it himself, knowing full well that should popular uprisings amount to the scale of that against Mubarak, the military will seek to placate the masses through cosmetic change of the presidency rather than cede control. The tight formation of Mubarak's reign took decades in the making. He built personal loyalties within the army, intelligence and administrative ranks that allowed him to form a tight and trusted inner circle, consolidating the executive powers he would later reap for the rest of his thirty-year tenure. For this reason, al-Sisi is best compared to Mubarak in the 1980s rather than Mubarak in the 2000s. With the fourth reshuffle across the army, administrative and intelligence services since 2015, al-Sisi does seem to be looking to mirror Mubarak's approach, but he does not yet have the personal control that allowed Mubarak centralized command powers. With the erosion of trust, personal gain and agendas, and high turnover of leadership positions, some fractures have been real and lasting. Smoothing over these cracks will go on to be a priority for al-Sisi and will present some destabilization for diplomatic engagement at the working level.

It is likely though that Egypt's human rights record may prove to be the real sticking-point in this crucial balancing act. The UK foreign policy apparatus has been criticized at home for its failures to report back on the efficacy of its private diplomacy approach regarding Egypt's controversial human rights record.[16] Since the Mubarak era, Britain has been accused of appearing too weak with Egypt on human rights and failing to hold its ally accountable. This has only become more contentious since the Arab uprisings placed Egypt's treatment of journalists and activists firmly in the spotlight. Public pressure on the UK government from human rights charities like REPRIEVE has mounted.[17] Yet, in recent years the UK has been more vocal than ever on Egypt in public fora. The UK International Ambassador for Human Rights, Rita French, has for the past consecutive years delivered her statements to the UN Human Rights Council, raising the UK's concerns over Egypt's violations as she did against the likes of China, Russia, Iran and Venezuela. In March 2020 Britain's ambassador called on Egypt to improve prison conditions and to lift restrictions on civil society, including by releasing all those detained for exercising 'their constitutional right to freedom of expression'.[18] Before that, in 2015, then British ambassador to Egypt, John Casson, publicly criticized the sentencing of three Al-Jazeera journalists accused of supporting terrorism. For the Egyptians, Casson's views were considered 'unacceptable interference' by Britain.[19] And still, the unresolved murder case of Italian Cambridge University student, Guilio Regini, remains at the centre of petitions and outcry by British academics at UK universities regarding the prospect of a boost in academic partnerships between British and Egyptian higher education institutions.[20]

'Promoting the values that Britain holds dear is not an optional extra ... [it] is part of who we are', wrote Boris Johnson as Foreign Secretary in a 2016 Foreign Office report on Human Rights and Democracy.[21] But for Human Rights groups, no policy could challenge this notion more than Britain's policy towards Egypt, and the criticism at home to prove UK's principles regarding Egypt only continues. Pressure and criticism at home, by the British public, will be an enduring struggle for London while continuing to define and defend the parameters of 'principled pragmatism' in the context of policy towards Egypt. It will require in part an ongoing public conversation whereby the paradigms through which Britain assesses its own leverage and influence in Egypt (and elsewhere) are made clear.

To walk along this tight rope is to lay bare the constrictions on Britain as an influencing force in the Middle East today. It is one thing to design a policy based on what is necessary and right, and quite another to develop one based on what is realistic and doable. Britain is more of a marginal player today than it was in 2010 when the Strategy Unit published its ambitious report. Partnerships and international coordination were highlighted throughout the strategic report, but it framed a future where the UK would use the strategy to 'give UK thought-leadership on Arab human development with the EU, UN and G8', 'take the lead in establishing an international consensus' and 'drive this agenda within the EU'.[22] But in reality regarding Egypt, much lies outside of UK's control.

Britain cannot act alone

As a member of NATO, G-7, G-20 and the UN Security Council and with the Commonwealth, Britain will continue to have a seat at virtually every international table of consequence despite Brexit, and it will do well to wield it to put forward the UK's principles for reform in Egypt that can lead to long-term stability. But in no scenario can Britain become a sole interlocutor on Egypt affairs, and neither can its principled objectives be realistically pushed forward without a degree of international coordination aside of those fora. The orbit that surrounds Egypt is made up of many competing priorities and interests, and the Egyptian regime has become accustomed to managing and paying lip service to each one. Unravelling them is key to opening the opportunities needed to play Britain's part. At a very simplistic level, the most important of these relationships for Cairo are Saudi Arabia, the United States, Russia and Europe. Whilst the bilateral relationship between Britain and Egypt can continue on the basis of both countries' shared interests, for Britain to stretch further into the reform agenda requires a careful calibration of the interests and concerns of all relevant actors.

The complex case of Egypt, with its impenetrable idiosyncrasies, was remarkably underestimated when responding to the upheaval that engulfed the region a decade ago. But it was further constrained by an assumption that the most important response would be the transatlantic one. The Egypt uprisings, in the wider context of the Arab Spring, was judged from London in terms almost entirely drawn from the UK debate at the time on Islam and modernity, Islam and democracy, and in the context of accusations against the British establishment of Islamophobia. It mired decision-making immensely and led eventually to a catastrophic overly simplistic miscalculation in backing the Muslim Brotherhood with a very narrow democratic mandate, while harming relationships with the Egyptian military elite and GCC allies.

Britain was not alone in miscalculating a response to the uprisings and events following 2011. Overall, events on the ground had vastly outpaced policymakers' ability to produce cohesive responses let alone coordinated strategies. The reactions by the United States and EU were slow and uncertain throughout the unfolding of events from 2011. Much of the flawed assessments were a symptom of a wider problem stemming from the ways the United States and EU (and the UK as a part of that) had long judged sources of insecurity in the region.

For one, Britain's assessment of Egypt had been interpreted through the prism of Washington, and by extension Israel since the 1970s. While Britain and Washington are both right to take note of Israel's reading of Egypt – after all Tel Aviv dedicates far more resource to analysing Cairo than London or Washington currently does – Israel's analysis can be heavily distorted by its own narrow national interests, namely securing the military and security cooperation along the Gaza strip and Egypt's Sinai desert, and cooperating across shared concerns regarding Hamas (which are now more closely aligned than ever following the total crackdown on all Muslim Brotherhood assets in the country since 2014). For this, Israel is most intimately familiar with Egypt's ruling military and the top echelons of the regime and intelligence community. Israel's insight is inherently weak on broader popular sentiment, and it has also become a blind spot for Washington and London, as both have spent too long developing Cairo policy primarily in the context of the Middle East Peace Process, and not enough on regional peace and security more broadly.

Since the early 1990s both the United States and EU have broadly converged on their approach to Egypt by relying on, and emphasizing, economic incentives for modernization and democratization. US president Biden's approach is much the same, with democracy and human rights at the centre of American foreign policy. Both the EU and United States have, over decades, sought to stimulate a democratic process through economic liberalization, and whilst they had not always reached the point of strategic coordination on Egypt, they were operating on the same paradigm. It was therefore no surprise that both the United States and EU, in the immediate aftermath of the uprisings in 2011, decided to mobilize efforts to support 'a reform agenda' via economic incentives. The greatest difference across the transatlantic has been EU's significant emphasis on conditionality or 'more for more' approach. Yet, this reliance on economic leverage and the inbuilt assumption that economic liberalization would transfer into political liberalization has always underestimated the importance of the sociopolitical and geopolitical constraints on such a policy. Specifically, for Egypt, other than the Israel factor, this means factoring in Saudi Arabia.

For Saudi Arabia, the United States and Europe's decision to allow for the rise of the Muslim Brotherhood in Egypt revealed two things that were significant and concerning for the Kingdom. First, that the West was prepared to abandon long-standing security arrangements and guarantees. Second, that Egypt in the hands of the Brotherhood posed a direct threat to the Kingdom's carefully crafted model of Islam and the state. It is hard to say whether the perspective of Saudi Arabia was on the agenda when the United States and EU devised their eventual response to the uprising. But what is clear is that since 2011, Saudi interests vis-à-vis Egypt – and that of the United Arab Emirates – can be the determining factor for the success of applying a more values-based policy. Riyadh's preparedness to financially assist the Egyptian military regime is based on the expectation that the Egyptians can continue to behave as a reliable bulwark against the Muslim Brotherhood and align their interests with the Kingdom's. This does not mean abandoning Britain's efforts to forge a path for Egypt's reform and ceding to Saudi and UAE policy. However, it does mean that in order to uphold the UK's values and principles and relay them most effectively to Cairo, Britain needs to identify where interests on Cairo align with not just European powers and the United States, but crucially too, Egypt's neighbourhood allies. The good news is that leaderships in the Gulf – namely Mohammed bin Zayed and Mohammed bin Salman – are spearheading a reform agenda of their own – towards social modernization and economic reform. If they achieve what they have set out to do, it will be in London's interests and Cairo's, and could dramatically recast the politics of the region.

Aligning policy with France and Germany on Egypt will be important to resourcing an agenda towards reform with Egypt. Together, Britain and Europe can wield influence on socioeconomic reform as both pose a valuable source of inward investment in Egypt. While the value of aid packages and soft loans are meagre when compared to Gulf funds, Europe and Britain carry reputational value that can encourage private investment. Egypt will be eager to maintain and encourage more of this support. Before the Covid-19 crisis, Egypt was showing signs of wanting to diversify beyond Gulf reliance. The economic uncertainty and the uphill recovery now as a result of both the Covid-19 economic hit and the impact on oil exports will increase Egypt's desire to seek capital investment from a wide range of economic partners beyond the Gulf states. What helps is that since 2016, the EU has adapted its rigid stance on conditionality making it easier to align with post-Brexit Britain on Egypt matters, at least for the time being. This is coupled with the fact that Saudi interference in Egypt affairs since 2011 has not been entirely popular on the Egyptian streets. This was most evident in the protests that erupted following the transfer of sovereignty of two Red Sea islands to the Kingdom in 2016. The Egyptian regime has since then felt the pressure to downplay the hold the Gulf states have on al-Sisi's domestic and regional politics and represent a more diverse portfolio of support and allies.

Transatlantic unity under the Biden administration will be crucial for the Iran file most immediately, but Britain should work to strengthen the alliance for its policies in the region overall, and work to build broad strategic alignment. Crucial to this will be to ensure that Britain is seen as a key cog in the transatlantic diplomatic machinery. With all the references from Boris Johnson to see Brexit as a chance to do things differently, British allies including the United States will be wondering what that means beyond the rhetoric. Biden's emphasis on democracy and human rights is a clear nod towards a values-based foreign policy for America, and this means Britain will need to complement US values in the medium term whilst ensuring it does not overtly harm the bilateral relationship with Egypt. How easy this proves to be will depend largely on the extent to which the United States will make the value on democracy and human rights conditional to future dealings with the administration. For Egypt and its Gulf allies, Biden's choice of cabinet nominees and advisers deepened concerns of a return to Obama's Middle East policies which were interpreted by Cairo to be pro-Iran and pro-Muslim Brotherhood. This, given that the region is broadly made up of three axes in tension with one another – the Israel-Gulf axis; the Iran axis; and the Turkey axis, means Team Biden will either need to choose what version of the Middle East to back, or smooth out the fault lines and reshape these three axes. Meanwhile, for Britain to effectively assert its influence in Egypt, it will be better doing it united with both the EU and United States. That has proven difficult in the current Middle East climate where neither a joined-up European approach to the region nor a shared transatlantic strategy has emerged in recent years.

With all this said, external powers cannot on their own build a peaceful Middle East. The UK and other international partners have also to recognize that the approach of prioritizing short-term stability is just that, short term. Cycles of unrest, counter-unrest and insecurity will continue to pose an ongoing challenge for policymakers for years to come. The need for gradual reform and the rule of law are part of underlying issues that have created an uncertain MENA. Britain can best wield what influence it does have by working with Cairo, not against it, and alongside key partners including those within the EU even though it is now out. Britain could go on for many years simply cooperating with Egypt on security and intelligence in the region, whilst investing in the country both in support of Egypt's general economic growth and UK's trade interests. It could continue to engage with Egypt politically on matters relating to the Middle East Peace Process and raise in private meetings UK's concerns over human rights in the country. This is a fair and a purely realist's approach to UK–Egypt relations, and it will reap benefits to post-Brexit Britain. But for 'Global Britain's' agenda – to secure peace and stability – some constructive pressure on the Egyptian regime to, for example, relax the NGO law to allow more chance for charities and civil society groups to receive funding from abroad, and introduce a fit-for-purpose counterterrorism law that will then allow for the emergency law to be lifted, can reap longer-term benefits for all parties. Such moves are critical for Britain to pursue a relationship with Egypt that can be true to some of the UK's principles towards peace and stability.

Generational friction – Embracing Egypt's future

A forward-looking policy on Egypt will do well to consider the growing gap between the old ruling elite for which Britain's current policy will still need to serve, and the new millennial and Gen Z (those born between 1996 and 2009) generations who increasingly remind us of how different they are to those who rule them. For the slow reforming countries like Egypt, the opportunities and progress will be in generational terms – not in ten to fifteen years, but in thirty and more. So, future-proofing Britain's policy – both in terms of values and actions – will then require knowing more about these younger generations.

For further incentive, in April 2019, UNICEF predicted that the most favourable period for the Middle East and North Africa will be 2018–40, when the dependency ratio of the population will be at its lowest, meaning that a large proportion of the MENA population will transition into their most productive years. In theory, this could open the potential for a 'demographic dividend' with increased shared wealth and expansion of opportunities. Nearly half of MENA's population today is under twenty-five. In 2015, it was estimated that one in five of the population in the region were between fifteen and twenty-four years, making MENA the region with the largest cohort at this age bracket. The UN predicts that this cohort has the potential to be 'agents of change', acting for a more 'prosperous and stable future' and playing their part in 'reaping the demographic dividend'. But this so-called dividend will not emerge automatically – it will need to be cultivated. Significant investment to create opportunities for this generation will be needed to realize this potential. Due to a growing elderly population, the 'window of opportunity' to benefit from the demographic dividend will begin to close in the second half of this century.

There is both an opportunity here and a demand for Britain to revitalize its engagement with the young people of Egypt. But there are two considerable obstacles to navigate or overcome – one more manageable than the other.

The first is that deeper understanding, beyond the myriad of youth surveys that now exist to infer trends across the region, is needed to establish what is consistent or different between millennial and Generation Z Egyptians to those generations before. In what ways – and in what direction – might they demand an acceleration of change. To reach a point for Britain to become an asset to this new generation, Whitehall and Foreign Office desks will drastically need to adjust to allow greater scope to study this generational cohort. It will require talking to different people, asking different questions and investing time in new inquiries.

Youth engagement is a subject that seems to matter to al-Sisi and his regime and so this shows it should matter to Britain too. Since 2013, al-Sisi has been keen to position himself as the advocate for Egyptian youth, looking to increase the role they play in government and leadership positions. With al-Sisi eager to show younger Egyptians entering senior positions than ever before, he has established a national leadership programme (the 'Presidential Programme for Rehabilitation of Youth for Leadership'), hosted a National Youth Conference and launched in 2017 'The World Youth Forum' – an annual global forum held in Egypt's popular resort, Sharm el-Sheikh, to engage global youth to supposedly bridge the gap between decision makers and young generations of the region.

Attitudes towards government, religion and culture, work, family and national and global politics appear to be setting the generations apart,[23] but the degree to which this may create new tensions or undermine stability will depend in part on the Egyptian regime's ability to catch up with more rapidly changing public opinion. British policy will need to build in flexibility to assess this, but here raises the second considerable stumbling block. Can Britain simultaneously placate and reassure the current Egyptian military elite whilst attempting to engage its youth? After all no matter how much al-Sisi's government prioritizes youth initiatives, there is still an underlying tension between the regime and Egypt's twenty-somethings. The regime recognizes a weakness in its hold over the younger generations who are innately globally connected and digitally minded. In the post-9/11 international and regional psyche, young people were seen as pressure-cookers and security threats rather than human resources and investments for the future. But in those twenty years this stigma has only alienated young people further and proved counterproductive.

We do not need polling to tell us that the vast majority of Egypt's youth are captivated neither by the Egyptian military nor by what ISIS has to offer. The demands and dreams of young Egyptians today are neither radical nor revolutionary. They are the aspirations of a pragmatic generation unlikely to fall for the false utopias or 'charismatic' leaders their parents once fell for. Britain can work constructively alongside Egypt's leadership to support the delivery on al-Sisi's promises, especially those that strive to switch a decades-long climate of fear into one of genuine hope. In the coming years, and after the long-term effects of the Covid-19 economic recession is clear, the youth of the region will need to see rhetoric turn to reality. The challenge of generational rifts in societies and the disconnect between them politically and socially are a shared issue for Britain and Egypt.[24] Both countries can learn from such a partnership if meaningfully constructed.

Many young people in Egypt desire and welcome a relationship with the UK that engages with British culture and widens horizons.[25] Across Egypt, Britain's reputation in educational quality could in the long term be better leveraged as part of serving a comprehensive stabilizing and reforming role. Britain's education market in Egypt is single-handedly kept in the game by the thousands of Egyptian nationals who choose to send their children to international and language schools and enrol on the International GCSE and A-level qualifications. As a part of youth engagement in the region, the UK should continue to welcome and encourage young people from Egypt to study in the UK, including through the Chevening scholarships programme. Such exchange offers potentially rewarding opportunity to positively influence future leaders and decision makers and help towards fostering a generation that could be a vibrant force for advancement in Egypt. Beyond that, Britain should commit to exploring innovative ways to partner with Egyptian businesses, universities and government officials to spearhead the shift towards youth-centred reform.

Conclusion

Egypt is where the balancing act between principles and pragmatism will be invaluable. A future policy depends now on Britain taking stock of what has been learnt in all these years, and recognizing Britain's limited leverage today while not being constrained by it. The relationship is one that will be anchored by mutual interests and concerns, especially around regional security and the ongoing threat of terrorism and Islamist extremism. Opportunities lie ahead for Egypt and Britain, namely the steady progress in Egypt's economy due to the commitment towards economic reform. But this has been achieved at the expense of political openness. The autocratic regime and political monopoly at the hands of the military might have sped up the economic reform agenda and forced through some law and order, but political instability due to brewing discontent among the Egyptian people leaves potential for future unrest. British policymaking will need to build in capacity to respond to flare-ups at the political level by learning from its flaws during the Arab uprisings of 2011, and this means supporting the current leadership, not abandoning it in favour of emerging opposition with limited democratic mandates. At the crux, this means building trust with the Egyptians in order to allow for constructive pressure from within for gradual political, social and economic reform.

Rather than an overhaul, Britain's approach, with a focus on a relationship with the ruling elite based on joint concerns including on security, trade and economic reform, would largely need to remain and form the basis of future engagement. The need for technical assistance in these areas has played to Britain's strengths so far, but

Britain needs an overarching political framework to ground all these initiatives under a coherent 'values-based strategy' – one that is ideally regional and not just bilateral and single issue.

The mechanisms to push through policy are also just as crucial as the content itself. Establishing a policy for Egypt will need to consider the limitations on Britain. Britain's marginal status today does mean that to influence any change in Egypt, it will need to align closely with EU partners, especially France and Germany, and the United States, but also Egypt's own regional allies, whilst keeping in mind other competing geopolitical interests – namely China and Russia. UK funds alone will have marginal leverage for development and any conditions if applied to Egypt. But if deployed in cooperation with EU funds, it will build scope for impact and influence. This should and can include in areas of human rights and political freedoms if Britain hopes to represent a values-based policy of engagement, but more work needs to be done to devise a coherent framework not just for policy towards Egypt, but for navigating the political idiosyncrasies of the Egyptian establishment. Criticism is possible, but Britain must do it with some degree of humility whilst recognizing its difficult legacy in Egypt.

15

Conclusion

Christopher Phillips and Michael Stephens

The world of the 2020s is defined by state competition and great power politics, and looks quite different from the post-Second World War international order, an order that has lasted for seven decades. As Professor Michael Clarke notes the era is dawning in which four great powers will shape the course of global affairs: The United States, China, Russia and India. Britain must create strategic space for itself amongst these big players, while adhering to its traditional relationship with the United States without being subservient. Additional pressures of the global coronavirus pandemic and the effects of climate change have tested states and international institutions as never before and have increased tensions rather than ushering in a new spirit of cooperation, particularly between China and the United States. The Middle East is not exempt from any of these challenges and, if anything with economies battered by consistently low oil prices, these states have become even more vulnerable to their effects than almost any other region on Earth. The Middle East is replete with both opportunity and challenge, but the unpredictable nature of global affairs makes it difficult to predict what the medium- and long-term trends that affect the region may be. When thinking about the Middle East's future there is a tendency to favour pessimism: rising populations, droughts and extreme weather patterns, stagnant economies, poor governance and the persistent problems of war and state fragility all give cause for concern. Indeed, when looking at the Middle East it can sometimes feel like there is such an overwhelming mass of problems to solve that it is impossible to know where to start.

For Britain, the first question to ask is whether engaging with these problems matters or not. This is not an unreasonable question given that the UK has problems of its own to focus on, and that its closest ally, the United States, has also asked the same question. In the 2020s arguments in favour of strategic retrenchment are finding willing ears and eager audiences. However, the authors contend that the Middle East is too important to be ignored, and that Britain gains far more by being involved in the region than by pulling away from it, with the caveat that there does need to be a serious rethink about how UK Middle East policy is constructed. A shift in zeitgeist is needed. And although it is uncomfortable to say it, the UK must rid itself of its white saviour complex that stems from a paternalist view of a region that is perennially unable to solve its own problems and needs constant attention. The states of the region have become more active, filling vacuums left by the end of American hegemonic influence, leading to interstate competition and power plays that are linked to the decline of Western influence in the region. There is no turning back this clock, and the UK must contend with this more activist turn among regional states (especially Turkey, Iran, Saudi Arabia, the UAE and Israel) as they jostle for position vis-à-vis each other. The UK can do its utmost to ensure that these rivalries do not become nuclear and can pressure these states to tone down their hostility. But London can at best mitigate the problems that have emerged; ultimately, it is up to the states of the region themselves to solve them.

There is an urge in the British foreign policy mindset to always be involved in every difficult conundrum, and to be 'in the room where it happens'. But there are now many questions that have arisen in regional affairs that do not require the UK's input, and that it cannot do much to solve. Although most policy officials already understand this, it is essential that the UK conceive of itself as middle power, albeit a middle power with first-rate capabilities and a highly favourable position in the international system. Understanding this should alleviate the burden of needing to be involved in every issue, all the time. After all in a time of such great global change even a great power (let alone the UK which has yet to define its own role in the world) will struggle to forge a regional policy that can adequately address the challenges of the Middle East region, while also seeing its own interests preserved. In short, it is acceptable for a reformulation of priorities which lead to a reduced conceptual burden on Britain. Then there is the key issue of capacity, which will inevitably be reduced as a result of the ongoing pandemic and the allocation of state resources to healthcare and the maintenance of prosperity. Like it or not, the UK will simply not have the resources to dedicate to foreign affairs and defence in the manner of years gone by. And so, if the current British approach to the Middle East is maintained the question will be how to do more with less. The authors believe that such a thing is impossible and that there is only one answer to this question, which is to do less but better.

Doing less, but better

If there is a single phrase that encompasses the book it is this. Doing less, but better defines the way in which we foresee Britain's engagement with the Middle East in the years ahead. We believe it is the most effective way to preserve British interests in an unstable and insecure region that despite its challenges remains of critical importance to British foreign policy.

The statement seems paradoxical and perhaps even heretical for those who believe in the concept of a Global Britain. For if the Middle East region is so critically important to the UK why do we, the authors, advocate dedicating less energy towards it? In order to counter this problem it is important to stress at this juncture what doing less does not mean. It does not mean retreating from the world, pulling up the draw bridge and forgetting about the Middle East because it is too complex. It does not mean ignoring the plight of refugees, or ceasing to act decisively against terrorist networks. For as Dr Louise Kettle points out, these challenges will be here for some time to come; we cannot simply ignore them. What we advocate is a far clearer sense of where and how Britain can have the most positive impact in the Middle East, and to double down on those areas where Britain can maximize its influence and leverage to ensure its prosperity and security as well as that of the region. All of the countries that have been discussed in this book are of interest to the UK whether it be through trade, exchange of knowledge, or training and capacity building. The authors have shown in each chapter that commercial opportunity exists, that security challenges remain, but that it is possible to focus on specific sets of opportunities that can be mutually beneficial to both London and the host country. In this way Britain's diplomatic effectiveness is maximized, and the money spent is better directed to the source where it will have most impact.

So where should Britain look? Well, the Gulf states should continue to be the main focus of Britain's attention, partly owing to historical ties and Britain's current security posture, but most importantly because that is where the most financial benefit is to be had. David Butter's chapter clearly shows that by volume of exports the UAE and Saudi Arabia are particularly important for British companies operating overseas. Britain should focus its efforts on ensuring that the Gulf remains prosperous, secure and redoubles its efforts to diversify away from hydrocarbon exports as a primary source of wealth. Britain's positioning as a global centre of green-tech and innovation should help in providing thought leadership and expertise that help ensure that the Gulf states are able to remain prosperous as they make this transition. The Gulf is a problematic place to be sure and as James Lynch notes with unequivocal certainty, the adherence of the six Gulf states to proper standards of human rights is still of deep concern. Moreover the fraternal squabbling amongst them is a headache that causes more problems than it solves. However, disputes among the GCC countries are their problem, and not Britain's. The UK should instead focus on where it can serve its core foreign policy objectives, by promoting British business, containing Chinese economic and security activity in the region, and ensuring security of hydrocarbons. As Borck and Stephens argue there will be an uncomfortable trade-off, which is the tacit admission that political reform is unlikely to be an area where Britain sees much success. But the UK can and indeed should hold the Gulf states to account when they behave in destabilizing ways outside their borders, which they are increasingly doing. Ensuring that states are upholding the international rules is an integral part of Global Britain (UK officials often talk about preserving 'the Rules Based Order'); moreover, the rise of China should not be read as a carte blanche for bad behaviour by authoritarian states.

Looking elsewhere in the region it is clear that Britain should try to prioritize states that provide an opportunity for economic engagement and could in time become vital regional pillars of stability, if their significant economic challenges are ameliorated. While the problems of Lebanon, Syria, Yemen, Iraq and Libya take up headlines, it is easy to forget that other countries could be better focuses for increased time and effort. In fact, redirecting efforts away from these less stable environments and doubling down on countries like Jordan, Oman and possibly Egypt with an increased focus on trade and prosperity seems a logical step. This would allow the prosperity component of Global Britain to be realized, while freeing up space for the FCDO to ensure that more energy is expended on making these relationships work. All three countries could do with as much support as possible from external actors in a manner which allows their own populations to benefit from the transfer of ideas and economic ties. Most importantly the UK should be a leading vector for job creation in these nations, which is crucial to seeing these countries prosper in the future. In February 2019 the UK hosted a conference focusing on Growth and Opportunity in Jordan, attended by a number of world leaders and global investors. The UK should look to expand on this kind of initiative, it is low cost but can lead to much gain, and no harm can come from increased engagement particularly in the form of expanded business opportunities, education and vocational training.

We do not recommend leaving the discussion there, and it would be incorrect to assume that Britain should simply double down on autocracies and make money. The region is too complex to be viewed through a simple trade-off between principles and pragmatism. Values do matter, and Britain should retain its own belief in democratic norms and protect an ideational component in its foreign policy. Given that democracies do exist in the region, and that it is absolutely within Britain's interests to promote them, there is no harm in forming a policy which promotes democratic norms (where applicable) and seeks to bolster democracies that are in danger of backsliding. However, as El Badawy cautions, it is more important to focus on how Britain can assist towards good-quality governance and an end to corrupt practices than simply creating the pretence of democracy, which is not a magic end state in and of itself. As Sudan and Algeria have shown, many millions of people still aspire for better and more accountable governance; in Lebanon, Iraq, Israel and Tunisia democracies still exist despite the political and social pressures that place them under great strain. It is imperative that the UK show its support for such democracies openly and repeatedly. It is in London's interest to consider ways to bring together the few democratic states in the region to share experiences, learn from each other, and most importantly to be recognized as walking the hard path that so many other states in the region continuously shun. Most monarchies in the region are treated with appropriate deference and respect; it should not be too difficult to raise the democratic nations of the Middle East onto a similar pedestal of respect and deference. Only by supporting those few states in the region that seek to implement and maintain democracy can the UK prevent a further backslide into the politics of authoritarianism and removal of freedoms that have become so fashionable among regional states since 2011.

The outlier here is Turkey, a democracy that has all the hallmarks of backsliding into an authoritarian dictatorship, but whose demographic size and NATO membership make it an absolutely crucial component of Middle East stability. The fact that Turkey has now had a series of serious diplomatic run-ins with the United States and France (not to mention the UAE, Israel and Saudi Arabia) places British interests in a conundrum. Bill Park's sober analysis is important; on its current trajectory Turkey is headed for regional isolation, despite its increased power projection across the region. The UK may have to spilt its approach towards Ankara, urging President Erdogan and his eventual successors to stay in the democratic club, while increasingly making clear when Turkey's regional activities constitute a serious concern to British security interests. There is no doubt that Britain's continued relationship with Turkey will require walking on a diplomatic tightrope, but as Park notes, Turkey's status as a joint

EU outlier makes it an attractive place for British investment and political engagement, this despite Ankara still being a part of the EU Customs Union. Turkey's myriad of economic challenges may well cause it to lower its strategic ambitions in the long run, but that cannot be taken for granted. In truth Britain may just have to accept that Turkey's current position is a perennial problem that can be better managed, but not solved.

Lastly the UK should pursue its security interests with the same determination of years gone by, particularly vis-à-vis international terrorist organizations such as Al-Qaeda and ISIS alongside a number of Iranian-backed militia groups. Transnational terrorist actors will continue to present a threat to the UK's security, be that through working to destabilize allies, targeting British nationals abroad or by producing radical propaganda that upsets Britain's domestic political environment. Sadly, as Kettle and Watling point out the next ten years will likely see a continued presence of such actors in Syria, Iraq, Yemen and Libya and extremist ideology will remain a problem across the region. There are many avenues of work that already exist in which Britain has cooperated effectively with regional states to shut down propaganda outlets and challenge the problems of extremism head on. If and when military action is needed, the current trajectory appears to be light footprint operations, or what Kettle terms 'Remote Warfare' working side by side with local actors, which is the most logical and correct approach. The question will remain as to how the UK goes about protecting itself in an era where the United States appears less inclined to military action in the Middle East, yet remains deeply committed to trying to solve the problems of Iran's nuclear programme. Sanam Vakil rightly points to a tension whereby Britain's European allies can certainly burden-share, but without the leadership of the United States, taking decisive action may prove extremely difficult. A critical component of the UK's counterterrorism and wider security posture remains rooted in a strong relationship with Washington, combined with a respectful engagement with regional states, slowly creating the conditions where they are able to take on the vast weight of counterterrorism efforts and establish deterrence on their own terms.

Pursuing agility ahead of strategy

If the reader finds that the above description does not sound much like a strategy, they would be correct. 'Doing less but better' is not a strategy, but more a collection of ideas that encompass an overall approach to the Middle East. We believe that creating an overarching strategy in a region as complex and diverse as the Middle East is a fruitless task. Instead this approach allows the UK maximum flexibility to pursue its objectives, while ensuring that the key interests that it seeks to promote (as part of Global Britain, or something else) are maintained. This will still render the UK vulnerable to 'events' in the Harold Macmillan sense of the term, meaning that policy will often be more reactive than prescriptive. But importantly when 'events' do occur, the UK will be able to better assess how to react to them and whether reacting at all is needed. This is especially the case with conflict, which time and again has caught the UK offguard and struggling to react appropriately.

Major international conflicts and wars such as have occurred in Syria, Yemen and Libya will require some form of UK response. It should not be the policy of the UK to turn its back on humanitarian disasters, and sitting back and doing nothing is not particularly global in outlook. However, a smarter more agile Britain, defining its policy through 'doing less but better', might have developed a better sense for when to intervene in these conflicts, and when not to. This goes back to our original point about Britain re-evaluating its need to be involved in absolutely every major debate that takes place. Such a policy would have guided Britain in a far more useful direction with regards to Syria, for example. London might well have spent less time deliberating over the form and shape of the Syrian opposition in the early years (knowing that Assad would never accept them), and dedicated more effort to humanitarian relief and counterterrorism efforts, which subsequently became – and indeed remain – the core interests that Britain held in the conflict. Likewise, in Libya, while recognizing the humanitarian imperative, the UK might not have pushed for a reckless regime change policy had it accepted the principle that its ambitions were too great, and its strategic end goals unclear. Libya and Syria serve as prime examples of Britain not stripping down these two conflicts to their bare strategic essentials, and then pursuing those essentials with more determination.

It is of course easy to make these criticisms with hindsight, and the authors accept that instability and conflict can often distract policymakers into dealing with immediate problems. Discussing highfalutin ideas is one thing, delivering them is of course quite another, especially when a country looks on the verge of civil war, or there is public pressure for the military or government to step in. Our formula of 'doing less but better' is hardly a catchy term that might motivate civil servants and politicians to go out and promote British interests. It is hard, for example, to imagine any ambitious British ambassador acknowledging that their host country is a diplomatic sideshow unworthy of adequate attention, and downsizing their presence to benefit the embassy operating in a neighbouring state. It is similarly challenging for a research analyst to admit that their years of expertise are largely irrelevant. To put it bluntly, what we advocate goes against the ethos of organizations like the Foreign Office (and the old Department for International Development) whose very purpose is to increase British engagement overseas and not reduce it. But the fact is that the UK will have to work with less resources for the foreseeable future, as a result of Covid-19 and other factors, and it is not feasible to continue in the manner of years gone by. Tough choices will have to be made, and the Middle East may well find itself low on the list of priorities, falling behind European security and Pacific security portfolios.

The UK's National Security Council (whose very existence is to provide an accountable moment in the policymaking process and set government on course to execute policy) will set the tone, and ultimately decide just how much time the UK can dedicate to Middle East affairs. If it comes to pass that the Middle East is indeed lower on the list of priorities, then the best way to ameliorate the potential log jam in decision-making on Middle East issues will be to decentralize policy and rebalance input from the National Security Council by placing more decision-making power into the hands of the regional hubs where Britain's main interests are centred. This will give the policy arms of the British state (be they security, trade, defence or diplomacy) more autonomy and an expanded remit to conduct their work even under reduced circumstances. The questions surrounding the National Security Council and its effectiveness in policymaking are beyond the scope of this book to solve, but we strongly believe that a Middle East policy that is more disaggregated from the centre, but guided by the principles of where the UK can and should do more is likely to be more successful and more adaptive to the highly tumultuous environment that is the Middle East.

Global and regional politics are changing fast, leading to uncertain outcomes and challenges that cannot easily be overcome. At the outset of this book we have made it clear that a need to re-evaluate was necessary because British policy in the Middle East cannot be a case of doing what was done in the past. Instead, overarching themes of reformulating Britain's diverse set of regional relationships in a manner that is more appropriate to the world of today and moves away from the colonial legacies of the past should be the guiding principle. Engaging through soft power and commercial initiatives with states that will benefit from British engagement, while being clear about where British security interests and values also matter. Although it is difficult to avoid trade-offs, hypocrisies and inconsistencies, particularly in the face of unforeseen events, being more flexible and adaptable will help to ameliorate such problems. It will be difficult to get a new approach to Middle East right. There will always be those who argue that the UK should be doing more, or that we should be doing less; those who argue that we should not work with the United States; or those who argue that we must have no difference of opinion with them. These are par for the course, and criticisms that any British policy must contend with in any normal healthy policy environment. What we assert is that Britain must be better at identifying the costs of engaging too broadly across the region, thereby spreading itself too thin and failing to adequately deliver on its key objectives.

Through this book we have sought to make both the policymaker and general reader alike aware of the challenges and opportunities for the UK in its Middle East policy, thereby making it easier to highlight the key objectives that will drive UK policy in the decade ahead. The Middle East does matter to the UK and will continue to matter whether we are distracted by Brexit, Covid-19 or some other national or global political crisis. Our hope is that this book lays the foundations for thinking about the region in a structured and comprehensive way for the next decade and serves as a baseline for thinking about how to reformulate Britain's relationship with the Middle East.

Notes

Chapter 1

1 General works on UK foreign policy include Gaskarth (2011), Owen and Ludlow (2017), Sanders (2017), Hill (2019). Recent Middle East-specific works include Straw (2019), Gaskarth (2016), Stansfield (2014), Strong (2015) and Wearing (2018).
2 See, for example, Kinninmont (2016) and Chalmers (2019).
3 House of Lords, 'The Middle East: Time for a New Realism', *Select Committee on International Relations HL Paper 159*, 2 May 2017, https://publications.parliament.uk/pa/ld201617/ldselect/ldintrel/159/159.pdf, accessed 10 May 2020.
4 Yougov polling, 25 November 2015, https://yougov.co.uk/topics/politics/articles-reports/2015/11/25/strong-and-continued-support-raf-air-strikes-syria

Chapter 2

1 Michael Stewart, quoted in Jones P., A. Shlaim and K. Sainsbury, *British Foreign Secretaries since 1945,* London: David & Charles, 1977, p. 192.
2 See Elizabeth Monroe, *Britain's Moment in the Middle East, 1914–71*, London: Chatto & Windus, 1981.
3 Anthony Parsons, *They Say the Lion: Britain's Legacy to the Arabs*, London: Jonathan Cape, 1986.
4 Plowden, *Miscellaneous Report No. 5* (1964), Cmnd.2276, pp. 2–3, par 9.
5 Quoted in Jones P. Avi Shlaim and K. Sainsbury, *British Foreign Secretaries since 1945*, London: David & Charles, 1977, p. 192.
6 See John Akehurst, *We Won a War: The Campaign in Oman 1965–1975*, Salisbury: Michael Russell, 1982.
7 *Hansard*, 24 May 1985, House of Commons Debates, Vol. 79, Col. 1281.
8 See Easa Al Gurg, *The Wells of Memory*, London: John Murray, 1998.
9 *Hansard*, 24 March 1980, House of Commons Debates, Vol. 981, Col. 406.
10 See Rosemary Hollis, *Britain and the Middle East in the 9/11 Era*, London: Wiley-Blackwell, 2010, pp. 168–9.
11 Ibid.
12 The Scott Report (the Report of the Inquiry into the Export of Defence Equipment and Dual-Use Goods to Iraq and Related Prosecutions) was a judicial enquiry commissioned in 1992.
13 'Interview given by Douglas Hurd', 4 March 1981, *Verbatim Service*, p. 2. The European Community's Venice Declaration broke new ground by calling for the recognition of the Palestine Liberation Organisation (PLO) and of the Palestinian right of self-determination.
14 See Azriel Bermant, *Margaret Thatcher and the Middle East*, Cambridge: Cambridge University Press, 2016.

15 Ibid., p. 156.
16 General Sir Peter De La Billiere, *Storm Command: A Personal Account of the Gulf War*, London: HarperCollins, 1992.
17 'UK's World Role: Punching above Our Weight', http://news.bbc.co.uk/hi/english/static/in_depth/uk_politics/2001/open_politics/foreign_policy/uks_world_role.stm.
18 The problems with this style of decision-making (and lack of minuting) were spelled out in *The Report of the Iraq Inquiry* HC 264 (2016) chaired by Sir John Chilcott. For a synopsis, see Executive Summary, pp. 54–6.
19 See 'Lawyers for Libyan Couple Welcome Government Apology over Illegal Rendition', *Law firm Leigh Day Press Release*, 10 May 2018, www.leighday.co.uk/News/News-2018/May-2018/Lawyers-for-Libyan-couple-welcome-Government-apolo
20 See, for example, Shane Brighton, 'British Muslims, Multiculturalism and UK Foreign Policy: "Integration" and "Cohesion" in and beyond the State', *International Affairs*, vol. 83, no. 1 (2007), pp. 1–17 and Frank Foley, *Countering Terrorism in Britain and France: Institutions, Norms and the Shadow of the Past*, Cambridge: Cambridge University Press, 2013.
21 Sherard Cowper-Coles, *Ever the Diplomat: Confessions of a Foreign Office Diplomat*, London: Harper Press, 2013, chapter 11.
22 'William Hague Arab Spring Statement in Full,' Politics.co.uk 13/10/11.
23 'Libya: Joint Statement by UK Prime Minister and French President', 28 March 2011. www.gov.uk/government/news/libya-joint-statement-by-uk-prime-minister-and-french-president; and Jason Davidson, 'France, Britain and the Intervention in Libya: An Integrated Analysis', *Cambridge Review of International Affairs*, vol. 26, no. 2 (2013), pp. 310–29.

Chapter 3

1 Speech to the 19th National Congress of the Communist Party of China, 18 October 2017.
2 Gideon Rachman, 'America, China and the Art of Confrontation', *Financial Times*, 17 December 2018.
3 Niall Ferguson, 'In This Cold War between Trump and China, Beware the Enemy within', *Sunday Times*, 10 March 2019.
4 Graham Allison, *Destined for War: Can America and China Escape the Thucydides Trap?*, Boston and New York: Houghton Mifflin Harcourt, 2017. See also a similar analysis a decade earlier in Richard E. Bush and Michael E. O'Hanlon, *A War Like No Other: The Truth about China's Challenge to America*, New Jersey: John Wiley, 2007.
5 Robert Kaplan, *The Return of Marco Polo's World: War, Strategy and American Interests*, New York: Random House, 2018.
6 Astrid H. M. Nordin and Mikael Weissmann, 'Will Trump Make China Great Again? The Belt and Road Initiative and International Order', *International Affairs*, vol. 94, no. 2 (March 2018), pp. 231–49.
7 See Bruno Macaes, *Belt and Road: A Chinese World Order*, London: Hurst, 2018.
8 Peter Frankopan, *The New Silk Roads: The Present and Future of the World*, London: Bloomsbury, 2018, pp. 87–95.

9 Raffaello Pantucci and Sarah Lain, *China's Eurasian Pivot: The Silk Road Economic Belt*, RUSI Whitehall Paper 68, London: Royal United Services Institute, 2017, pp. 30–46.
10 Will Doig, *High Speed Empire: Chinese Expansion and the Future of South East Asia*, Columbia, NY: Columbia University Global Reports, 2018.
11 Chinese Law Translate, *National Intelligence Law of the P.R.C. (2017)*, https://www.chinalawtranslate.com/en
12 'China General Nuclear Ready to Ramp up UK Ambitions', *World Nuclear News*, 6 December 2018.
13 See G. John Ikenberry, *After Victory: Institutions, Strategic Restraint, and the Rebuilding of Order after Major Wars*, Princeton: Princeton University Press, 2000.
14 Martin Jacques, *When China Rules the World: The End of the Western World and the Birth of a New Global Order*, 2nd edn, London: Allen Lane, 2009, p. 362.
15 Ibid., Chapter 13.
16 Vladimir Putin, speech to the Duma, Moscow, 18 March 2014.
17 Dmitri Trenin, *Should We Fear Russia?* Cambridge: Polity Press, 2014.
18 Having a GDP in 2017 of around $1.6 trillion as opposed to $2.6 trillion in Britain.
19 Igor Sutyagin and Justin Bronk, *Russia's New Ground Forces*, RUSI Whitehall paper 89, London: Royal United Services Institute, 2017, pp. 11–12.
20 Michael Burleigh, *The Best of Times, the Worst of Times: A History of Now*, London: Pan Books, 2018, p. 195.
21 A ninth enlargement is anticipated with the accession of North Macedonia to the alliance in 2020, bringing its membership up to thirty states.
22 Rodric Braithwaite, 'Russia, Ukraine and the West', *RUSI Journal*, vol. 159, no. 2 (April 2014), pp. 62–5.
23 'Russia Using Hired Guns to Fuel Libya Unrest', *The Times*, 14 March 2019.
24 See, for example, Misha Glenny, *McMafia: Seriously Organised Crime*, London: Vintage Books, 2009; Karen Dawisha, *Putin's Kleptocracy: Who Owns Russia?* New York: Simon and Shuster, 2014; Oliver Bullough, *Moneyland*, London: Profile Books, 2018.
25 Sutyagin and Bronk, op. cit., pp. 131–3.
26 See Lawrence Freedman, *Ukraine and the Art of Strategy*, Oxford: Oxford University Press, 2018.
27 United States Government, *US National Security Strategy*, January 2018 and Department of Defense, *US Defence Strategy*, January 2018.
28 Carla Norrlof, 'Hegemony and Inequality: Trump and the Liberal Playbook', *International Affairs*, vol. 94, no. 1 (2018), pp. 63–88; Arlie Russell Hochschild, *Strangers in Their Own Land*, New York: The New Press, 2016; Katherine J. Cramer, *The Politics of Resentment*, Chicago: Chicago University press, 2016.
29 Michael Kaplan, 'Jacksonian Nationalism and American Empire: Review Essay', *The New Jacksonian Blog*, 8 August 2010; Burleigh, op. cit., pp. 277–82.
30 Walter Russell Mead, 'The Jacksonian Revolt: American Populism and the Liberal Order', *Foreign Affairs*, vol. 96, no. 2 (2017), p. 3.
31 Dan Balz and Griff Witte, 'Europeans Fear Trump May Threaten Not Just the Transatlantic Bond, but the State of Their Union', *Washington Post*, 4 February 2019.
32 See Doug Stokes, 'Trump, American Hegemony and the Future of the Liberal International Order', *International Affairs*, vol. 94, no. 1 (2018), pp. 133–50; Gideon Rachman, 'The Trump Era Could Last 30 Years', *Financial Times*, 4 February 2019.
33 See Adrian Johnson, ed., *Wars in Peace*, London: Royal United Services Institute, 2014.

34 See the main judgements contained in Iraq Enquiry, Great Britain, and Sir John Chilcot. *The Report of the Iraq Inquiry: Report of a Committee of Privy Counsellors.* Dandy Booksellers Limited, 2016. Also, Michael Clarke, 'Planning and Fighting a War', *RUSI Journal*, vol. 161, no. 6 (December 2016), pp. 50–7.

35 In renouncing international agreements, Washington points in all cases to flaws and failings in them, which most allies would not dispute. The growing difference in thinking arises over whether failing arrangements are better than no arrangements. See Richard Haas, *A World in Disarray: American Foreign Policy and the Crisis of the Old Order*, London: Penguin, 2018, pp. 312–20.

36 McKinsey Global Institute, 'By Far the Most Rapid Shift in the World's Economic Center of Gravity Happened in 2000–10', 1 July 2012, https://globaltrends2030.files.wordpress.com/2012/07/nic-blog-mgi-shifting-economic-center-of-gravity.pdf; see also 'The World's Shifting Centre of Gravity', *The Economist*, 28 June 2012.

37 Extracted from *Statistica: The Statistics Portal* at https://www.statista.com/statistics/267898/gross-domestic-product-gdp-growth-in-eu-and-euro-area/

38 *The Economist*, 6–12 October 2018, pp. 18–19.

39 Adam Tooze, *Crashed: How a Decade of Financial Crisis Changed the World*, London: Allen Lane, 2018, p. 17.

40 Collectively, the 'mature economies', whose GDPs can be calculated, make up close to the global total of GDP, which is necessarily a matter of estimation. In 2018 the 'debt mountain' in relation to global GDP was estimated at 320 per cent.

41 David Goodhart, *The Road to Somewhere: The New Tribes Shaping British Politics*, London: Penguin Books, 2017, pp. 148.

42 Will Hutton and Andrew Adonis, *Saving Britain: How We Must Change to Prosper in Europe*, London: Abacus, 2018, pp. 29–30.

43 *OECD Economic Outlook*, Volume 2020, Issue 1: Preliminary Version, June 2020.

44 Ed Conway, 'Long-term Limbo Risks a Zombie Economy', *The Times*, 15 March 2019.

45 See Michael Clarke and Helen Ramscar, *Tipping Point: Britain, Brexit and Security in the 2020s*, London: I.B.Tauris/Bloomsbury, 2019.

46 Malcolm Chalmers, The Rules-based International Systems: What Are They? And How Do They Relate to Each Other?, *RUSI Briefing Paper*, 2019, pp. 35–6.

Chapter 4

1 Interview, Sir Christopher Meyer, London, 7 May 2019.

2 The National Security Capability Review, March 2018, p. 33.

3 The most notable example being John Mearsheimer and Stephen Walt, 'The Israel Lobby', *The London Review of Books*, vol. 28, no. 6 (March 2006).

4 Interview, Sir Malcolm Rifkind, London, 2 April 2019.

5 Eric Edelman, 'A Special Relationship in Jeopardy', *The American Interest*, 1 July 2010, https://www.the-american-interest.com/2010/07/01/a-special-relationship-in-jeopardy/

6 William Wallace and Christopher Phillips, 'Reassessing the Special Relationship', *International Affairs,* vol. 85, no. 2 (2009), p. 263.

7 Sir Humphrey, 'Britain and the US: The Relationship Runs Deep, Which Is Why It Is Often Difficult to See', *RUSI Commentary*, 29 May 2019, https://rusi.org/commentary/britain-and-us-relationship-runs-deep-which-why-it-often-difficult-see

8 Interview, Sir John Scarlett, London, 10 May 2019.
9 Sir Humphrey, 'Britain and the US: The Relationship Runs Deep, Which Is Why It Is Often Difficult to See', *RUSI Commentary*, 29 May 2019, https://rusi.org/commentary/britain-and-us-relationship-runs-deep-which-why-it-often-difficult-see
10 Walter Russell Meade, *God and Gold: Britain and America and the Making of the Modern World*, London: Atlantic Books, 2007, p. XII.
11 Robert Singh, 'The Strange Death of a Special Relationship', *The American Interest*, 29 March 2019.
12 Winston S. Churchill, *Conservative Mass Meeting: A Speech at Llandudno, 9 October 1948*, Europe Unite speeches 1947 & 1948, London: Cassell, 1950, pp. 416–18.
13 James Barr, '*Lords of the Desert: Britain's Struggle with America to Dominate the Middle East*', London: Simon and Schuster, 2018, p. 246.
14 Douglas Brinkley, 'Dean Acheson and the "Special Relationship": The West Point Speech of December 1962', *The Historical Journal*, vol. 33, no. 3 (1990), pp. 599–608.
15 Geoffrey Wheatcroft, 'Not-so-special Relationship: Dean Acheson and the Myth of Anglo-American Unity', *The Spectator*, 5 January 2013.
16 Anand Toprani, 'Oil and the Future of U.S. Strategy in the Persian Gulf', *War on the Rocks*, 15 May 2019, https://warontherocks.com/2019/05/oil-and-the-future-of-u-s-strategy-in-the-persian-gulf/
17 For example, Daniel R. DePetris, 'Americans Are Tired of Middle East Mayhem', *The National Interest*, 17 January 2019, and by Mara Karlin and Tamara Cofman Wittes, 'Ending America's Middle East Purgatory: The Case for Doing Less', *Foreign Affairs*, 11 December 2018.
18 Karl P. Mueller, Becca Wasser, Jeffrey Martini and Stephen Watts, 'U.S. Strategic Interests in the Middle East and Implications for the Army', *RAND*, 2017, p. 8.
19 Edward Luttwak, 'The Middle of Nowhere', *Prospect Magazine*, 26 May 2007.
20 US imports from Saudi Arabia of Crude Oil and Petroleum Products, US Energy information administration, https://www.eia.gov/dnav/pet/hist/LeafHandler.ashx?n=pet&s=mttimussa2&f=m
21 Karl P. Mueller, Becca Wasser, Jeffrey Martini and Stephen Watts, 'U.S. Strategic Interests in the Middle East and Implications for the Army', *RAND*, 2017, p. 11.
22 Christopher Phillips, *The Battle for Syria*, UK edition: Yale University Press, 2018, p. 72.
23 Jeffrey Goldberg, 'The Obama Doctrine', *The Atlantic* April 2016, https://www.theatlantic.com/magazine/archive/2016/04/the-obama-doctrine/471525/
24 For exact numbers, see Justin Bronk, 'Table of Military Assets in Elizabeth Quintana' and Jonathan Eyal, 'Inherently Unresolved, The Military Operation against ISIS', *RUSI Occasional Paper* October 2015, p. IX.
25 Trump on Syria: 'Let Someone Else Fight over This Long Blood-stained Sand', *CNBC News*, https://www.youtube.com/watch?time_continue=88&v=SK1PbIujJ1Q&feature=emb_title
26 'Press Release: Over 100,000 Reported Killed in Yemen War', *ACLED*, 31 October 2019, https://acleddata.com/2019/10/31/press-release-over-100000-reported-killed-in-yemen-war/
27 Clive Baldwin, 'How 15 Minutes of Courtroom Drama Stopped UK Arms to Saudi Arabia', *Human Rights Watch*, 21 June 2019, https://www.hrw.org/news/2019/06/21/how-15-minutes-courtroom-drama-stopped-uk-arms-saudi-arabia
28 The notable exception being Israel's capture of Syrian, Jordanian and Egyptian territory in 1967.

29 See Malcolm Chalmers, 'Which Rules? Why There Is No Single "Rules-Based International System"', *RUSI Occasional Papers*, 2019, pp. 7–8.
30 Holly Williams, 'Syrian Rebel Commander on Why U.S. Training Program Failed', *CBS News*, 29 September 2015, https://www.cbsnews.com/news/rebel-commander-weighs-in-on-why-u-s-training-program-failed/
31 Emily Knowles and Abigail Watson, 'No Such Thing as a Quick Fix: The Aspiration-capabilities Gap in British Remote Warfare', *Oxford Research Group Remote Warfare Programme*, July 2018, p. 10.
32 Prime Minister's statement on Libya, 28 February 2011, https://www.gov.uk/government/speeches/prime-ministers-statement-on-libya–2
33 See, for example, David Miliband, 'America Is Fueling Our Age of Impunity. Just Look at Yemen', *The Guardian*, 5 April 2019, https://www.theguardian.com/commentisfree/2019/apr/05/america-impunity-yemen or Robin Cook, 'Why I Had to Leave the Cabinet', *The Guardian*, 18 March 2003, https://www.theguardian.com/politics/2003/mar/18/foreignpolicy.labour1
34 For example in the United States, after CIA Briefing, Lindsey Graham, 'Corker Point Finger at MBS in Jamal Khashoggi Killing', *NBC News*, 4 December 2018, https://www.youtube.com/watch?v=JTi7vSzwvtc in the UK, see Crispin Blunt; or Sir Richard Branson Suspends Saudi Business Talks over Khashoggi Affair, *The Guardian*, 11 October 2018, https://www.theguardian.com/business/2018/oct/11/sir-richard-branson-suspends-saudi-business-talks-over-khashoggi-affair. For legislative implications, see, for example, 'Senate Votes to Condemn Saudi Crown Prince for Khashoggi Killing, End Support for Yemen War', *Washington Post*, 13 December 2018, https://www.washingtonpost.com/powerpost/senate-prepares-vote-to-curtail-us-support-for-saudi-led-military-effort-in-yemen/2018/12/13/cf934a96-fed7-11e8-862a-b6a6f3ce8199_story.html?utm_term=.7b906b98988e
35 'Putin and Saudi crown prince high-five at G20 summit', 30 November 2018, https://www.youtube.com/watch?v=rXiSafSqXAY
36 Thomas Mackie, 'If Looks Could Kill … NEVER Has Theresa May Looked So Awkward Meeting a Foreign Dignitary', *The Express*, 1 December 2018, https://www.express.co.uk/news/uk/1052960/theresa-may-awkward-meeting-saudi-crown-prince-MBS-g20-jamal-khashoggi-murder
37 Richard Norton-Taylor and Nick Hopkins, 'Defence Chief Signals Major UK Military Presence in Gulf', *Guardian Defence and Security Blog*, 18 December 2012, http://www.guardian.co.uk/uk/defence-and-security-blog/2012/dec/18/british-army-thegulf-defence
38 Gareth Stansfield and Saul Kelly, 'A Return to East of Suez? UK Military Deployment to the Gulf', *RUSI Briefing Paper*, April 2013, p. 5.
39 Ronen Bergman, 'US, UK Spied on Israel's Drone and Missile Programs', *Ynet News*, 31 January 2016, https://www.ynetnews.com/articles/0,7340,L-4759904,00.html
40 Patrick Porter, *Blunder: Britain's War in Iraq*, UK: Oxford University Press, 2018, p. 6.
41 Lorna Arnold and KatherinePyne, *Britain and the H-bomb*, London, UK: Palgrave, 2001, p. 53.
42 Secretary of Defense to the Secretary of State for Defence, 12 June 2018.
43 John Bolton, *Surrender Is Not an Option: Defending America at the United Nations*, Simon & Schuster, 2007, p. 210.
44 Walter Russell Mead, 'Trump's Jacksonian Withdrawal', *The Wall Street Journal*, 7 October 2019, https://www.wsj.com/articles/trumps-jacksonian-syria-withdrawal-11570487847

45 Ben Rhodes, 'The 9/11 Era Is Over', *The Atlantic*, 6 April 2020, https://www.theatlantic.com/ideas/archive/2020/04/its-not-september-12-anymore/609502/
46 Karl P. Mueller, Becca Wasser, Jeffrey Martini and Stephen Watts, 'U.S. Strategic Interests in the Middle East and Implications for the Army', *RAND*, 2017, p. 9.
47 Walter Russell Mead, 'Dialogues on American Foreign Policy and World Affairs: A Conversation with Former Deputy Secretary of State Antony Blinken', *The Hudson Institute*, 9 July 2020, https://www.hudson.org/research/16210-transcript-dialogues-on-american-foreign-policy-and-world-affairs-a-conversation-with-former-deputy-secretary-of-state-antony-blinken
48 See Borck & Stephens, 'The UK and the Gulf States', in Phillips & Stephens, ed., '*What Next for Britain in the Middle East*?'
49 Boris Johnson, 'Replace Iran Nuclear Plan with "Trump Deal"', says PM, *BBC News*, 14 January 2020, https://www.bbc.co.uk/news/uk-politics-51104386
50 Michael Stephens, 'Whether It Likes It or Not Europe Is Being Pushed and Pulled into America's Iran Policy', *War on the Rocks*, 1 August 2019, https://warontherocks.com/2019/08/whether-it-likes-it-or-not-europe-is-being-pushed-and-pulled-into-americas-iran-policy/
51 Jean-Loup Samaan, 'Coronavirus, Naval Forces, and Maritime Security in the Strait of Hormuz', *The Arab Gulf States Institute*, Washington, 27 April 2020, https://agsiw.org/coronavirus-naval-forces-and-maritime-security-in-the-strait-of-hormuz/

Chapter 5

1 Foreign and Commonwealth Office, About us, https://www.gov.uk/government/organisations/foreign-commonwealth-office/about
2 The current FCO strategy brings together a range of norms and values under one goal entitled 'Project our influence and demonstrate diplomatic leadership'. Foreign and Commonwealth Office single departmental plan, Updated 27 June 2019, https://www.gov.uk/government/publications/foreign-and-commonwealth-office-single-departmental-plan/foreign-and-commonwealth-office-single-departmental-plan-2019-20, accessed 25 May 2020.
3 Defined in the Washington Post as 'the sole single person hanging out with a couple'. '5 Reasons I Love Being the Third Wheel', *Washington Post*, 3 December 2015, https://www.washingtonpost.com/news/soloish/wp/2015/12/03/5-reasons-i-love-being-the-third-wheel/
4 'Get Brexit Done: Unleash Britain's Potential', The Conservative and Unionist Party Manifesto 2019, https://assets-global.website-files.com/5da42e2cae7ebd3f8bde353c/5dda924905da587992a064ba_Conservative%202019%20Manifesto.pdf
5 GDP first quarterly estimate, UK: April to June 2020, Office of National Statistics, https://www.ons.gov.uk/economy/grossdomesticproductgdp/bulletins/gdpfirstquarterlyestimateuk/apriltojune2020
6 The role of the FCO in UK government, written evidence from the Foreign and Commonwealth Office, 1 December 2010, submission to the Foreign Affairs Committee, https://publications.parliament.uk/pa/cm201011/cmselect/cmfaff/writev/fcogov/m12.htm
7 'William Hague Vows to Increase UK Influence in EU', *The Guardian*, 1 July 2010, https://www.theguardian.com/politics/2010/jul/01/william-hague-vows-to-increase-uk-influence-in-eu

8 'Invitation to Join the Government of Britain', *The Conservative Manifesto 2010*, https://conservativehome.blogs.com/files/conservative-manifesto-2010.pdf
9 'There Will Be No Downgrading of Human Rights under This Government', Foreign and Commonwealth Office, 31 March 2011, https://www.gov.uk/government/speeches/there-will-be-no-downgrading-of-human-rights-under-this-government
10 'Foreign Secretary Speech on Britain's Values in a Networked World', Foreign and Commonwealth Office, 1 July 2010, https://www.gov.uk/government/news/foreign-secretary-speech-on-britains-values-in-a-networked-world
11 The Foreign Secretary's Advisory Group on Human Rights, Foreign and Commonwealth Office, updated 18 February 2020, https://www.gov.uk/government/publications/the-foreign-secretarys-advisory-group-on-human-rights/the-foreign-secretarys-advisory-group-on-human-rights
12 'Britain Scraps Annual Assessment of Human Rights Abuses across the World', *The Observer*, 22 August 2010, https://www.theguardian.com/law/2010/aug/22/britain-scraps-human-rights-report
13 See, for example, 'UK Should Not Put Trade with Sudan Ahead of Human Rights', *The Guardian*, 16 August 2010, https://www.theguardian.com/commentisfree/2010/aug/16/sudan-britain-trade-human-rights
14 'Robin Cook's Speech on the Government's Ethical Foreign Policy', *The Guardian*, 12 May 1997, https://www.theguardian.com/world/1997/may/12/indonesia.ethicalforeignpolicy
15 'The Struggle for Middle East Democracy', *Brookings Institution*, 26 April 2011, https://www.brookings.edu/articles/the-struggle-for-middle-east-democracy/
16 'Obama Interview: The Ttranscript', *BBC World Service*, 2 June 2009, http://www.bbc.co.uk/worldservice/news/2009/06/090602_obama_transcript.shtml
17 The Hillary Clinton Doctrine, *Foreign Policy*, 6 November 2015, https://foreignpolicy.com/2015/11/06/hillary-clinton-doctrine-obama-interventionist-tough-minded-president/
18 'David Cameron's Cairo Visit Overshadowed by Defence Tour', *The Guardian*, 21 February 2011, https://www.theguardian.com/politics/2011/feb/21/cameron-cairo-visit-defence-trade
19 'Prime Minister's Statement on Libya', Cabinet Office, 28 February 2011, https://www.gov.uk/government/speeches/prime-ministers-statement-on-libya–2
20 'Dozens of Bahrain Arms Licences Revoked after Review', *BBC*, 18 February 2011, https://www.bbc.co.uk/news/uk-12502496
21 'David Cameron's Cairo Visit Overshadowed by Defence Tour', *The Guardian*, 21 February 2011, https://www.theguardian.com/politics/2011/feb/21/cameron-cairo-visit-defence-trade
22 See, for example, House of Commons Foreign Affairs Committee, British foreign policy and the 'Arab Spring', Second Report of Session 2012–13 para 155, https://publications.parliament.uk/pa/cm201213/cmselect/cmfaff/80/80.pdf
23 Elena Ianchovichina, *Eruptions of Popular Anger: The Economics of the Arab Spring and Its Aftermath. MENA Development Report*, Washington, DC: World Bank, 2018, http://documents.worldbank.org/curated/en/251971512654536291/pdf/121942-REVISED-Eruptions-of-Popular-Anger-preliminary-rev.pdf
24 'Prime Minister's Speech to the National Assembly Kuwait', Cabinet Office, 22 February 2011, https://www.gov.uk/government/speeches/prime-ministers-speech-to-the-national-assembly-kuwait
25 See United Arab Emirates: '"There is no freedom here": Silencing Dissent in The United Arab Emirates', *Amnesty International*, 18 November 2014, https://www.amnesty.org/en/documents/mde25/0018/2014/en/

26 'The White House and the Strongman', *New York Times*, 27 July 2018, https://www.nytimes.com/2018/07/27/sunday-review/obama-egypt-coup-trump.html
27 See 'A Saudi Prince's Quest to Remake the Middle East', *The New Yorker*, 2 April 2018, https://www.newyorker.com/magazine/2018/04/09/a-saudi-princes-quest-to-remake-the-middle-east. And 'Egypt's Military Rise to Power Partly Bankrolled by Emirates', audio recording suggests', *Daily Telegraph*, 2 March 2015, https://www.telegraph.co.uk/news/worldnews/africaandindianocean/egypt/11445060/Egypts-military-rise-to-power-partly-bankrolled-by-Emirates-audio-recording-suggests.html
28 'Saudi Arabia and UAE Prop Up Egypt Regime with Offer of $8bn', *Financial Times*, 10 July 2013, https://www.ft.com/content/7e066bdc-e8a2-11e2-8e9e-00144feabdc0
29 'UK Will Work with Egypt's New Rulers', says William Hague, *BBC*, 4 July 2013, http://www.bbc.co.uk/news/uk-23175224
30 'The UK and Egypt Sign Memoranda of Understanding', Foreign & Commonwealth Office, 6 November 2015, https://www.gov.uk/government/news/the-uk-and-egypt-sign-memoranda-of-understanding
31 'Egypt: Rab'a Killings Likely Crimes against Humanity', *Human Rights Watch*, 12 August 2014, https://www.hrw.org/news/2014/08/12/egypt-raba-killings-likely-crimes-against-humanity
32 'Freedom Is Still Flowering in the Arab Spring', Foreign and Commonwealth Office, 13 January 2012, https://www.gov.uk/government/news/freedom-is-still-flowering-in-the-arab-spring
33 'The White House and the Strongman', *New York Times*, 27 July 2018, https://www.nytimes.com/2018/07/27/sunday-review/obama-egypt-coup-trump.html
34 'UAE Told UK: Crack Down on Muslim Brotherhood or Lose Arms Deals', *The Guardian*, 6 November 2015, https://www.theguardian.com/world/2015/nov/06/uae-told-uk-crack-down-on-muslim-brotherhood-or-lose-arms-deals
35 'Tony Blair Eyes Abu Dhabi Office as He Looks to Expand Middle East Role', *Financial Times*, 23 June 2014, https://www.ft.com/content/8e7daff0-f78f-11e3-90fa-00144feabdc0
36 'UAE Anger at Britain Hits Business', *Financial Times*, 23 October 2012, https://www.ft.com/content/8e7daff0-f78f-11e3-90fa-00144feabdc0
37 'BAE Systems Fails to Win £6bn Contract to Supply Typhoon Fighters to UAE', *The Guardian*, 19 December 2013, https://www.theguardian.com/business/2013/dec/19/bae-systems-fails-contract-typhoon-figthers-uae
38 'Tony Blair Eyes Abu Dhabi Office as He Looks to Expand Middle East Role', *Financial Times*, 23 June 2014, https://www.ft.com/content/8e7daff0-f78f-11e3-90fa-00144feabdc0
39 'Muslim Brotherhood Review: A Tale of UK–UAE Relations', *Middle East Eye*, 17 December 2015, https://www.middleeasteye.net/news/muslim-brotherhood-review-tale-uk-uae-relations
40 'Updated Statistical Analysis of Documentation of Killings in the Syrian Arab Republic', Human Rights Data Analysis Group, 13 June 2013, https://hrdag.org/wp-content/uploads/2013/06/HRDAG-Updated-SY-report.pdf
41 'Russia, Backed by China, Casts 14th UN Veto on Syria to Block Cross-border Aid', *Reuters*, 20 December 2019, https://www.reuters.com/article/us-syria-security-un/russia-backed-by-china-casts-14th-u-n-veto-on-syria-to-block-cross-border-aid-idUSKBN1YO23V

42 Report of the United Nations Mission to Investigate Allegations of the Use of Chemical Weapons in the Syrian Arab Republic on the alleged use of chemical weapons in the Ghouta area of Damascus on 21 August 2013, United Nations, 16 September 2013, https://undocs.org/A/67/997
43 'House of Commons', Thursday, 29 August 2013, *Hansard*, https://publications.parliament.uk/pa/cm201314/cmhansrd/cm130829/debtext/130829-0001.htm
44 J. Strong, 'Interpreting the Syria Vote: Parliament and British Foreign Policy', *International Affairs*, 1123, 2015.
45 Public Opinion Drove Syria Debate, *YouGov*, 30 August 2013, https://yougov.co.uk/topics/politics/articles-reports/2013/08/30/public-opinion-syria-policy
46 J. Strong, 'Interpreting the Syria Vote: Parliament and British Foreign Policy', *International Affairs*, 1131, 2015.
47 ISIS: How 57 Per cent Came to Favour AirStrikes, *YouGov*, 26 September 2014, https://yougov.co.uk/topics/politics/articles-reports/2014/09/26/isis-how-majority-came-favour-air-strikes
48 See, for example, Iraq: Possible War Crimes by Shia Militia, *Human Rights Watch*, 31 January 2016, https://www.hrw.org/news/2016/01/31/iraq-possible-war-crimes-shia-militia
49 David Cameron Twitter account, 2 December 2015, https://twitter.com/david_cameron/status/672190400472420352?lang=en-gb
50 'Theresa May Earns Cold Reception in U.K. Parliament over Syria Attacks', *New York Times*, 16 April 2018, https://www.nytimes.com/2018/04/16/world/europe/theresa-may-uk-parliament-syria-corbyn.html
51 'Calais Crisis: Cameron Pledges to Deport More People to End "Swarm" of Migrants', *The Guardian*, 30 July 2015: https://www.theguardian.com/uk-news/2015/jul/30/calais-migrants-make-further-attempts-to-cross-channel-into-britain
52 'Migrant Crisis: UK Response Criticized by Senior Former Judges', *BBC*, 12 October 2015, https://www.bbc.co.uk/news/uk-politics-34502419
53 See, for example, 'EU Pushes Migration Talks with Tunisia, Egypt', *Reuters*, 20 February 2017, https://uk.reuters.com/article/uk-europe-migration-egypt-tunisia-idUKKBN15Z19L
54 'Promoting Human Rights Is Not about Who Can Shout the Loudest', *The Independent*, 10 December 2015, https://www.independent.co.uk/voices/promoting-human-rights-is-not-about-who-can-shout-the-loudest-a6767511.html
55 J. Kinninmont, 'The UK Needs a Smarter Approach to Human Rights in the Middle East and North Africa (2016)', *Chatham House*: https://www.chathamhouse.org/expert/comment/uk-needs-smarter-approach-human-rights-middle-east-and-north-africa
56 'The FCO's Administration and Funding of Its Human Rights Work Overseas', Foreign Affairs Committee, 5 April 2016, https://publications.parliament.uk/pa/cm201516/cmselect/cmfaff/860/86002.htm
57 National Security Strategy and Strategic Defence and Security Review 2015, https://assets.publishing.service.gov.uk/government/uploads/system/uploads/attachment_data/file/478933/52309_Cm_9161_NSS_SD_Review_web_only.pdf
58 Fourth Report of the Foreign Affairs Committee Session 2016–17. The use of UK-manufactured arms in Yemen: Response of the Secretaries of State for International Trade, Defence, Foreign and Commonwealth Affairs, and International Development, November 2016, https://assets.publishing.service.gov.uk/government/

uploads/system/uploads/attachment_data/file/568296/57525_Cm_9353_Web_Accessible_v0.3.pdf

59 Commons Research Briefing: UK Arms Exports to Saudi Arabia: Q&A, 10 July 2019, https://commonslibrary.parliament.uk/research-briefings/cbp-8425/

60 'Death Toll from Air Strike on Yemen Wedding Party Rises above 130: Medics', *Reuters*, 29 September 2015, https://www.reuters.com/article/us-yemen-security/death-toll-from-air-strike-on-yemen-wedding-party-rises-above-130-medics-idUSKCN0RT0XT20150929.'Saudi-led Coalition Admits to Bombing Yemen Funeral', *The Guardian*, 15 October 2016, https://www.theguardian.com/world/2016/oct/15/saudi-led-coalition-admits-to-bombing-yemen-funeral

61 Situation of human rights in Yemen, including violations and abuses since September 2014: Report of the Group of Eminent International and Regional Experts as submitted to the United Nations High Commissioner for Human Rights, 9 August 2019, https://documents-dds-ny.un.org/doc/UNDOC/GEN/G19/240/87/PDF/G1924087.pdf?OpenElement

62 'Humanitarian Crisis in Yemen Remains the Worst in the World', warns UN, *UN News*, 14 February 2019, https://news.un.org/en/story/2019/02/1032811

63 'Saudi Arabia Admits Using British Cluster Bombs in Yemen', *Financial Times*, 19 December 2016, https://www.ft.com/content/a268681a-c60a-11e6-8f29-9445cac8966f

64 'Britain Is Complicit in Saudi Arabia's War on Yemen', *The Guardian*, 13 June 2018, https://www.theguardian.com/commentisfree/2018/jun/13/britain-complicit-saudi-arabia-war-yemen-hodeidah. Situation of human rights in Yemen, including violations and abuses since September 2014: Report of the Group of Eminent International and Regional Experts as submitted to the United Nations High Commissioner for Human Rights, 9 August 2019, https://documents-dds-ny.un.org/doc/UNDOC/GEN/G19/240/87/PDF/G1924087.pdf?OpenElement

65 'Britain's Support for Saudi Arabia Is Making It Harder to Hold Russia to Account for War Crimes, Labour Says', *The Independent*, 26 September 2016, https://www.independent.co.uk/news/uk/politics/saudi-arabia-russia-war-crimes-labour-clive-lewis-hold-to-account-a7330506.html

66 'UK Minister Ignored Official Warning over Saudi Weapons Exports', court hears, *The Guardian*, 7 February 2017, https://www.theguardian.com/world/2017/feb/07/official-advised-uk-minister-to-suspend-saudi-weapons-exports-court-hears

67 See, for example, the statements of Boris Johnson, Foreign Secretary, *Hansard*, Commons Chamber, 26 October 2016, https://hansard.parliament.uk/Commons/2016-10-26/debates/9408b5f5-96ab-4565-9584-70d1944a3a27/CommonsChamber

68 'BAE Set to Brave Controversy by Attending Saudi Arabia Event', *Financial Times*, 17 October 2018, https://www.ft.com/content/b80cc26e-d1f3-11e8-a9f2-7574db66bcd5

69 'BAE Systems Will Go to the Saudi Ball', *BBC*, 16 October 2018, https://www.bbc.co.uk/news/business-45882301

70 National Security Strategy and Strategic Defence and Security Review 2015, https://assets.publishing.service.gov.uk/government/uploads/system/uploads/attachment_data/file/478933/52309_Cm_9161_NSS_SD_Review_web_only.pdf

71 Judgement Case No: T3/2017/2079 in The Court of Appeal (Civil Division) on Appeal from The High Court of Justice, Queen's Bench Division, Divisional Court, 20 June 2019, https://www.judiciary.uk/wp-content/uploads/2019/06/CAAT-v-Secretary-of-State-and-Others-Open-12-June-2019.pdf

72 'Trade Update: Written Statement', Elizabeth Truss, Secretary of State for International Trade, 7 July 2020, https://www.parliament.uk/business/publications/written-questions-answers-statements/written-statement/Commons/2020-07-07/HCWS339/
73 'How FCO Is Supporting the Government on Brexit', Foreign and Commonwealth Office, 1 November 2016, https://quarterly.blog.gov.uk/2016/11/01/how-fco-is-supporting-the-government-on-brexit/
74 '"Very Difficult" Differences in Brexit Talks – as UK Rejects Human Rights Link', *Sky News*, 5 March 2020, https://news.sky.com/story/very-difficult-differences-in-brexit-talks-as-uk-rejects-human-rights-link-11950298
75 House of Commons Foreign Affairs Committee: Global Britain: Human Rights and the Rule of Law: Thirteenth Report of Session 2017–19, 11 September 2018, https://publications.parliament.uk/pa/cm201719/cmselect/cmfaff/874/874.pdf
76 European Parliament Briefing: Human Rights in EU Trade Agreements: The Human Rights Clause and Its Application, July 2019, https://www.europarl.europa.eu/RegData/etudes/BRIE/2019/637975/EPRS_BRI(2019)637975_EN.pdf
77 'Commons Chamber', *Hansard*, 13 February 2019, https://hansard.parliament.uk/Commons/2019-02-13/debates/059B0ABD-3320-4753-891E-9AA429D07CB8/EUTradeAgreementsReplication
78 'Human Rights Are Getting Cut from Britain's Post-Brexit Trade Deal Negotiations', *The Conversation*, 31 October 2019, https://theconversation.com/human-rights-are-getting-cut-from-britains-post-brexit-trade-deal-negotiations-125165
79 'PM Seeks to Turbo-charge Trade between the UK and the Gulf', Prime Minister's Office, 5 December 2016, https://www.gov.uk/government/news/pm-seeks-to-turbo-charge-trade-between-the-uk-and-the-gulf
80 '£30 Billion: Trade Deals That Theresa May Is Doing in the Gulf Post-Brexit', *The Daily Express*, 5 December 2016, https://www.express.co.uk/news/politics/739967/Brexit-trade-deals-Theresa-May-Gulf-Middle-East-European-Union
81 Unlocking the full potential of the UK-GCC trade and investment relationship: Speech delivered by Secretary of State for International Trade, Dr Liam Fox at the UK-GCC PPP Conference in London, Department for International Trade, 19 April 2017, https://www.gov.uk/government/speeches/unlocking-the-full-potential-of-the-uk-gcc-trade-and-investment-relationship
82 'UK Government's Export Credit Agency Pinpoints GCC as a Priority Market', British Embassies Abu Dhabi and Dubai, 2 April 2018, https://www.gov.uk/government/news/uk-governments-export-credit-agency-pinpoints-gcc-as-a-priority-market
83 'UAE Calls on Early FTA with UK', *Khaleej Times*, 12 February 2020, https://www.khaleejtimes.com/business/local/uae-calls-on-early-fta-with-uk
84 'Joint Statement on UK – GCC Joint Trade and Investment Review', Department for International Trade, 5 November 2020, https://www.gov.uk/government/news/joint-statement-on-uk-gcc-joint-trade-and-investment-review
85 'Saudis Seek to Ease Investor Concerns after Royal Purge', *AFP*, 8 November 2017, https://www.france24.com/en/20171108-saudis-seek-ease-investor-concerns-after-royal-purge
86 'Saudi Arabia: UN Experts Urge Freedom for Loujain Al-Hathloul after 500 Days in Prison', UN Office of the High Commissioner for Human Rights, 27 September 2019, https://www.ohchr.org/EN/NewsEvents/Pages/DisplayNews.aspx?NewsID=25074&LangID=E

87 '"We Don't Have a Single Friend": Canada's Saudi Spat Reveals Country Is Alone', *The Guardian*, 11 August 2018, https://www.theguardian.com/world/2018/aug/11/canada-saudi-arabia-support-us
88 Jeremy Hunt Twitter account, 9 October 2018, https://twitter.com/jeremy_hunt/status/1049642482454224896?lang=en
89 Annex to the Report of the Special Rapporteur on extrajudicial, summary or arbitrary executions: Investigation into the unlawful death of Mr Jamal Khashoggi, United Nations, 19 June 2019, https://www.ohchr.org/EN/NewsEvents/Pages/DisplayNews.aspx?NewsID=24713
90 'Germany Rebuffs British Pressure to Sell Arms to Saudi Arabia', *Politico*, 20 February 2019, https://www.politico.eu/article/germany-rebuffs-british-pressure-to-sell-arms-to-saudi-arabia/
91 'Foreign Affairs Committee: Oral Evidence from the Foreign Secretary', HC 538, 31 October 2018, http://data.parliament.uk/writtenevidence/committeeevidence.svc/evidencedocument/foreign-affairs-committee/oral-evidence-from-the-foreign-secretary/oral/92185.html
92 'Saudi Arabia and the UK: Jeremy Hunt Is Not Telling the Truth about Arms Sales', *Middle East Eye*, 16 January 2019, https://www.middleeasteye.net/opinion/saudi-arabia-and-uk-jeremy-hunt-not-telling-truth-about-arms-sales
93 'UK on Collision Course with Saudis over New Human Rights Sanctions', *The Guardian*, 6 July 2020, https://www.theguardian.com/law/2020/jul/06/dominic-raab-to-annouce-uk-sanctions-against-human-rights-abusers
94 The UK sanctions list, UK government, https://www.gov.uk/government/publications/the-uk-sanctions-list, accessed 9 July 2020.
95 UK and Israel Sign Trade Continuity Agreement, Department for International Trade, 18 February 2019, https://www.gov.uk/government/news/uk-and-israel-sign-trade-continuity-agreement
96 'Report: Israel Asks UK to Include West Bank and Golan in Planned Free Trade Deal', *Times of Israel*, 15 February 2020, https://www.timesofisrael.com/report-israel-asks-uk-to-include-west-bank-golan-in-planned-free-trade-deal/
97 'British Arms Exports to Israel Reach Record Level', *The Guardian*, 27 May 2018, https://www.theguardian.com/world/2018/may/27/british-arms-exports-israel-new-record
98 'UN Right to Speak Out on Gaza Strike, Says Cameron', *BBC*, 4 August 2014, https://www.bbc.co.uk/news/uk-politics-28638491
99 'House of Commons Oral Answers to Questions, International Trade, Israel, Volume 681, 8 October 2020, https://hansard.parliament.uk/commons/2020-10-08/debates/D5965898-D63B-4838-8571-B51A97CF008F/Israel
100 'About That Much Vaunted U.S.–U.K. Trade Deal? Maybe Not Now', *New York Times*, 2 March 2020, https://www.nytimes.com/2020/03/02/world/europe/uk-us-trade-deal.html
101 'The US–UK Trade Talks Joe Biden Inherits', *Politico*, 14 December 2020, https://www.politico.eu/article/revealed-the-us-uk-trade-talks-joe-biden-inherits/
102 'Brexit Britain Faces the Gunboats', *Politico*, 22 January 2020, https://www.politico.eu/article/brexit-britain-faces-the-gunboats-trade-us-president-donald-trump-prime-minister-boris-johnson-iran-tariffs-sanctions/
103 '"We Don't Have a Single Friend": Canada's Saudi Spat Reveals Country Is Alone', *The Guardian*, 11 August 2018, https://www.theguardian.com/world/2018/aug/11/canada-saudi-arabia-support-us

104 Donald Trump Twitter account, 4 June 2020, https://twitter.com/realdonaldtrump/status/1213593975732527112?lang=en
105 'Britain "on Same Page" as US over Suleimani Killing, Says Raab', *The Guardian*, 5 January 2020, https://www.theguardian.com/politics/2020/jan/05/britain-sympathetic-to-us-over-killing-of-qassem-suleimani. Downing Street Distances Itself from Trump's Threat to Iranian Cultural Sites, *Press Association*, 6 January 2020, https://www.belfasttelegraph.co.uk/news/uk/downing-street-distances-itself-from-trumps-threat-to-iranian-cultural-sites-38837528.html
106 'Washington and Brussels Put Pressure on Brexit Britain', *Financial Times*, 22 January 2020, https://www.ft.com/content/6a9800c2-3d16-11ea-b232-000f4477fbca
107 MEPP: Statement by the High Representative/Vice-President Josep Borrell on the US initiative, The Office of the European Union Representative (West Bank and Gaza Strip, UNRWA), 4 February 2020, https://eeas.europa.eu/delegations/palestine-occupied-palestinian-territory-west-bank-and-gaza-strip/73960/mepp-statement-high-representativevice-president-josep-borrell-us-initiative_en
108 'Peace to Prosperity: A Vision to Improve the Lives of the Palestinian and Israeli People', January 2020, https://www.whitehouse.gov/wp-content/uploads/2020/01/Peace-to-Prosperity-0120.pdf
109 'Trump Plan's First Result: Israel Will Claim Sovereignty over Part of West Bank', *New York Times*, 28 January 2020, https://www.nytimes.com/2020/01/28/world/middleeast/israel-west-bank-annex-sovereignty.html
110 MEPP: Statement by the High Representative/Vice-President Josep Borrell on the US Initiative, The Office of the European Union Representative (West Bank and Gaza Strip, UNRWA), 4 February 2020, https://eeas.europa.eu/delegations/palestine-occupied-palestinian-territory-west-bank-and-gaza-strip/73960/mepp-statement-high-representativevice-president-josep-borrell-us-initiative_en
111 Release of US Proposals for Middle East Peace: Foreign Secretary's Statement, Foreign and Commonwealth Office, 28 January 2020, https://www.gov.uk/government/news/foreign-secretary-statement-on-release-of-us-proposals-for-middle-east-peace
112 Prime Minister's Questions, *Hansard*, 29 January 2020, https://hansard.parliament.uk/Commons/2020-01-29/debates/59978B62-B98C-44EB-8026-13560C37AD7C/PrimeMinister: 'Trump Plan's First Result: Israel Will Claim Sovereignty over Part of West Bank, *New York Times*, 28 January 2020, https://www.nytimes.com/2020/01/28/world/middleeast/israel-west-bank-annex-sovereignty.html
113 'Remarks by President Trump and Prime Minister Netanyahu of the State of Israel in Joint Statements', *White House*, 28 January 2020, https://www.whitehouse.gov/briefings-statements/remarks-president-trump-prime-minister-netanyahu-state-israel-joint-statements/
114 'Middle East Peace Plan, House of Commons', *Hansard*, 30 January 2020, https://hansard.parliament.uk/commons/2020-01-30/debates/EECA3331-80B3-45C5-B823-95564EE73495/MiddleEastPeacePlan
115 'UK's Johnson Welcomes Deal to Normalize Israel–UAE Relations', *Reuters*, 13 August 2020, https://uk.reuters.com/article/us-israel-emirates-britain/uks-johnson-welcomes-deal-to-normalise-israel-uae-relations-idUSKCN2592KK
116 Joe Biden Twitter Account, 16 September 2020, https://twitter.com/joebiden/status/1306334039557586944?lang=en
117 'Biden Made Sure Trump Is Not Going to Be President for Four More Years', *New York Times*, 2 December 2020, https://www.nytimes.com/2020/12/02/opinion/biden-interview-mcconnell-china-iran.html

118 'The Man Who Would be Prime Minister', *Economist*, 20 August 2009, https://www.economist.com/britain/2009/08/20/the-man-who-would-be-prime-minister
119 Behind Global Britain: Public Opinion on the UK's Role in the World (2019), https://bfpg.co.uk/wp-content/uploads/2019/04/Behind-Global-Britain-Public-Opinion-on-the-UKs-role-in-the-world.pdf
120 'Home Secretary Priti Patel: I Want Criminals to Feel Terror', *BBC*, 3 August 2019, https://www.bbc.co.uk/news/uk-49213743
121 See, for example, John Kampfner's Review of Dominic Raab's Book on the Erosion of Civil Liberties: Big Brother's Inexorable March, *The Guardian*, 8 February 2009, https://www.theguardian.com/books/2009/feb/08/assault-on-liberty-review
122 See, for example, Foreign and Commonwealth Office Written question, *Hansard*, 24 June 2020, https://www.parliament.uk/business/publications/written-questions-answers-statements/written-question/Commons/2020-06-24/64267/
123 'Get Brexit Done: Unleash Britain's potential', The Conservative and Unionist Party Manifesto 2019, https://assets-global.website files.com/5da42e2cae7ebd3f8bde353c/5dda924905da587992a064ba_Conservative%202019%20Manifesto.pdf-
124 Dominic Raab Twitter account, 6 July 2020, https://twitter.com/DominicRaab/status/1280095228893040642
125 Human Rights Update: Written statement, Dominic Raab, 6 July 2020, https://www.parliament.uk/business/publications/written-questions-answers-statements/written-statement/Commons/2020-07-06/HCWS337/
126 De Minimis Self-Certification Form, Foreign and Commonwealth Office, 9 June 2020, http://www.legislation.gov.uk/ukia/2020/45/pdfs/ukia_20200045_en.pdf
127 'Get Brexit Done: Unleash Britain's potential', The Conservative and Unionist Party Manifesto 2019, https://assets-global.website-files.com/5da42e2cae7ebd3f8bde353c/5dda924905da587992a064ba_Conservative%202019%20Manifesto.pdf
128 'My Pledges To You, Keir Starmer Labour leadership campaign website, https://keirstarmer.com/plans/10-pledges/, accessed on 26 May 2020.
129 Ibid.
130 'Arab Fractures: Citizens, States, and Social Contracts', *Carnegie Endowment for International Peace* (2017), VI, https://carnegieendowment.org/files/Arab_World_Horizons_Final.pdf
131 Covid-19 Crisis Response in MENA Countries, 9 June 2020, *OECD*, https://www.oecd.org/coronavirus/policy-responses/covid-19-crisis-response-in-mena-countries-4b366396/
132 'Iraq: Rein in Security Forces to Prevent a Bloodbath', *Amnesty International*, 9 November 2019, https://www.amnesty.org/en/latest/news/2019/11/iraq-rein-in-security-forces-to-prevent-a-bloodbath/
133 'An Ambassador for Human Rights Won't Convince the World That Britain Cares', *The Guardian*, 23 May 2019, https://www.theguardian.com/commentisfree/2019/may/23/ambassador-for-human-rights-britain-foreign-office-middle-east

Chapter 6

1 UK Office for National Statistics, https://www.ons.gov.uk/economy/nationalaccounts/balanceofpayments/datasets/uktradegoodsandservicespublicationtables
2 UK Trade Agreements with Non-EU Countries, 29 January 2020, https://www.gov.uk/guidance/uk-trade-agreements-with-non-eu-countries

3 George Allison, 'British Tempest Combat Jet Project Gathers Pace', *UK Defence Journal*, 2 January 2020, https://ukdefencejournal.org.uk/british-tempest-combat-jet-project-gathers-pace/
4 The United Arab Emirates: Inward and Outward FDI, http://dhaman.net/wp-content/uploads/2016/02/UAE.pdf
5 Office for National Statistics, https://www.ons.gov.uk/economy/nationalaccounts/balanceofpayments
6 Office for National Statistics, https://www.ons.gov.uk/economy/nationalaccounts/uksectoraccounts/datasets/unitedkingdomeconomicaccountsbalanceofpaymentscurrentaccount
7 SIPRI Factsheets, International Arms Transfers, 2018, https://www.sipri.org/publications/2019/sipri-fact-sheets/trends-international-arms-transfers-2018
8 'Ministers Wilfully Disregarded Evidence Saudi Arabia Was Violating International Humanitarian Law – Emily Thornberry', *The Labour Party*, 20 June 2019, https://labour.org.uk/press/ministers-wilfully-disregarded-evidence-saudi-arabia-violating-international-humanitarian-law-emily-thornberry/
9 The Arab Investment & Export Credit Guarantee Corporation, UAE, February 2016, http://dhaman.net/wp-content/uploads/2016/02/UAE.pdf
10 'Gavin Gibbon, Saudi Arabia to Become "home of boxing"', says promoter Eddie Hearn, *Arabian Business*, 4 December 2019, https://www.arabianbusiness.com/sport/434769-saudi-arabia-to-become-home-of-boxing-says-promoter-eddie-hearn
11 CEIC, Saudi Arabia Foreign Direct Investment, https://www.ceicdata.com/en/indicator/saudi-arabia/foreign-direct-investment
12 Office for National Statistics, https://www.ons.gov.uk/businessindustryandtrade/internationaltrade/datasets/uktradeinservicesallcountriesnonseasonallyadjusted
13 Ahmed Kotb, 'Post-Brexit Egypt–UK Trade', *Al Ahram*, 30 January 2020, http://english.ahram.org.eg/NewsContent/2/9/362478/World/International/PostBrexit-EgyptUK-trade.aspx
14 https://www.cbe.org.eg/_layouts/15/WopiFrame.aspx?sourcedoc={E6A4460A-7D09-434C-9AB1-B3C843F581ED}&file=External%20Sector%20Data%20274.xlsx&action=default
15 This contract is unlikely to be materially affected by the planned takeover of Bombardier's rail division by France's Alstom, which was announced in early 2020, https://www.alstom.com/press-releases-news/2020/2/acquisition-bombardier-transportation-accelerating-alstoms-strategic
16 For example, the expansion of eligibility for the UAE's ten-year residency visa, https://www.internationalinvestment.net/news/4024435/uae-expands-residency-golden-visa-eligibility; and Saudi Arabia's offer to global corporations of fresh tax breaks and exemption from labour regulations, https://www.ft.com/content/b968a082-486b-4eb0-b268-e1f2377891d9

Chapter 7

1 For example, the EU mission to counter piracy off Somalia (EUNAVFOR) has been run from the UK Joint Forces Command at Northwood.
2 Ministry of Defence (2019), *Annual Report and Accounts* (HC2347), p. 16; Boris Johnson, 'PM Statement to the House on the Integrated Review', 19 November 2020.
3 See, for example, Theresa May, 'Prime Minister's Speech to the Gulf Co-operation Council 2016', 7 December 2016, available at https://www.gov.uk/government/

speeches/prime-ministers-speech-to-the-gulf-co-operation-council-2016, accessed 20 February 2020.

4 House of Commons Library (2016), 'UK Relations with the Gulf', debate pack number CDP 2016-0097, 29 April 2016, available at https://researchbriefings.parliament.uk/ResearchBriefing/Summary/CDP-2016-0097#fullreport, accessed 18 December 2019, p. 2.

5 HM Government (2017), 'United Kingdom Strategic Export Controls Annual Report 2016', HC 287, available at https://assets.publishing.service.gov.uk/government/uploads/system/uploads/attachment_data/file/629853/Strategic_Exports_AR_2016_tagged.pdf, accessed 18 December 2019, p. 24.

6 Dominic Nicholls, 'UK's Future Commando Force: A Radical and "Lethal" New Unit to Fight Threats across the Globe', *The Telegraph*, 26 June 2020.

7 Ministry of Defence, *Annual Report 2018–19*, p. 41.

8 HM Government (2015), *National Security Strategy and Strategic Defence and Security Review 2015*, p. 6; HM Government (2018), *CONTEST: The United Kingdom's Strategy for Countering Terrorism*, p. 70; Noel Dempsey (2018), *House of Commons Briefing Paper: Defence Expenditure*, 8 November 2018, Number CBP 8175, p. 3.

9 For more, see https://theglobalcoalition.org/en/, accessed 18 December 2019.

10 Ministry of Defence (2019), *Ministry of Defence Annual Report and Accounts 2018–19*, HC 2347, available at https://www.gov.uk/government/publications/ministry-of-defence-annual-report-and-accounts-2018-to-19, pp. 30–1, accessed 18 December 2019.

11 Ibid., p. 31.

12 BBC News, 'Syria Conflict: UK to Give Extra £5m to Opposition Groups', 10 August 2012, available at https://www.bbc.co.uk/news/uk-19205204, accessed 20 February 2020.

13 This was after UN Security Council Resolution S/RES/2249 (2015) was agreed.

14 Most up-to-date information available at https://www.gov.uk/government/news/update-air-strikes-against-daesh, accessed 18 December 2019.

15 Data available at https://www.start.umd.edu/gtd/, accessed 13 October 2020.

16 Ibid.

17 Global Terrorism Database, available at https://www.start.umd.edu/research-projects/global-terrorism-database-gtd, accessed 3 October 2020.

18 Data available at https://www.unhcr.org/uk/syria-emergency.html, accessed 18 December 2019.

19 Alistair Burt, oral evidence to the House of Commons Foreign Affairs Committee on the Work of the Minister of State for the Middle East, 3 July 2018, Q39.

20 Data available at https://www.gov.uk/government/publications/factsheet-the-uks-humanitarian-aid-response-to-the-syria-crisis, accessed 18 December 2019. From 2018–19 the UK provided the people of Syria with 479,149 individual monthly food rations, 875,946 relief packages, 1,781,658 vaccines and 3,975,503 medical consultations. In addition, it provided 2,321,437 people with drinking water and 312,735 children were given access to education.

21 Data available at https://www.gov.uk/government/news/new-uk-aid-to-feed-millions-of-people-in-yemen, accessed 18 December 2019.

22 Details of UK contribution available at https://www.gov.uk/government/topical-events/daesh/about#humanitarian, accessed 18 December 2019.

23 Nawal al-Maghafi, 'How Chemical Weapons Have Helped Bring Assad Close to Victory', *BBC News*, 15 October 2018, available at https://www.bbc.co.uk/news/world-middle-east-45586903, accessed 18 December 2019.
24 Foreign and Commonwealth Office (2019), 'Statement on Iran Demarche', available at https://www.gov.uk/government/news/fco-statement-on-iran-demarche, accessed 18 December 2019.
25 BBC News, 'Iranian Officials Threaten to Seize British Oil Tanker', 5 July 2019, available at https://www.bbc.co.uk/news/uk-48882455, accessed 18 December 2019.
26 In breach of UN Security Council resolution 2231 (2015).
27 For more on this, see the Oxford Research Group's programme on remote warfare, https://www.oxfordresearchgroup.org.uk/pages/category/remote-warfare, accessed 18 December 2019.
28 Ministry of Defence, *Annual Report and Accounts 2018–19*, HC2347, London: TSO, 2019, p. 49.
29 House of Commons Defence Committee, *UK Military Operations in Syria and Iraq*, HC106, London: TSO, 2016, p. 23; Ministry of Defence, *Annual Report 2018–19*, p. 7.
30 Ibid., p. 7, 35.
31 Data available at https://www.gov.uk/government/topical-events/daesh/about#humanitarian, accessed 18 December 2018.
32 House of Commons Defence Committee, 'Oral Evidence: UK Military Operations in Mosul and Raqqa', HC 999, Tuesday 15 May 2018, London: TSO, 2018, Q47.
33 For more on this, see House of Commons Foreign Affairs Committee, 'Libya: Examination of Intervention and Collapse and the UK's Future Policy Options', HC119, London: TSO, 2016.
34 For more on lessons from history, see Louise Kettle, *Learning from the History of British Interventions in the Middle East*, Edinburgh: Edinburgh University Press, 2018.
35 Whilst the Ministry of Defence's (2018) 'The Good Operation', available at www.gov.uk, is a good example of communications within defence circles, this could be more effectively communicated to the public.
36 Any regional activities will also need to be aligned to a broader international strategy. An excellent plan for this process has been presented by the House of Commons Defence Committee (2020), 'In Search of Strategy – The 2020 Integrated Review', available at https://committees.parliament.uk/publications, accessed 7 October 2020.

Chapter 8

1 'Cameron "Anger" at Slow Pace of Turkish EU Negotiations', *BBC*, 27 July 2010, https://www.bbc.co.uk/news/uk-politics-10767768
2 'Blair Promotes Turkey's EU Membership', *Reuters*, 20 January 2007, https://uk.reuters.com/article/uk-turkey-blair-eu/blair-promotes-turkish-eu-membership-idUKL1688602520061216
3 2019 Country Report on Human Rights Practices: Turkey, *US Department of State*, 11 March 2020, https://www.state.gov/reports/2019-country-reports-on-human-rights-practices/turkey/
4 'Britain, Turkey, Sign Defence Deal to Develop Turkish Fighter Jet', *Reuters*, https://uk.reuters.com/article/uk-britain-eu-turkey-bae-idUKKBN15C0IM, 28 January 2017

5 Burak Ege Bekdil, 'Turkey to Rolls Royce: Let's Renegotiate Terms for TF-X Fighter Support', *Defense News*, 12 December 2019, https://www.defensenews.com/industry/2019/12/12/turkey-to-rolls-royce-lets-renegotiate-terms-for-tf-x-fighter-jet-support/
6 'UK Has Sold $1bn of Weapons to Turkey since Coup Attempt', *Middle East Eye*, 11 May 2018, https://www.middleeasteye.net/news/exclusive-uk-has-sold-1bn-weapons-turkey-coup-attempt
7 Bill Park, 'Erdogan Comes to London: Europe's Troubled Outliers Offer Mutual Comfort', *Platform for Peace and Justice*, 29 May 2018, http://www.platformpj.org/erdogan-comes-to-london-europes-troubled-outliers-offer-mutual-comfort/
8 Ayse Nur Dok, 'How Turkey–UK Relations Will Evolve in the Post-Brexit Period', *TRT World*, 16 May 2018, https://www.trtworld.com/turkey/how-turkey-uk-relations-will-evolve-in-the-post-brexit-period-17470
9 Bill Park, 'Can the US–Turkey Relationship Survive Erdogan and Trump?', *Platform for Peace and Justice*, 9 August 2018, http://www.platformpj.org/can-the-us-turkey-relationship-survive-erdogan-and-trump; for some background to the cooling of Turkey–West relations, see also Bill Park, 'Turkey's Isolated Stance: An Ally No More, or Just the Usual Turbulence?', *International Affairs*, vol. 91, no. 3 (May 2015), pp. 581–600.
10 Foreign Secretary's joint press conference Turkish Foreign Minister, March 2020, https://www.gov.uk/government/speeches/foreign-secretarys-joint-press-conference-turkish-foreign-minister-march-2020
11 Dominic Nicholls, 'Britain Accused of Putting Trade Deals before Condemnation of Turkey', *The Telegraph*, 14 October 2020, https://www.telegraph.co.uk/news/2019/10/14/britain-accused-putting-trade-deals-condemnation-turkey/
12 '"Nothing Is Ours Anymore"; Kurds Forced Out of Afrin after Turkish Assault', *The Guardian*, 7 June 2018, https://www.theguardian.com/world/2018/jun/07/too-many-strange-faces-kurds-fear-forced-demographic-shift-in-afrin
13 Mesut Ozcan, *Harmonizing Foreign Policy: Turkey the EU and the Middle East*, Aldershot: Ashgate, 2008; Ozlem Terzi, *The Influence of the European Union on Turkish Foreign Policy*, Aldershot: Ashgate, 2010.
14 Bill Park, 'Turkey and the Eternal Question of Being, or Becoming, European', in Trine Flockhart, ed., *Socializing Democratic Norms: The Role of International Organizations for the Construction of Europe*, Basingstoke: Palgrave Macmillan, 2005, pp. 232–48; Bill Park, 'The Security Dimensions of Turkey–EU Relations', in Michael Lake, ed., *The EU and Turkey: A Glittering Prize or a Millstone?* London: The Federal Trust, 2005, pp. 127–40.
15 Bill Park, 'Turkey and the US: A Transatlantic Future?', in Andrew M. Dorman and Joyce P. Kaufman, eds, *The Future of Transatlantic Relations: Perceptions, Policy and Practice*, Stanford: Stanford University Press, 2011, pp. 137–54; Bill Park, 'Turkey's New (De)security Policy: Axis Shift, Gaullism, or Learning Process?', in Andrew M. Dorman and Joyce P. Kaufman, eds, *Providing for National Security: A Comparative Analysis*, Stanford: Stanford University Press, 2014, pp. 254–70.
16 Omer Taspinar, 'Turkey's Middle East Policies: Between Neo-Ottomanism and Kemalism', *Carnegie Endowment for International Peace*, 7 October 2008, https://carnegieendowment.org/2008/10/07/turkey-s-middle-east-policies-between-neo-ottomanism-and-kemalism-pub-22209
17 Omer Taspinar, 'The Rise of Turkish Gaullism: Getting Turkish–American Relations Right', *Insight Turkey*, vol. 13, no. 1 (January–March 2011), pp. 19–25.

18 Behlul Ozkan, 'Turkey, Davutoglu and the Idea of Pan-Islamism', *Survival*, vol. 56, no. 4 (August–September 2014), pp. 119–40.
19 Ozgur Tufekci, *The Foreign Policy of Modern Turkey: Power and the Ideology of Eurasianism*, London: I.B. Tauris, 2017.
20 Mustafa Akyol, 'The AKP's Strange Bedfellows', *Al Monitor*, 25 January 2016, https://www.al-monitor.com/pulse/originals/2016/01/turkey-akp-old-enemies-turning-into-allies.html; Leela Jacinto, 'Turkey's Post-coup Purge and Erdogan's Private Army', 13 July 2017, https://foreignpolicy.com/2017/07/13/turkeys-post-coup-purge-and-erdogans-private-army-sadat-perincek-gulen/; Nafees Mahmud, 'How an Ultra-secularist Gained Clout in Turkey's Islamist Government', *Al Monitor*, 30 January 2020, https://www.al-monitor.com/pulse/originals/2020/01/turkey-ultra-secularist-man-said-to-be-behind-erdogan-policy.html
21 Alexander Murinson, 'The Strategic Depth Doctrine of Turkish Foreign Policy', *Middle Eastern Studies*, vol. 42, no. 6 (2006), pp. 945–64.
22 Bill Park, 'Turkey's Kurdish Complexes and Its Syrian Quagmire', in Michael M. Gunter, ed., *Routledge Handbook on the Kurds*, London and New York: Routledge, 2019, pp. 282–95. For insights into the evolution of Turkish policy towards the Syrian conflict, see Hassan Hassan, 'Turkey's Shifting Position in Syria', *Center for Global Policy*, 27 February 2018, https://cgpolicy.org/articles/turkeys-shifting-position-in-syria/; Sam Heller, 'Turkey's "Turkey First" Syria Policy', *The Century Foundation*, 12 April 2017, https://tcf.org/content/report/turkeys-turkey-first-syria-policy/?agreed=1; Bill Park, 'There Are No Clear Winners and Losers Yet in Syria', *Platform for Peace and Justice,* 13 October 2019, http://www.platformpj.org/there-are-no-clear-winners-and-losers-yet-in-syria/; Aaron Stein, 'Turkey's Evolving Syria Strategy: Why Turkey Backs al Nusra but Shuns IS', *Foreign Affairs*, 9 February 2015, https://www.foreignaffairs.com/articles/turkey/2015-02-09/turkeys-evolving-syria-strategy; 'Turkey's Operation in Syria: A Chess Game with a Shifting Balance of Power', *Al Jazeera*, 11 August 2019, https://studies.aljazeera.net/en/reports/2019/11/turkeys-operation-syria-chess-game-shifting-balance-power-191108120145362.html
23 Gozde Nur Donat, 'Erdogan: PKK Is the Same as ISIL – Both Are Terrorists', *Anadolu Agency*, 7 November 2014, https://www.aa.com.tr/en/turkey/erdogan-pkk-is-the-same-as-isil-both-are-terrorists/103609
24 'Turkey vs ISIS and PKK: A Matter of Distinction', Bipartisan Policy Center, July 2016, https://bipartisanpolicy.org/wp-content/uploads/2019/03/BPC-Turkey-ISIS-PKK.pdf
25 Michael Rose, 'Macron Says Time for Turkey to Clarify Ambiguous Stance on Islamic State', *Reuters*, 3 December 2019, https://www.reuters.com/article/us-nato-summit-macron-turkey-idUSKBN1Y71VE
26 Abdullah Bozkurt, 'ISIS Suspects Released in Big Numbers under Erdogan's Rule', *Stockholm Center for Freedom*, 24 April 2017, http://stockholmcf.org/isil-suspects-released-in-big-numbers-under-erdogans-rule/; Behlul Ozkan, 'Untangling Turkey's Middle East Allegiances', *Politico*, 23 December 2015, http://www.politico.eu/article/untangling-the-turkey-isil-connection/; David. L Phillips, 'Research Paper: ISIS-Turkey Links', 8 September 2016, http://www.huffingtonpost.com/david-l-phillips/research-paper-isis-turke_b_6128950.html; Merve Tahiroglu and Jonathan Schanzer, 'Islamic State Networks in Turkey', *Foundation for Defense of Democracies*, March 2017, http://www.defenddemocracy.org/content/uploads/documents/Islamic_State_Networks_Turkey.pdf; Ahmet S. Yayla, 'Try Erdogan at the International Criminal Court for Enabling ISIS', *The Investigative Journal*, 6 March 2020, https://

investigativejournal.org/try-erdogan-at-the-international-criminal-court-for-enabling-isis/; Amberin Zaman, 'For Turkey Which Is the Lesser Evil: ISIS or the Kurds?', *Wilson Center,* 4 March 2016, https://www.wilsoncenter.org/publication/for-turkey-which-the-lesser-evil-isis-or-the-kurds

27 Hevidar Ahmed, 'Senior Kurdistan official: IS Was at Erbil's Gates, Turkey Did Not Help', *Rudaw,* 16 September 2014, http://rudaw.net/english/interview/16092014; Dorian Jones, 'Islamic State Tests Turkey–Iraqi Kurd Ties', *Voice of America News,* 12 September 2014, https://www.voanews.com/middle-east/islamic-state-tests-turkey-iraqi-kurd-tie; Amberin Zaman, 'Masrour Barzani: Kurdish Independence Would Help to Defeat IS', *Al Monitor,* 2 July 2015, http://www.al-monitor.com/pulse/originals/2015/07/turkey-iraq-syria-kurdish-independence-help-war-against-isis.html; Amberin Zaman, 'The Iraqi Kurds' Waning Love Affair with Turkey', *Al Monitor,* 1 September 2015, http://www.al-monitor.com/pulse/originals/2015/09/turkey-iraq-kurdistan-krg-pkk-love-affair-over.html

28 Feyzi Baban and Wael Nawara, 'The Lost Promise of Turkey–Egypt Relations', *Al Monitor,* 24 November 2013, https://www.al-monitor.com/pulse/originals/2013/11/turkey-egypt-relations.html

29 Paul Iddon, 'The Significance of Turkey's Overseas Military Bases', *Ahval,* 13 July 2019, https://ahvalnews.com/turkish-military/significance-turkeys-overseas-military-bases

30 Uzay Bulut, 'Turkey Stabilising Libya? Think Again', *Gatestone Institute,* 22 November 2018, https://www.gatestoneinstitute.org/13337/turkey-libya-stabilization; Mustafa Gurbuz, 'Turkey's Policy towards a Fractured Libya', *Arab Center Washington DC,* 12 December 2017, http://arabcenterdc.org/policy_analyses/turkeys-policy-toward-a-fractured-libya/; Bill Park, 'What Is Turkey up to in Libya?' 26 February 2019, http://www.platformpj.org/what-is-turkey-up-to-in-libya/; and Bill Park, 'Turkey's Libyan Gamble: What's behind It and Will It Pay Off?', 6 January 2020, http://www.platformpj.org/turkeys-libyan-gamble-whats-behind-it-and-will-it-pay-off/, both *Platform for Peace and Justice.*

31 'Turkey's Gas Exploration off Cyprus Raises Tensions', *Reuters,* 14 October 2019, https://uk.reuters.com/article/uk-cyprus-turkey-ship/turkeys-gas-exploration-off-cyprus-raises-tensions-idUKKBN1WT21L

32 'Turkey Procures Its Third Drilling Vessel from UK', *Hurriyet Daily News,* 24 February 2020, https://www.hurriyetdailynews.com/turkey-procures-its-third-drilling-vessel-from-uk-152394

33 Senem Aydın-Duzgit and Nathalie Tocci, *Turkey and the European Union*, London: Palgrave, 2015.

34 Discussion with UK official, February 2020.

35 Sinan Ulgen, 'Negotiating Brexit: The Prospect of a UK–Turkey Partnership', *Turkey Project Policy Paper No. 11,* Brookings, March 2017, https://www.brookings.edu/wp-content/uploads/2017/03/ulgen-negotiating-brexit.pdf

36 Thierry Tardy, 'CSDP: Getting Third States on Board', *EUISS Issue* Brief, no. 6, March 2014, https://www.iss.europa.eu/sites/default/files/EUISSFiles/Brief_6_CSDP_and_third_states.pdf

37 'Trends in International Arms Transfers 2017', *Stockholm Institute of Peace Research Institute (SIPRI),* https://www.sipri.org/sites/default/files/2018-03/fssipri_at2017_0.pdf

38 Burak Ege Bekdil, 'Going It Alone: Turkey Staunch in Efforts for Self-sufficient Defense Capabilities', *Defense News,* 23 April 2017, https://www.defensenews.com/land/2017/04/24/going-it-alone-turkey-staunch-in-efforts-for-self-sufficient-defense-

capabilities/; 'Turkey: Domestic Arms Industry', *Global Security*, https://www.globalsecurity.org/military/world/europe/tu-industry.htm

39 World Bank Country Profile Turkey, 2020, https://wits.worldbank.org/CountryProfile/en/Country/TUR/Year/LTST/TradeFlow/ Import/Partner/all/; https://www.dacbeachcroft.com/media/823304/bilateral-trade-between-turkey-and-the-uk.pdf

40 These issues are explained fully in Catherine Barnard and Emilija Leinarte, 'EU–Turkey Customs Union', *The UK in a Changing Europe*, 8 June 2018, https://ukandeu.ac.uk/explainers/eu-turkey-customs-union; see also Ulgen, op. cit.

41 Matt Ward, 'Where Does the UK Rank in Foreign Direct Investment Statistics?', *House of Commons Library*, 4 April 2019, https://commonslibrary.parliament.uk/economy-business/where-does-the-uk-rank-in-foreign-direct-investment-statistics/

42 House of Commons Foreign Affairs Committee, *The UK's Relations with Turkey*, Tenth Report of Session 2016–17, HC615, p. 15, https://publications.parliament.uk/pa/cm201617/cmselect/cmfaff/615/615.pdf

43 Humeyra Pamuk and Phil Stewart, 'US Halts Secretive Drone Program with Turkey over Syria Incursion', *Reuters*, 5 February 2020, https://www.reuters.com/article/us-turkey-security-usa-drone-exclusive-idUSKBN1ZZ1AB

44 Richard Norton-Taylor, 'Terror Trial Collapses after Fear of Deep Embarrassment to Security Services', *The Guardian*, 1 June 2015, https://www.theguardian.com/uk-news/2015/jun/01/trial-swedish-man-accused-terrorism-offences-collapse-bherlin-gildo

45 Peter Apps, 'Syria's Assad Faces Growing Rebel, Foreign Threat', *Reuters*, 27 June 2012, https://uk.reuters.com/article/uk-syria-escalation/analysis-syrias-assad-faces-growing-rebel-foreign-threat-idUKBRE85Q11C20120627

46 Syrian rebels 'Aided by British Intelligence', *Sky News*, 19 August 2012, https://uk.news.yahoo.com/syria-rebels-aided-british-intelligence-041638306.html

47 Mark Curtis, 'A London Attacker's Links to UK Covert Operations in Syria and Libya', 7 June 2017, http://markcurtis.info/2017/06/07/update-a-london-attackers-links-to-uk-covert-operations-in-syria-and-libya/#_ftn8

48 Audit of the DoD's Accountability of Counter-Islamic State of Iraq and Syria Train and Equip Fund Equipment Designated for Syria DODIG-2020-06, https://www.dodig.mil/reports.html/Article/2085916/audit-of-the-dods-accountability-of-counter-islamic-state-of-iraq-and-syria-tra/; Shawn Snow, 'US Military Did Not Properly Store or Account for Nearly $715 Million in Weapons for Syrian Partners Fighting ISIS', *Military Times*, 18 February 2020, https://www.militarytimes.com/flashpoints/2020/02/18/us-military-did-not-properly-store-or-account-for-nearly-715-million-in-weapons-for-syrian-partners-fighting-isis/; 'Armed Conflict in Syria: Overview and US Response', *Congressional Research Service*, 12 February 2020, https://crsreports.congress.gov/product/pdf/RL/RL33487

49 Mark Mazzeti et al., 'Behind the Sudden Death of a $1 Billion Secret CIA War in Syria', *New York Times*, 2 August 2017, https://www.nytimes.com/2017/08/02/world/middleeast/cia-syria-rebel-arm-train-trump.html

50 http://www.mfa.gov.tr/sc_-15_-birlesik-krallik-in-pkk-karari-hk-sc.en.mfa.

51 Murat Yetkin, 'NATO Pledges Air Support as Turkey–Russia Rift Grows', *Yetkin Report*, 29 February 2020, https://yetkinreport.com/en/2020/02/29/nato-pledges-air-support-as-turkey-russia-rift-grows/

52 Patrick Wintour and Dan Sabbagh, 'UK Suspends Arms Exports to Turkey to Prevent Use in Syria', *The Guardian*, 15 October 2019, https://www.theguardian.com/world/2019/oct/15/uk-suspends-arms-exports-turkey-prevent-use-syria

53 Louisa Brooke-Holland, *UK Forces in the Middle East*, House of Commons Library Briefing, 15 January 2020, https://commonslibrary.parliament.uk/research-briefings/cbp-8794/
54 Paul Rogers, 'Against the Current', *London Review of Books*, 6 February 2020.
55 'Integrated Review of Security, Defence, Development and Foreign Policy', *Hansard*, 26 February 2020, https://hansard.parliament.uk/Commons/2020-02-26/debates/20022630000006/IntegratedReviewOfSecurityDefenceDevelopmentAndForeignPolicy
56 Douglas Barrie, 'UK Defence Review: Repent at Leisure', *International Institute for Strategic Studies*, 31 January 2020, https://www.iiss.org/blogs/military-balance/2020/01/uk-defence-review; Ian Bond, 'UK Foreign and Security Policy after Brexit', *Centre for European Reform*, 27 January 2020, https://www.cer.eu/publications/archive/bulletin-article/2020/uk-foreign-and-security-policy-after-brexit; Malcolm Chalmers, 'Taking Control: Rediscovering the Centrality of National Interest in UK Foreign and Security Policy', *Royal United Services Institute*, 10 February 2020, https://rusi.org/publication/whitehall-reports/taking-control-rediscovering-centrality-national-interest-uk-foreign; Harry Lye, 'UK Government Sets the Stage for Sweeping Defence Review', *Army Technology*, 20 December 2020, https://www.army-technology.com/news/uk-defence-review/
57 Global Britain: Delivering on Our International Ambition, 23 September 2019, https://www.gov.uk/government/collections/global-britain-delivering-on-our-international-ambition

Chapter 9

1 Ian Black, 'The Contested Centenary of Britain's "Calamitous Promise"', *The Guardian*, 17 October 2017, https://www.theguardian.com/news/2017/oct/17/centenary-britains-calamitous-promise-balfour-declaration-israel-palestine
2 Khalil Shikaki and Dahlia Scheindlin, Palestinian–Israeli Pulse: A Joint Poll (2016–2018) Final Report, PSR, January 2019, http://www.pcpsr.org/en/node/742
3 Ambassador Jonathan Allen, 'Reaffirming UK Commitment to a Two-state Solution Which Ends the Israeli–Palestinian Conflict', 20 February 2018, https://www.gov.uk/government/speeches/reaffirming-uk-commitment-to-a-two-state-solution-which-ends-the-israeli-palestinian-conflict
4 Anshell Pfeffer, 'Benjamin Netanyahu, the Undertaker of the Two-state Solution', *Haaretz*, 1 April 2019, https://www.haaretz.com/israel-news/israeli-palestinian-conflict-solutions/.premium-benjamin-netanyahu-the-undertaker-of-the-two-state-solution-1.7045749
5 Peter Beaumont, 'Three-quarters of Israeli Jews Oppose Detail of Palestinian State, Poll Shows', *The Guardian*, 20 October 2014, https://www.theguardian.com/world/2014/oct/20/israeli-jews-oppose-palestinian-state-poll-shows
6 Yolande Knell, 'US Stops All Aid to Palestinians in West Bank and Gaza,' *The BBC*, 1 February 2019, https://www.bbc.co.uk/news/world-middle-east-47095082
7 Patrick Wintour, 'UK's Key Role in Brokering UN Resolution on Israeli Settlements Confirmed', *The Guardian*, 28 December 2016, https://www.theguardian.com/world/2016/dec/28/uks-key-role-in-brokering-un-resolution-on-israeli-settlements-confirmed

8 Interview, FCO official.
9 Kame Hawash, 'The UK Is Quietly Changing Its Policy on Israel and Palestine,' *MEMO*, 5 April 2017, https://www.middleeastmonitor.com/20170405-the-uk-is-quietly-changing-its-policy-on-israel-and-palestine/
10 https://www.parliament.uk/business/committees/committees-a-z/commons-select/foreign-affairs-committee/inquiries1/parliament-2015/inquiry1/publications/, Written evidence from Middle East and North Africa Directorate, Foreign and Commonwealth Office (MEP0055)
11 The Office of the Prime Minister, PM meeting with Israeli Prime Minister Netanyahu, 6 February 2017, https://www.gov.uk/government/news/pm-meeting-with-israeli-prime-minister-netanyahu-6-february-2017
12 Jehan Alfarra, 'Is British Policy Shifting More towards Israel under Theresa May?' *MEMO*, 25 May 2017, https://www.middleeastmonitor.com/20170525-is-uk-policy-shifting-more-towards-israel-under-theresa-may/
13 Britain–Israel Trade after Brexit, *BICOM*, 13 December 2017, http://www.bicom.org.uk/analysis/britain-israel-trade-brexit/
14 Peter Beaumont, 'US Outnumbered 14 to 1 as It Vetoes UN Vote on Status of Jerusalem,' *The Guardian*, 19 December 2017, https://www.theguardian.com/world/2017/dec/18/us-outnumbered-14-to-1-as-it-vetoes-un-vote-on-status-of-jerusalem
15 Omar Dajani and Hugh Lovatt, 'Rethinking Oslo: How Europe Can Promote Peace in Israel and Palestine,' *ECFR*, 2017, https://www.ecfr.eu/page/-/ECFR226_-_RETHINKING_OSLO_-_HOW_EUROPE_CAN_PROMOTE_PEACE_IN_ISRAEL-PALESTINE.pdf
16 Alex Mostrous, 'UK Resumes £25m Aid to Palestinians,' *The Times*, 21 December 2016, https://www.thetimes.co.uk/article/uk-resumes-25m-aid-to-palestinians-ff533tjfk
17 Hugh Lovatt, 'Written Evidence from Hugh Lovatt, Policy Fellow and Israel/Palestine Project Coordinator at the European Council on Foreign Relations (ECFR) (MEP0024),' http://data.parliament.uk/writtenevidence/committeeevidence.svc/evidencedocument/foreign-affairs-committee/the-uks-policy-towards-the-middle-east-peace-process/written/49474.html
18 The Humanitarian Situation in Palestine – Exploring the Challenges and Coordinating the Response, *Forward Thinking*, 6 December 2018, http://www.forward-thinking.org/?p=5174
19 Interview Ambassador Husam Zomlot.
20 Interview FCO official.
21 Edward P. Djerejian et al., 'Two States or One? Reappraising the Israeli–Palestinian Impasse,' *Carnegie Endowment for International Peace*, 18 September 2018, https://carnegieendowment.org/2018/09/18/two-states-or-one-reappraising-israeli-palestinian-impasse-pub-77269
22 Written evidence from Hugh Lovatt, Policy Fellow and Israel/Palestine Project Coordinator at the European Council on Foreign Relations (ECFR) (MEP0024), http://data.parliament.uk/writtenevidence/committeeevidence.svc/evidencedocument/foreign-affairs-committee/the-uks-policy-towards-the-middle-east-peace-process/written/49474.html
23 Written evidence from Roger Higginson (MEP0004), http://data.parliament.uk/writtenevidence/committeeevidence.svc/evidencedocument/foreign-affairs-committee/the-uks-policy-towards-the-middle-east-peace-process/written/47205.html

24 Eran Etzion, 'EU–Israel Relations in the Trump Era', *Israeli–European Policy Network*, 2018, https://www.iepn.org/images/stories/papers/2018/eu-israel%20relations%20in%20the%20trump%20era%20-%20eran%20etzion.pdf
25 Israel/West Bank: 'Grant Palestinians Equal Rights', *Human Rights Watch*, 17 December 2019, https://www.hrw.org/news/2019/12/17/israel/west-bank-grant-palestinians-equal-rights
26 FAC: MEP0024.
27 FAC: Written evidence from Oxford Research Group (MEP0039)
28 FAC: Written evidence from Right Honourable Clare Short (MEP0037)
29 Foreign Affairs Committee, 'Oral Evidence: Israel and the Occupied Palestinian Territories: Prospects for 2014, HC 957', House of Commons, 14 January 2014, https://www.parliament.uk/documents/commons-committees/foreign-affairs/Israel-Palestine14Jan.pdf
30 'MPs Back Palestinian Statehood alongside Israel', *BBC News*, 14 October 2014, https://www.bbc.co.uk/news/uk-politics-29596822
31 Toby Green, 'What a Labour Government Recognising a Palestinian State Would Actually Mean', *The Jewish Chronicle*, 30 September 2018, https://www.thejc.com/comment/analysis/what-a-labour-government-recognising-palestine-would-actually-mean-1.470417
32 Anders Persson, 'If Not Now, When Should Europe Recognise Palestine?', *Al Jazeera*, 21 February 2018, https://www.aljazeera.com/indepth/opinion/europe-recognise-palestine-180221093922484.html
33 'The Oslo Accords, 25 years On: Time to Recognise the State of Palestine Alongside Israel', Letter in *The Times*, 13 September 2018, http://www.balfourproject.org/times-letter-13-september-the-oslo-accords-25-years-on-time-to-recognise-the-state-of-palestine-alongside-israel/
34 FAC: Written evidence from Liberal Democrat Friends of Palestine (MEP0067)
35 Sir Vincent Fean KCVO, Dan Rothem, Daniel Seidemann, Palestine in 2017 Settlements, Jerusalem and the case for recognition, Conservative Middle East Council, May 2017, https://cmec.org.uk/sites/default/files/field/attachment/CMEC%20Palestine%202017.pdf
36 FAC: Written Evidence from Palestinian Mission to the UK (MEP0072)
37 FAC: Written evidence from Council for Arab–British Understanding (Caabu) (MEP0030)
38 Donald Macintyre, Tony Blair: 'We Were Wrong to Boycott Hamas after Its Election Win', *The Guardian*, 14 October 2017, https://www.theguardian.com/world/2017/oct/14/tony-blair-hamas-gaza-boycott-wrong
39 Lee Harpin, 'Jack Straw Claims He Was Ditched as Foreign Secretary over His Backing for Dialogue with Hamas', *The Jewish Chronicle*, 20 November 2017, https://www.thejc.com/news/uk-news/jack-straw-claims-he-was-ditched-as-foreign-secretary-over-his-backing-for-dialogue-with-hamas-1.448383
40 Daniel Boffey, 'EU Court Upholds Hamas Terror Listing', *The Guardian*, 26 July 2017, https://www.theguardian.com/world/2017/jul/26/eu-court-upholds-hamas-terror-listing
41 'Hamas in 2017: The Document in Full', *Middle East Eye*, 2 May 2017, https://www.middleeasteye.net/news/hamas-2017-document-full
42 Ewen MacAskill, 'Palestinian Event in London Faces Ban over Hamas Links', *The Guardian*, 25 June 2017, https://www.theguardian.com/world/2017/jun/25/palestinian-event-in-london-faces-ban-over-hamas-links

43 Ian Geoghegan, 'EU Court Dismisses Hamas Appeal over Frozen Funds', *Politico*, 14 December 2018, https://www.politico.eu/article/eu-court-dismisses-hamas-appeal-over-frozen-funds/
44 Interview, former FCO official.
45 Interview, Nadia Hijab.
46 Daniel Sugarman, 'Revealed: GCHQ's Israel–UK Partnership', *The Jewish Chronicle*, 27 January 2017, https://www.thejc.com/news/uk-news/revealed-gchq-s-israel-uk-partnership-1.431416
47 Anna Ahronheim, 'British Warship Docks in Haifa as Part of Growing Cooperation with Israel', *The Jerusalem Post*, 22 November 2016, https://www.jpost.com/Israel-News/Politics-And-Diplomacy/British-warship-docks-in-Haifa-as-part-of-growing-cooperation-with-Israel-473381, UK–Israel relations after Brexit: Cyber security, Britain Israel Communications and Research Centre, April 2018, http://www.bicom.org.uk/analysis/uk-israel-relations-brexit-cyber-security/
48 Interview Israeli diplomat.
49 Noa Landau, 'In Era of Brexit and Tory Power, Israel Sees Shift in Relations with Britain', *Haaretz*, 6 March 2018, https://www.haaretz.com/israel-news/.premium-in-era-of-brexit-and-of-tories-israel-improves-relations-with-britain-1.6138494
50 Lee Harpin, 'Jeremy Hunt Condemns American Recognition of Golan Heights: "We Should Never Recognise Annexation of Territory by Force"', *The Jewish Chronicle*, 3 April 2019, https://www.thejc.com/news/uk-news/jeremy-hunt-condemns-american-recognition-of-golan-heights-donald-trump-1.482507
51 UK Delegation, 'Human Rights Council 34: UK Explanation of Voting on the Resolution Regarding Israel and the Occupied Palestinian Territories', *UN Human Rights Council*, 24 March 2017, https://www.gov.uk/government/news/human-rights-council-34-uk-explanation-of-voting-on-the-resolution-regarding-israel-and-the-occupied-palestinian-territories
52 Lee Harpin, 'Exclusive: Jeremy Hunt Announces UK Will Oppose Anti-Israel Measures at the UN Human Rights Council', *The Jewish Chronicle*, 21 March 2019, https://www.thejc.com/news/uk-news/jeremy-hunt-announces-uk-will-oppose-every-uh-human-rights-council-measure-on-israel-1.481834
53 Patrick Wintour, 'Charities Condemn UK over Refusal to Endorse Gaza Deaths', *The Guardian*, 22 March 2019, https://www.theguardian.com/world/2019/mar/22/charities-condemn-uk-over-refusal-to-endorse-gaza-deaths-report
54 Valentina Azarova, 'The UN Database on Business in Israeli Settlements: Pitfalls and Opportunities', *Al Shabaka*, 29 May 2018, https://al-shabaka.org/commentaries/the-un-database-on-business-in-israeli-settlements-pitfalls-and-opportunities/
55 Ian Black, 'UK Issues New Guidance on Labelling of Food from Illegal West Bank Settlements', *The Guardian*, 10 December 2009, https://www.theguardian.com/world/2009/dec/10/guidance-labelling-food-israeli-settlements
56 'Trade Agreements: Israel, Question for Department for International Trade', 2 May 2019, https://www.parliament.uk/business/publications/written-questions-answers-statements/written-question/Commons/2019-02-05/216949/
57 Patrick Wintour, 'UK Criticised for "Lacklustre" Response to Israel's West Bank Plans', *The Guardian*, 29 June 2020, https://www.theguardian.com/world/2020/jun/29/uk-criticised-for-lacklustre-response-to-israel-west-bank-plans
58 Ian Black, 'Just below the Surface: Israel, the Arab Gulf States and the Limits of Cooperation', *LSE*, 2019, http://eprints.lse.ac.uk/100313/

59 'Britain and France Welcome UAE Israel Deal', *The National*, 13 August 2020, https://www.thenational.ae/world/europe/britain-and-france-welcome-uae-israel-deal-1.1063442
60 Interview former FCO official.
61 'Oral Evidence: Israel and the Occupied Palestinian Territories: Prospects for 2014', HC 957 Tuesday, 14 January 2014, https://www.parliament.uk/documents/commons-committees/foreign-affairs/Israel-Palestine14Jan.pdf
62 The FAC enquiry was curtailed when a snap election was called and parliament dissolved in May 2017.
63 FAC: Written evidence from Daniel Seidemann, founder of the Israeli NGO, Terrestrial Jerusalem (MEP0060).
64 Interview, Israeli diplomat.
65 Interview, John Jenkins
66 Tom Phillips, 'There May Never be Peace', *Prospect Magazine*, 18 July 2012, https://www.prospectmagazine.co.uk/magazine/there-may-never-be-peace-israel-palestinians-jerusalem
67 Omar Dajani and Hugh Lovatt, 'Rethinking Oslo: How Europe Can Promote Peace in Israel and Palestine', *ECFR*, 2017, https://www.ecfr.eu/page/-/ECFR226_-_RETHINKING_OSLO_-_HOW_EUROPE_CAN_PROMOTE_PEACE_IN_ISRAEL-PALESTINE.pdf

Chapter 10

1 George Nathanial Curzon, *Persia and the Persian Question: Volume 1*, Cambridge: Cambridge University Press, 2016.
2 Ibid., p. 633.
3 Farekhdinne Azimi, 'British Influence in Persia, 1941–1979', *Encyclopædia Iranica*, online edition, 2012, available at http://www.iranicaonline.org/articles/great-britain-vi
4 Ibid.
5 James Onley, 'Britain and the Gulf Shaikhdoms, 1820–1971: The Politics of Protection', Center for International and Regional Studies, 2009, p. 4.
6 Britain's navy became reliant on oil instead of coal in 1914 greatly increasing their dependence on Iranian oil.
7 Keddie, 2006, pp. 125–35.
8 Mossadegh sought to renegotiate with the AIOC based on a fifty-fifty split. Similar agreements had been concluded with the Venezuelan government in 1948 and between the US government and Saudi oil company Aramco in 1950.
9 The post-coup oil agreement known as the Consortium Agreement of 1954 in essence confirmed a fifty-fifty profit sharing split along the lines advocated by Mossadegh.
10 Farekhdinne Azimi, 'British Influence in Persia, 1941–1979', *Encyclopædia Iranica*, online edition, 2012, available at http://www.iranicaonline.org/articles/great-britain-vi accessed on 25 February 2019.
11 Wm. Roger Louis, 'The British Withdrawal from the Gulf, 1967–71', *The Journal of Imperial and Commonwealth History*, vol. 31, no. 1 (2003), pp. 83–108.
12 Onley, p. 75.
13 Uzi Rabi, 'Britain's "Special Position" in the Gulf: Its Origins, Dynamics and Legacy', *Middle Eastern Studies*, vol. 42, no. 3 (May 2006), pp. 351–64; In advance of British

withdrawal, Iran had made an initial claim to Bahrain based on its historical control of the territory. This period would define future tensions with Iran. British policy sought to contain Iranian regional ambitions. Britain defended Bahrain and Qatar and saw the unification of the United Arab Emirates during this period, but was unable to prevent Iran's seizure of the three Persian Gulf islands of Abu Musa and the two Tunbs.

14 Shirin Hunter, *Iran's Foreign Policy in the Post Soviet Era: Resisting the International Order*, Denver: Prager, 2010, p. 22.
15 Hossein S. Seifzadeh, 'The Landscape of Factional Politics and Its Future in Iran', *Middle East Journal*, vol. 57, no. 1 (Winter, 2003), pp. 57–75.
16 Kenneth Katzmann, 'Iran's Foreign and Defense Policies', *Congressional Research Service*, 19 March 2019, https://fas.org/sgp/crs/mideast/R44017.pdf
17 Adam Tarock, 'Iran–Western Europe Relations on the Mend', *British Journal of Middle Eastern Studies*, vol. 26, no. 1 (May 1999), pp. 41–61.
18 Hunter, p. 143.
19 Bernd Kaussler, 'British–Iranian Relations, "The Satanic Verses" and the Fatwa: A Case of Two-Level Game Diplomacy', *British Journal of Middle Eastern Studies*, vol. 38, no. 2 (August 2011), pp. 203–25.
20 Tarock, 1999.
21 Judy Dempsey, 'Hint of Iran Sanctions Tugs at Trade Ties', *The New York Times*, 22 January 2006.
22 Hunter, 2010. p. 66.
23 Ibid., 148.
24 Ibid.
25 'Iran's Revolutionary Guards Arrest More Dual Nationals', *Reuters*, 9 November 2017.
26 'Iran: Targeting of Dual Citizens, Foreigners', *Human Rights Watch*, 26 September 2018.
27 'Britain Denies $500 Million Debt Linked to Bid to Free Jailed Aid Worker', *Reuters*, 16 November 2017.
28 Maysam Behravesh, 'Brexit, the EU and the Iran Nuclear Deal', *Middle East Monitor*, 5 April 2019, https://www.middleeastmonitor.com/20190405-brexit-the-eu-and-the-iran-nuclear-deal/
29 Jeffrey Goldberg, 'The Obama Doctrine', *The Atlantic*, April 2016.
30 Vagneur-Jones, 2019.
31 'German Iran Business Ties Growing Again', *DW*, 2 January 2018, https://www.dw.com/en/german-iranian-business-ties-growing-again/a-41998948
32 Mahsa Rouhi, 'Iran and America: The Perverse Consequences of Maximum Pressure', *IISS Survival Blog*, 10 March 2020, https://www.iiss.org/blogs/survival-blog/2020/03/iran-united-states-maximum-pressure
33 'Iran sanctions', https://www.treasury.gov/resource-center/sanctions/programs/pages/iran.aspx
34 'UK, France and Germany Create Payment System to Trade with Iran', *BBC News*, 31 January 2019, https://www.bbc.co.uk/news/business-47072020
35 Kelsey Davenport, 'Iran Newly Breaches Nuclear Deal', *Arms Control Today*, December 2019, https://www.armscontrol.org/act/2019-12/news/iran-newly-breaches-nuclear-deal
36 Michael Peel, 'European Powers Step Up Pressure on Iran over Nuclear Deal', *Financial Times*, 14 January 2020.
37 'PM: We Are Clear-eyed about Threat from Iran', *Gov.uk*, 7 December 2016.

38 Farhad Rezaei, 'Iran's Nuclear Agreement: The Three Specific Clusters of Concerns', *Insight Turkey*, vol. 20, no. 2 (Spring 2018), pp. 167–200.
39 Michael Safi, 'UK Flagged Tanker Seized by Iran Released and Heading for Dubai', *The Guardian*, 27 September 2019, https://www.theguardian.com/world/2019/sep/27/uk-flagged-tanker-seized-by-iran-in-july-released-leaves-bandar-abbas-port
40 Eva Pejsova, 'What the European Maritime Initiative in the Strait of Hormuz Tells Us about Brussel's Security Ambitions', *European Leadership Network*, 27 March 2020
41 Peter Walker, 'Saudi Arabia Oil Attack: Boris Johnson Says UK Believes Iran Responsible', *The Guardian, 23* September 2019, https://www.theguardian.com/politics/2019/sep/23/saudi-arabia-oil-attack-boris-johnson-says-uk-believes-iran-responsible
42 Ibid.
43 'Iran Appeals for $5billion IMF Loan as Deaths Near 4,000', *BBC*, 9 April 2020, https://www.bbc.co.uk/news/world-middle-east-52217600
44 Laura Rozen, 'Coronavirus Spurs Humanitarian Outreach to Iran', *Al-Monitor*, 18 March 2020, https://www.al-monitor.com/pulse/originals/2020/03/coronavirus-spur-humanitarian-outreach-iran.html

Chapter 11

1 The author would like to thank Karl Pike for his assistance in researching this chapter.
2 'Syria', *The Observatory of Economic Complexity*, https://oec.world/en/visualize/tree_map/hs92/import/syr/show/all/2010/, accessed 12 April 2020.
3 UK Diptel from Damascus to FCO, 'Syria – Homs', 27 May 2011; UK Diptel from Damascus to FCO, 'Syria: the Pace Quickens', 19 July 2011, referenced in Christopher Phillips, *The Battle for Syria: International Rivalry in the New Middle East*, London: Yale University Press, 2016, pp. 78–87.
4 Interview with Western official, October 2014.
5 Boris Johnson, 'Provision of Equipment to Syria Civil Defence and the Free Syrian Police: Written Statement – HCWS618', 26 April 2017, https://www.parliament.uk/business/publications/written-questions-answers-statements/written-statement/Commons/2017-04-26/HCWS618/, accessed 1 February 2019.
6 UK Diptel from Damascus to FCO, 'Syrian Economy: Assad's Weak Spot, and What More We Can Do to Squeeze It', 23 October 2011.
7 Interview with UK official, February 2015.
8 Hillary Rodham Clinton, *Hard Choices: A Memoir*, New York: Simon and Schuster, 2014, pp. 447–70.
9 'Syria: Humanitarian Crisis', *House of Lords Library Briefing*, 23 March 2018, https://researchbriefings.parliament.uk/ResearchBriefing/Summary/LLN-2018-0033
10 'UK Action to Combat Daesh', *Gov.uk*, https://www.gov.uk/government/topical-events/daesh/about; 'Airwars: US-led Coalition in Iraq and Syria', *Airwars,* https://airwars.org/conflict/coalition-in-iraq-and-syria/
11 Noel Dempsey, 'UK Defence Expenditure', House of Commons Library Briefing Paper Number CBP 8175 8/11/18.
12 King Abdullah II, 'Remarks by His Majesty King Abdullah IIat the State Banquet Hosted by Her Majesty Queen Elizabeth and His Royal Highness Prince Philip',

King Abdullah II Website, 6 November 2001, https://kingabdullah.jo/en/speeches/state-banquet-hosted-her-majesty-queen-elizabeth-and-his-royal-highness-prince-philip

13 Alistair Burt, 'Jordan: Military Aid: Written Question – 137187', 1 May 2018, https://www.parliament.uk/business/publications/written-questions-answers-statements/written-question/Commons/2018-04-23/137187/'UK to Donate £5 Million of Military Equipment to Jordan', *Forces Network*, 13 September 2018, https://www.forces.net/news/uk-donate-ps5-million-military-equipment-jordan

14 'Jordan', *The Observatory of Economic Complexity*, https://atlas.media.mit.edu/en/profile/country/jor/

15 Theresa May, '"Britain Will be a Partner You Can Depend On" – PM in Jordan', *Gov.uk*, 30 November 2017, https://www.gov.uk/government/speeches/britain-will-be-a-partner-you-can-depend-on-pm-in-jordan

16 'Jordan', *European Commission: European Neighbourhood Policy And Enlargement Negotiations*, https://ec.europa.eu/neighbourhood-enlargement/neighbourhood/countries/jordan_en

17 Shiv Malik and Alice Su, 'Abu Qatada Cleared of Terror Charges by Jordan Court and Released from Jail', *The Guardian*, 24 November 2014, https://www.theguardian.com/world/2014/sep/24/abu-qatada-cleared-terror-charges-jordan-court

18 'UK Aid Is a Lifeline for Many of Lebanon's Syrian Refugees, but We Can Do More with Its Influence', *Save the Children*, 13 December 2017, https://reliefweb.int/report/lebanon/uk-aid-lifeline-many-lebanon-s-syrian-refugees-we-can-do-more-its-influence

19 'Lebanon', *The Observatory of Economic Complexity*, https://atlas.media.mit.edu/en/profile/country/lbn/

20 'Lebanon', *European Commission: European Neighbourhood Policy and Enlargement Negotiations*, https://ec.europa.eu/neighbourhood-enlargement/neighbourhood/countries/lebanon_en

21 Philip Hammond, 'Gifting of Equipment to the 4th Land Border Regiment of the Lebanese Armed Forces: Written Statement – HCWS463', 12 January 2016, https://www.parliament.uk/business/publications/written-questions-answers-statements/written-statement/Commons/2016-01-12/HCWS463/

22 Alistair Burt, 'UK Welcomes Formation of New Government in Lebanon', *Gov.uk*, 1 February 2019, https://www.gov.uk/government/news/uk-welcomes-formation-of-new-government-in-lebanon

23 'Doing Business 2019: Training for Reform', *World Bank Group Flagship Report* (2019), http://www.worldbank.org/content/dam/doingBusiness/media/Annual-Reports/English/DB2019-report_web-version.pdf

24 Patrick Wintour, 'May Backs ally Jordan by Underwriting $250m World Bank Loan', *The Guardian*, 28 February 2019, https://www.theguardian.com/world/2019/feb/28/theresa-may-backs-ally-jordan-king-abdullah-underwrites-world-bank-loan

25 Omar al-Razzaz, 'Jordan: Doing Well by Doing Good', *The Economist*, 23 February 2019.

26 Curtis R. Ryan, *Jordan and the Arab Uprisings*, New York: Columbia University Press, 2018, Kindle Edition L4628.

27 'British Embassy Hosts Farewell for 24 Students Awarded Chevening Scholarships', *Jordan Times*, 13 September 2018, http://www.jordantimes.com/news/local/british-embassy-hosts-farewell-24-students-awarded-chevening-scholarships

Chapter 12

1 World Bank, 'Country Report: Iraq', https://databank.worldbank.org/views/reports/reportwidget.aspx?Report_Name=CountryProfile&Id=b450fd57&tbar=y&dd=y&inf=n&zm=n&country=IRQ, accessed 2 February 2020.
2 World Bank, 'Iraq: Systemic Country Diagnostic', 3 February 2017, p. 13, http://documents.worldbank.org/curated/en/542811487277729890/pdf/IRAQ-SCD-FINAL-cleared-02132017.pdf, accessed 2 February 2020.
3 Iraq Is Ranked 162/180 in Transparency International's Corruption Perceptions Index, https://www.transparency.org/country/IRQ, accessed 2 February 2020.
4 The rise of Iraq's informal economy has been apparent for over a decade, but the measures that might have curbed its growth have not been taken; see Robert Loonay, 'Economic Consequences of Conflict: The Rise of Iraq's Informal Economy', *Journal of Economic Issues*, vol. 40, no. 4 (2006), pp. 991–1007.
5 As defined by Sean McFate, *The New Rules of War: Victory in the Age of Durable Disorder*, New York: HarperCollins, 2019, pp. 25–40.
6 Orla Guerin, 'Isis in Iraq: Militants "Getting Stronger Again"', *BBC*, 23 December 2019.
7 Erica Gaston and Mario Schultz, 'At the Tip of the Spear: Armed Groups' Impact on Displacement and Return in Post-ISIL Iraq', *Global Public Policy Institute*, 18 February 2019, https://www.gppi.net/2019/02/18/at-the-tip-of-the-spear, accessed 20 February 2020.
8 As has been ongoing for some time, see Pesha Magid, 'How ISIS Still Threatens Iraq', *Foreign Policy*, 28 May 2019.
9 Interview with senior PMF politician, Baghdad, September 2019.
10 Renad Mansour, 'More Than Militias: Iraq's Popular Mobilization Forces Are Here to Stay', *War on the Rocks*, 3 April 2018.
11 Mohammad-Reza Madoudi, Head of the Iranian Trade Promotion Organization, 10 December 2018.
12 Not least in 2020, see Sofia Barbarani, 'Iraq Extends Ban on Iran Arrivals Amid Coronavirus Fears', *Al Jazeera English*, 22 February 2020.
13 Ibrahim al Jafaari, 'Speaking at the Royal United Services Institute', 14 September 2016, https://rusi.org/event/conversation-dr-ibrahim-al-jaafari-foreign-minister-republic-iraq, accessed 2 February 2020.
14 Charles Lister, 'All the President's Militias: Assad's Militiafication of Syria', *Middle East Institute*, 14 December 2017, https://www.mei.edu/publications/all-presidents-militias-assads-militiafication-syria
15 Omar al Nidawi, 'Finding a Way Forward in the Baghdad-Erbil Oil Dispute', *Middle East Institute*, 6 March 2019, https://www.mei.edu/publications/finding-way-forward-baghdad-erbil-oil-dispute
16 David Hadari and Benoit Faucon, 'Oil Falls to 12-Month Low on Coronavirus Concerns', *The Wall Street Journal*, 26 February 2020.
17 As would likely occur were the EU to implement its proposed 'European Green Deal', *The European Commission*, 11 December 2019, https://eur-lex.europa.eu/resource.html?uri=cellar:b828d165-1c22-11ea-8c1f-01aa75ed71a1.0002.02/DOC_1&format=PDF, accessed 1 March 2020; or as outlined in the UK's Energy White Paper, *Powering Our Net Zero Future*, London: HMSO, 2020, https://assets.publishing.service.gov.uk/government/uploads/system/uploads/attachment_data/file/943807/201214_BEIS_EWP_Command_Paper_LR.pdf, accessed 16 December 2020.

18 Dominic Evans, 'Iraq Says It Found 50,000 "Ghost Soldiers" on Payroll', *Reuters*, 1 December 2014.
19 Maya Gabeily, 'After Tough 2020, Iraq Eyes More Economic Pain Ahead', *Agence France Presse*, 17 December 2020.
20 Despite promises by the prime minister to punish such acts, activists have been murdered throughout 2020. Hisham al Hashimi (Renad Mansour, 'In Life and Death, Iraq's Hisham al-Hashimi', *Chatham House*, August 2020) was simply the highest profile example of many. The latest being Salah al Iraqi, see Maya Gabeily, 'Iraqi Activist Shot Dead in Baghdad', *Agence France Presse*, 15 December 2020.
21 Faleh Jabar, 'The Iraqi Protest Movement, From Identity Politics to Issue Politics', *LSE Middle East Centre Papers*, vol. 25 (2018): https://eprints.lse.ac.uk/88294/1/Faleh_Iraqi%20Protest%20Movement_Published_English.pdf
22 Sermons against corruption were interpreted (and privately briefed) as endorsing the protest movement as far back as Sistani's issued sermon of 30 September 2016, delivered at the Imam Abbas Shrine in Karbala, https://alkafeel.net/inspiredfriday/index.php?id=288&ser=2&lang=en, accessed 1 March 2020.
23 'Iraq: State Appears Complicit in Massacre of Protesters', *Human Rights Watch*, 16 December 2019, https://www.hrw.org/news/2019/12/16/iraq-state-appears-complicit-massacre-protesters
24 Ghaith Abdul-Ahad, 'After the Liberation of Mosul, an Orgy of Killing', *The Guardian*, 21 November 2017.
25 Qasem Soleimani, 'Gen. Soleimani Congratulates Ayatollah Khamenei and Muslims on ISIS Termination', *Khamenei.ir*, 21 November 2017, http://english.khamenei.ir/news/5283/Gen-Soleimani-congratulates-Ayatollah-Khamenei-and-Muslims-on
26 V. H. Rothwell, 'Mesopotamia in British War Aims, 1914–1918', *The Historical Journal*, vol. 13, no. 2 (1970), pp. 273–94.
27 Susan Pedersen, *The Guardians: The League of Nations and the Crisis of Empire*, Oxford: Oxford University Press, 2015.
28 Joel Rayburn, 'The Last Exit from Iraq', *Foreign Affairs*, vol. 85, no. 2 (2006), pp. 30–2.
29 Frederick Anscombe, *State, Faith and Nation in Ottoman and Post-Ottoman Lands*, New York: Cambridge University Press, 2014, pp. 209–10.
30 Kanan Makiya, *Republic of Fear: The Politics of Modern Iraq*, London: University of California Press, 1998, p. 151.
31 Susan Pedersen, 'Getting Out of Iraq – in 1932: The League of Nations and the Road to Statehood', *The American Historical Review*, vol. 115, no. 4 (2010), pp. 975–1000.
32 MB, 'British Interests in the Persian Gulf', *Bulletin of International News*, vol. 18, no. 19 (1941), pp. 1193–8.
33 TNA, CAB 79/11/24: War Cabinet, Chiefs of Staff Committee, Minutes of Meeting held Tuesday, 6 May 1941.
34 Stefanie Wichhart, 'Selling Democracy During the Second British occupation of Iraq, 1941–5', *Journal of Contemporary History*, vol. 48, no. 3 (2013), pp. 509–36.
35 Richard Aldrich, *GCHQ: The Uncensored Story of Britain's Most Secret Intelligence Agency*, London: Harper Press, 2010, pp. 148–68.
36 Stephen Blackwell, 'A Desert Squall: Anglo-American Planning for Military Intervention in Iraq, July 1958–August 1959', *Middle Eastern Studies*, vol. 35, no. 3 (1999), pp. 1–18.
37 Rob Johnson, *The Iran-Iraq War*, Basingstoke: Palgrave Macmillan, 2011, p. 188.
38 TNA, FO 8/6398: G H Boyce to Mr Renton, 30 October 1986.

39 Alex Wagner, 'UK, Russia Issue Draft Proposals To Revamp Iraq Sanctions Regime', *Arms Control Today*, vol. 31, no. 5 (2001), p. 22.
40 Tony Blair, 'The Blair Doctrine', Chicago, 22 April 1999, https://www.globalpolicy.org/component/content/article/154/26026.html
41 Attacks on Saudi Arabia have already been launched from Iraq, see Isabel Coles and Dion Nissenbaum, 'U.S.: Saudi Pipeline Attacks Originated From Iraq', *The Wall Street Journal*, 28 June 2019; more specifically the attack was carried out by Khateib Hezbollah. And Israel has alleged shipments of Iranian missiles.
42 'UK should do more in Iraq, says Committee', House of Commons, 5 February 2015, http://www.parliament.uk/business/committees/committees-a-z/commons-select/defence-committee/news/report-situation-in-iraq-and-syria-and-the-response-to-daesh/
43 'UK Aid Removing Daesh Explosives and Helping Iraqis Return Home', *Press Release*, 5 January 2019, https://www.gov.uk/government/news/uk-aid-removing-daesh-explosives-and-helping-iraqis-return-home
44 Office of National Statistics, 'UK Trade with Iraq, 2018', https://www.ons.gov.uk/economy/nationalaccounts/balanceofpayments/bulletins/uktrade/may2019#explore-uk-trade-in-goods-country-by-commodity-data-for-2018-with-our-interactive-tools

Chapter 13

1 For example, Diana Alghoul, 'Prince Charles' Visit to the Gulf Says "Business as Usual" for Britain and the GCC', *Middle East Monitor*, 14 November 2016, https://www.middleeastmonitor.com/20161114-prince-charles-visit-to-the-gulf-says-business-as-usual-for-britain-and-the-gcc/
2 For example, Roast baby camel, 'Your Highness? Moment a Saudi Royal Offered "Delicacy" to Charles … and if HRH Got the Hump, He Didn't Let It Show', *The Daily Mail*, 17 March 2013, https://www.dailymail.co.uk/news/article-2294997/Roast-baby-camel-Your-Highness-Moment-Saudi-royal-offered-delicacy-Charles–HRH-got-hump-didnt-let-show.html
3 'The Arab World A Perspective from Britain', *Yougov*, 25 September 2017, https://d25d2506sfb94s.cloudfront.net/r/8/YouGov_ArabNews_UK_Perception_Arab_World_Data_Tables.pdf
4 For example, Boris Johnson, 'We Can't Afford to Ignore Our Dynamic Friends in the East', *The Telegraph*, 21 April 2013, https://www.telegraph.co.uk/comment/columnists/borisjohnson/10009124/We-cant-afford-to-ignore-our-dynamic-friends-in-the-East.html
5 For example, Emily Thornberry, 'Saudi Bombs Are Decimating Yemen. Yet May's Glad-handing Goes on', *The Guardian*, 5 April 2017, https://www.theguardian.com/commentisfree/2017/apr/05/saudi-arabia-bombs-yemen-theresa-may-trade
6 Roberts, D. B. 'Bucking the Trend: The UAE & the Development of Military Capabilities in the Arab World', *Security Studies*, vol. 29, no. 2 (2020), https://doi.org/10.1080/09636412.2020.1722852
7 Prime Minister's visit to Bahrain and the Gulf Co-operation Council, 5 December 2016, https://www.gov.uk/government/news/prime-ministers-visit-to-bahrain-and-the-gulf-co-operation-council
8 Prime Minister's speech to the Gulf Cooperation Council, 7 December 2016, https://www.gov.uk/government/speeches/prime-ministers-speech-to-the-gulf-co-operation-council-2016

9 James Lansdale: Why Saudi Crown Prince Mohammed bin Salman's visit matters, *BBC News*, 7 March 2018, https://www.bbc.co.uk/news/world-middle-east-43235643
10 Jamal Khashoggi: All you need to know about Saudi Journalist's Death, *BBC News*, 24 February 2021, https://www.bbc.co.uk/news/world-europe-45812399
11 'Exeter Academic Jailed for Spying Filing Formal Complaint', *BBC News*, 7 May 2019, https://www.bbc.co.uk/news/topics/czdjzwvzdw9t/matthew-hedges-case
12 'Iran Seizes British Tanker in Strait of Hormuz', *BBC News*, 20 July 2019, https://www.bbc.co.uk/news/uk-49053383
13 Saul Kelly and Gareth Stansfield, 'A Return to East of Suez? UK Military Deployment to the Gulf', *Royal United Service Institute Briefing Paper,* April (2013).
14 Mark Sedgwick, 'Britain and the Middle East', in Jack Covurrabias and Tom Lansford, eds, *Strategic Interests in the Middle East: Opposition or Support for US Foreign Policy*, Aldershot: Ashgate Publishing Limited, 2007, pp. 3–25.
15 Saul Kelly and Gareth Stansfield, 'A Return to East of Suez? UK Military Deployment to the Gulf', *Royal United Service Institute Briefing Paper*, April (2013).
16 See BBC, 'Arms Sales Fuel BAe's Profits', 25 February 1999; C.R.G. Murray, 'UK's Relations with Saudi Arabia and Bahrain', written evidence submitted to the Foreign Affairs Select Committee, Session 2012–13, 7 January 2013.
17 The Office for National Statistics, https://www.ons.gov.uk/economy/nationalaccounts/balanceofpayments/adhocs/007716additionalcountrydatafortradeingoodsandservicesbetween1999and2016
18 'Gulf States Are Becoming More Adventurous Investors', 15 June 2019, *The Economist,* https://www.economist.com/middle-east-and-africa/2019/06/15/gulf-states-are-becoming-more-adventurous-investors
19 '$45bn Qatar Investments in UK', says minister, *Middle East Monitor*, 11 January 2019, https://www.middleeastmonitor.com/20190111-45bn-qatar-investments-in-uk-says-minister/
20 'Factbox: Qatar's Investments in Britain – Barclays, Sainsbury's, Harrods and IAG', *Reuters Factbox*, 19 February 2020, https://uk.reuters.com/article/uk-iag-qatar-stake-investments-factbox/factbox-qatars-investments-in-britain-barclays-sainsburys-harrods-and-iag-idUKKBN20D1EC
21 Robert Sharratt, 'The Gulf Investor Deception: How Barclays and Credit Suisse Avoided a Govt Bailout during the 2008 Financial Crisis', *Coinmonks*, 2 January 2019, https://medium.com/coinmonks/how-barclays-and-credit-suisse-avoided-a-govt-bail-out-during-the-2008-financial-crisis-501aedda491e
22 'Sandhurst's Sheikhs: Why Do So Many Gulf Royals Receive Military Training in the UK?' *BBC News*, 26 August 2014, https://www.bbc.co.uk/news/magazine-28896860
23 Department for Business Energy and Industrial Strategy, Section 4 Gas, January to March 2020, p. 29, https://assets.publishing.service.gov.uk/government/uploads/system/uploads/attachment_data/file/894947/Gas_June_2020.pdf
24 For example, Tokhir N Mirzoev; Ling Zhu; Yang Yang; Tian Zhang; Erik Roos; Andrea Pescatori; Akito Matsumoto, 'The Future of Oil and Fiscal Sustainability in the GCC Region', *IMF Policy Paper*, 6 February 2020, https://www.imf.org/en/Publications/Departmental-Papers-Policy-Papers/Issues/2020/01/31/The-Future-of-Oil-and-Fiscal-Sustainability-in-the-GCC-Region-48934
25 Lord Mayor of London heads to Gulf to strengthen trade and investment ties, 9 February 2020, https://news.cityoflondon.gov.uk/lord-mayor-of-london-heads-to-gulf-to-strengthen-trade-and-investment-ties/

26 For example, UK arms used in the war in Yemen, The Campaign against Arms Trade, https://www.caat.org.uk/campaigns/stop-arming-saudi/uk-weapons-used
27 Prime Minister's speech to the Gulf Co-operation Council 2016, 7 December 2016, https://www.gov.uk/government/speeches/prime-ministers-speech-to-the-gulf-co-operation-council-2016
28 'Full Interview: Saudi Arabian Prince Turki Al-Faisal on U.S. Foreign Policy | Full Interviews', *CNBC*, 13 October 2019, https://www.youtube.com/watch?v=BV2nwr-Q4k8&feature=emb_err_woyt
29 See Michael Stephens, 'The Arab Cold War Redux: The Foreign Policy of the Gulf Cooperation Council States since 2011', *The Century Foundation*, https://tcf.org/content/report/arab-cold-war-redux/
30 PM call with Emir of Qatar,8 August 2019, https://www.gov.uk/government/news/pm-call-with-emir-of-qatar-8-august-2019
31 Iran Crisis, 'We Will Not Lament Soleimani's Death', Boris Johnson says', *Sky News*, 5 January 2020, https://news.sky.com/story/iran-crisis-trump-described-as-a-terrorist-in-a-suit-as-aggression-escalates-11901729
32 See, for example, Mohammed al Yahya, 'The Iran Deal Is Iran's Nuclear Bomb', *Al Arabiya English*, 3 November 2015, https://english.alarabiya.net/en/views/news/middle-east/2015/11/04/The-Iran-deal-is-Iran-s-nuclear-bomb.html
33 Prime Minister seeks new chapter in relations with the Gulf on visit to Bahrain, 4 December 2016, https://www.gov.uk/government/news/prime-minister-seeks-new-chapter-in-relations-with-the-gulf-on-visit-to-bahrain
34 For example, Rosie Garthwaite and Ian Anderson, 'Coronavirus: Alarm over "invasive" Kuwait and Bahrain Contact-tracing Apps', *BBC News*, 16 June 2020, https://www.bbc.co.uk/news/world-middle-east-53052395; Ben Hubbard, 'Someone Tried to Hack My Phone. Technology Researchers Accused Saudi Arabia', *The New York Times*, 28 January 2020, https://www.nytimes.com/2020/01/28/reader-center/phone-hacking-saudi-arabia.html; Mark Mazzetti, Nicole Perlroth and Ronen Bergman, 'It Seemed Like a Popular Chat App. It's Secretly a Spy Tool', *The New York Times*, 22 December 2019, https://www.nytimes.com/2019/12/22/us/politics/totok-app-uae.html
35 James Lynch, The Third Wheel, in Phillips & Stephens, '*What Next for Britain in the Middle East?*' pp. 55–68.
36 'UK Government Accused of Phoning Saudi Arabia to Apologise after Imposing Human Rights Sanctions', *The Independent*, 10 July 2020, https://www.independent.co.uk/news/uk/politics/uk-saudi-arabia-human-rights-ben-wallace-yemen-war-crimes-a9611221.html
37 Sir Bernard Jenkin, 'Replacing the "Golden Age" Policy towards China', *RUSI Commentary*, 27 May 2020, https://rusi.org/commentary/replacing-golden-age-policy-towards-china
38 See, for example, Karen Young, 'The Gulf's Eastward Turn: The Logic of Gulf-China Economic Ties', 14 January 2019, The American Enterprise Institute.
39 Abdelaziz al Uwaisheg, 'The Gulf's Position in a Fragmented New World Order', *Arab News*, 22 June 2020, https://www.arabnews.com/node/1693791
40 Simeon Kerr, 'UAE Caught between US and China as Powers Vie for Influence in Gulf', *The Financial Times*, 2 June 2020, https://www.ft.com/content/1ff119ff-50bf-4b00-8519-520b8db2082b
41 For example, Abdelaziz al Uwaisheg, 'China–US Rivalry Needs Defusing to Revive Global Economy', *Arab News*, 2 June 2020,https://www.arabnews.com/node/1683726

42 Jason Bordoff, 'The 2020 Oil Crash's Unlikely Winner: Saudi Arabia', *Foreign Policy Magazine*, 5 May 2020, https://foreignpolicy.com/2020/05/05/2020-oil-crash-winner-saudi-arabia/

Chapter 14

1 Frederic C. Penfield, 'England's Absorption of Egypt,' *The North American Review*, vol. 165, no. 493 (1897), pp. 682–94. *JSTOR*, www.jstor.org/stable/25118924, accessed 4 May 2020.
2 'EU–Egypt Relations: Initialing of New Association Agreement', IP/01/123 https://ec.europa.eu/commission/presscorner/detail/en/IP_01_123
3 http://www.mfa.gov.eg/Missions/uk/london/embassy/en-GB/BilateralRelations/modernhistory/
4 'UK–Egypt Announce Joint Economic Partnership', *British Embassy Cairo*, 20 January 2020, https://www.gov.uk/government/news/uk-egypt-announce-joint-economic-partnership
5 'UK–Egypt Joint Statement on Economic Cooperation', https://assets.publishing.service.gov.uk/government/uploads/system/uploads/attachment_data/fie/859337/UK–Egypt_Joint_Statement_on_Economic_Cooperation.pdf; https://www.londonstockexchange.com/london-stock-exchange-welcomes-egypts-sovereign-green-bond-sustainable-bond-market?lang=en
6 'British Armed Forces Minister Bolsters UK–Egypt Defence Ties', *British Embassy Cairo*, 13 June 2019, https://www.gov.uk/government/news/british-armed-forces-minister-bolsters-uk-egypt-defence-ties
7 'Egypt's Sisi, Britain's MI6 Chief Talk Furthering Intelligence Cooperation', 9 November, 2020, https://egyptindependent.com/egypts-sisi-britains-mi6-chief-talk-furthering-intelligence-cooperation/
8 See evidence submitted by the Foreign and Commonwealth Office to the Foreign Affairs Select Committee (FASC) on 8 December 2011 on 'British Foreign Policy and the "Arab Spring": The Transition to Democracy', https://publications.parliament.uk/pa/cm201012/cmselect/cmfaff/writev/arab/as07.htm
9 Also known as The Mubarak Plan (1990, 1998). See United Nations General Assembly, 20 October 2000, official records of First Committee, 19th Meeting, https://www.un.org/unispal/document/auto-insert-189795/
10 FASC, 'British Foreign Policy and the "Arab Spring"', p. section 43. 8 December 2011.
11 John Bew, *Realpolitik: A History*, UK: Oxford University Press, 2015; Duncan Kelly, 'August Ludwig von Rochau and *Realpolitik* as Historical Political Theory', *Global Intellectual History*, vol. 3, no. 3 (2018), pp. 301–30.
12 Data forecast as of March 2020. 'International Food Policy Research Institute "Covid19 and the Egyptian Economy"', https://www.ifpri.org/publication/covid-19-and-egyptian-economy-estimating-impacts-expected-reductions-tourism-suez-canal
13 Latest official figures available on Central Agency for Public Mobilization and Statistics (CAPMAS), https://www.ifpri.org/publication/covid-19-and-egyptian-economy-estimating-impacts-expected-reductions-tourism-suez-canal
14 Dr Maha Azzam statement, 26 September 2019, https://www.middleeastmonitor.com/20190926-calls-for-uk-to-protect-protesters-in-egypt/

15 See Arab Barometer, Arab Opinion Index and ASDA'A BCW Arab Youth Survey. Together each of these surveys report a gradual increase in attitudes against Islam in daily politics of the region.
16 See House of Lords Select Committee on International Relations, 'The Middle East: Time for New Realism', 2 May 2018.
17 For example: 'Foreign Office Reveals "Step-change" in Egypt Approach', 22 July 2016, https://reprieve.org.uk/press/foreign-office-reveals-step-change-in-egypt-approach/
18 'UN Human Rights Council 43: Item 4 General Debate', 10 March 2020, https://www.gov.uk/government/speeches/un-human-rights-council-43-item-4-general-debate
19 Damien Gayle, 'Egypt Summons UK Ambassador in Row over Al-Jazeera Convictions', *The Guardian*, 30 August 2015, https://www.theguardian.com/world/2015/aug/30/al-jazeera-convictions-egypt-summons-uk-ambassador
20 Ben Quinn, 'British Universities Criticised over Pursuit of Egyptian Links', *The Guardian*, 22 August 2018, https://www.theguardian.com/education/2018/aug/22/uk-colleges-accused-of-ignoring-human-rights-abuse-in-egypt
21 'Human Rights and Democracy: The 2016 Foreign & Commonwealth Office Report', Preface by Boris Johnson, https://assets.publishing.service.gov.uk/government/uploads/system/uploads/attachment_data/file/630623/Human_Rights_and_Democracy_Report_2016_accessible.pdf
22 FASC, 8 December 2011.
23 Arab Barometer, Arab Opinion Index and ASDA'A BCW Arab Youth Survey.
24 'A Global Generation Gap', *Pew Research*, 24 February 2004, https://www.pewresearch.org/global/2004/02/24/a-global-generation-gap/
25 'The Middle East: Time for New Realism', 2 May 2018.

Select Bibliography

Richard Aldrich, *GCHQ: The Uncensored Story of Britain's Most Secret Intelligence Agency*. London: Harper Press, 2010.

Christopher Hill, *The Future of British Foreign Policy: Security and Diplomacy in a World after Brexit*. London: John Wiley & Sons, 2019.

Frederick Anscombe, *State, Faith and Nation in Ottoman and Post-Ottoman Lands*. New York: Cambridge University Press, 2014.

John Bew, *Realpolitik: A History*. Oxford: Oxford University Press, 2015.

Ian Black, *Enemies and Neighbors: Arabs and Jews in Palestine and Israel, 1917–2017*. London: Atlantic Monthly Press, 2017.

Michael Clarke and Helen Ramscar, *Tipping Point: Britain, Brexit and Security in the 2020s*. London: I.B. Tauris, 2019.

George Nathanial Curzon, *Persia and the Persian Question: Volume 1*. Cambridge: Cambridge University Press, 2016.

Jamie Gaskarth. *British Foreign Policy: Crises, Conflicts and Future Challenges*. London: John Wiley & Sons, 2013.

Jamie Gaskarth, 'The Fiasco of the 2013 Syria Votes: Decline and Denial in British Foreign Policy'. *Journal of European Public Policy* 23.5 (2016): 718–34.

Christopher Hill, *The Future of British Foreign Policy: Security and Diplomacy in a World after Brexit*. London: John Wiley & Sons, 2019.

Rosemary Hollis, *Britain and the Middle East in the 9/11 Era*. London: Wiley-Blackwell, 2010.

Will Hutton and Andrew Adonis, *Saving Britain: How We Must Change to Prosper in Europe*. London: Abacus, 2018.

Robert Kaplan, *The Return of Marco Polo's World: War, Strategy and American Interests*. New York: Random House, 2018.

Kanan Makiya, *Republic of Fear: The Politics of Modern Iraq*. London: University of California Press, 1998.

Elizabeth Monroe, *Britain's Moment in the Middle East, 1914–71*. London: Chatto & Windus, 1981.

David Owen and David Ludlow, *British Foreign Policy after Brexit: An Independent Voice*. London: Biteback Publishing, 2017.

Mesut Ozcan, *Harmonizing Foreign Policy; Turkey the EU and the Middle East*. Aldershot: Ashgate, 2008.

Christopher Phillips, *The Battle for Syria: International Rivalry in the New Middle East*. London: Yale University Press, 2016.

Patrick Porter, *Blunder: Britain's War in Iraq*. Oxford: Oxford University Press, 2018.

Walter Russell Meade, *God and Gold; Britain and America and the Making of the Modern World*. London: Atlantic Books, 2007.

Curtis R. Ryan, *Jordan and the Arab Uprisings*. New York: Columbia University Press, 2018.

David Sanders and David Patrick Houghton, *Losing an Empire, Finding a Role: British Foreign Policy since 1945*. London: Macmillan International Higher Education, 2016.

Gareth Stansfield, 'The Islamic State, the Kurdistan Region and the Future of Iraq: Assessing UK Policy Options'. *International Affairs* 90.6 (2014): 1329–50.

Jack Straw, *The English Job: Understanding Iran and Why It Distrusts Britain*. London: Biteback Publishing, 2019.

James Strong. 'Interpreting the Syria Vote: Parliament and British Foreign Policy'. *International Affairs* 91.5 (2015): 1123–39.

Ozlem Terzi, *The Influence of the European Union on Turkish Foreign Policy*. Aldershot: Ashgate, 2010.

Adam Tooze, *Crashed: How a Decade of Financial Crisis Changed the World*. London: Allen Lane, 2018.

Dmitri Trenin, *Should We Fear Russia?* Cambridge: Polity Press, 2014.

Ozgur Tufekci, *The Foreign Policy of Modern Turkey: Power and the Ideology of Eurasianism*. London: I. B. Tauris, 2017.

David Wearing, *AngloArabia: Why Gulf Wealth Matters to Britain*. London: John Wiley & Sons, 2018.

Index

Abbas, Mahmoud 65, 112, 114
King Abdullah of Jordan 143, 147, 234–5 n.12
Abraham Accords 109, 121
Acheson, Dean 42
activism 3, 58, 100, 125, 145
aerospace sector 17, 70, 98. *See also* BAE Systems
Afghanistan 16, 23, 35, 43, 46, 90, 125, 128, 139, 142, 160, 171
Africa 29–30, 33, 182, 184
  Africa-focused investment 75
  Djibouti 29, 87
  monorail system 76
  North Africa 67, 78
  Somalia 100, 173, 184
Ahmadinejad, Mahmood 127–9
airstrikes 45, 59–60, 67, 85, 88, 142, 215 n.47, 216 n.60
Algeria 67, 70–1, 73, 78, 87, 109, 202
allies 1, 3–5, 8, 43, 48, 51, 65, 92, 99–100, 103, 124, 127, 143, 146, 149, 173, 193
  Arab 19
  Assad's 141–2
  British 8, 24, 55, 146
  European 21, 33, 35, 39, 106–7, 127, 161, 203
  Gulf 140
  London 7, 142
  Middle Eastern 144
  NATO 51, 98
  regional 82, 87, 141, 197
  of the United States 3, 161
  Western 3, 20, 25, 105, 140, 142
al-Nusra Front. *See* Jabhat al Nusra group
Amnesty International 68
Anglo-Iranian Oil Company (AIOC) 125, 232 n.8
Anglo-Iraqi Treaty of 1848 158
Ansar Allah (Houthi) movement 44–5, 60, 86, 89, 129, 132
antagonism 28, 33, 39
anti-ISIS 3, 100, 142–4. *See also* Islamic State of Iraq and Syria (ISIS)
Arabian Peninsula 20, 160, 179
Arab–Israeli conflict 14–16, 18, 21, 43
Arab League 25, 111
Arab Nationalism 14, 151, 158
Arab Partnership Unit/Arab Human Development 185–6, 191
Arab Peace Initiative (API) 111
Arab Spring 24–6, 56–7, 61, 85, 87, 89, 109, 188–9, 191
Arab uprisings of 2011 1–2, 24–5, 55, 57, 67, 76, 145, 172, 190, 196
Arafat, Yasser 18, 116
arms deal/defence export 17–18, 47, 61, 69, 77, 103, 162, 168. *See also* Al Yamamah arms deal; trade policy
  European companies 70
  licences 57, 61, 64, 103
  MENA countries in 73
  UK–Gulf 170–1
  UK–Turkey 103, 106
Arms Trade Treaty 61
Asia 28–9, 31, 36, 39, 48, 83, 170
al-Assad, Bashar 25, 32, 45, 58–9, 85, 87–8, 91, 99, 106, 129, 139–42, 144, 146–7, 153, 186, 204
Atlantic Alliance 32, 34
Atomic Energy Act of 1946 49
Australia 30, 72
Australia Group 88
authoritarian/authoritarianism 9, 43, 56, 66, 68, 114, 172, 175–6, 179, 189, 201–2

BAE Systems 17, 61, 71, 73, 98
  Tempest 70
al-Baghdadi, Abu-Bakr 142
Balfour Declaration 109, 117
Barghouti, Mustafa 114
BBC 1, 5, 148

Belgium 76, 120
Brussels 97, 102
Belt and Road Initiative (BRI) 29
Ben Ali, Zein al-Abidine 24, 56–7
Bicom pro-Israel organization 120, 229 n.13
Biden, Joe 3, 28, 35, 49–52, 66, 82–3, 90, 102, 107, 116, 133, 147, 157, 174, 178, 192–3, 219 nn.116–17
bilateral relationships 6, 13, 18, 28, 63–4, 82, 92, 98, 101–5, 113, 121, 123, 125–6, 129–34, 130, 162, 168–9, 179, 182, 191, 193. *See also specific countries*
bin Hussein, Faisal 157
bin-Laden, Osama 20
bin Nayef, Mohammed 75
bin Salman, Mohammad (Crown Prince) 46–7, 63, 74–5, 99, 167, 173, 193
bin Zayed, Mohammed 58, 169, 193
Biological and Toxins Weapons Convention 88
Black, Ian 6, 8
Blair, Tony 2, 21–4, 35, 48, 56, 67–8, 97, 107, 118, 159
Bolton, John 49, 130
Bombardier company 76, 221 n.15
bombing campaigns 3, 89
Borck, Tobias 6, 9, 50, 201
Boycott, Disinvestment and Sanctions (BDS) movement 110, 120
boycotts 21, 113, 118–20
BP oil and gas company 16–17, 58, 76
Branson, Richard 75, 211 n.34
Brexit 1–3, 5, 8, 25, 27–8, 36, 38–9, 55–6, 60–2, 65, 67–8, 78, 92–3, 103, 107, 113, 120, 123–4, 128, 147, 151, 170, 191, 205. *See also* post-Brexit Britain
Brexit effect 61–2, 113
referendum 60, 62, 112, 167
and UK's security 81–3
Withdrawal Agreement 62, 82
British Aerospace. *See* BAE Systems
British Airways 17, 74, 130–1
British Council 1, 5, 148
British Empire 7, 170
British forces. *See* Her Majesty's Government (HMG); *specific forces*
British Muslims 24
The British Royal Family 165, 169
British Special Forces 83–5, 104, 106, 142, 160, 168. *See also specific forces*
'British values' 1–2, 4–5, 7, 55–6, 58–60, 66–8, 176
Brown, Gordon 2, 21–2, 24, 56
Brown, Nathan 115
Burt, Alistair 113, 222 n.19, 235 n.13
Bush, George W. 18–19, 22–4, 35
Butter, David 5, 8, 201

Cameron, David 4, 24–5, 55–7, 59, 61, 64, 66–8, 97, 140–1, 166–7, 169, 215 n.51
on Libyan regime 57
national security 59–60
and Sisi 58
on use of chemical weapons 59, 141
visit to Turkey 97
Canada 63, 65, 140
Lord Caradon 15
Carter, Jimmy 44
Carter doctrine 43
Casson, John 190
Chalmers, Malcolm 39, 46
chemical weapons
Cameron on use of 59, 141
in Syria 25, 88–9, 91, 140, 215 n.42
Chemical Weapons Convention (CWC) 88
Chevening Scholarships Programme of UK 148, 184, 196, 235 n.27
Chilcott Inquiry 23–4, 92, 207 n.18, 209 n.34
China 3, 13, 33, 36, 38–9, 47–8, 50, 56, 59, 70, 73, 75–6, 103, 117, 130, 147, 175–8, 190, 197, 199, 201
Beijing 3, 28–30, 36, 50, 175, 177–8
and British nuclear power plants 30
and Eurasia 28–9
2015 investment in Europe 36
May's visit (early 2018) to 99
rules-based international order 31
and the US 28–9, 34, 50, 162, 170, 177–9, 199
Churchill, Winston 42
civil war(s) 25, 87
in Libya 33
Syrian 32, 39, 58, 129, 139, 141, 145

Clarke, Michael 4, 8, 199
climate change 35, 55, 134, 199
Clinton, Bill 21–3, 35
  Clinton Parameters of 2001 111
Cold War 27, 31, 50, 99
  US–China 28
  US–Soviet 28
commerce/commercial 13, 17, 29–31, 55, 58, 61–2, 64, 69, 77–8, 81, 89, 100, 125, 130, 132, 134, 147, 171, 178, 186, 201, 205
Common Security and Defence policy (CSDP) 81, 102
Conservative Friends of Israel 112
Conservative Middle East Council 119
Conservative Party 16–17, 24, 56, 66, 82, 99
  manifesto (2019) 67
Consortium Agreement of 1954 232 n.9
Cook, Robin 56
  foreign policy of 66–7, 213 n.14
Corbyn, Jeremy 67, 74, 116, 120
corruption 8, 57, 63, 75, 151–2, 154–5, 161, 170, 186, 188, 237 n.22
Council for Arab-British Understanding 118
Council of the European Union 81
counterterrorism (CT) 24, 44, 83–7, 90, 93, 124, 129, 135, 185, 187, 194, 203. *See also* national security of UK; terrorism/terrorists
  against Daesh 85–7
  Iraq 84–5
  Syria 85
Covid-19/coronavirus pandemic, impacts of 1, 5, 27–8, 30, 33, 50, 52, 66–7, 78, 107, 120, 124, 145, 151, 166, 176–7, 179, 184, 187, 193, 199, 204–5, 220 n.131
  collapse of oil prices 68, 154, 170
  contraction of UK GDP 56
  economic cost of 68
  economic recession 36–9, 68
  in Egypt 187–8, 196
  in Gaza 110
  government spending during 5
  in Gulf 170
  in Iran 133–4
  in Iraq 163
  in Lebanon 147
  refugee crises 89–90, 146
  and tourism 187–8
Crimea, Russian-occupied 31–2, 120
Curzon, George Nathanial, *Persia and the Persian Question* 123
cyber-attacks 88, 129
Cyprus/Cypriot 33, 48, 85, 97, 101–2, 104, 106, 117
  sovereign base areas (SBAs) 101, 105

Daesh 84–6, 92, 156, 160. *See also* Islamic State (IS)
  Global Coalition against 84–7
  and Iraq 152–3, 159
  in Syria 153
Davutoglu, Ahmet 99
decarbonization 78–9
decision-making process 22–3, 204, 207 n.18
defence policy of UK. *See also* arms deal/defence export
  defence engagement 83
  defence spending 4, 15–18, 61, 82–4, 107
  with Gulf 171
  with Saudi Arabia 60–1, 89
  with Turkey 98
de la Billiere, Sir Peter 19
democracy 43, 57–8, 60, 62, 91, 119, 139–40, 142–3, 145, 148, 158, 189, 191–3, 202
Democrat Administration 35
Department for International Development (DfID) 67, 113, 142, 185, 204
Department for International Trade (DIT) 61–2
diplomacy 5–6, 8, 16–17, 32–3, 39, 49–50, 59, 83, 119, 133, 156, 162, 201, 205
  diplomats 1, 15, 34, 48, 55, 60, 115, 117, 139–41, 156
DP World London Gateway 70
Dual Containment (Iraq and Iran) 21
dual nationals/nationality 128, 134
Dubai Expo 2020 74
Duncan, Alan 97, 104

E3 50–1, 124, 130–1, 133–4
Ease of Doing Business index of World Bank (2019) 147

Eastern Mediterranean Gas Forum 101
East of Suez 8, 15, 42, 47, 83, 126, 167–9, 179
East Port Said industrial zone 76
Economic Association Agreements 70
economy/economics 8, 13, 28–9, 36, 47, 50, 52, 140, 177
  aid-dependent (PA) 114
  Asian 36, 39
  British 1–2, 8, 13, 16, 24, 37, 48, 65, 103, 125
  Chinese 29–31, 162
  Covid-19 recession 36–9, 68, 78, 196 (*See also* Covid-19/coronavirus pandemic, impacts of)
  debts/loans 14, 29–30, 36–7, 88, 129, 160–1, 193
  decarbonization 78–9
  economic crisis 27, 31, 36–7, 56, 168
  economic growth 36–7, 130, 152, 161, 187–8, 194, 236 n.4
  Egypt 185–9, 196
  global economy 29, 36–8, 78, 123, 166, 170
  in Gulf 171, 177–8
  hydro-carbon dependent 166, 168–70, 179, 201
  international 1, 38
  of Iraq 151–5, 157, 161–2
  mature economies 37, 209 n.40
  non-hydrocarbon 79
  Russian 31, 33
  Turkey 6, 103
Eden, Anthony 14
education system 143–4, 148, 158, 177, 182–4, 189–90, 196, 202, 222 n.20
Egypt 3, 5, 7, 9, 14, 24, 46, 58, 60–1, 67, 69–71, 73, 78, 87, 100–1, 112, 121, 140, 147, 172–3, 201
  Cairo 76, 101, 181, 183–6, 191–4
  demographic dividend 194–5
  economic reform 185–9, 194, 196
  education market of UK in 196
  EU–Egypt Association Agreement 184
  GDP of 187–8
  generational friction (Gen Z) 194–6
  Green Bond 184
  history of Britain in 182–5
  impact of Covid-19 in 187–8
  Memorandum of Understanding (MoU) 185
  monorail system 76
  relationship with UK 9, 181–5, 189–4, 194, 196–7
  Sinai Peninsula 185–6, 192
  trade and investment 75–6 (*see also* trade policy)
  UK–Egypt Association Agreement 184
El-Badawy, Emma 5, 7, 9, 202
Embassy 77, 116, 204
  British 88, 113
  Iranian 88
  Tehran 127
  Tel Aviv 113
  UK 124
  US 51, 98, 111, 113, 127, 132
employment/jobs 37, 77–8, 104, 143, 151–2
  job creation 155, 202
  unemployment 152, 188
Erdogan, Recep Tayyip 8, 99–100, 104, 202
  visit to the UK 98
Etzion, Eran 115
Eurasia 28–9
Europe 4, 21, 28–9, 31, 33–4, 38–9, 42, 52, 70, 98, 101–2, 109–10, 124, 127, 129, 131, 133, 141, 167, 170, 181, 191, 193
  decline in terrorist attacks 86
  impact of Covid-19 78
  ISIS attacks in 60
  security 34, 39, 60
  2015 Chinese investment in 36
  and the US 50–2
European Bank for Reconstruction and Development 76
European Convention on Human Rights (ECHR) 62
European Council on Foreign Relations (ECFR) 114–15, 122
European Counter Terrorism/Cybercrime Centres 82
European Economic Community (EEC) 16
European Investment Bank 76
European Security and Defence Policy. *See* Common Security and Defence policy (CSDP)

European Union (EU) 1, 20–1, 24–5, 27, 30, 36, 48, 62, 65, 67, 81–2, 92, 97, 101–2, 105, 123–4, 131
Britain's departure from 1, 3–4, 8, 62–3, 76, 81, 99, 101–2, 105, 147–8
economic development schemes 145
EU–Jordan compact 143–4
members/membership 70, 98, 101, 104, 107, 116–17, 120
trade agreements 62, 70
Iran-EU 131
tariff-free/quota-free 70
and the United States 66, 102, 191–2
withdrawal agreement 82
Europol agency 82
Expo 2020. *See* Dubai Expo 2020
extremism/extremists 25, 37, 81, 84, 86, 110, 171, 173, 186, 188, 196, 203

Falklands War 16
fatwa 127, 156
financial technologies (fintech) 170, 178
First World War 13, 157, 182. *See also* Second World War
Five-Eyes intelligence community 30, 82
force for good, Britain's 22, 56, 67
Foreign and Commonwealth Office (FCO) 4, 17–18, 56, 60–2, 67, 97, 110, 116, 118, 161, 163, 185–6, 201, 212 n.6, 212 nn.1–2, 217 n.73
Human Rights and Democracy report 56
Overseas Business Risk – the Occupied Palestinian Territories 120
Strategy Unit paper 185, 191
warning to Iranian British 128
foreign investment 38, 151–3, 155
foreign policy 22, 46, 49, 113, 192
British 2–5, 27–8, 30, 36, 38, 63, 123, 127, 154, 165–6, 175, 181, 200, 202, 206 n.1 (Ch 1)
post-Brexit 166
towards Middle East 167, 178
US influence on 65–6
of Cook 66
goals of UK 186
national security (*see* national security of UK)
prosperity agenda 55–6, 58, 61–3, 66
values 1–2, 4–5, 7, 55–6, 58–60, 66–8, 176, 193
of Iran 126–7
Turkish 99
the US 4
Fox, Liam 62, 217 n.81
France 8, 14, 21, 37, 42–3, 45, 51, 73, 76, 82, 88, 98, 100–1, 103, 109, 112, 117, 120, 124, 130, 134, 140–1, 144, 174–5, 193, 196, 202
Franco-British strategic competition 39
Free Syrian Army 91
Free Trade Agreement (FTA) 26, 62–3, 65, 69–70, 107. *See also* trade policy
Friends of Al-Aqsa 118
Future Commando Force, UK's 83

Gaddafi, Muammar 23, 25, 43–4, 57, 104–5, 172, 186
Gaza/Gaza Strip 18, 64, 110, 113–14, 118, 192
Covid-19 outbreak 110
Gaza–Israel conflict 110–11, 116
Marches of Return protest 110, 119
Geneva, UNHRC in 119
geopolitics 27–30, 38, 142, 144–5, 169, 171, 175, 178, 192, 197
Germany 21, 25, 37, 51, 60, 63, 70, 73, 82, 103, 105, 120, 124, 130, 134, 140, 142, 148, 193, 197
and Turkey 98, 104
Global Britain 1, 55, 65, 67, 106–7, 113, 135, 162, 181, 200–1
Global Coalition against Daesh 84–7
Global Human Rights Sanctions 64, 67
Golan Heights 35, 64, 89, 112, 119
The Good Operation 223 n.35
Government Communications Headquarters (GCHQ) 101
Government of National Accord (GNA) 100–1
Great Britain 17, 42, 123, 125
great power 1, 3, 28, 31, 36, 38–9, 50, 162, 199–200
great recession 36
Greece/Greek 21, 100
Athens 47, 49, 101
dispute between Turkey and 101
Greenblatt, Jason 112

Gross Domestic Product (GDP) 6, 29, 31, 36–7, 56, 72, 82, 146, 152, 187–8, 208 n.18, 209 n.40, 212 n.5
GSK company 76
G20 summit 47, 211 n.35
Gulen movement 104
Gulf 1–2, 4, 6, 9, 14–20, 35, 39, 42–3, 45, 47–8, 51, 57–8, 61–2, 64–5, 67, 77, 83, 89, 92, 100, 106, 109, 124, 134, 147, 156, 159–60, 162, 175, 177–9, 181, 201
  Arab/Persian 18, 20–1, 24, 43, 47, 51, 69–72, 74, 78, 121, 125–7, 129–30, 132–3, 165, 169, 174
  economic system 171, 178
  global competition 176–8
  growth in the UK exports to 78
  Gulf Crisis of 2017 167, 173
  Gulf Strategy (2015) 47–8, 51, 167, 175–6, 178
  human rights in 175–6
  hydro-carbon dependent economy 166, 168–70
  impact of Covid-19 170
  International Maritime Security Mission 45, 51
  May's visit to 131
  oil and gas resources 170
  outward investment 79
  relationship with UK 165–75
  trade 5, 16, 70, 77 (*see also* trade policy)
Gulf Cooperation Council (GCC) 6, 25, 58, 62, 69, 71, 77, 130, 167, 173–5, 177, 191, 201
Gulf War 19
  legacies of 1990–1 20–1

Haftar, Khalifa 100
Hague, William 24, 56–8, 68
  irreducible core, human rights 56, 60
  on values 56
Hamas (Islamic Resistance Movement) 110–11, 114, 117–18, 173, 192
Hammond, Philip 60
Hashd Al-Shaabi. *See* Popular Mobilization Forces (PMF)
al Hashimi, Hisham 237 n.20
Hassassian, Manuel 121
Healey, Denis 15
Hearn, Eddie 74
Heath, Edward 16, 167
hegemony, US 3, 13–14, 21, 43–5, 165, 167, 174, 200
Her Majesty's Government (HMG) 13–15, 17, 19, 21–6
Hezbollah 3, 21, 25, 89, 110, 127, 129, 132, 144–5, 147
Hezen Parastina Gel (HPG). *See* People's Defence Forces
Higginson, Roger 229 n.23
Hijab, Nadia 118
HMS Jufair, Royal Navy base 83
Hollis, Rosemary 8
  Britain and the Middle East: Policy in the 9/11 Decade 2
House of Commons 24, 116–17
  Defence Committee 223 n.36
  Foreign Affairs Committee 60, 104, 116
House of Lords Select Committee on International Relations 2
Houthi movement. *See* Ansar Allah (Houthi) movement
HSBC banking company 76
Huawei controversy in 2018 30
humanitarian/humanitarian crisis 59, 60, 81, 87, 105, 114, 124, 133, 141, 159–60, 172, 204
  non-humanitarian 141
human rights 55–7, 60–1, 66–8, 73, 97, 99, 107, 135, 139–40, 142–5, 148, 165–6, 170–1, 197. *See also* Foreign and Commonwealth Office (FCO)
  abuse/abuser 5–6, 45, 58, 119, 176
  and Brexit 62
  in Egypt 190, 192, 194
  EU trade agreements 62
  in Gulf states 175–6
  irreducible core of UK foreign policy 56, 60
  in Saudi Arabia 63, 65
  Turkey's record 102
  violations 67, 127, 132
  in Yemen 216 n.61, 216 n.64
Human Rights Act (HRA) 62
Human Rights Advisory Group 56
Human Rights Watch 128

Hunt, Jeremy 63, 119, 128, 218 n.88
Hurd, Douglas 18, 21, 206 n.13
al-Husri, Sati 158
King Hussein of Jordan 18
Hussein, Saddam 19–20, 22, 43, 45, 88, 127, 159, 168

IMF 19, 30, 133
imperial/imperialism 15, 20, 157–8, 182–3
 anti-imperialism 14
 imperial era, end of 13–14
India 14, 33, 36, 56, 70–1, 74, 78, 123, 158, 170, 175, 182–3, 199
Indian Ocean 14, 17, 29
Indonesia 29, 36
Indo-Pacific tilt 4, 50, 177
INSTEX (special-purpose vehicle) 131
intelligence agency of UK 84, 88, 101
intelligence sharing, UK 18, 24, 82–3, 113
Intermediate Nuclear Forces (INF) Treaty (1987) 35
international community 38, 90, 112, 129, 135, 140, 154–5, 159
international law 18, 30, 64–6, 110, 116, 119–21
International Maritime Security Mission 45, 51
international system 31–2, 35, 41, 49, 200
interventions, UK 4, 35, 50, 68, 101, 126, 159
 in Kosovo 22
 in Libya 25, 92
 military 13, 46, 57, 59, 67, 90, 140, 158
 in Sierra Leone 22
Iran/Iranian 1–6, 8–9, 14, 16, 20–1, 25, 44–5, 52, 65, 67, 78, 86, 106, 109–10, 113, 123, 133–5, 139, 142, 144, 146–7, 153–4, 156, 173–4, 179, 189–90, 200, 233 n.13
 ballistic missile activities 89, 123, 126, 132, 134, 159–60
 Chieftain tanks case 88, 129
 Covid-19 outbreak 133–4
 Curzon's travel through 123
 cyber warfare 129
 detainment policy 128
 escalation against Trump's administration 132
 Grace 1 tanker seize by UK 89, 132
 Green Movement (2009) 127
 Iranian Revolution 88, 123, 125–9, 159
 nuclear deal/programme 8, 35, 39, 45, 51, 90, 126–34, 171, 173
 policy of containment of (2011) 46
 post-revolutionary system 126, 130
 Prince Charles's visit to Bam 128
 regional stability of 88–9, 134–5
 relationship with UK 124–6
 seize of UK tanker *Stena Impero* 89, 132
 supply of arms by Britain 18
 and the United States 156–7
Iran–Iraq War 159, 168
Iraq/Iraqis 1, 3, 7–8, 14, 18–20, 22, 25, 35, 43–6, 48, 59–60, 67–8, 73, 78, 89–91, 106, 124, 132, 139, 142, 148, 151–2, 171, 184, 186, 189, 201–3, 236 nn.3–4
 Baghdad 20, 84, 100, 132, 151, 153–6, 158, 160–2
 client–patron system 151–2, 154–5
 corruption 151–2
 counterterrorism 85
 Counter Terrorism Service (CTS) 160
 and Daesh 152–3, 159
 economic system of 151–5, 157, 161–2
 Erbil 154
 Fallujah 84, 152
 Golden Division in 46
 impact of Covid-19 in 163
 invasion of 23–4, 128
 invasion of Kuwait 13, 18–19, 159
 and Iran 153
 Iraqi Armed Forces 19, 85
 Iraqi Security Forces 85, 91
 Iraq War 3, 5, 67, 84, 87–8, 131, 188
 KRG 154, 160, 162
 League of Nations 157–8
 Ministry of Peshmerga Affairs 83
 Mosul 84, 100, 152, 159–60
 Non-Combatant Evacuation Operations 156
 nuclear capability of 88
 oil market 152, 154
 Peshmerga 46
 PMF (*see* Popular Mobilization Forces (PMF))
 Protest Movement 151, 163

government's violence against protestors 155, 157
Ramadi 84, 152
relationship with UK 157–63
Republican Guard Corps 19
risks and uncertainty in 154–7
in 2020s 152–4
supply of arms by Britain 18
terrorist attacks in 86
unemployment of youth 151
UN weapons inspectors to 20
Ireland 56, 117
IRGC 128–31
Islamic Republic of Iran (IRI) 18, 43, 124, 126, 129, 135
Islamic State (IS) 25, 39, 46, 84–5, 109, 117, 184
Caliphate 39, 84, 142, 146
and Turkey 100, 104–5
Islamic State of Iraq and Syria (ISIS) 1, 7, 43–4, 85, 134, 139, 142, 146, 173, 195, 203. *See also* anti-ISIS
attacks in Europe 60
Iraqi territory under (2014) 59, 129
Islamic State of Iraq and the Levant (ISIL) 84
Islamophobia 102, 191
Israel Defence Forces 119
Israeli–Palestinian conflict 1, 3, 18–19, 45, 51, 109–10, 113, 117, 148. *See also* Palestine/Palestinians
equal rights 111, 115
Marches of Return protest 110, 119
one-state solution 110–11
OPTs (*see* Occupied Palestinian Territories (OPTs))
peace agreement 111
two-state solution 110, 112–15, 117, 120–1
Israel/Israelis 3, 6, 8, 14–16, 18, 21, 26, 41, 44–5, 48, 51, 56, 58, 65, 67, 69–71, 73, 86, 89–90, 101, 109, 116–22, 127–8, 134, 139, 147, 156, 177, 186, 192, 200, 202, 210 n.28
annexation 65, 112, 114–15, 117, 119
Gaza-Israel conflict 110–11
Jerusalem 35, 41, 51, 64, 110–11, 113, 115, 120–1
nation-state law 110
Prince Charles's (Prince of Wales) visit to 119
Prince William's visit to 119
relationship with UK 118–19, 218 n.95, 231 n.47
and Saudi Arabia 62–4
self-defence 119
Tel Aviv 111, 113, 192
and terrorism 112–13
trade agreement with the UK 64
Turkish trade 104
Italy 25, 33, 37, 73, 101, 103, 117
Izz al-Din al-Qassam 117

Jabhat al Nusra group 104–5, 144, 146
Jacksonian nationalism 34–5, 49
Japan 29–30, 41, 72, 76, 175
Javid, Sajid 145
Jenkins, John 121
Jews/Jewish 14, 112, 115–16, 183
Jihadism/Jihadists 141–2, 144, 146
Johnson, Boris 65–8, 75, 82, 116, 120–1, 128–9, 132–3, 169, 190, 193, 240 n.31
Johnson, Lyndon 15, 64–5
Joint Comprehensive Plan of Action (JCPOA) 6, 44–5, 51, 88–90, 124, 127, 157, 173–4
and nuclear programme of Iran 129–34
Joint Trade and Investment Review (UK and GCC) 63
Jordan 7–8, 14, 18, 24, 60, 65, 70, 73, 86–7, 100–1, 105, 113, 121, 139, 141–7, 201
Amman 7, 143–4
EU-Jordan compact 143–4
Hashemite Kingdom of 46, 143
'Jordan: Growth and Opportunity – the London Initiative 2019' conference 147, 202
Jordanian Quick Response Force 91
relationship with UK 143, 148–9
Joshua, Anthony 74

Kerry, John 111–12
Kettle, Louise 4, 8, 200, 203
Remote Warfare 203
Al-Khalifa, Hamad bin Issa 169
Khamenei, Ali 128

Khashoggi, Jamal, murder of 3, 46, 51, 63–4, 75, 167, 211 n.34, 218 n.89
Khatami, Muhammad 127–9
Khomeini, Ayatollah 43, 126–7
Kosovo 22, 59, 159
Kurdistan Freedom Hawks 105
Kurdistan Worker's Party. *See* Partiya Karkeren Kurdistane (PKK)
Kurds/Kurdish 19–20, 102, 148
  KRG 154, 160, 162
  Turkey against 100
Kushner, Jared 51, 112, 116
Kuwait 14, 21, 43, 69, 87, 89, 91, 130, 159
  Iraqi invasion of 13, 18–19, 45, 159

Labour government 5, 15–16, 56, 167, 176
Labour Party 21, 24, 46, 59, 61, 74
  anti-Semitism 110
Lebanon 3, 7–8, 21, 45, 60, 67, 70, 89, 113, 124, 129, 139, 141–8, 186, 189, 201–2
  impact of Covid-19 147
  Lebanese Armed Forces (LAF) 83, 91, 144–5
  relationship with UK 144–9
Levant 8, 139, 143, 145–6, 148, 181
Liberal Democrat Friends of Palestine 117
Liberal Democrats 24, 36, 59
liberalization (economic/political) 127–8, 175, 179, 192
Libya 1, 16, 23, 25, 32–3, 35, 39, 43–6, 60, 68, 87, 89, 92, 100–2, 104–5, 140, 172–3, 185–6, 201, 203–4
  Cameron against Libyan regime 57
Libyan National Army (LNA) 100
Littoral Response Groups 83
London 1, 3, 5–9, 34, 41–2, 45–8, 50–2, 88, 103, 106, 112–13, 116, 124, 140, 142–4, 146–7, 149, 162, 167, 169–70, 172, 175–7, 179, 192, 204
  London Agreement 18
  real-estate market 168, 178
  Whitehall 57, 128, 134, 159, 167, 178, 182, 195
Lovatt, Hugh 229 n.17, 229 n.22
Luttwak, Edward 43
Lynch, James 5, 8, 176

Maastricht Treaty (1992) 81
Macmillan, Harold 203
Macron, Emmanuel 59, 100, 131, 133
Major, John 18
al Makhtoum, Mohammed bin Rashid 169
Malaysia 29–30
Malta 117
Mandate for Palestine in 1947 14
maritime security 89, 91, 101–2, 106, 129, 132, 134, 174
Marjai'yah 155–6
Mashal, Khaled 118
May, Theresa 47, 59, 61, 67, 130, 147, 167, 169, 175
  and Kerry 112
  and Netanyahu 113
  turbo-charge trade 62
  visit to Gulf 131
  visit to Turkey 97
Mead, Walter Russell 34–5, 49
Mediterranean 33, 39, 60, 70, 101–2, 105
MI6-CIA 23, 125, 185
The Middle East 58, 60–1, 65–8, 70, 73, 78, 81–3, 87, 89, 98–9, 109, 122, 124, 133–4, 158, 165–6, 172–4, 176–7, 181–2, 184–5, 188–9, 191, 194, 199–201, 203, 205
  Bahrain 14–15, 25, 57, 69, 73–4, 83, 87, 89, 106, 109, 121, 170–1, 173, 233 n.13
  Manama 110, 167, 169, 171
  Nuclear Weapon Free Zone 186
  peace plan 65
  post-Brexit UK in 106–7
  UK–Middle East security relations 83–4, 87, 92, 171
  values in policy of 55–6, 67
Middle East North Africa (MENA) region 4, 50, 69–71, 75, 91, 139, 147, 185, 194
  arms markets 73
  decline in terrorist attacks 86
  global arms importers 73
  UK's trade with 71–3, 76–7
Middle East Peace Process (MEPP) 21, 23–4, 65, 109, 116, 121, 124, 186, 192, 194, 219 n.107, 219 n.110
migration/migrants 25, 60, 124, 141, 169–71, 185–6

Missile Technology Control Regime 88
Moore, Richard 185
Morocco 24, 70–1, 78, 87, 109
  British exports to 75–6
Morsi, Mohamed 24, 55, 58, 100, 172, 183
  massacre of Morsi's supporters 58
Mossadegh, Mohammad 14, 123, 125–6, 232 n.8
Muasher, Marwan 115
Mubadala investment company 79
Mubarak, Hosni 56–8, 183, 185–6, 189–90
Mubarak of Egypt 24
The Mubarak Plan 241 n.9
al Muhandis, Abu Mahdi, killing of 132
Muslim Brotherhood (MB) 3, 58, 100, 173, 191–2

Nagorno–Karabakh conflict 102
Nasser, Gamal Abdel 14, 182–3
National Intelligence Law 30
nationalism 86, 99, 125. *See also specific nationalism*
national security of UK 55, 59–60, 63, 66–7, 140. *See also* foreign policy; security policy
  and Brexit 81–3
  British forces (*see specific forces*)
  CT (*see* counterterrorism (CT))
  against Daesh 84–6
  National Security Council 204–5
  National Security Strategy 33, 60–1
  training programmes 91
  UK–Gulf 171–2
  UK–Middle East 83–4, 87, 92, 171
  UK–Turkey 104–5
NEOM mega-city project, Saudi Arabia 75
Netanyahu, Binyamin 65, 111–13, 121, 229 n.11
The Netherlands 21, 37, 73
New Labour 21–4, 159
New Syrian Army. *See* Revolutionary Commando Army
NGO 56, 194
9/11 attacks 13, 23, 35, 50, 84, 128, 189
Nixon Doctrine 43
no-contact policy 117–18
non-proliferation, nuclear 124, 134, 174, 184
non-state actors 3, 13, 46, 59, 119, 126–7, 129, 132
North Atlantic Treaty Organization (NATO) 16–17, 19, 22, 25, 32–3, 35, 43, 51, 82, 92, 98–105, 107, 159, 191, 202
Northern Ireland 22–3
Norway 21, 37, 118
Nuclear Non-Proliferation Treaty 88
Nuclear Suppliers Group 88
Nusra Front (Al-Qaeda in Syria) 25, 105

Obama, Barak 25, 35, 44, 48–9, 56, 111–12, 130, 140–1
Oborne, Peter 64
Occupied Palestinian Territories (OPTs) 110, 114, 118–21, 186
  impact of occupation 113–14
Office for National Statistics (ONS) 71
oil and gas sector 5, 29, 31, 69, 71–2, 74, 76, 78, 168, 170
  oil prices 2, 16, 31
    collapse due to Covid-19 68, 154, 170
    crash in Iraq 154, 157
    increase of global 16
Oman 7, 14–15, 23, 69, 73–4, 83, 87, 106, 121, 130, 147, 168, 170, 173, 201
  Exercise Saif Sareea 3 in 91
  Muscat 7, 47, 174
  UK-Oman Joint Defence Agreement 91
one-nation 66
Operation Agenor 51–2
Operation Ajax 125
Operation Desert Fox 22
Operation Desert Storm 19
Operation Ellamy 92
Operation Enduring Freedom-Philippines 50
Operation Inherent Resolve 50, 142
Operation Peace Spring 106
Operation Protective Edge 64
Operation Sentinel 50–2
Operation Shader 84
Operation Telic 84
Organisation for the Prohibition of Chemical Weapons (OPCW) 88
Organisation of the Islamic Conference 111

Organization of Petroleum Exporting Countries (OPEC) 16
Oslo Accord 21, 111, 114, 117, 230 n.33
Ottoman Empire 13, 99, 125, 157

Palestine Expo in London (2017) 118
Palestine Liberation Organisation (PLO) 18, 21, 111, 114, 117
Palestine/Palestinians 6, 14, 18, 21, 23–4, 67, 112, 114–15, 117, 121
  as independent state (recognition) 116–17
  and Israel (*see* Israeli–Palestinian conflict; Israel/Israelis)
  non-Jewish communities 109
  parity of esteem 117
  pro-Palestinian protests 120
  refugees 144
Palestinian Authority (PA) 24, 70, 101, 110, 113–15, 117, 121
pan-Arabism 109
Paris Accord 35
Park, Bill 6, 8, 202, 225 n.22
Partiya Karkeren Kurdistane (PKK) 91–2, 99–100, 104–5
Patel, Priti 66, 220 n.120
peace process 6, 21, 65, 109, 111, 115, 121, 184. *See also* Middle East Peace Process (MEPP)
People's Defence Forces 105
People's Protection Unit. *See* Yekineyen Parastina Gel (YPG)
Peres, Shimon 18
Perincek, Dogu 99
Persia. *See* Iran/Iranian
Persian Constitutional Revolution (1905–11) 125
Phillips, Christopher 5, 7–9
Phillips, Tom 122
Plowden Report 14–15
Poland 33, 37
policymakers/policymaking 1, 28, 48, 55–7, 60, 67, 102, 128, 145, 148, 155, 175–6, 189, 191, 194, 205
political Islam 173, 189
Pompeo, Mike 130
Popular Mobilization Forces (PMF) 59, 129, 153, 156, 163
Portugal 117
post-Brexit Britain 5, 9, 18, 26–7, 37–9, 50, 68, 77, 82–3, 98, 123, 129, 133–5, 148, 171, 178, 193–4. *See also* Brexit
  foreign policy 166, 176
  Global Britain 181
  in Middle East 106–7
  trade agreements 70, 130–1
  UK–Turkey relationship 99, 101–5
Powell, Colin 19
pragmatism 4–6, 8, 13, 26, 46, 126–7, 130, 185, 190, 195–6, 202
Presidential Programme for Rehabilitation of Youth for Leadership 195
Prime Ministerial Trade Envoys 62
Prince Charles (Prince of Wales)
  visit to Bam, Iran 128
  visit to Israel 119
Prince William 119
protests/protesters 5, 57–8, 67, 88–9, 149, 189, 193
  Gezi Park protests (2013) 97
  Iraqi Protest Movement 151, 155, 163
  2009 presidential elections 128
  violence of government in Iraq against 155
Public Investment Fund 70, 75, 79
Putin, Vladimir 31–2, 34, 47
  2014 Duma speech 33
Pym, Francis 17

Al-Qaeda 1, 20, 23–5, 160, 173, 203
  Hayat Tahrir as-Sham 146
  Jubhat al-Nusra 144, 146
  Syrian (al Qaeda-affiliated group) 104
Qajar period (1789–1925) 125
Qasim, Abd al-Karim 158
Qatar 14–15, 35, 69–71, 73–4, 77–8, 100, 104, 106, 114, 130, 133, 141, 166–8, 172–4, 233 n.13
  Doha 172–3
Quartet (the US, Russia, the EU and the UN) 24, 117–18

Raab, Dominic 5, 64, 67, 98, 120–1
radicalism/radicalization 24, 87, 102, 143, 146, 173
Reagan, Ronald 17–19, 47

Realpolitik 49, 187
rebels/rebellion 15, 25, 57
  anti-Assad rebels 142
  Chechen rebellion 32
  Houthi 172
  moderate armed 141
  Syrian 91, 104–5
  Yemeni 106
refugees 25, 102, 109, 111, 171
  crisis 87, 90, 98, 139, 141–4
  Jordan 87
  Lebanon 87
  Palestinian 144
  Syrian 60, 87, 98, 105, 141–4, 146
  Turkey 87
regional policy 8–9, 45, 178, 200
regional security 29, 44, 81, 86, 91, 124, 127, 129, 134–5, 151, 159, 179, 187
regional stability 13, 45–6, 59, 81, 83, 87–90, 93, 179
  of Iran 88–9, 133, 135
  refugee crises 87, 90
  weapons of mass destruction 87–9
remote warfare approach 81, 83, 90–3, 203
Revolutionary Commando Army 46
Reza Shah Pahlavi, Mohammad 43, 125–6
rights-based approach 115
Riyadh Ritz Carlton 63, 75
Rossiyskaya Gazeta of 2015 33
Rouhani, Hassan 127, 129, 133
Royal Air Force (RAF) 83, 85, 101, 106
Royal Navy 83, 168
rule of law 16, 19, 23, 31, 63, 66, 97, 194
rules-based international order 31, 62, 107, 201
Russia 3, 13, 20, 25, 28, 32–3, 38, 45, 47, 50, 56, 59, 90, 100, 103, 117, 123, 125, 130, 141–2, 146–7, 162, 190–1, 197, 199
  in Britain's foreign and security policy 31
  economy of 31, 33
  introduction of *Iskandar-M* missiles 33
  Kremlin 31–2
  Moscow 3, 32–3, 146
  revanchist 31–2, 34
  Russian-occupied Crimea 31–2, 120
  trade and investment 73
  and Turkey 102
  and the US 34
  wild-west capitalism in 32

al Sadr, Muqtadr 155
Safavid dynasty (1501–1722) 125
el-Said, Hala 75
Salman Rushdie affair 127
sanctions policy 22–3, 124, 159
Saudi Arabia 1, 3, 17, 20, 24, 26, 35, 39, 43, 45, 47, 51, 58, 69, 71, 74, 77, 83, 86–7, 89, 106, 109, 121–2, 126, 130, 141, 146–7, 153, 166, 168, 170, 172–5, 177, 191–3, 200–2, 238 n.41
  airstrikes by Saudi-led coalition (2015) 60
  and Canada 63
  drive for diversification 74
  human rights in 63, 65
  and Israel 62–4
  NEOM mega-city project 75
  Riyadh 20, 44–5, 57, 60, 64, 130–1, 173, 192
  and UAE 130
  UK's (trade) relationship with 63–4, 70–5
    defence sales 60–1, 89
  VAT in 78
  women's right to drive in 63
Saudi Aramco company 75
scholarship(s)
  Chevening Scholarships Programme of UK 148, 184, 196, 235 n.27
  Jordan-only 148
  military-focused 43
Schwartzman, Stephen 75
The Scott Report 206 n.12
Second World War 14, 19, 41–2, 159. *See also* First World War
secularism 86, 91
Security Capability Review of 2018 41
security cooperation 7, 58, 64, 91, 104, 160, 175, 189, 192
Security, Defence, Development and Foreign Policy 107
security policy 33, 47–9, 52
  American/the US 34–5, 41, 43–4, 52

Britain 2–8, 29–31, 35, 38–9, 46, 49, 140, 143, 160 (*see also* national security of UK)
European 34, 39
Gulf 51
regional (*see* regional security)
security threats 7–8, 49, 140, 153, 195
Seidemann, Daniel 121
Shah of Iran. *See* Reza Shah Pahlavi, Mohammad
Shamir, Yitzhak 18
Sharon, Ariel 23–4
el-Sheikh, Sharm 184, 195
Shell oil and gas company 16–17, 76
Shia Muslims 19, 86, 106, 156
attacks on 84
Short, Clare 116
Sierra Leone 22, 59
Singapore 69
al-Sisi, Abdel Fattah 58, 75, 100, 172, 183, 186–7, 189–90, 193, 195
Sistani, Ayatollah 155–7, 237 n.22
small- and medium-sized enterprises (SMEs) 77
Soleimani, Qassim, killing of 65, 132–3
Son, Masayoshi 75
South Korea 76, 103
sovereign base areas (SBAs), Cyprus 101, 105
sovereignty 29, 35, 46, 59, 65, 114, 193
Soviet Union 13, 15, 31, 42–3, 117, 158–9
Finlandisation policy 33
Spain 21, 70, 103, 117
Special Relationship (UK and US) 8, 15, 41–2, 50
sponsorship deals 74
Starmer, Keir 67. *See also* Labour Party
state-building 139, 143–4
State of Palestine. *See* Palestine/Palestinians
Stephens, Michael 6, 8–9, 50, 201, 212 n.50
Stockholm International Peace Research Institute (SIPRI) 73
Straits of Hormuz 132, 162
Strategic Defence and Security Review (SDSR) 22, 82–4
Straw, Jack 23, 118, 128
Stuart, Michael 15
Sudan 60, 67, 87, 100, 109, 184, 186, 202
Suez Canal 14, 42–3, 182, 188
Suez Crisis of 1956 42, 182–3
Sulaimani, Qasim 45, 156, 174, 219 n.105
protest against assassination of 151
Sunni Islam 46, 59, 86, 151–3
Sweden 117, 142
Switzerland 72, 118
Syria 1, 3, 7–8, 25, 33, 43–6, 48, 58, 60–1, 87, 89–92, 100, 102, 104, 109, 124, 132, 134, 140, 144–9, 153, 173, 201, 203–4
chemical weapons in 88–9
civil war 32, 39, 58, 129, 139, 141, 145
counterterrorism 85
Daesh in 153
Damascus 59, 88, 140–1, 147, 153
failing of UK in 139–42
Ghouta chemical attack (2013) 59
Idlib 89, 98, 105–6, 146
IS threat in 100
Syrian refugees 60, 87, 98, 105, 141–3, 146
terrorist attacks in 86
Trump on 210 n.25
and Turkey 104, 106
Syrian Democratic Forces (SDF) 46, 91–2, 100, 104–5, 142
Syrian Opposition Coalition (SOC) 141
Syrian Train and Equip Programme 105

Taliban 23, 146, 160
Tamarod protest movement 58
tax/taxation 17, 37, 78
Tehran 4, 44, 88–9, 106, 124–35, 146, 174
terrorism/terrorists 1, 8, 13, 18, 38, 46, 57, 81, 98, 118, 131, 135, 160, 166, 171, 173. *See also* counterterrorism (CT); *specific organizations*
EU databases of 82
Global Terrorism Index 85–6
and Israel 112–13
Lockerbie bombing in 1988 23
9/11 attack 13, 23, 35, 50
suicide bombings 24
terrorist attacks 20, 84
in Iraq 86

Russian civilian aircraft (2015) 184
in Syria 86
UK–Turkey cooperation against 104–5
Teyrebazen Azadiya Kurdistan (TAK). *See* Kurdistan Freedom Hawks
TF-X Turkish fighter programme 98
Thatcher, Margaret 16–20, 47
Thornberry, Emily 120
Timber Sycamore program 105
Tory/Tory manifesto 56, 59
tourism 153, 170, 187–8
trade policy 1, 3–5, 19, 28–9, 35, 48, 51, 201, 210 n.20, 239 n.25. *See also* Free Trade Agreement (FTA)
Abu Dhabi 58
agricultural production 70
bilateral (*see* bilateral relationships)
British (exports/imports) 1, 5, 15, 64, 71, 103, 120, 123
advertisement 77
arms/defence (*see* arms deal/ defence export)
with Gulf 5, 78, 168–71
with Iraq 161–3
with Israel 64
with Jordon 143
leading export markets 72
with Lebanon 144, 147
with MENA region 71–3
merchandise trade 71–2
with Morocco 75–6
with non-EU countries 220 n.2
with Qatar 168
services exports/destinations 69, 72
with Turkey 98, 104
UK-GCC 217 n.81
US/UK 65–6
counter-trade deal 17
Egypt 75–6
EU trade agreements 62, 131
INSTEX (special-purpose vehicle) 131
and investments/investors 1, 55, 58, 63, 69–71, 74–7, 79, 129, 134
outward 70, 79, 104
Iran-Tehran 128, 130
Saudi Arabia 60–1, 63–4, 70–5
and Israel 62–4
surpluses 69, 72, 74
trade-offs 4, 6, 176, 182, 188, 201–2, 205
UAE 70–1
transatlantic relationships 35, 42, 52, 99, 101, 192–4
Treaty of Golestan (1813) 125
Treaty of Paris (1857) 125
Treaty of Turkomanchy (1828) 125
Trump, Donald 28, 31, 34–5, 44–5, 49, 51–2, 59, 65–6, 89–90, 102, 107, 111–13, 116, 119–20, 124, 129–33, 145, 156, 173, 219 nn.104–5
maximum pressure policy 49, 89, 129–31, 133, 135, 157, 173
on Syria 210 n.25
Tunisia 24, 56, 70, 87, 140, 202
Turkey 1, 3, 5–6, 8, 26, 33, 39, 48, 60, 69–71, 73, 86, 133, 141–2, 146–8, 153–4, 200, 202, 225 n.22
AKP 99
Ankara 6, 98, 100, 102–4, 106, 202–3
arms trade 103
dispute between Greece and 101
and EU 102–3
foreign policy of 99
formal expeditionary bases 100
human rights record 102
and IS in Syria 100, 104–5
and Israel 104
and jihadi 104
Milliyetci Hareket Partisi (MHP)/ Nationalist Movement Party 99
relationship with Britain 8, 97, 102–7
Cameron's visit to 97
defence deal 98
May's visit to 97–8
Ministry of Foreign Affairs (MFA) 105
post-Brexit 99
Raab's visit to 98
security relations 104–5
trade 98, 104
Turkish Republic of Northern Cyprus (TRNC) 97
UK–Turkish Strategic Partnership 97–8
and Russia 102
and Syria 104
troubled relationship with different countries 98
UK Foreign Direct Investment 104–5
and the United States 98, 102, 104, 107

Turkish Aerospace Industries (TAI) 98
Turkish Republic of Northern Cyprus (TRNC) 101
Typhoon fighter jet deal 17, 58, 63, 70

UK Export Finance 62, 77, 161
UK Middle East policy 5, 9, 47, 50, 56, 68, 199, 205
Ukraine 32
UK Special Forces 83–5, 104, 106, 142, 160, 168
unilateralism 45, 117
United Arab Emirates (UAE) 3, 14–15, 26, 45, 57–8, 69, 71, 74, 78, 100, 106, 109, 121, 130, 133, 166, 168, 172–4, 192, 200–2, 233 n.13
  Abu Dhabi 57–8, 63, 70, 74, 110, 173
  anf Turkey 104
  Dubai 74
  Palm Jumeirah, Dubai 77
  and Saudi Arabia 130
  ten-year residency visa 221 n.16
  trade and investment 70–3, 76–7
  UK Export Finance team in 62
The United Nations (UN) 59, 67, 101, 116, 141
  General Assembly 114
  humanitarian plan 87
  Independent International Commission of Inquiry 88
  Millennium Development Goals (MDGs) 22
  partition resolution of 1947 116
  Refugee Agency 87
  resettlement programmes 60
United Nations Human Rights Council (UNHRC), Item 7 119
United Nations Security Council (UNSC) 15–16, 19, 59, 65, 68, 100–1, 113, 117, 120–1, 131, 141, 191
  Resolution 242 15, 112
  Resolution 425 21
  Resolution 1284 22
  Resolution 1441 23
  Resolution 2334 112
  Resolution S/RES/2249 222 n.13
  Responsibility to Protect doctrine 57
The United States 3, 8–9, 13–16, 19–22, 25, 33, 36–7, 39, 42, 44–7, 56, 59–60, 70–1, 73–4, 82, 88–90, 92, 100–1, 103–5, 109–10, 112, 116, 119, 121, 124, 126, 129, 133, 139–42, 144, 146, 151, 153, 156, 158–9, 161–2, 165, 167, 174–7, 197, 199, 203, 205, 211 n.34
  and British 34, 36, 127–8
  and China 28–9, 34, 50, 162, 170, 177–9, 199
  and EU 66, 102, 191–2
  and Europe 50–2
  influence on British policy 65–6
  invasion of Iraq (2003) 128
  and Iran 156–7
  killing of Soleimani 65, 132–3
    Tehran's revenge after 133
  nuclear/non-nuclear sanctions 130–1, 133–4
  policymakers 48
  and Russia 34
  security 34–5, 41, 43–4, 52
  supremacy 42
  trade and investment 72–3, 76
  and Turkey 98, 102, 104
  US CENTCOM region 48
  Washington 3–4, 14–15, 20–1, 23, 28, 34–5, 41–3, 45–8, 50–2, 98, 101–2, 107, 111–13, 116, 131–2, 134, 140, 152, 161–2, 168, 177–9, 192, 203, 209 n.35
Unite Trade Union 74
Universal Security System 46
US Middle East Policy 50
USSR 43, 159

Vakil, Sanam 5–6, 8, 203
Venezuela 190
Vietnam 15, 30, 36
Vodafone company 76

Wagner Group 32
Wallace, Ben 98
war crimes 45, 60–1
  chemical weapon 59, 141
  Yemen conflict 60
war on terror 13, 22, 24, 84
warships 101
Wassenaar Arrangement 88
Watling, Jack 5, 7–9, 203
Weapons of Mass Destruction (WMD) 20, 23, 25, 87–90

West Bank 3, 6, 18, 64–5, 109, 111–16
 Israeli annexation of 115
 Ramallah 110, 114
wialyet al-faqih 156
Wilson, Harold 15, 167
World Bank 19, 30, 76, 187

Xi Jinping 28

Al Yamamah arms deal 17, 47, 73, 168
Yazidis 59, 84
Yekineyen Parastina Gel (YPG) 91, 99–100, 153
Yemen/Yemenis 1, 14–15, 25, 39, 45, 48, 55, 73, 86–7, 89, 91, 106, 109, 124, 129–30, 134, 172–3, 186, 201, 203–4, 215 n.58
 airstrikes by Saudi-led coalition (2015) 60
 and British arms 60–1
 Houthis in 89, 129, 132
 human rights in 216 n.61, 216 n.64
 Saudi/Emirati war (2015) in 130, 132
Yougov polling UK (2015) 206 n.4 (Ch 1)

Zaghari-Ratcliffe, Nazanin 88, 128
Zarif, Mohammad Javad 131
Zomlot, Husam 114